Praise for *Baseball Maverick*

"Steve Kettmann expertly takes you along the fascinating journey of a true Renaissance man. From combat to the roots of modern analytics to rebuilding the New York Mets—I'll let you decide the most difficult of such pursuits—Sandy Alderson is a compelling case study of leadership." —Tom Verducci, *Sports Illustrated*

"[A] lively chronicle." —*Newsday*

"Alderson has long been a baseball man, but his education, time in Vietnam and being the first nonplayer to challenge the supremacy of players in traditional scouting always set him at a distance. His is a story of fathers, sons and American service . . . *Baseball Maverick* . . . stands on its own, a worthwhile journey of an important figure Kettmann clearly and understandably admires." —Howard Bryant, *ESPN The Magazine*

"Sandy Alderson stumbled into baseball, but as Steve Kettmann shows so adroitly, he's put a best foot forward everywhere he's marched in the game. If, under his aegis, Alderson's Mets can finally come back to glory, it will cap the career of a man who has not only led his teams, but led the whole sport." —Frank Deford

"Steve Kettmann has given us so much more than a baseball book or biography; he has given us a fascinating look into one of the game's great minds. Sandy Alderson defies any simple description, but Kettmann has brilliantly painted a portrait that ties together the Marine, the scholar, the general manager, and the maverick streak that binds them together." —T. J. Quinn, ESPN

"A timely account of how GM Sandy Alderson has revived the entire New York Mets organization and transformed the team into a pennant contender . . . Extremely well written and unflaggingly interesting, the book will appeal insight into what GMs do and int major league baseball teams are bu

BASEBALL
MAVERICK

Also by Steve Kettmann

One Day at Fenway: A Day in the Life of Baseball in America

BASEBALL MAVERICK

How Sandy Alderson
Revolutionized Baseball
and Revived the Mets

STEVE KETTMANN

Grove Press
New York

Published simultaneously in Canada
Printed in the United States of America

ISBN 978-0-8021-2518-7
eISBN 978-0-8021-9256-1

Grove Press
an imprint of Grove Atlantic
154 West 14th Street
New York, NY 10011

Distributed by Publishers Group West

groveatlantic.com

15 16 17 18   10 9 8 7 6 5 4 3 2 1

For
Sarah

I found Sandy fascinating. He had such a different way of looking at things. It doesn't seem unique now because we're used to it, this is what you expect GMs to be, but back then, you talk about a maverick, this was a maverick. He was smart enough to know what he didn't know, but he was also smart enough to question what everyone perceived to be as givens. He had the self-confidence to question things and look for a better way. I knew I was never going to be as smart as Sandy. Every day that I went in, I was going to learn something that was going to make me better.

—Billy Beane

We must learn to see with the eyes of today, and not insist on looking through the dusty spectacles of yesterday.

—Eric Walker, *The Sinister First Baseman*
& Other Observations

A lot of this statistical stuff is overkill. If you get on base and hit for power, you're a good offensive player. If you're a pitcher, you do the opposite: You don't walk anybody and you keep the ball in the ballpark.

—Sandy Alderson

CONTENTS

BASEBALL
MAVERICK

Sandy Alderson (right), then a Dartmouth undergraduate, visited Vietnam in the summer of 1967. His father, John Alderson (left), violated strict rules to take him up in his B-57 for a strafing run.

PROLOGUE

THE MEANING OF
A WORLD SERIES

Anytime a baseball team makes it to the World Series, it counts as sweet vindication. That was especially true in 2015 for the New York Mets, their fans, and everyone around the team. Yes, it was agonizing to lose to the Kansas City Royals in five games, despite holding leads in four of those games, but after six straight losing seasons, six straight years of watching *other* teams in the playoffs, the Mets had finally taken a headlong dive into the future with their giddy run to the World Series. Later would come time to hash out questions of off-season contract offers, the Rubik's Cube of payroll math, and how to capitalize on a future loaded with both promise and risk; the overriding emotion around the team in late 2015 was a combination of relief and excitement that the club was once again a team to watch, a team that had truly been, as absolutely everyone could now agree, revived. The Mets were fun and entertaining and sexy. They were a team that all but screamed: Watch us! Wait till you see what's coming next!

The symbol for the revival was their Fantastic Four of hard-throwing young starters, all of them throwing 96 and harder with a nasty arsenal of complementary pitches (and a Fantastic Five if Zack Wheeler could come back from Tommy John surgery sometime in 2016, as projected).

Matt Harvey, who gets mentioned here first since he turned the first and last games of the 2015 World Series into high theater, loved the almost campy drama of his Dark Knight persona, until he didn't. Superhero movies are often about characters with both special powers and all-too-human vulnerabilities, and Harvey has made high art of showcasing both before a New York sports public eager to have him turn into the reincarnation of Broadway Joe Namath: dashing and funny, the man of the moment, unstoppable when it came time to take over a game. Harvey's love of the spotlight, his need to make things interesting for himself, left him in a precarious place at times during the 2015 season, but by wintertime he could cool his heels knowing he'd turned in a fascinating, impressive season, more than enough to earn him Comeback Player of the Year honors.

We watched Harvey in Game 1 of the Series against the Royals and it was like Superman around Kryptonite, his special powers clearly on the wane. Then, in Game 5, hoping to stave off a season-ending loss, Harvey looked like an action-figure toy whose power has been switched back on. That look in the eyes that Pedro Martinez likes to talk about with pitchers going into big games was there again, and so was an almost ridiculous command of all four of his pitches, starting with a fastball that was once again explosive, hitting 98 miles per hour. Earlier in the Series, Mets pitchers had trouble getting the contact-happy Royals to swing and miss at anything. Harvey struck out the side twice. He did more than dominate—he mesmerized, even when he finally started to run out of gas later in the game. Maybe it was a mistake for manager Terry Collins to let Harvey go back out there in the ninth inning. For sure it was a mistake to leave him in the game even after he walked speedy Lorenzo Cain to bring up the tying run with no outs.

But for sheer drama, for light-it-up emotional spectacle, no Mets fan or indeed no fan of baseball would ever forget the indelibly etched memory of Harvey's fierceness in the dugout, jumping around in his agitation, crying out "No way!" were they going to take him out of the game. To call such moments mere theater is to miss the point. Great teams and great players are built on such moments.

Harvey saw himself as the staff ace in 2015, but that could just as easily have been amazing Jacob deGrom, the converted shortstop who came out of nowhere like a meteorite crashing down in the middle of the Mets' world and changing everything. Here was another onetime "unpolished gem," as general manager Sandy Alderson put it to me, a talented player acquired in the Omar Minaya years whose progress year by year just kept accelerating to where he nabbed Rookie of the Year honors in 2014.

Where Harvey was part football player, the type to clench his fists at his side and let out with a yell like Mel Gibson in *Braveheart*, deGrom had about him the look of an artist—a very determined artist. Maybe it was the impossibly lithe form: six-foot-four and an alleged 180 pounds, with those long stork legs. Pitching well is mostly a mental challenge, as everyone knows, mostly a question of summoning a sublime level of concentration, and deGrom had an artist's ability almost to levitate, to lift himself through concentration, willpower, and imagination to a plane where he did things that should not have been quite possible. Yes, he had the physical tools, but in leading the 2015 Mets to the National League pennant, it was his preternatural concentration that enabled him to bounce back and beat arguably the best two pitchers in baseball, Clayton Kershaw and Zack Greinke, to propel the Mets through the 2015 National League Division Series. For me deGrom's superhero name had to be the Silver Surfer, because he elevated above everyone else and was from Florida and had some of the laid-back cool-dude air of a surfer.

The left-hander in the group, Steven Matz, was still a chalk outline of a big-leaguer in 2015, having—incredibly; you almost have to Google it and stare at it yourself—pitched in only six regular-season games before taking the hill for the Mets in the 2015 postseason. Matz had the look of a player from a different era. I saw a resemblance to the young Joe DiMaggio back in his San Francisco Seals days, a quality both of gentleness and aloofness in his demeanor, as if his athletic gifts were still somewhat a mystery even to him. Matz announced himself to the baseball world with a major-league debut to tickle the delight of any kid on a playground conjuring how it was going to be for him one day: Pitching at Citi Field, fifty miles from where he grew up on Long Island as a Mets fan, Matz not only pitched his way to his first major-league victory, holding the Reds to two runs over $7^2/_3$ innings, but also went 3-for-3 at the plate, with a double and four RBIs. He even slid hard into second to break up a double play.

For his second start, pitching at Dodger Stadium, Matz did his best Sandy Koufax impression, throwing six shutout innings in the Mets' thrill ride of an 8-0 win. A weird strain of his lat muscle left that auspicious two-start career opener hanging in the air until September, when Matz returned from the DL for four more starts, finishing with an ERA of 2.27, before he stepped into the glare of October baseball and three times pitched well enough to win. During the World Series he stayed at his childhood home on Long Island and even handed out candy to kids on Halloween. Matz was a marvel of technique, a wizard of technical purity; watching him pitch, his motion spun with the balance and force of a gyroscope. More than the other young guns, he looked ready to repeat the exact, effortless motion again and again forever, with close to technical perfection. So he might as well be called Iron Man, a superhero protected by his technical prowess. True, he seemed fragile at times, requiring a long road back from Tommy John surgery, but the Mets were eager to see how his startling precociousness would evolve over the coming seasons.

It was funny how in the age of Twitter and instant opinion, flashed all over the place, what seemed true at the time, then was quickly disavowed as overblown, often proved in the end to be just as true as it first seemed. Noah Syndergaard's first World Series pitch, that high fastball to the Royal's Alcides Escobar to open Game 3 at Citi Field, illustrated the syndrome beautifully. In concept and execution, the explosive rising fastball that Syndergaard uncorked to the screen was sublime in its perfection. Analyst Tom Verducci had commented on the Fox broadcast just seconds earlier, "I wouldn't be surprised to see this fastball in on Escobar. Announce yourself right away if you're Noah Syndergaard."

Syndergaard announced himself, all right. The talk later about whether he was head-hunting with the pitch was preposterous. The ball sailed to the screen, never on target to hit Escobar, and in fact flew over the spot where his wrists had been, not his head. It was way too high to cause any damage. As d'Arnaud told me, "I couldn't have caught it." But when the Royals chose to make an issue of the pitch in the aftermath of the Mets' victory in Game 3, it only amplified the impact of Syndergaard's pitch. Lost in the hubbub was the undeniable fact that Syndergaard looked wobbly in the early going, so it wasn't as if the message pitch got him going, but he found his groove later and did what no other Mets pitcher could in the Series and picked up a victory.

Interview-room postgame quotes are usually flat and useless, but not this time. Syndergaard proceeded with quiet dignity to throw out the unwritten rule that says in a case like this you lie. He calmly explained that he had talked with d'Arnaud going into the game about their plan and said: "How do you feel about high and tight for the first pitch and then a curveball for the second one?" Fair enough. Escobar had been crowding the plate, daring to be backed off.

It was true that baseball had changed, and a dirty play like Chase Utley ignoring the bag on his way to breaking Ruben Tejada's leg in Game 2 of the NLDS, once widely accepted, would have no place in the game moving forward. But pitching inside was the very foundation of pitching, and it couldn't be taken away, especially not a mere message pitch, as opposed to an actual beanball. Bob Gibson would throw pitches like that just because he didn't like the way someone looked at him. Syndergaard was doing his job, he was announcing himself in the mind game of October competition and when some of the Royals started spouting off about the pitch being "unprofessional" (Alex Rios) and the like, it was laughable. In fact, studied on replay, that was clearly a very *professional* message pitch, really one of the more spectacular message pitches you could ever throw.

"I feel like it really made a statement to start the game off, that you guys can't dig in and get too aggressive because I'll come in there," Syndergaard said in the interview room after Game 3, then upped the ante with: "If they have a problem with me throwing inside, then they can meet me sixty feet, six inches away. I've got no problem with that."

Syndergaard had served notice on the Royals and the baseball world that these Mets were a force, not just a fad. In a sense Syndergaard was reclaiming for the Mets a key chord of New York City swagger and mojo that Roger Clemens had snatched from them years earlier in Queens. Mike Piazza was a great Met, but in the all-important area of postseason theater we will forever see him flashing Clemens a bewildered, timid look as a shard of his bat was flung back toward his feet as he dutifully trotted down the line toward first base in Game 2 of the 2000 World Series, and seemed oddly out of it as both benches cleared and Clemens offered the all-time absurd explanation, "I thought it was the ball." He was throwing the *ball* at Piazza? That's supposed to make sense?? The Mets may have won only one game in the 2015 Series, as they had won only one in the 2000 Series against the Yankees, but Syndergaard's gunslinger theatrics gave the Mets and their fans a feeling of having been more than up to the challenge— and hungry for more. Syndergaard, aware of what buzz he had generated among fans, took to Twitter just after the 2015 season and announced, "New York City: This is not the end, but the beginning of something special."

Sandy Alderson had been saying for years that you could never truly enjoy a winning season except in retrospect, and in 2015 that formulation took on new meaning: The Mets had every reason to be confident about where they were headed as a team, but it would take years to know how far they would go in backing up that confidence. Alderson had raised eyebrows by asserting in a private meeting that the team needed to approach the 2014 season with the mindset that they would win ninety games, then a year later the Mets had hit ninety wins on the last day of the season. Now going forward the Mets' loaded starting pitching was impressive enough that the team could be penciled in for ninety wins, once Alderson made the necessary round of offseason moves to bolster offense and defense. The more interesting question, looking ahead past 2015, was how the long-term experiment the Mets had embarked on after Alderson took over in late 2010 would continue to evolve.

The Mets, with the Cubs just behind, had doubled down on an approach that combined all the bells and whistles of an informed, nuanced application of analytics and massive new stores of data available to teams, yet at the same time reinvented analytics-driven baseball to include a healthy respect for the human element. To a new breed of fan, used to consuming baseball in his or her own *Matrix*-like cubicle, cut off from the real world except via digital stream, this might have sounded quaint, like escorting grandpappy across the street from the old folks' home to get in a little (very slow) bowling. The flood of information available via detailed pictures and statistics might have blinded some to a bedrock truth about watching baseball, which is that the game will always surprise you—and it is in watching how individuals react to those surprises, the character and resourcefulness they show or don't, that baseball happens. So many outsiders were being brought into baseball, toting Ivy League credentials and brash self-confidence, they tended to think like these new-age fans and discount the human side, but the Alderson approach amounted to a counter-argument to that tendency.

The Mets clearly had been "revived" for the 2015 season through the patient work of Alderson and his trio of assistants—Paul DePodesta, J. P. Ricciardi and John Ricco; the good fortune of having an intriguing stash of talent in the farm system (credit to predecessor Omar Minaya); and the disciplined, patient approach to develop that talent. It was considered outlandish when I declared on the cover of this book's hardcover edition that the Mets had been "revived," with people arguing that nothing had happened yet. I disagreed then—and disagree now. You don't call a home run a home run only when it clears the fence; sometimes you know at contact the ball is gone, deep over the wall, and such was the case with the transformation of the Mets from reeling team in reconstruction mode to talented bunch needing a jolt of trade-deadline help. It was. always a given, if you knew him, that Alderson was one way or another going to make damn sure that happened with the Mets in 2015.

It just so happened that through a combination of luck and hard work I had the opportunity to document in this book much of what Alderson was up to season to season, from late 2010 when he took the Mets' GM job to the 2015 World Series appearance. Nowhere in the pages will you find Alderson referred to as a "genius," despite what some claimed I said, because as an expert on Alderson I never saw him as a genius, but more of an everyman—smart, yes; quick, no question; but someone toiling like most of us with all-too-human limitations and failings. What he did unquestionably have was a fascinating life story that made him who he was, a story explored in these pages from the scrub brush of Vietnam, where he was a marine officer late in the Vietnam War, to Harvard Law, to a California law firm where he soon found himself squaring off with the irrepressible Charles Finley, then owner of the A's—all before he even got started as a general manger.

It will take years to determine just what Sandy Alderson's legacy in the game will be. What is clear is that now that the Mets have morphed from sub-.500 straggler to World Series contender, far more people will take the time to connect the dots and look at where Alderson came from, from his early days with the A's, when he was at the center of revolutionizing baseball decision-making and management; to his time in the commissioner's office and in San Diego; to his joining the Mets. If the Mets end up establishing that 2015 was more than a one-off, if they can achieve more October success, the Alderson template will gain wider currency.

I'm confident that will happen, because I've had an inside look at the philosophy over five years and I believe it's sound. Trendy ideas are always dangerous. Alderson set in motion new approaches, taken further and popularized by his protégé Billy Beane, which led to a buzz that transcended baseball, but it is in the workshop of day-to-day baseball operations that those different ideas will be ultimately evaluated. It just may be that baseball executives who buy into a sabermetrics-above-all-else approach stunt their own perspective. It just may be that they hurt their competitiveness. As a front-office executive for one 2015 playoff team put it in a private conversation, "Let all these teams think they're reinventing the wheel with all that sabermetric shit, and meanwhile we'll keep winning." The new schoolers may at times fall in love with what they think is fresh and smart and powerful, and forget that building a team will always be a complex and intuitive act, best handled with a healthy respect for meeting people on their own terms, whether the team in question is a group of Navy SEALS, a corporate department, or a baseball team.

The New York Mets under Alderson have been an experiment in arguing that talent develops best when it can be developed across the board, from the talent of ticket sales people to marketing people to brilliant young stats guys to scouts and of course players. As I explore in some depth, this is an ethos that Alderson developed and deepened during his years in the Marine Corps, including serving in a leadership post in Washington side by side with future top generals like Peter Pace and James L. Jones.

It was in this context, the development of human capital, that the Mets' 2015 World Series appearance needed to be considered. They had a plan and they stuck with it. They were going to work to develop every prospect they had by at least 30 percent, and the net effect of that progress would be a collective quantum leap forward for the organization in homegrown talent. It was fair then to point to the organization's minor-league winning record in 2014, the best in baseball, as a precursor to coming success at the big-league level. The development of talented young players accelerated still further during the high-stakes games of October. Postseason experience was the ultimate performance enhancer, particularly if you viewed winning the World Series as far and away the primary goal of any baseball team or any baseball player, as opposed to putting together a good winning percentage during the regular season.

For all the prattling in the press about how field managers didn't matter, Alderson was flexible enough to give Terry Collins and his coaching staff considerable autonomy to make key decisions and manage his team. Yes, Collins left Harvey in one batter too long in Game 5 of the World Series, but the choice did not immediately burn in infamy, seen instead as an unfortunate capper to a great season: A manager has to manage. Following the World Series the Mets announced Collins was getting a contract extension. Just after the season, the Mets' rivals, the absurdly talented Nationals, pulled a surprise move and named Dusty Baker their manager, even though a sizable body of thought out there had it that Baker was overrated. The Nationals apparently weren't worried about that. Baker was not just a three-time Manager of the Year with the San Francisco Giants, before stops with the Cubs and the Cincinnati Reds; he also had a knack for engaging people and leaving them upbeat and excited, as I saw firsthand when the Wellstone Center in the Redwoods in California, where I'm codirector, published his 2015 book *Kiss the Sky: My Weekend in Monterey at the Greatest Concert Ever.* The trend back toward managers who were strong characters who had learned from experience may have run at odds with what were seen as *Moneyball* tenets, but after all, Alderson did make his name in Oakland as a GM working closely with law school grad Tony La Russa, a man as flinty and competitive and strong-willed as they come.

Flexibility is a hallmark of good management. The story of the Mets explored in this book ended up being a great baseball tale, full of the slow-building excitement of gathering talent and then developing it, carefully and calmly, without rushing the pace. The pop of a fastball exploding into a catcher's mitt reverberates through the pages as we track the progress of Harvey, deGrom, Syndergaard, and Matz, along with hard thrower Zack Wheeler, hoping to make it back into the Mets rotation sometime after the 2016 All-Star break. A fan hungry for more information and understanding can load up on little details likely to make watching the Mets over the coming, exciting years even more enjoyable.

But at the same time, this is a book about more than baseball. It's a book about thinking for yourself, bucking conventional wisdom again and again, and insisting on following certain principles that you have laid out for yourself. In other words, it is a book about what it means to be a true maverick. It's also a book about being true to yourself. For example, I once asked Alderson in a quiet moment which big-league manager he'd have for his club if he could pick anyone alive, and he told me he might have to go with Joe Maddon. But when word spread just after the 2014 season that Maddon was leaving Tampa Bay, Alderson refused even to consider talking to him about managing the Mets, since he had just given Collins a contract extension and wanted to stand by him. Later I wondered about that upright choice, especially when Maddon electrified the Cubs and their fans and turned that franchise around.

But in the end Terry Collins did a masterful job in 2015 as well. He went head-to-head with Maddon in the National League Championship Series, and his team prevailed in spectacular fashion. You don't always have to reach for the exciting new thing to be smart.

Sometimes it's about sticking with someone and trusting him or her to keep evolving in a role. I think the Mets' success will lead people beyond baseball to look to Alderson's insights for new directions in smart, forward-thinking leadership. Just what conclusions those readers might come to I have no idea, but I was lucky enough to have deep access to a great story, and I think readers who follow Alderson on his long journey will come away with some fresh thoughts to apply to their own lives about what is smart and what is not.

PART I

THE MARINE SHAKES UP BASEBALL IN OAKLAND

The Marines
are looking
for a few
good men
...for officer training

Sandy Alderson saw combat as a young Marine officer late in the Vietnam War and then in the early 1970s served at the Marine Barracks in Washington, where he was being groomed to be a future high-ranking general—and was featured in this recruitment poster.

1

KHE SANH

In 1955, the year the Brooklyn Dodgers won their only World Series, a rollicking, seven-game classic against the New York Yankees, military pilot John Alderson and his young family were living on an Air Force base in Osaka, Japan, listening to the games on the radio. Four days after the Series, the Yankees set off on a six-week barnstorming tour through Asia, and when they played in Osaka, John Alderson was on hand to watch with his son, Richard "Sandy" Alderson, all of seven years old. Sandy had his eye on that day's Yankees third baseman, a vinegary little guy from California named Billy Martin.

"Some Americans were razzing Martin," Sandy Alderson says now. "When he looked over to the stands to give it right back, the hitter smoked one right past him."

This was just ten years after the end of World War II, and for the Aldersons the fenced-in base was alienating. But for all the sense of jarring separation from the local Japanese, they did have one thing in common: baseball. Sandy attended third grade in Osaka and it was his first chance to play organized baseball. He'd been tossing the ball around with his father since he was small, but finally he was playing in real games. Baseball had been introduced in Japan late in the nineteenth century and was deeply established by the 1940s. "We would occasionally play Japanese teams," Alderson told me. "They would kick our butt. They were much better than we were."

The Aldersons traced their roots back to England and Wales. John Alderson grew up not far from Niagara Falls, New York, and was a pitcher for Gasport High School, which was where he was said to have squared off against a good left-hander starting for South Park

High in Buffalo by the name of Warren Spahn. On February 1, 1943, with the morning papers showing pictures of the RAF's night bombing of Berlin and headlines about Joseph Goebbels' "brutal" push for total mobilization of the German adult population, John enlisted in the U.S. Army Air Corps and learned to fly the twin-engine AT-10 at Moody Field in Georgia in preparation for flying B-24s in Europe. He joined the Forty-Fourth Bombardment Group in England, but arrived too late to take part in its most famous mission, Operation Tidal Wave, a coordinated low-altitude attack in August 1943 on nine oil refineries in Romania in which more than fifty aircraft were lost. "I wasn't there yet, thank God, because that was a tough mission," John told the *New York Daily News*. "I'm no hero."

Hero or not, he flew thirty-two missions in World War II. Home after the war, he enrolled at the University of Washington in Seattle and of all things became a drama major. "Either he wanted to meet girls or it seemed an easier option than some other things," Sandy explains. John set his sights on one of the stars of the department, Gwenny Parry, who grew up in Denver, her parents recent immigrants from Wales. In 1947 John had a role in the school production of *The Philadelphia Story*, and he may not have been able to act a whit but, based on a picture in the yearbook, at least he looked good in tails and seemed to be enjoying himself immensely. He and Gwenny were soon married, and she gave birth to Sandy that November. They were living in Denver when John was recalled to duty to fly B-26 bombers in the Korean War. Sandy, his mother, and his sister, Kristy, born in December 1951, stayed behind until John was transferred to Japan.

Next up after Japan was eight months at Chanute Air Force Base in Rantoul, Illinois, which afforded John and Sandy the chance to go to a doubleheader at Comiskey Park, where Sandy rooted against the visiting Yankees. Later, at Shaw Air Force Base in South Carolina, Sandy played Little League and his father coached him. John taught Sandy always to be aware of the situation. If you were on first base running to second on a ground ball, you hustled. Sandy might have learned the lesson too well. He was eleven years old and went in hard to second to break up a double-play chance—and elbowed the kid playing second. His coach flipped out. No son of *his* was going to play like that. John made Sandy ride the pine the rest of the day.

In 1960 the Milwaukee Braves played an exhibition game against the Cincinnati Reds at Capital City Stadium in Columbia, South Carolina, near Shaw AFB. Sandy was starstruck to see Hank Aaron, his idol, and tracked him down getting into a cab with his teammates Billy Bruton and Wes Covington. "I knew all these guys by heart," Alderson says. "The Braves were my team. I was a twelve-year-old kid asking for an autograph on a ball, and they signed it and gave it back."

Soon the family had moved again—this time across the Atlantic for three years at Alconbury Air Force Base in England. Overseeing the base's Babe Ruth team was Ed Ellis, a colonel from Alabama who took a liking to young Alderson. Up until this time Alderson had been called Sandy or sometimes Rick. But when Colonel Ellis took to calling him "Richie," which he hated, there was not much he could do. Soon everyone was calling him "Richie," including the colonel's two sons, Buster and Rip, good friends of his.

The Alderson family left England in early 1964 when John was reassigned to CIA headquarters in Langley, Virginia, working a desk job in the U-2 spy-plane program, a staffing choice that sounds like some kind of Joseph Heller joke about the genius for ineptitude that is military bureaucracy. John Alderson as a desk jockey? John, predictably, "hated" it. Sandy tried to take the move in stride.

"By that time we had moved so many times I had gotten used to it," Sandy says now. "Since you don't have any other experience and don't know anything other than this periodic movement from place to place, it wasn't that traumatic. But it had its impact. You develop a group of friends someplace and then go someplace else and develop a new group and the old group tends to fall by the wayside. It does make one very adaptable. That's a positive. But it probably stunts long-term relationships as well, and that's a negative."

The family decided to live in Falls Church, Virginia, where the Ellis family had also settled after leaving Alconbury. "We could have lived anywhere in the Washington area," Alderson says, "but we ended up getting this temporary apartment in a dumpy apartment complex in Falls Church, so I could go to high school where I'd have some friends." Alderson had a year and a half at Falls Church High, playing both football and baseball. Flipping through the school yearbook offers an intriguing glimpse: His senior picture captures a young man grappling with shyness, having come to the school long after most friendships had been formed. He's good-looking in the scrubbed, athletic, all-American way of *Good Will Hunting*–era Matt Damon, his tie impeccably knotted, his dark hair just past crew cut length, his half-smile starting to form into the sort of crooked grin useful for punctuating the occasional sarcastic one-liner.

"He was outgoing, he was social, but he wasn't real effervescent," says Tom Bradley, the star pitcher on the Falls Church High baseball team and Alderson's best friend. "He fit in really well. You always do when you play a sport."

The two sat next to each other in algebra, taught by a retired Navy rear admiral named Stephen Tackney, whom Alderson remembers walking around the room listing to one direction. All through class, the two would smirk and wisecrack, and Bradley would keep squeezing one of those squeaky hand-strengthening gadgets. "We got thrown out of the admiral's class a few times for talking and laughing," Alderson recalls.

"He was really smart, but also a little bit of a troublemaker," remembers the cocaptain of the cheerleading squad at Falls Church High at the time, then known as Linda Huff. "He would get Tom Bradley in trouble in Admiral Tackney's Algebra 2 class. It wouldn't bother him if he got kicked out of class. He still got an A."

One of the surprises of the Falls Church yearbook is that there is no mention anywhere of "Sandy" Alderson. He's always "Rich." For that he had Colonel Ellis to thank.

"I ended up at the same high school as his kids, so I couldn't escape it," he says.

"Poor kid!" remembers Linda. "He came and everybody called him 'Richie' and he really hated it. To this day good friends from high school call him Richie and they know he hates it. He just really didn't like it. He tried to be 'Rich.' I called him 'Rich.'"

She still calls him Rich. Linda and Sandy started dating on Halloween night their senior year, though Alderson took her home early so he could go hang out with his friends Rip Ellis and Tom Bradley, or that at least is the way Linda remembers it. She forgave him for that lapse. They were married four years later and celebrated their forty-fifth anniversary in December 2014.

"He changed his name back to Sandy when he went to Dartmouth," Linda says. "I called him 'Rich' the first year and a half. I still call him 'Rich,' instead of 'honey' or something. I just can't look at him and say, 'Sandy, pass the butter,' and we've been married since 1969."

"When she calls me a printable name, that's what she calls me," Alderson confirms.

Like many his age, Alderson took a summer job after he graduated high school in 1965, but his was a little unusual: working in the basement of the Central Intelligence Agency. It is not a job he has ever disclosed publicly, prior to the publication of this book. One of the issues with the CIA was that anyone who stepped into the building at Langley had to have clearance, even low-level workers, like interns or support staff. That made it preferable for family members of those already working in the building to be brought in as employees. Since John Alderson's assignment to the U-2 spy-plane program meant the entire family had already been vetted, the way was clear for Sandy to take a job there. Clearance levels corresponded to how high in the headquarters building you were allowed to go; Alderson worked in the basement. So if U-2 flights revealed something interesting, as they had in April 1965 when they discovered SAM-2 sites protecting Hanoi and Haiphong Harbor, that would not fall within Sandy's sphere. Nor would he have likely been privy to wires on August 28, 1965—the day Bob Dylan was booed in Forest Hills, New York, for going electric—with information and analysis of a U.S. action in the Mekong Delta that claimed the lives of more than fifty Viet Cong.

Alderson's job was to collect incoming cables from embassies, consulates, and aid offices around the world and code them to be distributed to the right analysts, who worked together in an area of the basement that looked a lot like a newsroom, humming with energy and activity. Talking about it now, Alderson downplays the work as being mostly trivial. "The cables that I was reading had to do with stuff like the wheat crop in Egypt is lousy this year," he says. Then again, the cables offered what had to have been a highly educational glimpse of the ways of intelligence analysts: habits of mind, modes of expression, as well as a road map of the topics and areas that CIA analysts around the world felt worthy of study and dissection. Anyone who spent a summer reading such cables at that age and at that moment of heightened geopolitical tension would have to emerge from the experience smarter and possessing fewer illusions about the ways of the world.

Alderson's tenth-grade French teacher in England had a Dartmouth alumni magazine that he leafed through one day. "That was the first I'd heard of Dartmouth," he says. So he applied to Dartmouth, Stanford, and Yale, and only got into Dartmouth, where he studied history on a Navy ROTC scholarship. His first couple of years, he was more interested in playing baseball—first on the freshman team, then for one year on the varsity—than he was in studying. He was a second baseman, better in the field than up to bat. After two years of ROTC he faced an important choice: He could continue to work toward being a Naval officer or he could opt to become a Marine officer instead. He chose the Marines and it gave him a newfound motivation to study. "I got religion somehow," he says.

Alderson's father could stomach only so much time at a desk before he got himself transferred in the summer of 1965, just after Sandy graduated high school. John wound up as an adviser for a squadron of B-57 Canberras at an Air National Guard Base near Hutchinson, Kansas. A year later John was transferred to the Philippines and then Vietnam, joining the U.S. Air Force's Thirteenth Bomb Squadron, dubbed the "Devil's Own Grim Reapers." By Sandy's sophomore year at Dartmouth, John was back to flying combat missions, his squadron of B-57 bombers deployed in Vietnam for two months at a time, then back to the Philippines. As a military dependent, Sandy could jump transport planes and visit his family in the Philippines on his breaks from school and did that often. If he could get that far, he started thinking, why not continue on to Vietnam? The war was the biggest story in the United States, and Alderson wanted to see for himself what was going on. All he needed was a visa to get into Vietnam. "I was curious and adventurous," he says. "I figured, 'All right, I'll be a freelance journalist!'"

Despite having no experience, he lined up a letter of introduction from a newspaper in Hutchinson, Kansas, and was able to secure a visa. But when he showed up at the Saigon Army Press Office in the summer of '67, the press officer told him: "You've got to have two letters to be accredited. And by the way, we know you're not here as a journalist, you're just screwing around."

With no accreditation, Alderson had no access to military transportation in South Vietnam. But Colonel Ellis, the man who had inflicted years of "Richie" torment on him, was stationed in Saigon at that time and arranged for him to hop a short military flight to the base at Phan Rang where John Alderson was stationed, flying night bombing missions to disrupt movement along the Ho Chi Minh Trail in North Vietnam. Ninety-four B-57Bs had been deployed for the war, including many from the Royal Australian Air Force. Sandy showed up at the base, located on the South Vietnamese coastline looking out at the South China Sea, near the ruins of a twelfth-century Cham temple. John was thrilled to see his son; he couldn't wait to get him up in the air on a test hop. One of the rare pictures of Sandy in Vietnam shows him sitting in the rear seat of a camouflaged B-57, cockpit ajar, wearing a flight helmet and grinning broadly, and John in a flight suit, the picture of fly-boy cool and confidence. This was just before John ignored the rules and took Sandy up in the B-57.

"That was a major no-no," said John's good friend Don Graham, who also flew B-57s out of Phan Rang. "You don't take up a civilian in a combat situation, even if that's your own son. I'm amazed they even did that. Imagine if anything had happened!"

John showed Sandy what the B-57 dive-bomber could do with some hair-raising bombing runs over those twelfth-century ruins, though not actually dropping any bombs. They also did strafing runs, John operating the .50-caliber machine guns—but not over land. "That was out in the South China Sea," Sandy explains. "He wasn't *that* cavalier."

John did everything he could to make Sandy queasy.

"He tried to make me throw up," Alderson says.

"I took him up and got him sick, which was exactly what I wanted to do," John crowed to the *New York Daily News*. "But it was very enjoyable. I know Sandy'll never forget it."

That week at his father's base in South Vietnam did indeed stay with Alderson. His father would fly off on night bombing runs and Alderson, nineteen at the time, would hang out at the hooch with a fun-loving squadron of Australians, hearing tales of action they'd seen. Rather than concluding he'd been foolish to try to talk his way into a press pass to cover the war in Vietnam, Alderson vowed to give it another try.

Instead of one letter from a newspaper editor vouching for his credentials, he would show up in front of that same press officer in Saigon a year later with two such letters. He'd still be a college kid, but in the meantime he'd have worked to make himself smarter about Vietnam. He asked for and received permission to construct his own independent study course on Vietnam at Dartmouth in the spring of 1968. This was shortly after the decisive phase of the war, the January 1968 Tet Offensive, a massive coordinated campaign of North Vietnamese attacks, despite an agreement to have a cease-fire during Tết , the Vietnamese New Year celebration. U.S. forces were caught off guard and fierce fighting raged all through February, especially during the battle for the city of Huế in central Vietnam, home of the walled Imperial Citadel, where Vietnamese emperors had lived and ruled from the first decade of the nineteenth century up until 1945, when Ho Chi Minh declared Hanoi the capital. U.S. forces prevailed at Huế and inflicted huge losses on the North Vietnamese, but Tet marked a decisive turning point in attitudes back home.

For the course Alderson read the work of many journalists, figures like Bernard Fall, the Austrian-born expert on Vietnam who reported from Southeast Asia and taught at Howard University. Fall flew back to Vietnam in February 1967 and asked an officer "where the action was," as R. W. Apple later reported in the *New York Times*. Fall was out on patrol with a company of Marines, dictating book notes into a tape reporter, when he stepped on a mine and was instantly killed. His last words were: "We've reached one of our phase lines after the firefight and it smells bad. . . . Could be an amb—"

Alderson was intrigued by Fall and Graham Greene, the Oxford-educated former journalist who had come back to Saigon sixteen years earlier after reporting in the field and hunkered down in room 214 of Saigon's French colonial hotel, the Continental, to write *The Quiet American*. Alderson in 1968 was not quite on board with Greene's thesis of America as a blundering innocent abroad, but he found it interesting, and the novel's hypnotic prescience was not lost on him, as when a character observes, "The French may hold, poor devils, if the Chinese don't come to help the Vietminh. A war of jungle and mountain and marsh, paddy fields where you wade shoulder-high and the enemy simply disappear, bury their arms, put on peasant dress."

For Alderson there was a palpable thrill in walking the halls of the Continental right after he arrived in Saigon. "I went there because I was a Graham Greene fan," he told me. From his room at the Continental he could walk one block to the Rex Hotel, where foreign correspondents gathered at the rooftop bar and where the famous press briefings known as the "five o'clock follies" occurred. "The people who went to those press briefings were the people you'd see on CBS or NBC, network correspondents," he says. "I was big into that. I really thought that was fascinating. I did go out in the field with some of these TV people."

Like Greene, he wanted to be out and about as much as he could, not cooped up in a hotel. Alderson arrived in May during the Mini–Tet Offensive and captured developments in Saigon during his first forty-eight hours there for an article he published in the *Dartmouth*, his student newspaper. CONG CLOBBER SAIGON AS ALLIES DIG IN, read the headline, and a short editor's note followed, explaining that "Alderson is spending several months in Vietnam and will be sending THE DARTMOUTH regular dispatches." The article began:

> SAIGON—For several days, parts of this city have been absorbing a renewed offensive by Vietcong and North Vietnamese regulars, a follow-up to the murderous "Tet offensive." While most of the city is vulnerable at night, during the day fighting is centered in the suburbs and in Saigon's sister city, Cholon. Thus much of the city carries on as usual, even as smoke billows only blocks away.

The article is competent enough, if unspectacular. The surprise comes in the vividness of the quotes from U.S. soldiers. "This morning I saw six or seven rangers run a hundred meters across an open rice paddy and then swim a stream to catch two VC who tried to break contact," one helicopter gunship pilot told him. "They shot the hell out of both of them."

Soon after filing his dispatch from Saigon, Alderson caught a military transport to Da Nang and headed up to the Imperial City of Hué, along the banks of the Perfume River, a place of grace and beauty, at least up until a few months before Alderson arrived. I visited the place myself in 2010, and even then there was a haunting poetry to once regal gardens fallen into neglect. Deep within the inner reaches of the elaborate Citadel complex, I poked through a half-renovated building that had been the royal reading room, a red-slatted fence marking space before the red-squared wall of windowed sliding doors over which a massive pagoda-style roof lifted to the skies. Many in the United States are familiar with the Vietnamese name "Nguyen," thinking it like "Jones" in being merely popular, but the name spread far and wide because the Nguyen dynasty ruled Vietnam from 1804 until 1945. Its seat of power was this Citadel.

Michael Herr, author of the classic study *Dispatches*, arrived in Vietnam not long before Alderson did in 1968 and soon was on his way to the massive Imperial Citadel. This was right after the Tet Offensive had started, and Herr caught a ride to get to the action and wound up with a group of Marines fighting its way into Huế, passing by hundreds of dead civilians and feeling the blast of na-palm being dropped within a hundred meters of their position. "Up on the highest point of the wall, on what had once been a tower, I looked across the Citadel's moat and saw the NVA [North Vietnam-ese Army] moving quickly across the rubble of the opposing wall," Herr wrote. "We were close enough to be able to see their faces. A rifle went off a few feet to my right, and one of the running figures jerked back and dropped. A Marine sniper leaned out from his cover and grinned at me."

Three months later Sandy Alderson showed up on a bicycle. Seriously: He rented a bicycle and went pedaling around to get a look for himself at the Imperial Citadel. "I would just bicycle around Huế City," Alderson says. "It was totally destroyed, but it wasn't deserted by any means. I bicycled through the Imperial City and along the Perfume River, basically what a tourist would do, except for the fact there was a war going on."

Based in Da Nang with a military press pass, Alderson showed up at the military press office each morning to see what press excursions were planned that week. "It was like going to a hotel in the Catskills, and you could sign up for a variety of different activities," Alderson re-calls. One day he might be out on one of the huge gunships nicknamed "Puff the Magic Dragon," looking down into the emerald-green rice paddies fanning out in every direction and waiting to hear the thunder of the rapid-fire .50-caliber mini-guns opening up on a perceived threat hiding in the tree line. Another day, he might tag along on an Opera-tion Ranch Hand sortie dropping the toxic defoliant Agent Orange. It was May 1968 and back in America young men his age were doing everything they could to avoid having to come fight in what they saw as a pointless war, some fleeing to Canada, many burning their draft cards. Alderson was fleeing deeper into the war, catching press flights to famous firebases like Con Thien and Khe Sanh.

"It was like a college student going to Europe," Alderson says now. "This was the biggest thing going on in the world at that time. Really it was like an adventure. I've always liked doing what other people don't."

Khe Sanh was near the border with Laos, just south of the 17th parallel dividing North Vietnam from South Vietnam at the time. In January 1968, General William Westmoreland had declared it a priority to hold the Khe Sanh firebase at all costs, for psychological reasons, even with an estimated forty thousand North Vietnamese closing in on the five thousand Marines at the base. The only U.S. hope was air power. An estimated 100,000 tons of bombs were dropped around the perimeter of the base, as well as 158,000 high-caliber shells. Khe Sanh was seen at the time as so important, it even showed up in Walter Cronkite's famous February 27, 1968, *CBS Evening News* commentary about Vietnam, when he declared, "We are mired in stalemate," and President Johnson concluded that if he'd lost Cronkite, he'd lost the American people. "Khe Sanh could well fall, with a terrible loss in American lives, prestige, and morale," Cronkite said. "It is increasingly clear to this reporter that the only rational way out then will be to negotiate, not as victors, but as an honorable people who lived up to their pledge to defend democracy, and did the best they could."

Michael Herr also visited the famous firebase. "Khe Sanh was a very bad place then, but the airstrip there was the worst place in the world," he wrote in *Dispatches*. "If you were waiting there to be taken out, there was nothing you could do but curl up in the trench and try to make yourself small, and if you were coming in on the plane, there was nothing you could do, nothing at all."

Three months later when Alderson caught a C-130 transport to Khe Sanh, the furious bombing had slowed down, but not died out. The landing strip, the key to survival during the pivotal seventy-seven-day siege in February, had become infamous. Coming in for a landing, Alderson could see the hulks of other C-130s that had attempted the same landing and been destroyed by incoming fire, often killing everyone on board. "So the C-130s would land and come to a stop for like thirty seconds," he says. "They would dump their passengers, gear, and supplies and take right off."

Alderson spent only one night there. At Khe Sanh, that meant sleeping in a bunker: Everything on that firebase was dug down deep, underground, covered by layers of timber and sandbags. The shelling might have let up from the heaviest days of the siege, but you never knew when a stray might land right on top of where you were sleeping. "It was harassment fire," Alderson says now. "The North Vietnamese weren't trying to dislodge the firebase; they were just trying to make the Marines nervous and keep them down in the bunkers."

Above all he recalls waking up at night and having to pee. He couldn't hold it all night.

"You could hear the rats running around all over the place on the floor of the bunker, so at night you didn't even want to put your foot down from the cot," he recalls. "I woke up and had to take a leak, but thought, 'Oh shit, I don't want to get a rat bite.' I wasn't going to go to the head. I was just going to get outside the bunker, take a leak, and get back in. You didn't want to get caught outside."

Alderson did not file a story from Khe Sanh. His output as a reporter was limited to that one article he'd published in the *Dartmouth* upon arriving. "I quickly realized I wasn't really competent," he says. "I didn't want to comment on the war. I didn't want to be an apologist for it to a bunch of undergraduate readers." Alderson had learned a thing or two about accepting how little he knew.

2

POSTER BOY

One morning during his senior year at Dartmouth, Alderson was studying at the library when a group of students at the same table got up and walked away. He noticed they'd left behind a scrap of paper. Curious, he unfolded the note and read: "That guy across from you is Sandy Alderson, the biggest militarist on campus." He was more perplexed than angry. He could have pointed to many ROTC types far more militaristic than he was. Were they fans of Graham Greene? No way. Reading the note reminded Alderson once again of how much he was an outsider. He was apart from the experience of the great mass of the student body. He supported the war, if only because his father was part of it. He had hoped to attend the Air Force Academy and become a pilot like his father, but when it came time for his eyes to be tested, he flunked. He was color-blind.

His graduation from Dartmouth was rained out, leading to a modified, scaled-down ceremony inside. Alderson had been commissioned a couple of days earlier with more than one hundred other ROTC students, including one other Marine, and reported to Quantico two weeks later for training at The Basic School. Alderson finished first out of 250 in his group of officers, the "honor man," a distinction that did not go unnoticed, given how rigorous the training had been: Up until the Tet Offensive, it had emphasized rural warfare, but by the time Alderson was at Quantico, the Marine Corps had built a model Vietnamese village with thatched huts. There was classroom study of tactics, but most of the work was in the field. Walt Zorkers, who went through the training about the same time as Alderson, recalled that it also included classes on leadership. "That was the only time I had that," Zorkers says. "Later I went to Harvard Business School, but no one ever taught me anything at Harvard Business School about being a leader. They made me a technician. The only place I got leadership training was at The Basic School at Quantico."

Alderson was gung ho to get to Vietnam, but instead found out he was being sent to Monterey, California, for eight months of intensive study of Vietnamese, six hours a day, taught by native speakers. "I took a test during Basic School at Quantico and made the mistake of scoring too high," Alderson says.

Before reporting to Monterey on January 1, Sandy and Linda were married on December 20, 1969, in Falls Church, Virginia, spending one night there and then hitting the road. They did all their Christmas shopping in two days and celebrated the holiday in Florida. They spent one night in New Orleans and saw the damage that Hurricane Camille had inflicted along the coast a few months earlier. "We went the southern route and did it in four days," Linda recalls. "I remember driving through L.A. and saying, 'Oh my god, I know all these streets. Here's Hollywood and Vine.' We drove up to Monterey and had dinner at our first Denny's ever."

Zorkers remembers a banquet late in his and Alderson's time studying in Monterey where the guest speaker was a general. Zorkers and Alderson wrote their names and serial numbers on a napkin, with a note begging to be sent to Vietnam, and handed that to the general. They were both Ivy Leaguers, the best in their class at Vietnamese. "Sandy and I were both of the same mind: We're here, so let's not waste this opportunity," Zorkers remembers. "Sandy at the time was probably more conservative and more supportive of a very unpopular war. I, on the other hand, objected quite a bit to the war. But if there were going to be any more Marine officers left in Vietnam, we thought we would like to be among them, because we thought we could do the best job."

"The whole time I was in Monterey it was like: 'Shit, I'm not going to get to Vietnam! I've done all this training and I'm not going!'" Alderson says. "I was totally pissed off. So I was constantly calling people to say, 'Hey, don't forget about me.'"

In Monterey Alderson was forever trying to tune in California Angels night games, which would come in and out, since by then his high school friend Tom Bradley was pitching in the big leagues, compiling a 4.13 ERA for the Halos that summer. Alderson would drag Zorkers up to San Francisco, a two-hour drive, to watch the Giants play at Candlestick Park. That was the summer that Willie Mays had his last good season, bouncing back at age thirty-nine to hit .291 with twenty-eight homers, but the Giants sputtered to a third-place finish. "I never got excited about baseball," Zorkers remembers. "Sandy was in love with the sport. He was just a baseball junkie."

Finally their orders came through. Alderson, sent to WestPac in Okinawa, was out of his mind with frustration. He called a gunnery sergeant in Hawaii to plead his case. "This is bullshit!" Alderson recalls yelling. "I've taken Vietnamese for eight months! And you're going to send me to frigging Okinawa?" His appeal was successful. "The gunnery sergeant said, 'Screw it! Send the guy south.' That's how I got to Vietnam."

John Alderson, when he heard the news, decided he had to get out to California to see his son before he deployed. He was stationed at MacDill Air Force Base in Tampa, Florida, and somehow talked his way into clearance to fly a B-57 cross-country. Along the way Alderson and his friend Don Graham stopped off at McConnell Air Force Base in Kansas to refuel. A young crew chief tried to ground them, since red hydraulic fluid was leaking out of the landing gear, rendering it inoperable. Alderson ripped up the official forms grounding the plane.

"We weren't here," John Alderson told him. "You didn't see us. You didn't talk to us."

By that night they were in Monterey.

"That was my dad," Sandy Alderson says. "He was so different from me. It's one of the things I admire. I didn't try to emulate him necessarily, but I really admired him for who he was."

Sandy Alderson was named a platoon commander in 2nd Battalion, First Marines within days of arriving in Vietnam on September

21, 1970, and deployed to a base in the Marble Mountain area just south of Da Nang. The landscape was not the jungle most Americans associate with Vietnam, but a mixture of low scrub grass and sandy dirt near My Khe beach, dubbed "China Beach" by the Americans. You don't have to have come any closer to serving in the military than binging on war movies like *Platoon* to know that the new lieutenant is always going to be viewed with blunt, open skepticism by his men. Alderson understood all too well the need to earn their respect. On his second day out on patrol, they came across a box mine and he personally took care of exploding the thing with a C-4 charge and fuse. He lit the fuse and hurried away to watch it blow.

"Nothing happened," Alderson recalls. "If you were the one that set the charge and it didn't blow, you were the one who had to go fix it."

The problem was: What if the fuse was still smoldering? What if you went back to check on it and it exploded? "I was on all fours crawling up to this thing and pulling the fuse out of the blasting cap," he says. "That was testimony to my incompetence, but that's what happens with people who first get there: Crazy stuff happens."

Typically the platoon would move out at night and be out on patrol one or two days, establishing a camp, if necessary, with observation posts. They searched for small VC units looking to set up a rocket launcher near the helicopter base at Marble Mountain. "We never saw any big units," recalls John Grinalds, operations officer of the battalion at the time. "Most of them were smaller Viet Cong units, local militia who had been in the area for a while, trying to control the nighttime hours while we controlled the daytime hours. This was a shadow government that worked at night. It was almost like flipping the shades on a window, they flip one way and then flip the other; one way it's VC in control, one way we were in control. Viet Cong would set out booby traps: box mines, with artillery mines in them that would go off, or dynamite in them, all kinds of different explosives. The explosion would kill anyone in a ten- to fifteen-meter radius. It was very, very tough on the Marines. It was nothing you could put your arms around like a unit. You couldn't capture them or kill them."

I asked Alderson how many men he lost as a platoon commander.

"When I was a platoon commander I didn't lose a single one," he said.

Alderson was not fired at much in Vietnam. He did earn a Bronze Star for his actions during a flare-up that occurred when helicopters were called in to evacuate his platoon, but downplayed the medal. "It really wasn't a big deal," Alderson says now. "It's not like bullets were whizzing by or anything." His first reaction, in fact, had been that some jackass in one of the helicopters had fired off a rocket by mistake. However, it became clear that Vietnamese along a nearby tree line were firing their way. "I carried a .45, and at that point I grabbed somebody's M16 and started firing," he says. "That was pretty much it."

The tide was ebbing, the war shifting toward an end game with the Marines about to be pulled out. Plotting an orderly retreat takes organization and discipline, and by that point in the war both were fraying. Alderson found himself disappointed in much that he saw. As his friend Walt Zorkers pointed out, young Marine officers were prepared to lead and Alderson wanted that opportunity. Instead, he found the organization of the battalion slipping toward the absurd, even by the standards of men at war. Within weeks of Alderson's appointment as platoon commander, everything changed. Through one of the frequent rotations, as more experienced men were sent home, the company was often devoid of experienced officers, so Alderson was promoted from platoon commander to company executive officer, the number two man of the entire company, since his eight months of language training in Monterey made him more senior than any other officer other than the CO. Three weeks later, the game of musical chairs continued. A more senior officer rotated in to become XO, and Alderson went back to being a platoon commander. Soon he was moved back to XO and then yet another rotation ensued—you can almost hear the music playing and stopping abruptly—and this time, First Lieutenant Alderson suddenly became company commander. Establishing his authority was no easy task, given the certainty that another rotation would come before long.

It came in less than two weeks—Alderson, just like that, was told to go back to commanding a platoon.

Not so fast, he said. Alderson hadn't wound up first in his class at officer-training school by tilting at windmills. He believed in the Marine Corps and its mission. But he had been around the military most of his life and knew weak leadership when he saw it; the constant shifts in leadership were hurting unit effectiveness and morale. Most officers in Alderson's position would have swallowed their objection to the ongoing farce; go along to get along is the mantra of anyone looking to make a career in the military. That was not Alderson's mind-set. Something welled up in him from down deep, an anger, an outrage, whenever he saw someone doing things by the book with no common sense.

"Look, you can't keep changing platoon commanders every two weeks," Alderson told his commanding officer. "Without any continuity, there's no leadership. There's no training. There's no readiness and there's no effectiveness."

Speaking out in this way was not something one did as an officer in the Marine Corps, but Alderson's CO told him it would not be held against him. "I appreciate you making this point," Alderson was told. "It won't affect your future."

Alderson was naive enough to believe him. Instead of commanding a platoon, he was made a civil affairs officer, where he could use his Vietnamese-language proficiency. He went about his duties and tried to put the episode behind him—and then he received his fitness report. The gung ho former "honor man" was given a report that was critical and cited Alderson's outspoken remarks. It was a rebuke, and Alderson was not about to take it without putting up a fight. He invoked a seldom-used Marine tradition, at least for officers, dating back to its origins as part of the Navy, and "requested mast," that is, he demanded the right to go over the head of his commanding officer and tell his story to the regimental commander.

Colonel P. X. Kelley, commander of the First Marines, was a formidable figure. As a battalion commander in Vietnam, he'd earned the Silver Star, the Legion of Merit, and the Bronze Star. Later he would rise to be commandant of the Marine Corps. He was a Marine's Marine, tough but fair. Alderson made his case. Kelley heard him out.

"You know what?" Kelley finally said. "I agree with you, Lieutenant. You're absolutely right."

How often did a Marine officer request mast? "On a scale of one to ten, that would be probably a one," Kelley told me in early 2013. "Most would not do that, unless they felt it was for the good of the Corps and the good of the unit."

Kelley did more than back Alderson up. He became his energetic advocate. "He was an extraordinarily good platoon commander," Kelley told me. "His leadership skills were absolutely perfect. He could lead anyone anywhere."

Alderson was given the plum job of working with the regiment's intelligence officer, John Grinalds, a former all-state high school football player who grew up in Georgia and graduated with honors from West Point as salutatorian. "He was my alter ego," Grinalds told me. "When I wasn't doing something, he was doing it. When he wasn't doing something, I was doing it. He was obviously a very, very talented officer."

Alderson remembers feeling out of the loop. "I was in the dark half the time," he says now. "As an assistant regimental intelligence officer, I was basically nobody."

To this day Alderson talks about Grinalds with a certain amount of awe. Like others Alderson would admire and seek to emulate, Grinalds combined the qualities of a gifted athlete and second-in-his-class West Point smarts with a sensibility that was both tough and refined. Grinalds gave me crisp, lucid descriptions of the war and added this thought: "I remember the whole time I was there I never heard a bird sing. Not once. I don't know why that was. It could have been the violence and gunfire scared them away. I don't know. I did hear ducks and geese one time. But never a songbird."

Alderson was in Vietnam with the Marines less than eight months, from September 21, 1970, to May 10, 1971, when the First Marines were redeployed to Camp Pendleton in California. The day he left, the Associated Press moved an article on the wires about President Nixon's troop reductions in Vietnam, noting that American forces had numbered more than 543,000 at their peak but by then had been reduced to 267,100. Also that day, the *New York Times* carried a short report on a young monk in Huế City, near where Alderson had ridden around on a bicycle, who had set himself on fire to protest the war.

Once Alderson's tour ended, he wanted to go where Linda was, which was back in D.C. After graduating in 1969 from Mary Washington College in Fredericksburg, Virginia, she landed a job with American Management Systems, gaining an early education in code writing and the power of computers.

Alderson spent only a couple weeks at Camp Pendleton before being transferred, with the help of John Grinalds, to Marine Barracks, Washington, D.C., known in the Corps as Eighth and I. President Thomas Jefferson is said to have personally chosen the site for the Marine Barracks in March 1801. An aura of history pervaded the place, and anyone assigned there knew he had been tapped on the shoulder and marked for success. As Linda Alderson sums it up, "You had to look good in the uniform and you had to be really smart."

There was something in Alderson's nature that argued against going career military, a part of him that rebelled against the idea of never being able to tell someone to go screw himself if you thought he was dead wrong. Then again, peering at pictures of the young Sandy Alderson in his Marine Corps dress uniform, an inescapable conclusion leaps out: This man belongs in that uniform. Alderson could easily have wound up as a high-ranking Marine general. That, after all, was the role to which Alderson's contemporaries at Eighth and I ascended. Alderson arrived in May 1971 and took over the Special Ceremonial Platoon from Peter Pace, also a former platoon commander in Vietnam, who had just been promoted. Later in his time at Eighth and I, Alderson served as executive officer to another up-and-comer named James L. Jones. Pace would later rise to the military's top post, chairman of the Joint Chiefs of Staff. Jones later served as Supreme Allied Commander Europe, commandant of the Marine Corps, and national security adviser to President Obama.

"He was a brilliant officer and a great leader," Jones told me. "He really had the respect of his senior peers as well as his subordinates and was primed to do some really great things if he stayed on active duty. Through adversity and pressure, Sandy Alderson was a very cool customer."

As commander of the Special Ceremonial Platoon, Alderson oversaw the Marine silent drill team, a color guard unit, and a unit called the Body Bearers, and also oversaw several Marines assigned to the White House, where he regularly attended military ceremonies during the Nixon years. They were also involved in ceremonies at the Tomb of the Unknown Soldier and traveled throughout the country, putting on displays at military bases and sporting events.

The U.S. Marine Corps silent drill unit that Alderson commanded in 1971 represented graceful, synchronized movement of the highest order, like the balletic perfection of a Cirque du Soleil performance. "It's as close as you can get to zero-defect performance, because they expect perfection every time you go out there," Jones told me. "The lieutenant put in charge is very carefully picked and that's why Sandy Alderson got the job."

The temptation is strong to equate "discipline" in the military sense with the laughably perverse *Animal House* version, namely a very young Kevin Bacon (who else?) bending over in his skivvies during initiation at the rich, stuck-up fraternity house, getting whacked hard on the ass with a paddle, and squeaking out, "Thank you, sir! May I have another?" But what about the discipline of an individual trying to relax into the calm of perfection? At Eighth and I, Alderson had men under his command who came from all corners of the country and all walks of life; some were smarter than others, some more gifted physically, some more driven. Each had weaknesses and quirks that could get in the way of the unit coming together. Yet they overcame them; the individual became more the individual by losing itself in the whole.

It's intriguing to start thinking about "discipline" as simply the ability to say no to an impulse if the goal is the larger good, for example laying off an outside pitch to help the team by collecting a walk. As a Marine, Alderson internalized a deep conviction that holding back from impulsive behavior can be as important as taking action. Eighth and I was even more of a formative experience than commanding troops in Vietnam for Alderson; he was there far longer than he was in Vietnam, he points out, and the kind of crisp teamwork that he'd been disappointed not to see enough of in Vietnam was very much on display at Eighth and I.

Consider the death of former president Lyndon B. Johnson on January 22, 1973, and its aftermath, when more than forty thousand people streamed by his coffin lying in state at the Capitol Rotunda. An honor guard of four officers stood at attention around the coffin, each stock-still, eyes locked. One of them was Sandy Alderson. "You're only on for half an hour at a time," he says. "The key was not blinking. That was the tough part." Picture Alderson standing at attention next to LBJ's body and trying not to blink, and the word "discipline" takes on new meaning. It becomes a lot easier to understand why, moving forward a few years, this man might have strong views on plate discipline.

Alderson had become a conduit through which the pride of others flowed, and that role taught him a new humility, a new awareness of the necessity sometimes to place the needs of the group before the need of the individual. He found that it was easier and more satisfying to be proud not of oneself, but of what one had accomplished through close and exacting teamwork. Even on the day when Alderson became a poster boy for the Marines, he did not set out alone from Marine Barracks, but instead with his men and three other officers, including a captain. One of the shots taken that day showed a ramrod-straight Alderson bedecked with medals facing the camera flanked by four other Marines, all of them in white gloves and white pants. That became a new recruitment poster, with the words: "The Marines are looking for a few good men . . . for officer training."

Posters for the Marines were iconic. Alderson said that with so many famous recruiting posters, the one featuring him hardly stood out, but the Marine Corps circulated it widely. "It was a very famous poster of him in his dress blue uniform that was standard all over the Marine Corps," James L. Jones told me. "You'd see that all over the place."

* * *

Alderson ended up at Harvard Law School in the same "Why not?" spirit behind so much in his life. "I took the law boards in college because everybody else was taking them," he says. "I did pretty well, so I thought, 'I'll apply to some law schools and see if I get in.'" When he applied in 1969, the University of Virginia and Harvard accepted him. Yale turned him down (and yes, he's still steamed about that). Late in his time at Eighth and I, he reapplied to the law schools. The University of Virginia now refused to reaccept him. He was ticked off—and he took action. Alderson had read an article in the *Washington Post* by a military affairs correspondent who struck him as showing some promise, so Alderson called up the paper and got the reporter on the phone to rail about schools denying admission to Vietnam veterans who had been admitted earlier, but had put off their studies to serve in the war. "This is bullshit!" he told the reporter.

"I called the dean at UVA and said, 'I've gone to the *Washington Post*. This is a situation that I'm not going to tolerate!' Five days later I got an acceptance from Harvard, but I also got a letter back from UVA saying, 'We reconsidered your application and you've been admitted,' and I was able to go back and say, 'Take a hike!'"

It meant a lot to Alderson that Harvard honored its earlier commitment. He and Linda moved to Cambridge and soon he was a Red Sox fan. He even grew his hair out. Walking by a Cambridge post office one day, he saw the Marine Corps recruitment poster featuring himself. "At the time my hair was about four inches long," he said. "It wasn't a political statement, believe me. I let it grow out because I was tired of getting haircuts two or three times a week."

3

HOLY TOLEDO!

They went out too fast. Sandy Alderson and his friend and mentor Roy Eisenhardt took off with the nearly nine hundred others in the first annual San Francisco Marathon on July 10, 1977, setting out from the eastern edge of Golden Gate Park. The two men ran shoulder to shoulder toward the sea, down the easy slope of John F. Kennedy Drive. Even when they neared the pounding surf of Ocean Beach and headed south on the Great Highway toward Lake Merced, the excitement carried them along almost without effort. Both men were intent on cracking three hours for the marathon. That meant averaging 6:52 per mile. "We went out at about 5:50s without even realizing it, and at ten miles I looked and thought, 'Oh my god, this is good and this is bad,'" Eisenhardt told me. "We had a great time at the end of ten miles, but at an expense."

Alderson and Eisenhardt had done the work, but with each passing mile it was becoming clear the prospect of cracking three hours was looking questionable. The two men had by then run together hundreds of times in the two years since the law brought them together. Harvard Law had passed in a blur for Alderson. A man who was not intimidated by Vietnam, as either a student journalist or a Marine lieutenant, nonetheless found himself rocked back on his heels by the world he encountered at Harvard Law from 1973 to 1976. Alderson never felt the sense of fitting in at law school that he had felt in the Marines. "I can't say that I totally enjoyed the experience," he says. "It was a big change from the Marine Corps. I enjoyed my fellow students, and the professors there were incredible, but it didn't inspire any passion for the law. In fact, at the time I thought I should have gone to business school."

The summer after Alderson's second year of law school, he clerked at a prominent San Francisco firm, Farella Braun & Martel, where Eisenhardt was a partner. To many at the firm, it seemed inevitable that Eisenhardt and Alderson would become close. Both had graduated from Dartmouth, both had served as officers in the Marine Corps, both had attended elite law schools, both had agile senses of humor, and both were athletic. "How could you not like him?" Eisenhardt asks now. On their lunch breaks the two ran all the way from the Chinatown YMCA to the Golden Gate Bridge and back, a nine-mile run.

"It was amazing to me," Linda Alderson told me. "Roy took Sandy under his wing right away when he was a summer clerk. I was working full time, but I went out to California for a couple of weeks and Roy took us to Hawaii on a business trip. He took me, too. I have a picture of the three of us."

What attracted Alderson to Farella Braun & Martel was above all its location in San Francisco, where by that point his best friend from high school, Tom Bradley, was pitching for the Giants. Bradley was coming off an attention-getting run with the Chicago White Sox, where his feats included surviving as part of a three-man starting rotation and giving teammate Rich Gossage the nickname "Goose." Bradley finished a respectable 13-12 for the Giants in 1973 and even edged Tom Seaver at Shea Stadium that August in a taut affair that had the *New York Times* gushing, "Tom Bradley—the Latin scholar of the San Francisco Giants—came, saw and conquered the New York Mets yesterday in a 1–0 pitching duel against Tom Seaver."

Bradley was heading into his third year with the Giants by '75, but by the time Alderson arrived in town to start his clerkship, Bradley had been shipped out to Triple-A Phoenix. "I left my fastball back at Candlestick Park, I have to say," Bradley told me. "Back then we didn't have the protection players have now with agents. My arm just never came back."

Sandy and Linda needed somewhere to stay when they moved to San Francisco, and Eisenhardt offered his place. "Roy heard me calling Sandy 'Rich,' so he started calling Sandy 'Rich,' too, like, 'Do you know when Rich is coming home?'" Linda says. "I thought that was funny." This was a man who took up countless pursuits over the years, from carpentry to piano to languages to computers, and mastered each in turn. "He was very impressive. He was incredibly accomplished as an attorney and as an individual," Alderson says. "A latent edge revealed itself from time to time. Was I his protégé? I'd say yes. Ultimately, I owe my entire professional career to Roy."

Eisenhardt specialized in business law; taught at Boalt Hall, the UC Berkeley School of Law, his alma mater; and coached freshman crew. So what had he seen in Alderson? "My belief was you can get to a certain level just by being smart and memorizing stuff, but without intuition you don't get to the final step of being an effective lawyer," Eisenhardt says. "What I would look for was that ability to make conceptual leaps, and I saw that in Sandy."

Eisenhardt was drawn to Alderson's sense of humor. "There are plenty of different types of humor," he said. "There's everything from the Three Stooges to Gene Wilder. Sandy's sense of humor I would put in the subtle one-liner category, where it's below the radar. This little piercing insight comes out, phrased in a way that gives you a recognition about what's really been going on, and then he lets it lie. He doesn't follow it up with a big belly laugh that requires you to laugh as well. It just comes in and then exits stage left."

Charlie O. Finley's Oakland A's were always a colorful train wreck of a club, scruffy and entertaining, talented and tough, united in their resentment of a miserly owner who was garish and unconventional, but also brilliant enough to build teams that won and won unforgettably. As a kid growing up in San Jose, I was lucky enough to attend one game of the 1972 World Series, cheering on Gene Tenace's heroics in a Series the A's won in seven, their first of three straight World Series titles. I loved the zany flair of those teams with colorful nicknames like "Catfish" for Jim Hunter, having no idea the name was cooked up by the showman Finley, complete with a cheerfully bogus backstory.

Finley would kick around all sorts of crazy ideas with his cousin Carl, who ran the A's front office almost single-handedly. "Dad and Charlie wanted baseball to be entertaining," Carl's daughter, Nancy, told me. "The game needed to be jazzed up several degrees. The designated hitter came out of these conversations. Nothing was considered a 'stupid' idea. Anything could be thrown out."

Finley brought traces of genius to his work, but he had the problem of the true visionary: He saw the future too well. For him it flashed before his eyes so vividly that he was forever disappointed at how slowly others caught up to his ideas. Some, admittedly, were better off forgotten, like orange baseballs and "Harvey," a mechanical rabbit that would pop up near home plate with a basketful of fresh baseballs for the umpires. Many of the innovations Finley pushed—night World Series games, brightly colored uniforms—were resisted at the time, but accepted as a given long after he'd been hounded out of the game by a baseball establishment that saw him as an interloper. Finley worked as his own general manager and burned up the phone lines from Chicago with his deal-making, but invariably he alienated his players with his tightfistedness. "He seemed to get his way when he wanted to make a trade for somebody," says Steve Vucinich, equipment manager of the A's, who started as a bat boy and ball boy the year the A's came to Oakland. "Most of the time it was a successful trade. You also have to take the fact that he didn't pay anybody. He told me once, 'Steve, you save your pennies so you can spend your thousands.'"

Bruce Jenkins, longtime sports columnist for the *San Francisco Chronicle*, started covering the A's in the '70s. "I can't imagine there's been anyone in the history of sports who was so obsessed with cutting everything, getting by on the absolute least he could get away with, while not even living there, living in Chicago, and yet just dominating with the team that he put together," Jenkins said. "Here's a half-drunk blowhard from Chicago—this guy is going to change the game in ways that are so meaningful? I resented the hell out of it. At the same time he was a brilliant businessman, very successful throughout his life, a complex cat. There's no one way to come up with an opinion with Finley because there's always a flip side."

Jenkins was at the Oakland Coliseum on June 15, 1976, when Finley, sizing up the implications of the coming age of free agency in baseball, decided he wanted to unload his high-priced talent all in one swoop and announced that day he was selling his stars Joe Rudi and Rollie Fingers to the visiting Red Sox for $1 million each and Vida Blue to the Yankees for $1.5 million. Such moves would become standard before long, but Commissioner Bowie Kuhn negated the deal. There wasn't much for Finley to do but look for an exit strategy. Rudi, Fingers, and Blue were all gone by the 1978 season, part of an exodus of talent following the World Series–winning years. The A's limped through '77 and '78 well south of .500 under a succession of forgettable managers (Bobby Winkles?), and in 1979 dropped to an almost Mets-in-'62 level of futility, 54-108, the only consolation being that almost no one saw them play that year (season attendance: 306,763) and not many heard them either. Finley, who did not attend a single A's game that year, even in Chicago, did so little to promote the team that he was sued by local governments and the commission they appointed to run the Coliseum. Single-game attendance dropped as low as 653.

Finley was demoralized, but he pulled one more brilliant move, hiring as his new manager for the 1980 season Billy Martin, a man who just might have been as smart, ornery, and unpredictable as he was. Though he will forever wear pinstripes in the imagination of baseball fans, Martin was born near Oakland in Berkeley, and his major breakthrough came when Casey Stengel, then managing in the Pacific Coast League, took an interest in him. Stengel schooled the young Martin in hard-nosed baseball and the lessons stuck. "If Case told me to run through a brick wall—I mean if he said, 'Billy, I think you can do it'—I'd give it a try," Martin once said. After Stengel's Oakland Oaks won their first pennant in years with a young Martin on the squad, Stengel was hired by the Yankees in 1949 and soon brought Martin to play for him there. Anyone who doubts that force of personality dictates events on a baseball field just has to study the way Martin, a scrawny second baseman, became a team leader and a key part of the 1950s Yankees, going on such a hitting rampage in the 1953 World Series, a Yankees victory over the Brooklyn Dodgers, that he had to be named Series MVP. Martin loved the nightlife, so much so the Yankees eventually unloaded him, thinking him a bad influence on Mickey Mantle. By 1980 Martin had already managed Minnesota, Detroit, and Texas, and the Yankees—twice. Energized by Martin's leadership, the 1980 A's got off to an 18-11 start.

Grappling with a divorce, Finley needed to sell the team. Cornell Maier, chairman of Kaiser Aluminum in Oakland, started looking to put together a group that could keep the A's in Oakland. One of the local businessmen Maier approached in July 1980 was Walter A. Haas Jr. of San Francisco, who at the time was chairman of Levi Strauss, founded by his great-granduncle Levi Strauss. Haas, a clear-eyed businessman who steered Levi Strauss to a new international profile, also happened to be a man deeply committed to philanthropy, having founded a foundation with his wife, Evelyn, all the way back in 1953. Haas was a Giants fan. He was not much interested in the A's. But he knew if Oakland lost the team to Denver or New Orleans, an already struggling East Bay would be far worse off.

"He cared about the quality of life for everyone in the Bay Area, so it was beyond what team he liked," his son Wally told me.

Haas agreed to be part of a group, but Maier came back with the news that Finley only wanted to sell to Haas, not an ownership group.

"Walter turned him down flat," Wally says. "He said, 'I'm still involved with Levi's, I'm not looking to run a team.'"

Walter was together with his family, including his son Wally, his daughter, Betsy, and Betsy's husband, Roy Eisenhardt, and told them the story of his saying no to Finley.

"Roy and I looked at each other," Wally recalled. "He said, 'You did what? You turned him down?'"

"Well, of course," Walter said.

"Well, wait a minute, Dad," Wally said. "We'll run the team. You don't have to run the team, if that's really your issue."

The family conferred, and finally Walter said, "You mean I literally could just be sitting in the stands eating peanuts and drinking a beer and second-guessing you guys?"

"Absolutely."

The die was cast. Eisenhardt said the family had spent time mulling different ways to give back to the community and saw an opportunity. "Investment in the A's probably leveraged into $150 million to $200 million of value conferred on that community just by virtue of having something to be proud of and the gap it filled in a lot of people's lives," Eisenhardt told me. "That's how we discussed it: We can leverage this into a whole lot of good stuff. I want to be very clear: To start off, our goal could not be to win the World Series, because winning a World Series to me was a false chase. The philosophy that I was extending on Walter's behalf was to establish a winning culture and make the team an asset that people were proud of."

Eisenhardt figured he'd help negotiate the sale and oversee the transition and then get back to life as it was. Wally was working at Levi's in community relations, good preparation to create a community relations department for the A's, but at the time he had been looking to change jobs. "I really wanted to get into sports," Wally told me. "So much so, ironically, I literally was starting to take a correspondence course from the Columbia School of Broadcasting on how to become an announcer. You'd send a tape in and then they'd critique it and you'd have another lesson. It was ridiculous. I stopped after one time because I got this tape back from my instructor"—and here, telling the story, he slipped into a cartoonish, cheesy voice— "'Well, Wally Haas, that's a real good start!' So disc jockey, L.A., plastic crap. I said, 'I can't do this.'"

As more progress was made on the sale, Eisenhardt realized he needed some legal help with aspects of the deal, so he turned to his protégé, Sandy Alderson. "I didn't want to be my own lawyer," Eisenhardt said. "I asked Sandy if he would be the attorney on the transaction. There were a lot of i's to dot on the whole thing. I wanted someone responsible."

Soon Roy and Wally were flying to Chicago to meet with Finley. One of the imperatives of the deal that was very clear to Roy and Wally was that they needed to keep talks out of the papers, which they knew could blow up any potential sale. "My job at the end of this deal was to babysit Charlie," Wally told me. "I was thirty-two years old and he almost killed me. He was so perfect for Chicago, let me put it that way. He was married still, but he had an ex–Miss California on his arm who was about twenty-eight. Here's a guy who had gone through quadruple bypass surgery. He was just the showman of showmen. Every time you go to a restaurant he wanted to make sure everybody knew he was there. He drank like a fish. Bourbon. Brown all the way. We'd come back after a night in the bars. I'd be staggering. He'd call me up in my hotel room—the room was literally spinning a couple of those nights—and he'd say, 'Haas, I've got one more thing.' I finally said, 'Charlie, fuck you, I'm going to bed.'"

Wally showed up the next day at the lawyers' office to sign the documents finalizing the sale.

"Look, Charlie, if you can keep this a secret, we'll buy you dinner in San Francisco Friday night before the Saturday press conference," Wally told him.

Back in San Francisco, Wally and Roy realized they had a problem: Where could they possibly go for dinner without having it hit the papers? They seized on the notion of Walter's private dining club in North Beach, called the Villa Taverna, tucked away in an alley half a block from the Transamerica Pyramid. It was a place for San Francisco's old money, in many ways a bizarre choice for a meal with Finley, but it worked out. Wally and Roy arrived first to find the place empty except for them. Finley showed up and looked around, smiling.

"You guys gotta lotta class!" Finley called out. "You bought this place out!"

Wally was sweating: "I thought to myself: 'OK, now what do we do? Do we go along with it and hope that nobody shows up? Or do we tell him?' I said: 'Fuck it. Let's go along with it.' I kept looking over at the door. Nobody came in for the two hours we were there, so he never knew."

Finley was in fine form at the press conference to announce the $12.7 million sale in August 1980, lamenting, "I'm having to leave because of the idiotic, astronomical, unjustified salaries today. But I don't think I could be leaving the team in better hands." Tom Boswell, writing in the *Washington Post*, described incoming team president Eisenhardt as "the consummate handsome blow-dry smoothie" and dutifully reported the Haases' plan to build the A's back up through the farm system, but mocked Eisenhardt for downplaying the cross-bay rivalry with the Giants and saying he hoped "mutual success would 'create a synergy between the teams.'"

Wally Haas still chuckles at one of the little surprises of that day. A young college student approached with his résumé, wanting the Haas family to hire him. He was at the time announcing Cal games on radio—and actually had called A's games on ten-watt KALX as well. What struck Wally at the time was the fresh-faced young man's "shock of reddish-brown hair, almost permed." His name? Larry Baer, who would go on to lead the San Francisco Giants to World Series titles in 2010, 2012, and 2014, rising to CEO.

Finley was so unpredictable, all bets were off on the sale going through until it was signed and delivered. To close the transaction, thirty-two-year-old Sandy Alderson was flown to Chicago as the lawyer representing the Haas family on the deal. "He was kind of bombastic," Alderson says. "Charlie was concerned that we wouldn't wire the money in time for him to get interest for that day. He kept threatening me: 'If it's not wired by such and such a time, if it's not closed, I'm going to void the deal!' He was bouncing around trying to bully everyone, including Roy and me. Finally we did get the money transferred in time, but it was one of those deals where you're not absolutely sure it will get done until it is done."

For Alderson it was a chance to get his own look at a figure he'd been hearing about for years. He'd been in the Bay Area in the summer of '75 working as a summer clerk at Farella Braun and then, back in Cambridge for fall semester, rooted for Boston in the ALCS against Oakland, which the Red Sox swept. Finley may have been bombastic, but he was his own man. In meeting Finley, Alderson did what he always did: He sized him up and imagined himself in Finley's shoes. He liked Finley's ideas and his fearlessness. He wondered what a man like Finley could do if he kept the flair for originality and the love of innovation, but reined in the personal irregularity, if he stopped penny-pinching to great extremes and thought instead about building a team that could last.

* * *

One of the boldest moves the new A's ownership group took when Walter Haas bought the team from Charlie Finley in August 1980 was to decide they were going to feel perfectly at home thinking like the fans they were. They were not grizzled, tobacco-chewing baseball veterans muttering under their breaths about the way things used to be. They had not spent decades behind home plate perfecting a pose of wry disengagement. They *cared*. They loved sports. They were thrilled at the prospect of being in on the action. This might have made them seem naive to some, but it gave them distinct advantages: They did not have to imagine how the fans they were trying to cultivate might feel about something. They knew because they were fans, too. They asked themselves: What would be the coolest possible thing we could do? What would be so fun, such a kick, it would excite any fan and have them eager to follow the A's? The answer came to them with a cry of "Holy Toledo!"

They kept in mind a core truth worth remembering: Nothing builds loyalty to a club like having a character in the broadcast booth fans love like part of the family. They wanted Bill King. They thought back to their own experiences of sports over the years and how often it was King, born and raised in Illinois but a fixture in the San Francisco Bay Area since the late 1950s, who had so often animated their favorite moments and given them such delicious flavor. King's signature call was "Holy Toledo!" As award-winning broadcaster Ken Korach recalled in his book *Holy Toledo*, "Night after night his voice would carry excitement and energy, like a jazz saxophonist commanding a room with a solo that built to a crescendo . . . '*Holy Toledo!*'"

King had called both Raiders and Warriors games for years. "I was a huge fan," Wally told me. "What made it so interesting was he could paint a picture like nobody's business. You could *see*, it was in such detail. It was not just the play-by-play, it was the color he added at the same time and doing it all in this machine-gun style."

Wally and Roy Eisenhardt were focused on getting King—and wanted to team him up with another great broadcaster, Lon Simmons, he of the rumbling bass voice and dry sense of humor. "I would call Lon sort of an abstract painter in his broadcasting style, and I considered Bill more a pointillist, somebody who connected all these minute dots into a panoramic portrait," Alderson told me.

Long before Alderson was ever listed in the A's media guide as a vice president, he was a key adviser and confidant to Eisenhardt. The two would kick around ideas during their runs or basketball games. Eisenhardt saw it as more an intellectual partnership than a mentor-protégé relationship. "I thought of us as peers," Eisenhardt told me. "The only difference between Sandy and me is I had eight years in age on him and he had done things I hadn't done. I wasn't in combat. That's an experience that it's hard to even think about what it must be like."

Having the Marine Corps in common not only deepened the bond between them, it also gave them a lens through which to see many of the challenges inherent in building the A's franchise. "We talked about how good it was for people to have an experience where they're mutually interdependent, as opposed to hierarchically connected, you know, 'My boss shit on me so I'm going to shit on you,' that kind of thing," Eisenhardt said. "You can really learn a lot from the horizontal interconnection in the Marine Corps. You learn not to overreact or underreact to anything, because other people are counting on you."

They also talked about pride. They were both proud of their time in the Marines. Why not make the community proud of the A's? To do that, they reached an agreement with KSFO, the powerhouse station in the market—"K-S-F-O in *Sannnn Frannnn*-cis-co"—rather than having A's games on a small-signal FM station.

Bolstering their radio presence was just one facet of a larger effort they undertook to energize fans in every way they could imagine. They hired sports marketing consultant Matt Levine, who used techniques he'd honed working in consumer product marketing (he'd been an executive at Scott Paper Company in Philadelphia) and international business consulting (McKinsey & Company), to explore why fans go to sporting events and what they hope and expect to get out of the experience.

"Winning is everything," Ray Kennedy wrote in an April 1980 *Sports Illustrated* article. "That has been the rallying cry in the front offices as well as the front lines of professional sports for so long that it is the turnstile equivalent of In God We Trust. And for obvious reasons. As any ticket taker well knows, more victories equals more fans equals more profits. Elementary, no?

"No. Dumb, unimaginative and hopelessly antediluvian thinking, says Matthew Levine, president of Pacific Select Corp., a marketing consultant firm that specializes in the sports business. 'Winning isn't everything,' he insists. 'In fact, only 25% of the fans come out solely because a team is winning.'"

Among the other findings from Levine and his coworkers, based on interviews with roughly three hundred thousand fans, the article reported:

- More than half of the people who consider themselves loyal sports fans never attend a game.
- Sportswriters are much less influential than either they or the teams think they are.
- At any given game 15% to 20% of the fans are there to "relieve pressure and tensions."
- Today's young adults (18 to 30 years old) don't know how to watch a game.
- The free-agent shuffle is destroying the sense of stability and continuity that fans thrive on.

Eisenhardt called Levine and suggested he come out to an A's game to meet him and Wally Haas. So there Levine was, two weeks after the August 1980 sale, for a midweek game against the Texas Rangers. Paid attendance: 2,443. "There were not a thousand people at the game," Levine says. "I met Wally, but Roy was doing the grilling, sizing me up: 'What would you do? What are your thoughts? Could you help staff this place?'"

"We resonated," Eisenhardt says. "He was a guy I could talk to who wasn't encumbered with 'Well, this is how you do it in baseball.' He was thinking more broadly. It doesn't mean every idea worked, but what Matt provided was somebody I could talk to outside of baseball who you could test ideas on. One of the ideas was: We could get Bill [King]. And Matt knew Bill and set up a meeting."

Eisenhardt and King also resonated. "I think it really was Roy's personality," Alderson says. "Bill King saw himself as kind of a Renaissance man. I'm sure that's how he viewed Roy, an accomplished guy who had a lot of different interests. They became very close friends."

Family history helped dictate the Haas family's community-minded approach. Loeb Strauss, born in 1829 in Bavaria, immigrated to the United States and before long was set up in San Francisco as the representative of the family wholesale dry-goods business. Loeb, who changed his name to Levi within a few years of arriving in America, was constantly innovating, eventually experimenting with durable denim pants he may actually have cut out himself, and he was committed to philanthropy, donating substantial sums to charities including the Home for Aged Israelites and the Roman Catholic and Protestant Orphan Asylums.

Levi Strauss died in 1902 and turned over his company to his nephew Jacob Stern, whose daughter Elise married Walter A. Haas Sr., who in turn took over in 1928. The family business thrived on his watch. "My grandfather would always bring a transistor radio when he had to go to the opera or symphony," Wally told me. "People thought he was hard of hearing when in fact he was just listening to the Giants game."

The 1960s adopted Levi's and made them famous. The family philosophy was: If you feel you've been lucky, why not pass some of that luck on? A 1978 article in *Forbes* quoted Wally's brother, Peter Haas, as saying, "I know a lot of people agree with Milton Friedman that a company's only responsibility is to make money. Well, we disagree completely."

"Really at the end of the day the reason why my dad bought the A's, more than giving his son and son-in-law a new job, was he really did worry that with Oakland being such a complicated and distressed community, it would be devastating for them to lose the A's," Wally says. "Maybe by keeping the A's here, if we ran it the way that we ran Levi's, which was essentially being really good corporate community citizens and giving back to the community, we could make the A's a community asset."

So many franchises had been family-owned in the postwar years, resistance to change was endemic in baseball. The Stoneham family owned the Giants in New York and San Francisco, the O'Malleys owned the Dodgers in Brooklyn and Los Angeles, the Busch family owned the Cardinals, and the Yawkeys owned the Red Sox. The family atmosphere extended to sports reporters, who were often invited to parties and given World Series rings if the team won. There was a "culture of continuation," as Steve Vucinich put it to me.

Teams were built around strong personalities who did not want to be questioned by their underlings. The organization the Haases inherited from Finley had a front office of six people: Mickey Morabito, traveling secretary and PR man, brought to Oakland by Billy Martin; Walter Jocketty, director of minor-league operations; Ted Robinson, who handled promotions and group sales as well as doing some backup radio broadcasting; Lorraine Paulus, who handled ticket operations; Lorraine's assistant; and Finley's cousin Carl. "Carl was a smart baseball man and businessman and he ran the entire operation," Jocketty told me. "He was the guy that kept things going in Oakland all those years. He always had to answer to Charlie, as we all did, by phone." Jocketty himself never met Finley until the press conference announcing the sale of the team to the Haas family.

"I'll never forget walking into the office the first day," Wally says. "I said, 'Roy, I'm really worried about the employees. We've got to make them feel at ease.' So I walked into the offices and I figured the receptionist would be the first person I'd see. The receptionist was a cardboard sign that said, 'Dial 0 for assistance.' We walked into Charlie's office and it was this dusty room with a bunch of books lined up along the wall and the bookends were two World Series trophies, real World Series trophies. It looked like a bomb had been dropped."

As team president, Eisenhardt urged people to be creative in their problem solving and to never be afraid to surprise him. "I used to tell everybody who worked for me, 'I expect you to make mistakes, and if you make no mistakes, that's not necessarily good, because it means you're not taking any risks,'" Eisenhardt told me.

He divided up the organization into four quadrants: community relations, finance, marketing and fan relations, and baseball. Wally Haas made an immediate impact working in community relations, getting players out among fans in Oakland and the East Bay and also instituting a range of brand-new initiatives, from literacy programs to a complaints desk at the ballpark. Former Washington Capitals marketing executive Andy Dolich was hired to take over marketing. Later, Kathleen McCracken was hired as CFO to round out the team. For the baseball quadrant, Eisenhardt would groom Sandy Alderson.

Everything was changing, even if not everyone in baseball understood that just yet. In 1975, five years before the Haas family bought the team, arbitrator Peter Seitz handed down the Messersmith decision, which in effect rendered baseball's reserve clause null and void. Up to then teams could simply renew a player's contract, even if he had not signed a new one, which kept salaries down. Once the onslaught of appeals against Seitz's ruling in the case of Andy Messersmith and Dave McNally was exhausted, Major League Baseball and the Players Association signed an agreement in 1976 allowing all players with six years of big-league experience to become free agents. Charles Finley understood the coming age of free agency would make being a baseball owner much more expensive, but even he could not have foreseen how dramatically the landscape would be remade.

Salary arbitration, which the owners had agreed to in 1973 to discourage holdouts and attempt to fend off universal free agency, was an area where being smart and doing your homework paid off. No one denied Finley was smart, but in his last two years as owner he had lost all ten of his arbitration cases. The new guys would be more diligent. "I'd been writing documents for years with arbitration clauses," Eisenhardt told me. "That wasn't a big deal." The new A's group had key arbitration cases that year with Tony Armas and Mike Norris, who could potentially land major salary increases. Armas led the team in RBIs with 109 and Norris won twenty-two games.

Eisenhardt asked Alderson to work on the cases along with a partner at the firm, Alan Harris, known as a skilled litigator.

"At some point Alan was pulled away because of a trial,'" Alderson recalls. "So I ended up doing most of the work." Then Alderson and Eisenhardt decided to bring in veteran baseball man Tal Smith to consult, but for the most part the young lawyer was on his own. Nonetheless, he and the A's won both cases. Armas had asked for a raise to $500,000 from $37,000 the previous season and was awarded $210,000. Norris, seeking $450,000, wound up with $300,000.

Eisenhardt hesitated to hire Alderson full time.

"He didn't think the firm would appreciate the fact that he was taking a lawyer with him," Alderson says. "That was his hesitancy. But my attitude was 'Hey, I can always be a lawyer. Why not try this?'"

4

HOOKED UP WITH APPLE

In late 1980 Matt Levine approached Fred Hoar, Apple Computer's vice president of communications, with a win-win scheme: The A's would get free Apple computers and Apple would get reams of free media attention from the advent of computers in baseball. "I want to put Apple on the map in a way it's never been," Levine told Hoar. "I want to get you more than $1 million of PR for a handful of pieces of equipment."

Hoar passed him to the Apple II product manager, a huge Dallas Cowboys fan who loved the idea of marrying statistical analysis of sport with computers. He asked what Levine needed, which amounted to three Apple II Plus computers and accessories.

"Can you wait around?" he asked Levine.

"What do you mean?"

"If you give me fifteen minutes, I'll give them to you today."

It was all in keeping with Eisenhardt's request to Levine when he hired him as a consultant. "I talked to him about the fact that we tried to do all this analysis of players' statistics and so forth, but it all became so anecdotal and impressionistic," Eisenhardt says. He told Levine at the time: "What I'd like to do is just have a system where we record every pitch and what happened. Then we can write some program where we could query the database and find out: How many ground balls does a left-hander hit to the left side?"

To implement their plans, they needed not only the computers but a modem connection to a PDP-10 mainframe computer at Digital Equipment Corporation in Philadelphia that would crunch the numbers every night based on the information gathered and spit data back out. Levine also had to write software to run these computers, and fortunately, he had the perfect partner. After the flattering *Sports Illustrated* article about Levine had come out, he was contacted by a scientist named Richard D. Cramer, who had a degree from Harvard, a PhD from MIT, and a passionate interest in baseball statistics. Cramer started crunching baseball numbers on computers in the 1970s, and he was an early member of the Society for American Baseball Research (SABR) and a cofounder of its Statistical Analysis Committee.

"He said, 'Maybe we can partner,'" Levine recalls. "So he and I became partners in STATS Inc.: Sports Team Analysis and Tracking System."

The acronym was Levine's idea; developing the software for what came to be known as the Edge 1.000 system fell to Cramer. As Alan Schwarz wrote in *The Numbers Game*, "Cramer tackled the input algorithms. Pete Palmer, Cramer's SABR friend at the American League statistics house, wrote the FORTRAN mainframe code."

As Levine pointed out, the Edge 1.000 system was basically doing what former Baltimore Orioles manager Earl Weaver used to do. "He'd have all these cards about matchups," he said. "The computer could automate them and make them available for the play-by-play broadcasters as well as the manager, as well as the staff. That's what was new."

Another priority was to upgrade the system for selling tickets. The Finley-era approach was to print out tickets for every game of the season all at once and put them in shoe boxes. "Roy had decided that selling tickets out of shoe boxes was not exactly the way he wanted to do things," says Linda Alderson. "Roy hired me to do exactly what I had graduated up the computer ladder to do, which was interface between the guy he had hired to be ticket manager and these guys he had hired to write the code. We had to be able to make special packages of tickets, not just individual tickets or season tickets. It was absolutely brand new. The Toronto Blue Jays came to look at our system at the A's to study it."

From a paltry 306,763 fans in 1979 to 842,259 a year later in Billy Martin's first season as A's manager, turnout continued to grow, reaching 1.3 million in 1981, the first full season with the Haas family as owners. Andy Dolich, executive vice president of business operations, oversaw an effort to improve as many aspects of the fan experience at the ballpark as possible. They upgraded the food and replaced old, broken seats with new orange seats, part of a million-dollar upgrade to the stadium, including $250,000 for a state-of-the-art scoreboard where they could feature something called dot racing. They also brought music to the ballpark in a new way. "As far as I know, we were the first team to start it," Eisenhardt told me. "We started playing 'Celebration' when we would win and played it when a guy hit a home run."

In the early '80s, the future radio talk show host Rush Limbaugh was working for the Kansas City Royals in group sales. He also started playing music between innings, complete with sound effects, as Zev Chafets explained in his book *Rush Limbaugh: An Army of One*, but it did not go over well with the Royals. "They didn't like it when I played Michael Jackson," Limbaugh told Chafets. "They used to say, 'Where do you think we are, Oakland?'"

The fans responded to Billy Martin's heart-on-his-sleeve style, so the team decided to go for it and soon "Billy Ball" was born. "The point of the advertising program was not to come up with some gimmicky promotional thing, but to create the sense that the team had a lot of personality and cared about the fans," Eisenhardt said. The A's were 18-3 by the end of April, a record, and they were having a blast. *Chronicle* sportswriter Bruce Jenkins still can't believe what he saw—or averted his eyes from—on A's charter flights back then. "A typical A's team charter in the Billy Martin era: You're heading east, it's mayhem, Billy's in his cups, wicked card games in the back, two completely buxom, comely stewardesses with their tits hanging out," Jenkins says. "In the back you have Billy with these tawdry but beautiful stewardesses."

It was a fun time to be around the A's and Levine felt a sense of finally breaking through. For years he'd gone door-to-door trying to find owners of sports teams who would hear him out and try his ideas, and he'd had quite a few successes by then. But this was something that could have an impact on baseball for years to

come. Their innovations on multiple fronts could—and did—prove
influential.

To move forward with the computer experiment Eisenhardt
had requested, Levine needed someone to sit in the radio booth
with announcers Bill King and Lon Simmons and feed data into
the computer. They posted notices at college campuses around the
Bay Area and ended up hiring Jay Alves, who had played baseball at
Half Moon Bay High and was the statistician for the football team.
He graduated from the University of Arizona in 1977 and worked
for two years as a weekend sports anchor on Channel 9 in Tucson.
Alves started in August 1981 as the A's "Apple computer operator,"
as he was listed in the 1982 media guide. "I traveled with the club,"
Alves says. "I sat with Bill and Lon and would give them information.
The computer would crash in the middle of the game and then you'd
have to redo the whole thing. You had those floppy disks. It was the
green screen computer, the very beginnings of Apple. At the time
it was just to track pitches and to track locations, thinking that you
could eventually use that as a tool for pitchers and defensive place-
ments, which is what they do now. It was mostly a broadcast tool."

"The A's had every statistic you ever wanted, Jay Alves sitting
up in the booth with us," Simmons told me. "We had enough information, we could have carried on a broadcast six or seven hours
after the game."

Billy Martin was old school all the way and let everyone know
how crazy he found all this stuff with computers. "He found it threatening because he had it all up in his head," Eisenhardt told me. "I
kept telling him, 'Billy, this isn't for you, I'm not trying to change
anything you do. This is for us to help us understand.'"

Alderson started full time with the A's in October 1981, five
months after Linda gave birth to their son, Bryn, but the full extent of
his role at the time was understated. The version that reporters often
accepted was that he came to the A's as a "general counsel," which
made sense; it just didn't tell the full story: Eisenhardt always had
in mind for Alderson to be more than merely a lawyer. The first A's
media guide that mentions Alderson, the 1982 guide, lists him fourth
on the depth chart, with the title "Vice President & General Coun-

sel," behind only Eisenhardt (president), Wally Haas (executive vice president), and Carl Finley (vice president, baseball administration).

"Roy was doing both things at the time, running the organization and sort of playing GM," Wally Haas explained to me. "He realized he couldn't do that, so he brought Sandy on to be the GM. It was the greatest move he made, frankly."

"I told Sandy, 'I can't call you the general manager,'" Eisenhardt remembers. "I wanted him to be running the entirety of it. I think that was the job I designed for him."

"He didn't say, 'Would you be the general counsel?'" Alderson recalls. "It was really, 'I need some help over here. Would you be willing to come over and help me out?' There wasn't a job description. I just did whatever was needed. I had a kind of open portfolio. I was really learning the business, learning baseball, and doing it quietly. I didn't have any single area of responsibility. There wasn't much for me to screw up other than a few contracts."

At first under the Haas family ownership, Billy Martin was general manager as well as field manager, taking over the title from Finley himself. "I didn't want that title," Eisenhardt told me. "It implied a baseball knowledge. Billy didn't want a general manager looking over his shoulder. That was a free giveaway. I said, 'OK, fine, kicking and screaming, I will give in.'" Managing many of the same players who just two years earlier had finished the 1979 season with a dismal mark of 54-108, Martin in 1981 was both an excellent tactical manager, making all the right moves, and a charismatic motivator. Martin led the A's to the ALCS for that strike-shortened season and was giddy to be facing his old team, the Yankees. It was, clearly, one of Martin's finer hours, even if the Yanks did sweep the A's in three straight games. "Of course we're disappointed," Martin told reporters afterward. "I'm disappointed because we didn't play the way we had during the year. That's the frustrating part. . . . We'll be there next year."

Jay Alves, the team's computer operator, was enlisted to help Alderson prepare for the arbitration case with Rickey Henderson, coming up in February 1982. "There wasn't computer-generated data then," Alderson says. "We had to create that ourselves. The statistical analysis we were doing for salary arbitration was pretty basic. There was some fear that if you got too esoteric, it would be portrayed by the other side as deceptive."

Alderson squared off against a team of six lawyers including Steve Fehr, whose brother Donald Fehr assisted the Players Association in the Seitz decision. "He just blew them away," Alves says. "On our side it was just Sandy and me, the bobo, handing him pieces of paper when he needed them. Sandy was a lawyer, but he was also a baseball man. These other lawyers came in and I just realized, 'They don't know the game nearly as well as Sandy does.' He had briefs ready that I had typed up on the word processor, arguments that should have been brought up that he'd thought of, and these other lawyers didn't even think of them."

The problem was Henderson, then twenty-three, was too damn good. He'd led the A's in batting average (.319) and on-base percentage (.408) in the strike-shortened 1981 season. The arbitrator awarded Henderson the salary he sought, $535,000, the third highest ever awarded by an arbitrator at that point, rather than the $350,000 the A's had put forward. "I of course was devastated that we lost," Alderson recalls.

In 1981 the A's had come flying out of spring training and won their first eleven games, on their way to an 18-3 April. In 1982 they were 11-11 in April and twelve games under .500 and dropping by June 24. Martin's mojo had left him. "As great as he was in '81, the greatest ever, to my mind, he was just that bad in '82, and just that nasty, drunk and swearing at his own players in the hotel lounge," Bruce Jenkins told me.

Martin became increasingly erratic and more and more of a challenge for A's ownership.

"I think partly why Roy brought Sandy on frankly was so he had somebody else also to deal with Billy Martin, who was a complicated guy, as good a manager as you could ever have, but also obviously had this other side of him," Wally Haas says. "So Sandy got the short straw."

Eisenhardt could see something slipping away.

"I loved Billy," he says. "He had some problems that caused his personality to change. He managed by intimidation, and intimidation as a leadership style works up to a point, then the players figure out how to sit down at the other end of the bench. The half-life of that style is definitely measurable. In '80 he had done a great job with the team and in '81 he did a great job with the team. In '82 things started to fall apart."

Martin flew off the handle when Alderson offered support to Tony Phillips after Martin sent him down to Triple-A to discipline him for arriving late to a game. "When Billy got wind of my conversation with Phillips, he went nuts," Alderson says. "I was only trying to be helpful to the kid, helping him deal with it and taking him to the airport, just to soften the blow a little bit. Besides, Billy was late to the ballpark all the time. I didn't tell Phillips, 'Hey, you shouldn't have been sent down.' There was none of that."

Back in New York, George Steinbrenner was sending out indications that he might want Martin to manage the Yankees for a third time. The A's were at home against the Brewers on a Thursday afternoon in August and gave up five unearned runs in a 10–6 loss. Martin was in a dark mood afterward.

"Billy had a tax problem," Steve Vucinich says. "I think he wanted an extension or some money and Sandy said no, and it just pissed off Billy and he started drinking in his office. The next thing we knew the office was destroyed. The TV was broken, pulled off the wall; the refrigerator was on its side. Billy had cut himself and there was blood on the walls."

"I think Billy's whole second-half behavior was about Sandy," says Bruce Jenkins. "You talk about two opposites! This guy is taking over?"

"It was a big deal. Is Billy the manager or is he the manager and the general manager?" Alderson remembers. "And it wasn't clear, really. Pretty much by default it was Billy running the show."

Martin had enjoyed free rein and did not like having his authority questioned. He asked for a definition of roles. Alderson called Martin's attorney, Eddie Sapir.

"I can remember saying something lawyerlike, like, 'We're going to stand by the four corners of the contract.' It was such a cheap response," Alderson says. "There was nothing in the contract that talked about Billy being the general manager. I wasn't really part of the decision-making group at the time, but Billy viewed me as a real threat. There's no question about that. That's why he blew up when I got involved with Phillips. That's when he blew up and destroyed his office."

The A's announced in October 1982 that Martin would not be back as manager, despite having three years left on his contract. Alderson's time to make his mark had come. The most important next step was hiring a replacement for Martin, and to compile a list of candidates, Alderson says, "most of our information came from Peter Gammons," then a baseball writer for the *Boston Globe*. The A's interviewed Jim Leyland, Jim Fregosi, Jimy Williams, Steve Boros, Hal Lanier, Ed Nottle, and Ray Miller. They put together a good group; every one of their candidates, except Nottle, the A's Triple-A manager at the time, would soon end up with a big-league managing job.

5

COMPUTER HELPS A'S
ZAP TIGERS

Early in his time with the A's, Alderson had let it be assumed that he knew less than he actually did about baseball; it was easier to learn that way and far better to surprise people than to have them muttering about how wildly you'd overstated your level of understanding. This strategy in part had to do with the environment around the A's then, the cocksure Billy Martin embodying the idea that only a baseball lifer could really know the game, but it was fundamental to the Alderson code, drilled into him as a boy and above all as a Marine: Take on a job only when you believe you can do it well. Never make a promise until you're ready to fulfill it.

Alderson's core beliefs about baseball started with the precept that it was smart not to swing at bad pitches, but instead to force a pitcher to come to you on your own terms; a hitter could be aggressive, even violent, but better to attack a hittable pitch after working the count than simply to flail away at anything that came up there. It was a philosophy that fit him to a T. Even in conversation, Alderson rarely replies to a comment or question unless he knows what he wants to say, and given the right opening, he seldom fails to pounce. The more he thought about examples from his own years as a baseball fan, the more he thought about Baltimore Orioles manager Earl Weaver, a pioneer of statistical analysis who led the Orioles to victory in the 1970 World Series. Weaver also authored three books.

"If you go back and read about Earl Weaver, his strategy was basically get people on base and hit a three-run homer," he says.

"There was another influential manager at the time, Gene Mauch, who was a proponent of small ball—bunt 'em over, get 'em over, yadda, yadda, yadda. Mauch never won a pennant. Plus, I always thought that the home run was more entertaining, although the Mauch approach can also be entertaining with these little elements. Everybody gets to clap when a guy gets a single. Everybody gets to clap when he steals second. Everybody gets to clap when he gets bunted to third. And then what happens? The next hitter can't get him in from third with less than two outs. Baloney! You get a couple guys on and hit a bomb. That's how you win games."

Alderson was an early reader of Bill James, the influential numbers guru. James started out putting his baseball thoughts down on paper while working as a night watchman at the Stokely–Van Camp pork and beans factory in Lawrence, Kansas, and attracted all of seventy-five purchases when he took out an ad in the *Sporting News* promoting his self-published first book, *1977 Baseball Abstract*. James would never quite shake the rough edges of a guy who penned his bon mots and crunched his numbers in a factory that produced 90 million cans of pork and beans annually while other, less worthy individuals, as he saw it, were paid salaries by newspapers to sit in the press box. As influential as his love of numbers would be, James also spawned a school of sportswriting that saw as one of its imperatives a need to napalm-blast newspaper sportswriters with scorn. "If all of the newspaper stories that have been written about Billy Martin were put in a pile in the middle of New Jersey, it would be the best place for them," James wrote in one of his early *Abstract*s.

"His condescension comes through in his prose," *Washington Post* critic Jonathan Yardley wrote in 1982. Yardley also noted: "For six springs James, a practitioner of a black art called sabermetrics, 'the mathematical and statistical analysis of baseball records,' has been publishing an 'abstract' of the previous season's statistics. Up to now he has been his own publisher." Starting in 1982, the *Abstract* was published by Ballantine.

James had a furious energy that won him die-hard adherents. There was something almost lovably cloddish in the way that James, fulminating about "hokum" spewed by others, could interrupt himself to go off on tangents like this one in 1982 on names, inspired by a mention of Milwaukee's Gorman Thomas: "Did you know that players named Thomas have hit 682 home runs in major league play, the ninth highest total for any surname? They passed Mays last May with their 669th and are closing in on the Joneses, whose first in 1982 will be their 700th. The top ten names for home runs are Williams (1,762), Robinson, Johnson, Smith, Jackson, Aaron, Ruth, Jones, Thomas and Mays. More stuff you'd never know if you didn't read the *Baseball Abstract*."

Alderson ordered an early *Bill James Baseball Abstract* by mail and credits James with introducing him to rigorous statistical analysis of baseball. But James was off in Kansas, which was a long ways away from California. Alderson needed someone in California to develop these ideas into practical applications, and he found that someone on his commute back and forth to work.

His house on Green Street was well situated for a quick drive through the heart of San Francisco and onto the Bay Bridge with its sweeping views, and Alderson loved those drives. "I'd go up to Broadway and through North Beach past Carol Doda's—where a bunch of Marines spent an evening in 1971, on the corner of Columbus—down to the Embarcadero Freeway, the Bay Bridge, and the East Bay," he says. "I could get from Green Street to the Coliseum in twenty to twenty-five minutes. It was an easy commute, picturesque route, and about the right amount of time to listen to NPR."

The local NPR affiliate, KQED, had a recurring five-minute segment by someone named Eric Walker, who would discuss his thoughts on baseball and statistics during morning drive time. Walker's segment, sponsored by Kaypro computers, was syndicated to about twenty other stations and led to his being asked by Celestial Arts, a small publisher in Millbrae, just south of San Francisco, to do a book. *The Sinister First Baseman* was published in 1982.

Alderson first heard Walker on the radio and then picked up a copy of his book and liked what he saw. *The Sinister First Baseman*, great fun to read now, is all over the place. Written in prose that is by turns baroque and Victorian, it careens here and there with undisguised glee. As former Giants manager Frank Robinson put it in his foreword, "This is a baseball book that incorporates mythology, Greek philosophers, anatomy, history, and anthropology, to name only a few of the subjects touched on seriously, sarcastically, or just plain humorously." Often reading Walker, he sounds so much like the guy next to you on BART talking about UFOs that it takes a little work to notice that, yes, he's actually making a lot of sense: "I repeat: a fan's *only* right is to *buy* or *not buy*," he writes at one point. "Disagree with that, and the Kremlin would love to talk with you at length. I am just as frustrated as you—and very possibly a lot more so—with the brainlessness in the current baseball scene . . . *but we don't own the game*."

The best line in the whole book might be: "We must learn to see with the eyes of today, and not insist on looking through the dusty spectacles of yesterday." Walker was well aware that the importance of on-base percentage was hardly a new idea. What was new was technology. With personal computers now becoming available, and already being used by the Oakland A's as he was writing, rigorous analysis of data could add depth and detail to the study of how the game was actually played and what actually worked and did not.

Walker was a free spirit, not without his quirks, who felt comfortable going to great lengths to get his ideas across, even with very little validation that the rest of the world found them interesting or valuable. He was part of a tradition going back to Branch Rickey, who hired a number cruncher named Allan Roth and came up with on-base percentage. Walker had grown up a baseball fan in New York, gotten away from it, then fallen back in love later in life, armed with an engineer's mentality and an eagerness to probe more deeply. The event that changed his life was reading a book called *Percentage Baseball* by Earnshaw Cook. "It was a terrific book," he told me. "Cook was an extremely clever man and, as he admits in the introduction, one of the worst writers in the world. He came close to getting a job with the Kansas City A's and he talked himself out of it by being too arrogant. This book, written about the time Bill James was getting ready to go to elementary school, laid the groundwork: The laws of nature are the laws of nature, math is math, physics is physics, the way it works is pretty much the way it works."

Frank Deford had given Cook's ideas a big plug back in the March 6, 1972, issue of *Sports Illustrated*, writing, "For more than a decade Earnshaw Cook, a retired Baltimore metallurgist, has been trying to convince baseball's bosses that playing the sacred percentages is, to be blunt, dumb baseball. In 1964 Cook brought out a 345-page book, *Percentage Baseball*, that was full of charts, curves, tables and complicated formulas that sometimes went on for the better part of a page. The book dared to suggest that either: a) baseball is not using the best possible odds on the field, or b) mathematics is a fake."

For example, Deford continued, "The sacrifice bunt is one of the least productive plays in baseball. The fact that it is negative strategy, says Cook, 'is validated beyond reasonable doubt.'"

Walker agreed about the sacrifice bunt—and then some. He argued that the ultimate key to winning in baseball was to avoid outs and to put runners on base. Never give an out away, he argued. "In baseball, some numbers are known, some are not, and the meaning of most of them can be debated," Walker wrote. "But there's one number everyone knows and agrees with: three. Three outs and you're gone. Period. The end. All runners cancelled, all theories moot, all probabilities zero. That number must, in any rational evaluation of the game, dominate planning."

This was the kind of lucid insight, polished to a gemlike clarity, that Alderson could put in his back pocket and carry around with him. Walker had worked with the San Francisco Giants as a consultant preaching the importance of on-base percentage. "I was on good terms with [manager] Frank Robinson," he told me. "I was kind of a fixture in his office. There's the chair, there's the desk, and there's Eric Walker." Walker enjoyed talking to Robinson, but he never had much influence with Giants general manager Tom Haller and was on the lookout for a more receptive GM.

Walker wrote to the A's in 1982 offering to do some number crunching for them, having no idea if he'd ever hear back. He did. "I sent them a letter of inquiry," Walker told me. "I was told after the fact that Sandy had listened to me on the radio and was familiar with my book."

"Hash me up a sample of what you can do," Alderson told Walker during their first meeting at the A's offices.

For his sample, Walker produced a thirty-two-page report in September 1982 that he sent to Alderson—earning, he recalls, $500 for his work. Walker could not have known that Alderson once spent a summer at Langley reading and sorting CIA cables from all over the world, but clearly he was evoking clandestine intelligence work when he stamped an upper-case CONFIDENTIAL across the top of the first page of the report, followed by THE OAKLAND ATHLETICS: A QUANTITATIVE ANALYSIS BY MATHEMATICAL METHODS.

"It is elementary that the more runs a team scores and the fewer runs it gives up, the more games it will win," the first page of Walker's report began. "Less elementary is the fact that this relationship can be quantified. The statistical equation relating runs, opponents' runs, and win-loss percentage is:

$$P = \frac{(R - OR)}{(R + OR)} + (.5)$$

"In modern times, to be a realistic contender a team must be capable of approximately .600-level baseball; lower percentages can sometimes win Flags, but .600 is a realistic level."

One of Walker's key conclusions in the report was that, compared to offense and pitching, the impact of defense on winning games is "generally much overestimated"—at least when one focused on regular-season competition, which was what Walker was doing. Given the emphasis on offense, then, Walker focused on that season's A's players and also on potential trade targets, relying on a statistic he created called "SX" for "scoring index," generated using figures for at bats, walks, hits, total bases, and games played.

The Walker report was pointed on the topic of Tony Armas, acquired by Finley from the Pirates in an eight-player swap early in 1977. He tied for the league lead in homers in 1981 and was fourth in 1980. Walker preferred the upside of young Mike Davis, who hit .400 in limited action. "At almost any currently plausible performance levels, Davis' value is significantly higher than Armas'," Walker wrote.

"Experience has proven again and again that (over 1000 BFPs) career levels are the best predictors of coming results; Armas' good 1980 should not obscure the point. Unless Davis bombs badly, he clearly should displace Armas."

When Walker turned in the report, Alderson read it and told him, "I thought this was interesting." Two and a half months later, the A's traded Armas and Jeff Newman to the Red Sox for Carney Lansford, Garry Hancock, and a minor-leaguer.

Walker's most directed recommendation of a player to acquire was catcher Ron Hassey, in his fifth season with the Indians. The argument was that the A's needed to upgrade and, of the options, "Hassey is essentially it," Walker wrote. "Reliable report has it that his defense is at least very adequate, and his mediocre 1982 season should not obscure his strong and consistent career record." Then in a note that could have anticipated Oakland's eventual acquisition of Jeremy Giambi, he added: "His slowness as a runner is a liability, but one can't have everything."

Walker was paid $5,000 a year to generate information and analysis for Alderson and the A's. "I never got very much feedback," Walker told me. "At the time for all I knew I was just throwing rocks in a dark cave."

The relationship—and the reports—continued for years. He and Alderson would talk periodically throughout the year, meeting a few times, though not on a set schedule. "My impressions were: Here's a guy who speaks in complete grammatical sentences and expresses his thoughts clearly," Walker says. "That registered with me. Very few people do that. You could see he was a very intelligent guy, and you could sense even through the velvet, there was iron there."

I asked Walker how much Alderson's thinking shifted over the years as Walker worked on ever more sophisticated analytical tools to assist in baseball decision-making.

"I don't think it shifted a lot," Walker said. "I think he was onto this from the very beginning. It's self-proving. It's like the law of gravity. You can argue about it all you want, but when you drop the rock, it falls. What analysis is about is understanding what helps to win ball games. It has to do with locating the best ballplayers. To this hour, walks are still underrated. Another shibboleth that gets passed around is that everyone understands the importance of walks. The *under*valued part has always been walks."

"After reading Earl Weaver and reading *The Sinister First Baseman* and reading Bill James, it became clear to me that the Earl Weaver approach was superior and you could establish that mathematically," Alderson told me. "Once you established a correlation between on-base percentage and slugging percentage with run production, then you also established a correlation between gross run production and win-loss percentage, and it became apparent that the best approach was high on-base percentage and hit the ball out of the ballpark, as opposed to batting average, as opposed to the hit-and-run and bunting.

"For somebody like me, who was looking for a structure for talent evaulation, it wasn't like I had to jettison twenty years of history in the game or a more traditional approach to the game, because I hadn't been in the game. It was easier for somebody like me to go all in on this new approach. I wasn't searching for a philosophy so much as a process by which one could make good baseball decisions. That process would involve information from a variety of sources, and what would those sources be and how would the different strands of information be weighted? Do you rely exclusively on a scout who has been doing it for fifteen years? Do you rely on some guy in Kansas who has come up with a different approach? Or do you try to come up with a way to utilize both?"

To know for sure, Alderson had to understand both the guy in Kansas and his own scouts. Fortunately he had a job with a major-league team and could do just that. He could read James and Walker and then go watch baseball side by side with professional scouts who had spent decades studying—and thinking about—the game. It was like the difference between reading a book like Michael Herr's *Dispatches* in a campus library in America and taking a bike ride through Hué.

Alderson gave himself a game plan to maximize his chances of absorbing information and perspective from baseball people without putting people off, and he stuck to it with all the discipline of someone standing attention at the corner of Lyndon Johnson's coffin.

"One, I kept my mouth shut.

"Two, I didn't dress like a lawyer, which fit in nicely with the Haas family and Roy Eisenhardt.

"Three, I tried to stay in decent shape, because acceptance comes in different ways. One, you're nonthreatening; two, you're respectable; three, in this case, trying to maintain some fitness without trying to mimic what was going on around me.

"Four, I waited for opportunities to make a contribution. As Peter Ueberroth once told me, 'Half of the battle is showing up.'"

Showing up meant a lot of things. Sometimes it meant getting into his car and driving an hour and a half to Modesto to sit next to a scout and watch A's prospects in game situations. "I would go watch games, even though I wouldn't really know what in the hell I was looking at," he says. "But I did have some basic principles in mind that were coming out of Bill James and Eric Walker. So it wasn't so much scouting for tools as it was actually seeing a player who had only been a statistical entity, not a human being."

Alderson and the Haas family, in choosing a manger for the A's in 1983, may have gone a little too far in the direction of choosing someone who would represent a departure from Billy Martin. Steve Boros, interviewed first, had done his homework about the team's new regime, and he figured that if he mentioned computers, he'd have an edge; he was right. "We picked Steve Boros, who is now deceased, a great guy whose distinguishing quality may have been that he was an English literature graduate from the University of Michigan," Alderson says. That December at the winter meetings, once the A's had hired Boros, the *Times* quizzed him on his literary taste and informed readers that his favorite novel was *The Great Gatsby* and his favorite play was *Death of a Salesman*. Boros fit right in with Renaissance men like Eisenhardt, but Alderson smiles thinking about the team's Boros period.

"Steve would never argue with an umpire," he told me. "He refused. He said, 'Look, they're not going to change their minds, so I'm not going to argue with them.' I kept saying, 'Look, Steve, this is part of the theater of the game and you have to do this. This is part of what fans expect, it's what players expect, it's part of your leadership role, it's part of what you do as a surrogate for fans.' I tried to get into this sort of intellectual discussion with him about arguing with umpires. I finally said, 'Just one day decide you're going to do it. Get in front of the mirror and practice, and just recognize that it's not about principle, it's not about something fundamental in your personal ethos, this is just part of the entertainment.'"

The transition from Martin to Boros opened the way for a major leap forward in how much the A's used computers as an analytic tool on the baseball side. Jay Alves was pleased to find Boros a far more receptive audience to all that they'd already been working on. "Billy didn't care," Alves said. "He was a gut guy. But when Steve Boros was hired, he had a lot of interest, and I would give him stuff from time to time."

Soon Matt Levine's promise to Apple about getting reams of free publicity came through in spectacular fashion. The media attention was so abundant and breathless, it soon became a joke around the team.

A brief sampling:

COMPUTERBALL IS HERE!, *Sport*, April 1983
COMPUTER HELPS A'S ZAP TIGERS, *Miami Herald*, May 13, 1983
THE COMPUTERS OF SUMMER, *Newsweek*, May 23, 1983
COMPUTERS GRAB PLACE IN BASEBALL, *USA Today*, September 28, 1983

The *Newsweek* article, which reached the widest audience, focused on Boros and White Sox manager Tony La Russa as the first two skippers in baseball to use Apple II Pluses, noting, "The A's inadvertently ushered in the computer era when they bought a system called Edge 1.000 for their broadcast team two years ago. . . . Today both teams employ computer operators who, by dint of some furious keyboard tapping, manage to record a highly nuanced, pitch-by-pitch account of each game."

Ray Kennedy, writing about Boros in *Sports Illustrated*, observed, "Though traditionalists may shudder at the thought, it was inevitable that such a stat-happy pursuit as baseball would plug into a data bank. And Boros, forty-six, a Michigan grad who plans to take classes in computer science during the off-season, is in the forefront of a new wave of enlightened technocrats who are rewiring the game."

Like a lot of magazine articles, this one oversold the trend it was trying to highlight. Baseball was a long way from being rewired. The traditionalists were correct in pointing out that a lot less had changed than had remained fundamentally the same. A manager would always have to play at least the occasional hunch, but those choices would increasingly be made against a backdrop of precise information a manager could choose to heed or ignore as he saw fit. The true rewiring of baseball would take much longer. For that to occur, advances in technology were needed that could lead to a quantum leap forward in data collection and in new ways of seeing the game, akin to how the space telescope gave us previously unimaginable glimpses of the cosmos.

6

THE GOOGLE OF BASEBALL

What the Haas family ownership pursued in the 1980s, with Alderson in the middle of the operation, was ahead of its time. Now their approach would be summed up as the Silicon Valley model: Find smart and creative-minded people, put them together in a work environment where they are taken care of and encouraged to love their jobs, give them plenty of space to try ideas that might be good or bad, and then build a community of people inspired to see the organization as innovative, fun, and effective. "The Haas family ran Levi Strauss in a very progressive way, very sensitive to their employees' well-being," Alderson says now. "I think that's how we looked at the A's. Google and Apple and these other places in Silicon Valley today are a contemporary version of what was going on with the Haas family forty years ago. But—this is probably my age speaking—it appears a little less genuine at Google and Apple. It has a lab rat feel to it, where everything is manipulated for productivity, like the contented cow gives more milk."

Alderson, a man hungry for new ideas to try out, found a steady supply of them in A's executive Karl Kuehl (pronounced "keel"), a leathered baseball veteran but also, surprisingly enough, a freethinker. Born in Monterey Park, California, Kuehl was a player-manager in the Northwest League starting at age twenty-one and later managed the Montreal Expos for part of a season, albeit to a disastrous 43-85 record, before he was removed in favor of Charlie Fox. Kuehl headed player development for the A's from 1983 to 1995, but he was a fount of fresh ideas.

Ray Karesky was working at a hospital in Phoenix in the spring of 1984 when the A's started making inquiries about implementing an employee-assistance program. As it happened, Karesky administered the hospital's EAP, which focused on offering support and counseling to employees going through issues with substance abuse and other personal problems. Karesky, a licensed psychologist, had a master's degree in education from Harvard and a PhD in counseling psychology from Arizona State University. Kuehl called him up to say the A's would like to meet with him to talk about his EAP work. "I was a casual sports fan, so it wasn't like 'Oh my god!'" Karesky says now.

Alderson and Kuehl made an odd duo. "Karl was so thoroughly baseball, it oozed out of his pores, and Sandy was very new to baseball," Karesky recalls. "But they shared some values, including the idea that if you took care of people, it was good for the club."

They had a list of detailed questions about EAP, its scope, its effectiveness, its risks and rewards. "They asked me about my background, and I told them I worked a lot with disturbed adolescents," he says. "They looked at each other, smiled, and said, 'Perfect.'"

Two days later, Kuehl called and asked him to catch a flight to Albany, New York, to meet with Oakland's Double-A minor-league team.

"It wasn't just that Sandy was an innovator; he was willing to act quickly," Karesky told me. "Other teams could take months and years to try to work it out. My boss at the hospital said, 'You can't go! You don't have a contract!' I went anyway."

One of the first people he met in Albany was Keith Lieppman, manager of the team, who later succeeded Kuehl as farm director. There in Albany he also met an unusual character from New York, a writer named Harvey Dorfman the A's hired to work as the first mental skills coach in baseball. "Karl recommended him, and my attitude at the time, frankly, was anything Karl wanted to try, I was willing to try," Alderson told me.

Dorfman was nothing like the German-accented egghead psychiatrist stereotype and used his Bronx accent and offbeat sense of humor to put ballplayers at ease. His message, reiterated in countless ways, was to practice clearing the mind of distraction and visualize positive outcomes. As he said at the time, "Ask any coach and he says 80 percent of the game is mental . . . yet they have never had anyone working full time on that part of the game."

"Harvey was sort of an odd duck," Alderson says. "He reminded me immediately of Phil Silvers as Sergeant Bilko. He had the same bigger-than-life personality. It wasn't just that he looked like Silvers. He sort of acted like him, too. Eventually he ended up with the same relationship with others in the organization that Bilko had with his Army peers. He was this wacky guy that everyone followed and revered. Harvey was Phil Silvers in a baseball uniform."

Dorfman grew up in the Bronx, far more interested in following the Bombers than his studies. He ended up teaching English at Burr and Burton Seminary in Manchester, Vermont, and wrote about baseball. As Rick Wolff noted in a 2011 *New York Times* remembrance, "Dorfman was conversant in the current best sellers and would routinely quote chapter and verse from famous philosophers about life's challenges."

Kuehl met Dorfman in Vermont, through Lieppman, and later collaborated with Dorfman as coauthor of *The Mental Game of Baseball: A Guide to Peak Performance*, which explains, "The key, then, is for a player to regulate his mental performance as he regulates his physical performance. He must learn the strategies and skills required for controlling himself and his situation in the ball game. He must handle worry and anxiety, often based on the pressures of performing; he must take responsibility for that performance; he must approach his game with commitment, concentration, and confidence. As we said, this is not an easy task, but it's a necessary one. . . ."

Dorfman never claimed to be a psychologist (he called himself a "stretch," not a "shrink") and was forever interested in absorbing what insight he could from authors. As a well-read individual, he was familiar with a classic text in the area of mental preparation for high performance, *Zen in the Art of Archery* by Eugen Herrigel, one of the first books to introduce Zen ideas to Europe and the United

States, inspiring more popularly read titles like Robert Pirsig's *Zen and the Art of Motorcycle Maintenance*.

The A's took a proactive approach to mental-health work. Dorfman and Karesky did not sit by waiting to deal with problems as they arose. They were encouraged to travel to where different teams in the organization were playing and get to know the players and other personnel well. "My instincts told me if they don't get to know me, they're not going to trust me, and they're not going to use me," Karesky explains. "I became very much a creature of baseball operations, not just the organization. It proved to be a good model, getting involved with baseball operations; a lot of the counseling takes place informally."

Dorfman ultimately moved on, frustrated that the A's were not willing to risk riling their field managers by having him work directly with major-leaguers. "His whole time with us was as a minor-league coach," Alderson says. "He was exposed to the major-league level, but he never had any responsibilities with the major-league team or the major-league players. That's ultimately what caused him to leave Oakland."

The A's under the Haas family had a top-to-bottom commitment to making such programs work. There were, however, glitches. It was clear the foundation of any counseling program was confidentiality. No ballplayer would talk to a counselor about what was really going on in his life without faith that he could speak in private with no betrayal of confidence. Trust had to be 100 percent. Karesky could not be asked to leak information from private sessions. Alderson and Kuehl had to be completely trustworthy as well.

"If they don't trust Sandy and Karl, they're not going to trust me," Karesky says. "That was put to a test early. Others in the organization didn't necessarily see it that way. They thought I worked for the club, and I should give information."

Alderson told Karesky not to worry.

"Ray, this is not your problem," he said. "I will deal with it. You just do what you do."

Karesky heard that Alderson went to the mat to back him up, and the matter was no longer an issue. Alderson to this day speaks very highly of Karesky and the work he did over many years for the A's, including developing one of the first Spanish-language counseling programs in baseball. There was a ferment of ideas, and much of the innovative spirit was driven by Karl Kuehl.

"Karl was very influential in all this, saying, 'We should try this!'" Alderson told me. "He was an amazing guy. He was hard-nosed and conventional in many ways, but he was such a forward thinker in so many other ways."

Alderson's time in the Marine Corps developed in him a commitment to foster talent at all levels, from the grounds crew to community relations to the guys who played music between innings. It was all forward-thinking and high-minded, the emphasis on a horizontal structure, but there was also the adrenaline rush of competition to keep the pulse rate going. "Alderson smiled at a lot of things, but it always carried some sort of meaning, because there was an edge to him," Bruce Jenkins of the *Chronicle* says. "You paid attention to Sandy, because you'd better be alert. Lord knows he always was. That made him a stimulating guy to be around."

Their innovations in that period also included installing the first weight room in baseball. Alderson had noticed a surge in power in the early 1980s from former Red Sox catcher Carlton Fisk, he of the famous wave-it-fair home run. Fisk attributed his increase in home runs to weight training, Alderson recalled, but because he'd worked out in the off-season and not kept it up during the regular season, his numbers tailed off. "That's when the light went off," Alderson says. "We have to put something together for the off-season and we have to find a way to maintain that conditioning during the season."

In 1982 the Raiders had left Oakland—and the Coliseum—creating some space, so the A's put in weight-lifting equipment for their players and anyone else who wanted to use it, a group that included Alderson and Eisenhardt. It was not extensive, a small space with what Alderson calls "an odd collection of different machines, pulleys, and dumbbells." Given the importance of weight training to the contemporary game, it's almost comical how suspicious old-time baseball people were of any sort of weight lifting. Dave McKay, one of the A's coaches, took on the extra duties of being strength and conditioning coach.

"In those days hotels didn't have health clubs and spas and all that, so Dave's main responsibility as strength and conditioning coach was to wake guys up on the road, load them into a van, and drive them to Gold's Gym or whatever," Alderson says. "It wasn't like he was formally trained. But McKay was physically fit and took care of himself, and knew his way around weights, and had trained in the context of a baseball career. He wasn't in the weight room in the ballpark in Oakland coaching guys. He was a resource."

As part of the settlement of the 1981 strike, baseball's rules called for "compensation picks" when teams lost valuable players to free agency. The A's, having just lost Tom Underwood to a free-agent signing, had a pick coming in 1984 and claimed right-hander Tim Belcher, selected by the Yankees in the first round and then inadvertently left exposed. It was a brassy move by Alderson, something the old-boys network of GMs would never have done, and it made the A's a better team. "He worked the rule," Jay Alves says. "Then three years later we traded Belcher to the Dodgers for Rick Honeycutt, who became an important part of the club."

As a new GM, especially one coming from outside of baseball, Alderson was not about to throw his weight around when it came to choices on which players to draft. He freely admitted to lacking a scout's or baseball lifer's eye for evaluation. But in leading the discussion over whom to pick, he could move the thinking toward his frame of reference. As it happened, the expected first overall pick in the June 1984 amateur draft was a raw-boned redhead named Mark McGwire, who had been putting on a show with his moon shot homers for USC, hitting an eye-popping thirty-one for the Trojans his junior year. The three teams most interested in McGwire were the Mets, choosing first, and the A's and the Padres, choosing tenth and eleventh, respectively.

Dick Wiencek, the A's scouting director, loved McGwire. He lived in Claremont, California, near where McGwire had gone to high school, and often saw him play at USC. In fact, Wiencek insisted the other A's scouts go see him as well. Alderson got a first-hand look at McGwire during a UCLA-USC Pac-10 game—and he checked his numbers. What Wiencek and other scouts kept talking about was McGwire's ability as a pure hitter with power; that was great, Alderson thought, but still better was that he was a pure hitter with power who also had a great eye. His freshman year at USC, McGwire had more walks than strikeouts. Over his entire three-year career at USC, he finished with eighty-three walks to go with 168 hits, a highly valuable complement to his fifty-three homers and 147 RBIs.

The A's were considering McGwire, Shane Mack, and Oddibe McDowell. When the Mets opted not to draft McGwire, worried that he wouldn't sign with them, the A's pounced. "Mark McGwire was a power guy who got on base," Alderson says now. "McGwire was *the* power guy in that draft, but there were some reservations about him among some scouts because of Jeff Ledbetter, another power hitter, who had been drafted a year or two earlier from Florida State and not panned out."

Alderson, always a gatherer of information, liked to wait to get a feel for the landscape before asserting himself. There were always certain fixed points around which his evolving perspective could pivot, and one of those was the A's mercurial leadoff man. Rickey Henderson was an Alderson type of player all the way, getting on base and scoring runs and also hitting home runs. "Rickey was a great base stealer because he was on base all the time," he says. "That was the icing on the cake. Those qualities were valuable. They weren't fundamental. Rickey's probably the greatest player I ever saw because of his on-base qualities and his power and his speed. He had it all."

The A's were not quite ready to build their future around Rickey, the hometown hero who set a major-league record in 1982 by stealing 130 bases. Before the 1983 season, they offered him a seven-year deal for more than $10 million. He turned that offer down and opted to go to arbitration for a third straight year instead. The truth was team owner Walter Haas would have dug deeper to re-sign Rickey if the will was there, but a few in the A's leadership were put off by some of Rickey's eccentricities and a belief that he would sometimes give less than full effort. "We had this feeling that he just didn't represent us that well and he was a loose cannon," Alderson says. Rickey was an All-Star again in '84, playing for the $950,000 one-year salary he'd been awarded in arbitration, and going into the off-season it was time to look to trade him.

Alderson flew to Los Angeles in November '84 to meet at Dodger Stadium with Al Campanis, then the club general manager, and manager Tommy Lasorda. The Dodgers, offering pitcher Alejandro Peña and a position player, thought they had the inside track on Henderson. Heading into the annual winter meetings in early December, held that year at the Hyatt Regency in Houston, the consensus was that there was not going to be much excitement. Then the Rickey rumors started flying. Campanis, knowing that the Yankees and a slew of other teams were also after Henderson, tried to set a deadline with the A's of eleven o'clock Tuesday morning on the second day of the meetings.

Alderson played his strong hand. With the Dodgers' offer in pocket, he got down to business with the Yankees—the problem was which players should he ask for? Fortunately, Alderson was a man who liked to read widely, scouring sources that other general managers ignored. Four years earlier a Canadian named Allan Simpson, who had spent three summers with the semipro Alaska Goldpanners while also working as sports editor of the *Fairbanks Daily News-Miner*, had the crazy idea of starting an all-baseball publication in his garage. He moved to the Vancouver area in 1980 to do just that, founding the *All-America Baseball News*, which would soon morph into *Baseball America*. By 1983 it was up to six thousand subscribers but still widely seen as a fringe publication. Alderson paid attention and noted that *Baseball America* had been on target with a number of its projections. He had little faith in the ravaged A's scouting network of that era, still recovering from Finley-era neglect. So going into his meeting with Yankees general manager

Clyde King and his assistant Woody Woodward, he boned up on its ranking of Yankee prospects.

"I just asked the Yankees for the first five guys from *Baseball America*'s list of the top Yankee prospects!" he says. "*Baseball America* had just started being published and everybody in baseball said, 'Oh, this is bullshit, they don't know anything.' But objective third parties have got to have some validity."

The trade worked out well for the A's. They wound up with Jay Howell, Jose Rijo, Stan Javier, Eric Plunk, and Tim Birtsas, an infusion that helped the club build toward its dominance later in the decade. Henderson signed a five-year, $8.6 million contract with George Steinbrenner and was in for a lively time in New York.

One move Alderson made before the '85 season was to trade two minor-leaguers to the Giants for thirty-five-year-old slugger Dusty Baker. "He was the first nonplaying GM I had," Baker told me. "It kind of showed me the changing times in basic baseball, which never has gone back. Before it was ballplayers, probably the smarter ballplayers, with a good head, with education, with a business mind, and they also had somebody backing them up on the business side of the game, but then Sandy was the first guy I met who was all from the business side."

Baker was a former Marine, and the first time he went into Alderson's office to talk to him, he saw the Marine recruitment poster featuring Alderson. Baker, whose five years as a Marine reservist included time as an MP in Shreveport, Louisiana, was taken aback at first.

"He seemed like a professor type, not a Marine type," he told me. "I had big-time respect for him because at the time he was in he had to be extremely tougher than he looked. He never wore it on his sleeve, but I knew it was in there."

One of Baker's teammates, Dave Kingman, offered a glimpse of Alderson's evolving thinking. The A's signed Kingman in early '84 after he was released by the Mets, and he led Oakland that year with thirty-five homers and 118 RBIs. Each of the next two seasons Kingman topped thirty homers and ninety RBIs, but he just didn't get on base; he had thirty-three walks in '86 and a .210 average. "We didn't re-sign him because his on-base percentage was .255, and instead we signed Reggie Jackson," Alderson says. Jackson's on-base percentage in 1986, playing for the California Angels, was .379, to go with eighteen homers. "We signed Reggie, even though his power numbers were going way down, because his on-base percentage was still very high."

At that point they were still feeling their way. "It wasn't a pervasive thing where everything we did was a function of this system or of a bunch of numbers," Alderson says. "There were basic principles that we tried to adhere to and we were looking at players from a statistical perspective. But as time went on, Eric Walker began to develop some more sophisticated models. Among the first things Eric did for us was to incorporate adjustments in the data for league and park factors."

That big *Newsweek* article on the coming age in baseball had cited two managers who used computers as a tool in sizing up patterns, Steve Boros of the A's and Tony La Russa of the Chicago White Sox. Boros lasted into the '84 season, then was replaced as A's manager by his bench coach, Jackie Moore, who in turn lasted until '86. La Russa, born in Tampa, Florida, played part of six seasons, mostly for the A's, and finished with a .199 average. He had a law degree and was more cerebral than most baseball lifers and every bit as intense as Alderson. Once the White Sox fired him after their 26-38 start to the '86 season, the A's hired him to replace Jeff Newman.

The A's were twenty-one games under .500 going into La Russa's first game as A's manager, in Boston on July 7, 1986, and faced the challenge of going against 14-1 Roger Clemens, who led the league in strikeouts. La Russa insisted on a bold move. In May the Phillies had released Oakland-born pitcher Dave Stewart, and Alderson signed him to a minor-league contract that month. Stewart, drafted originally by the Dodgers as a catcher, had been traded twice by then and had never won more than ten games in a season. His career record stood at 30-35. La Russa wanted him on the mound to face Clemens at Fenway, and his hunch paid off: The A's won, 6–4, Jose Canseco and Kingman both homered, and Stewart outpitched Clemens.

Roy Eisenhardt, the law professor turned A's executive who brought Alderson into baseball, prepared to step down as president in 1986. The shift, though long planned, was still jarring; Eisenhardt had so much to do with creating the identity of the Haas-family-owned A's, but once he passed leadership of the team to his brother-in-law, Wally Haas, Alderson had a counterpart who was as ferociously competitive as he was.

7

EARTHQUAKE

A block away from the San Francisco house where Sandy and Linda Alderson lived for most of the 1980s is a sports bar called the Bus Stop Saloon, right at the corner of Union and Laguna Streets, well known as a gathering spot for San Francisco Giants fans. Alderson rooted for the Giants when his high school best friend, Tom Bradley, was pitching for the team in the early 1970s. But once the Haas family brought Alderson into the A's organization, his stance on the Giants shifted. Early in the 1984 season, Alderson stopped by the Bus Stop to catch some of an A's game, but it wasn't on the TV. Instead, they had on the Detroit Tigers, who had won thirty-five of their first forty games that year. Still, this was the Bay Area, not Michigan.

"How about turning on the A's game?" Alderson asked the bartender, not mentioning that he lived a block away or that he was the A's general manager.

"Aw, shit!" the bartender barked at him. "We're not watching the A's. They're terrible! We're watching Detroit."

Alderson did not even bother to give the bartender a piece of his mind.

"I just walked out," he says now. "That was 1984. It was the last time I set foot in that place."

The San Francisco Giants always had a way of looking down on the Oakland A's, who did not arrive in California until 1968, a full decade after the Giants moved from New York. To the world, San Francisco had long been the glamour city, cosmopolitan and beautiful, and even when the Giants played at concrete-slab Candlestick Park, far away from downtown, the "SF" still counted for something. The A's were the not-quite-invited guests at a swank cocktail party, garish and crude Charlie Finley laughing too loud over by the hors d'oeuvres table. Even under the Haases, a socially prominent San Francisco family, the suggestion was that if the Bay Area could not support two teams, sooner or later the East Bay interlopers had to go.

The A's had five straight losing seasons under their belt going into 1987, but three days before the start of the season they made a five-player swap with the Chicago Cubs, trading three minor-leaguers for starting pitcher Dennis Eckersley and a journeyman infielder named Dan Roan. Eckersley, thirty-two by then, had slipped to 6-11 with a 4.57 ERA for the Cubs the year before and was not impressive in spring training, especially against the A's. The Cubs wanted to work a twenty-one-year-old prospect named Greg Maddux into their rotation and considered Eckersley expendable. Eckersley fit right in with the A's. He was born in Oakland and attended high school in nearby Fremont, and he was consummately California in all the right ways, from the dashing looks to the hyperactive mound presence to the joyous command of baseball lexicon ("I threw him a cookie!") to the spectacular verve with which he would rip himself after a disappointing outing. Eckersley, with more than twelve seasons in the big leagues, had always been a starter, including a 20-8 record for the 1978 Red Sox, and Alderson traded for him thinking he could start with the A's or be a long man in the bullpen.

"Eckersley wasn't pitching much in spring training because he'd pulled an oblique swinging the bat," Alderson recalls.

Eckersley, only twenty years old when he broke into the big leagues, had enjoyed the nightlife at least as much as the next guy, but just before he wound up with the A's, he'd confronted his alcoholism. In January 1987, he entered a treatment center in Rhode Island and later told *Sports Illustrated*, looking back, "I'm prepared to explain that I am an alcoholic. . . . I could have lost my wife, my career, everything. Instead, I finally started growing up."

La Russa was never a full-fledged adherent of Alderson's baseball philosophy, and the field manager and general manager clashed at times. But overall, La Russa was a great fit for the team, primed to think differently about baseball, as aware of statistics on matchups as anyone. Getting him in an A's uniform made a huge difference, but the team faltered at the start of the '87 season, losing five straight, the kind of belly-flop beginning to a year that can get a manager in hot water with the higher-ups. Sure enough, La Russa was informed that Walter Haas, Wally Haas, and Alderson would be stopping by to see him to talk about it. "We just came here to make sure you're all right," Walter told him.

Eckersley's two starts with the A's in 1987 did not go well and he was lost in the bullpen much of the season. Pitching coach Dave Duncan had suggested to La Russa that Eckersley could be good in the bullpen, and then A's closer Jay Howell went down with shoulder trouble. "Initially we had him for depth, and then Dave and Tony turned him into one of the best closers in history," Alderson says.

The other major event in 1987 was the arrival of the Bash Brothers as a cultural phenomenon. The year before, Oakland's fifteenth-round pick, Jose Canseco, had won Rookie of the Year honors with thirty-three homers, 117 RBIs, and a whole lot of charisma. McGwire followed that up in 1987 with one of the all-time great rookie seasons, hitting a rookie-record forty-nine home runs, adding 118 RBIs to lead the team (Canseco had 113 that year), and also showing what a classic Alderson player he was with a team-leading seventy-one walks, a .289 average, and on-base percentage of .370. Like Canseco a year before, he was named Rookie of the Year. "From the very beginning we were kind of put against each other as competitors," Canseco told me. "Who's better? Who's this? Who's that? Who is the number one Bash Brother?"

The A's finished the '87 season at .500, a step up after five straight losing seasons, and moved into the off-season ready to upgrade. Wally Haas points to baseball's 1987 winter meetings at the Hilton Anatole Hotel in Dallas as the key to the team's rebuilding effort. Early in the meetings Alderson packaged two of the pitchers picked up in the Rickey Henderson trade, Rijo and Birtsas, and sent them to the Reds in exchange for veteran slugger Dave Parker, finalizing the deal after hours of talks.

The Mets thought they had engineered a deal to send Jesse Orosco, Mookie Wilson, and Rafael Santana to the Los Angeles Dodgers in exchange for Bob Welch, a former first-round pick who had finished that season 15-9 with a 3.22 ERA. When that swap was spurned by the Dodgers, the Mets stepped up an intense effort, meeting with nine teams, including Oakland, to try to arrange a more complicated deal. "Let's get this straight," Alderson told them. "We're here trying to do the same thing you want to do." The A's were after Welch, too, ready to deal sought-after shortstop Alfredo Griffin, and Alderson stayed in Dallas even after the meetings officially wrapped up on Wednesday to try to close the deal.

Alderson had been pressing his case to Dodgers general manager Fred Claire since the recent GM meetings in Florida, where they'd gone running together. "Sandy was a good jogging companion, and you always gained something when you engaged him in conversation," Claire wrote in his book *Fred Claire: My 30 Years in Dodger Blue*. "As it turns out, we were a little too engrossed in our discussions during this particular run and got lost. . . . The key part of my discussion with Alderson had focused on one aspect of the deal: Welch to the A's, Griffin to the Dodgers."

Wally Haas had left the winter meetings at the normal close, not staying late with Alderson and his special assistant, Ron Schueler. He called the hotel room in Dallas very late at night to see if they'd finally completed the deal. Schueler answered the phone and told him the trade had been finalized.

"I could hear Sandy in the background, saying, 'Now what did we just do again?'" Wally told me.

"Well, that's real reassuring, Schu!" Wally said at the time.

The Mets received Jack Savage from the Dodgers and Kevin Tapani and Wally Whitehurst from the A's; the Dodgers picked up Griffin and Jay Howell from the A's and Jesse Orosco from the Mets; and the A's landed Bob Welch and Matt Young from the Dodgers.

"We got on the plane going back and we actually got applause," Alderson says. "We felt like we'd taken some major steps."

Heading into the 1988 season, the A's raised eyebrows by going with an untested rookie at shortstop, Walter Weiss, born in Tuxedo,

New York, and drafted by the A's in the first round of the 1985 draft. "Everyone said we couldn't win with a rookie shortstop," Alderson recalls. "That was the year Walt Weiss was Rookie of the Year."

The A's eased to a 6-6 start in '88, and then it was like the warp drive engaging in a *Star Trek* movie: *Whoosh!* They won eighteen of their next nineteen games, including a fourteen-game winning streak, and were in first place to stay. By May 9, Bob Welch had already won five games, Eckersley had twelve saves, Canseco had nine home runs and thirty-two RBIs. They clinched the AL West on September 19, Stewart winning his nineteenth game that day. The A's steamrolled the Red Sox in the ALCS, winning all four games once they got past a tense Game 1 with Dennis Eckersley called on to close. Canseco homered in three of the four games, and in the game he didn't connect the A's got homers from McGwire, Carney Lansford, Ron Hassey, and Dave Henderson.

The A's developed an unmistakable swagger, not only showing up at your ballpark convinced they were going to beat you, but carrying on as if they fully expected to walk off with your girlfriends, too. Winning 104 games in the regular season will do that for you. That was the attitude they brought to Dodger Stadium to open the World Series on October 15. L.A. manager Tommy Lasorda was forced to sit his best power hitter, Kirk Gibson, who led the team in homers that year with twenty-five but had sprained his right knee. Mickey Hatcher took his place in left field and started the game off with a jolt, hitting a two-run homer in the bottom of the first off Stewart. Canseco made up for that in the second, blasting his first career grand slam to put the A's up 4–2. The Dodgers added a single run in the sixth, but going into the ninth the A's still had a one-run lead—Eckersley, called on to close, got two quick outs before walking pinch-hitter Mike Davis.

Behind the A's dugout, Sandy and Linda Alderson were sitting with their young son, Bryn, and Wally Haas was sitting with his wife, Julie. Wally had learned never to watch games with his family; he wasn't always fun to be around. In Oakland he and Alderson watched games together in the owner's box along with former Giants and Angels manager Bill Rigney, a man who had seen everything in his many years in the game, and team physician Allan Pont. "Anyone else, beware coming in there, because it got so intense," Wally told me. But at Dodger Stadium, Wally was sitting with Julie.

The great Dodger announcer Vin Scully had said during his game broadcast that Kirk Gibson's sprained knee was so bad, he was probably not even available to pinch-hit. Gibson, listening to Scully as he sat in the clubhouse getting treatment, decided to take a few swings, just to see, and then let Lasorda know he was available to bat. Once Davis walked, the Dodger Stadium crowd of 55,983 heard Gibson's name announced as the hitter and went into a state of delirium. Eckersley worked it to a full count and decided to come in with a backdoor slider.

As soon as Gibson swung, pandemonium broke out. Everyone was jumping around. Alderson had trouble seeing what had happened. "Bryn was sitting on my lap, so it was hard for me to get up and watch it go out," he told me.

Unbeknownst to Wally, Julie hid her head below the seat rather than watch. It was all too nerve-wracking.

"Did he hit it out?" she asked Wally, truly not knowing.

"No, he didn't hit it out!" he yelled. "They're cheering Canseco's great catch! No, he didn't hit it out! Those are all A's fans dressed in blue!"

He went on in that vein, sprinkling his outburst with some colorful language.

"The place was as loud as Chavez Ravine probably ever got," he says. "I lost it. I snapped. It was not a pretty picture. So I got mine later that night, because Rig and my father and I went back to the hotel and tried to drown our sorrows. I went up to my room and found out that Julie had locked me out, which quite frankly was what I deserved. She was going to leave the next day, she was so upset, and got into one of those commuter vans and it caught on fire on the way to LAX, so she couldn't even leave. She had to come back and watch [Orel] Hershiser stick it to us the next game. Believe me I was a nicer person that night."

Hershiser was masterful in Game 2, pitching a three-hit, complete-game shutout. The Series moved to Oakland for Game 3 and Mark McGwire won it in the ninth with a home run, but that was about all Oakland had to cheer before the Dodgers won the next two to close it out in five. It was a crushing way to end a season. The A's were sure they had the better team, and many in baseball agreed, but they'd been outplayed. There was no solace to be had. Alderson seethed. Wally Haas seethed. "If you guys don't cool it and stop living and dying with every pitch," Pont eventually told Alderson and Wally, "you're going to both die of heart attacks."

Nothing teaches like pain and disappointment, and going into 1989 the A's had learned a lot. They got off to an 18-7 start and once again looked unstoppable. The key moment in the season involved Alderson: Four and a half years after trading Rickey Henderson to the Yankees, Alderson brought him back. The June 21 swap with the Yankees cost the A's outfielder Luis Polonia and pitchers Eric Plunk and Greg Cadaret, but heading into the postseason with Henderson leading off, the A's had a much different look.

The A's and Giants were two teams that could hit—that much was clear going into Game 1 of the World Series. San Francisco first baseman Will Clark had one of the sweeter left-handed swings you'll ever see and had just led his team over the Cubs in the NLCS. Former Met Kevin Mitchell backed him up, and behind him the Giants had third baseman Matt Williams, just coming into his own after three seasons of bouncing up and down. But whereas the A's threw out proven ace Dave Stewart in Game 1, the Giants countered with Scott Garrelts. "The one thing the Giants didn't have, they didn't have any dominating starting pitching," Alderson says.

There was nothing very startling about Oakland's systematic dismantling of Garrelts in Game 1; Stewart, meanwhile, held San Francisco to five hits in pitching a complete-game shutout. Game 2 looked a lot like Game 1: Again the A's pounded out five runs against the Giants starter, this time forty-year-old Rick Reuschel, known as Big Daddy. Rickey Henderson led off the first with a walk, stole second, and scored on a Carney Lansford double, and the A's never looked back. Up by two games in the Series, they turned their focus to heading across the Bay Bridge to San Francisco for Game 3 two days later, the first World Series game in San Francisco since Bobby Richardson snagged a line drive off Willie McCovey's bat to end the '62 World Series.

I was in my apartment on the third floor of an old Victorian in San Francsico when the temblor hit at 5:04 on October 17. As a veteran of many quakes, I was more curious than worried, trying to gauge where on the Richter scale this one would hit. I was lucky not to be at Candlestick. The old concrete slab was engineered to handle the stresses of an earthquake, but few among the sixty-two thousand on hand knew that. Many described hearing a roar.

"When it started to shake, my first thought was that people were stomping their feet on the third deck," Alderson says. "Then it got stronger and it became pretty clear it was an earthquake, having been through a few. I didn't notice light columns swaying or any of that. At some point it stopped and there was an eerie silence, then a roar from the crowd. Immediately after the earthquake, the lights went out and I thought, 'Wow, maybe the game will be delayed until the next day because the lights went out.'"

Many players had wives or girlfriends in the family section, located under an expanse of Candlestick concrete, and rather than risk having it fall on them, they were evacuated onto the field. Players and team officials were also brought down. As bad as it seemed at first, the damage was relatively contained. The *Chronicle* headline the next day screamed HUNDREDS DEAD—quadrupling the actual number—and in the aftermath there was a widespread feeling of relief that the quake had not resulted in more fatalities.

For many baseball fans, it felt odd when the Series resumed at Candlestick following a ten-day hiatus. Once again Dave Stewart was the starter, and the A's erupted with five home runs to win 13-7. The A's jumped ahead early in Game 4, Rickey Henderson hammering Don Robinson's third pitch of the game to left field for a leadoff home run. The A's jumped to an 8–0 lead and held on to win 9–6.

The sweep was above all a vindication for the Haas family and all the resources—and time and talent—they had pumped into rebuilding the team. The farm system had been a shambles, and with a lot of painstaking work, they turned it into a rich source of talent that could produce three straight American League Rookies of the Year. The Haases spent heavily to make the Coliseum a far more enjoyable place to see a game, and they built a community relations department to get involved in lives as a force for positive change and hope. The East Bay had suffered more from the earthquake than San Francisco itself, and the celebration of the A's victory—though muted, given the natural disaster—was a balm to many. "The earthquake was unquestionably a tragedy for the Bay Area, and it took years to rebuild after destruction on that scale," Alderson says.

One year later, the A's were back again for their third straight World Series appearance, a feat matched in the last century only by the New York Giants, the Philadelphia A's, the St. Louis Cardinals, the Baltimore Orioles, the Finley-era Oakland A's, and—repeatedly—the Yankees. The A's in 1990 won 103 games and once again they were loaded, with McGwire (39) and Canseco (37) leading the home-run attack, and Rickey Henderson adding twenty-eight from the leadoff position to go with a batting average of .325 and on-base percentage of .439. Dave Stewart and Bob Welch, both thirty-three that year, anchored the pitching staff, and Welch finished 27-6 to win the Cy Young Award. The A's swept the Red Sox in the ALCS, Stewart winning Game 1 at Fenway and Game 4 in Oakland, both against Roger Clemens, to garner MVP honors.

They were on a roll when they arrived at Riverfront Stadium in Cincinnati for Game 1 of the World Series against the Reds, and just as Stewart had stifled the Red Sox, now Jose Rijo, who'd been with the A's from '85 to '87, overpowered them. They lost Game 1 7–0 and were swept in four with no A's hitter other than Rickey Henderson (.333) getting going. Canseco had one hit, a homer, to bat .083 in the Series and was benched for Game 4. Rijo won the first and fourth games and was named MVP. "Hershiser beat us twice in the '88 World Series and was clearly the dominant pitcher," Alderson says. "And in '90 we got beat by Jose Rijo. One guy dominated."

That A's era came to a dramatic end on the night of August 31, 1992, during a home game against the Orioles. Shortly before his first at bat of the game, Canseco was called back from the on-deck circle and Tony La Russa gave him the news that he had been traded to the Texas Rangers for power hitter Ruben Sierra, pitchers Bobby Witt and Jeff Russell, and $400,000 in cash. No one was more stunned than Canseco, who did not believe the A's would actually trade him, despite the rumors. It seemed hard to believe a run of futility was in store, but such are the rhythms of the game. The A's lost the '92 ALCS to Toronto and did not make it back to the postseason until 2000. Walter Haas, the benevolent team owner, had decided that he wanted to sell the team before he died, rather than passing on yearly losses to other family members, and as his health worsened, so did the team's chances of reloading in the style that marked those back-to-back-to-back World Series teams.

Most peopled assumed that *Juiced*, the steroid tell-all memoir that I wrote with Jose Canseco, was his first book, but actually, it was his second. Canseco and McKay coauthored a paperback called *Strength Training for Baseball*, published in February 1990, that was a practical guide for ballplayers wanting to add strength, complete with cheesy cover photo featuring Canseco in a muscle shirt showing off his biceps. The book contains a warning on page 159 that takes on added interest in retrospect. "A word about steroids, don't use them," Canseco and McKay wrote. "Steroids may create the illusion of great gains in short periods of time, but they have a debilitating effect on your body chemistry, and in the long run you will be much worse off for having used them."

The passage offers a strange kind of time capsule from that era. As late as early 2005, when *Juiced* was published, the standard position on steroids in baseball, even among a lot of smart and informed fans and a lot of skeptical, well-meaning journalists, was: *We just can't know what these guys do to themselves behind closed doors.* The book was widely attacked the week it came out, especially its claim that a majority of active ballplayers had used performance-enhancing drugs, despite former Padre slugger Ken Caminiti's assertion in a groundbreaking *Sports Illustrated* article by Tom Verducci that not only had Caminiti "won the 1996 National League Most Valuable Player award while on steroids he purchased from a pharmacy in Tijuana, Mexico," but that "at least half the guys are using steroids." Then came the bombshell events that followed: Mark McGwire was among the players who showed up in Washington for nationally televised hearings before a congressional subcommittee and seemed to shrink before the eyes of a nation, talking with numbing repetition about not being there to talk about the past. Rafael Palmeiro jabbed his finger for emphasis as he asserted with soap-opera drama at the hearings, "I have never used steroids! Period!" Within a few months came his suspension after reports he'd tested positive for the steroid Winstrol, a Canseco favorite. Palmeiro was a juicer, just as Canseco had said he was. Finally, perceptions were shifting toward a more accurate reflection of reality, helped along by the excellent reporting of the *San Francisco Chronicle* Balco team of Lance Williams and Mark Fainaru-Wada, the *New York Daily News* investigative unit under Teri Thompson of T.J. Quinn, Michael O'Keeffe, and Christian Red, and, finally, Howard Bryant's book *Juicing the Game*.

In retrospect it probably makes sense that denial held on as long as it did. The fact is, drug use is a very private affair. Through most of the Steroid Era in baseball, the widespread use of needles to inject steroids or human growth hormone was in fact kept under tight wraps. Pedro Gomez, now an on-air reporter for ESPN, has been a vocal critic of steroid use in baseball. He's known as one of the leading "hawks" arguing that any former steroid user should be banned from consideration for the Hall of Fame. Even Gomez had to admit that when he was covering the Oakland A's for the *San Jose Mercury News* from 1990 to 1994, including covering the 1990 World Series, the mind-set was that steroids simply did not exist in the game.

"That was a football thing," he said. "I don't remember a single conversation where we talked about this guy is on steroids or that guy—not one," he said. "It just wasn't on our radar. And I never remember fans saying, 'This guy's on steroids.' That didn't happen either. Guys talked about spending the whole off-season lifting weights and coming back bigger, and you took them at their word. Years later we knew we had made a mistake, but not then. Players went to extraordinary lengths to hide this."

I was startled to hear a similar point being made by Ray Karesky, who spent years in the A's organization counseling ballplayers—all under the cover of confidentiality—on drug issues and other problems. "Players would share with me some amazing things they wouldn't share with anybody," he told me. "Nobody ever came up to me and talked about steroids. They knew that this was something to not talk about."

Alderson says that in the days of the Bash Brothers in Oakland, no one was inclined to take at all seriously any rumors of steroid use that might have circulated here and there. "At the time there wasn't any concern at all about what else might be going on other than physical training," he says. To the extent that steroid use in sports was gaining attention, the focus was on the National Football League. A New Jersey congressman, William Hughes, had been hearing alarming reports of growing steroid use among high school athletes, and introduced the Anabolic Steroid Control Act of 1990, which classified anabolic steroids as a so-called Schedule III drug, making steroid use without a prescription illegal. The Act was signed into law in November 1990 by President George H.W. Bush.

The following season, Commissioner Fay Vincent cracked down on steroids as well, sending a memo to all teams declaring that Major League Baseball now included steroids in the category of dangerous illegal drugs: "The possession, sale or use of any illegal drug or controlled substance by Major League players and personnel is strictly prohibited. Major League players or personnel involved in the possession, sale or use of any illegal drug or controlled substance are subject to discipline by the Commissioner and risk permanent expulsion from the game. . . . This prohibition applies to all illegal drugs and controlled substances, including steroids."

Up to that point, steroids were neither illegal nor banned by baseball; by 1991 they were both. Vincent himself—ousted in 1992 as commissioner—had not been greatly concerned about steroids in baseball, but wanted baseball to take a proactive approach to all drug abuse. Vincent had first been alerted to the issue during the 1988 postseason when fans at Boston's Fenway Park taunted Jose Canseco with cries of "Ster-oids!" Canseco turned it all into his usual high theater, flexing his muscles for the crowd, and denied steroid use. Everything to do with Canseco was such a sideshow, it was hard for anyone to know what to make of the charges, which had started with *Washington Post* columnist Tom Boswell's October 1988 assertion on a television program that Canseco had used steroids. Boswell had tried to publish allegations about steroid use by Canseco in his newspaper, but higher-ups quashed the idea on the ground that he had no proof.

A's owner Wally Haas remembers being surprised when the fans at Fenway Park cried out "Ster-oids! Ster-oids!" to taunt Canseco during the American League Championship Series shortly after Boswell made the accusation, struck that one accusation should inspire that kind of reaction. Alderson was starting to wonder by then if it might be a case with Canseco of where there was smoke there was fire. But he had no notion of how to assess the validity of such speculation. He was a man who loved information, accurate, detailed, credible information, and when it came to suggestions of steroid use, all he had was hazy conjecture. On a personal level Alderson liked Canseco, and had trouble believing he had it in him to inject himself with steroids. Talking about the issue now, Alderson was especially adamant on two points: Team officials never factored in rumors about possible steroid use in discussions about trading Canseco, and never in Mark McGwire's time with the A's did Alderson suspect him of steroid use. Even when revelations about McGwire later came out, all indications were that he only started using steroids later in his career when back trouble kept him out of the lineup, not in the Bash Brothers era.

"We know a lot more now about PEDs than we did twenty years ago," Alderson told me. "But what do we really know even today? We don't know shit. How can players test negative and then be caught with one performance-enhancing substance or another? When I answer these questions it's like, 'OK, color me stupid.' Did I suspect McGwire of using steroids? No. Does that make me stupid? Maybe. His brother was in the NFL. He hit forty-nine homers as a rookie. We were all about creating stronger players through weight training, there's no question about that. But the possibility that steroids were involved never came to my mind until later."

T.J. Quinn, a former Mets beat writer for the *New York Daily News* who went to work the steroid beat for years as part of the *News* investigative team and in recent years on ESPN, has broken as many stories on PEDs as anyone. Quinn thinks it's important to avoid revisionism in talking about steroids in baseball more than twenty years ago. "There definitely was a naiveté in baseball at the time, and anytime anyone wants to hold Bud Selig or anyone else accountable, they have to remember that," Quinn says. "There was no real anti-doping movement then. WADA, the World Anti-Doping Agency, was not created until November 1999. There is this real revisionism that somehow everybody should have done more and said more in those late '80 and early '90s. That said, the Oakland A's of that era clearly benefited from steroid use, and you cannot look at their accomplishments without an asterisk, whether you hold someone accountable or not."

Focusing on Alderson, Quinn was at a loss to know where to come down on the legacy of his Oakland years. "Sandy was just so much smarter than anyone else in baseball that if anyone was going to get it, it was going to be him," he said. "There is a higher standard for him. He's not your average guy. That said, at the time there was no testing and there was no punishment. Baseball had no PED policy. If he did have suspicions, what was he supposed to do?"

8

PASSING THE TORCH

Back in his early days as a highly touted Mets prospect, a 1980 first-round pick impressing everyone with his raw physical gifts, Billy Beane started thinking he'd love to be a general manager. He was eighteen, his first year in the organization, when general manager Frank Cashen came out to meet the minor-leaguers wearing a bow tie and monogrammed shirt. Beane was blown away by the aura Cashen had, the aura of a decision maker, a creative thinker, a man who built things. Out in the outfield, he told his fellow prospects, "This is the guy you want to be, right there."

Beane had kicked around by early 1989 and spent most of the previous season playing Triple-A ball for the Toledo Mud Hens. Now he was getting a shot with the A's, taking batting practice at Scottsdale Community College that spring training, when he looked up to get his first glimpse of the architect of that year's powerhouse A's. "I'm out on the field hitting and here comes this guy with a Panama hat and shorts on," Beane told me. "Nobody did that back then. No GM wore shorts. That was a position where it was still your Sunday best in spring training. If somebody told you this guy was a Harvard Law graduate who went to Dartmouth, the first time you see him you would expect completely different dress. It was very unpretentious. Being from San Diego, I thought that was the coolest thing in the world. That alone was enough inspiration to want to be a GM so I could choose if I wanted to wear shorts to work."

Old-school general managers like Cashen had impressed Beane, but he had trouble relating to older guys with paunches, "old bow-tied East Coast lawyer types," as he put it. Alderson was a new breed.

"It wasn't like he chatted with me," Beane remembers. "But I found myself drawn to this guy. His presence had a very self-assured casualness that I thought was fascinating."

Beane won one Cactus League game with a walk-off hit in extra innings and broke camp for the big-league club, but saw only limited duty with the A's that season, missing some time with a wrist injury and getting sent out to Triple-A Tacoma before being called up again in late August. "Where you been?" Rickey Henderson asked him, not knowing he'd been sent down. Beane was not on the postseason roster, but earned a ring when the A's beat the Giants in the World Series. One number that jumps out, looking at Beane's stats now, is: eleven. That's his career total in major-league walks, over 315 plate appearances, and all the walks came in 1986 when he played eighty games for the Twins.

"Billy was not a player that anybody would really want today," Alderson says. "He never walked. He didn't hit for power. Putting aside his talents, which were considerable, he just didn't have an approach. He didn't get it at that time, which he would admit today."

Beane came to his second spring training with the A's, 1990, looking for a way to feel better about his future. "One of the things about baseball that's challenging, if you're somewhat restless intellectually, is there's a lot of down time," Beane says. "Friends from high school were finishing college, some on their way to law school, and here you are. Even when I signed, I never thought that playing was going to be the end-all."

Beane's breakthrough moment came on the back diamond at Phoenix Municipal Stadium, midway through a morning that started out with a chill in the air that soon gave way under the bracing desert sunlight. The clack of bat on ball was reverberating from different points around the practice field in that comforting ritual of spring. Beane started asking Ron Schueler, Alderson's special assistant, what exactly his job entailed. It was a good question, since Schueler wore a lot of hats with the team: throwing batting practice, serving as sounding board for Alderson, and also doing a lot of advance scouting for the team by going ahead to observe the tendencies of its next opponents.

"I'm the advance guy, though we're looking for someone to free me up to do some other stuff," Schueler told him.

Beane back then had a fresh-faced eagerness and a ready grin, and up until that moment he'd been talking just to talk, one of the rituals of spring, like stretching, dinner at the Pink Pony, and late-night cocktails at the Downside Risk. But this conversation had turned meaningful.

"As I sat there talking to him, I was thinking, 'One thing I love about the game, I love evaluation,'" Beane told me. "I had a lot of admiration for Sandy and I'd already decided I wanted to be a general manager."

When most fans think of baseball scouts, they picture a variation on the traditional "bird-dog" scout, freelance talent evaluators forever on the lookout for future big-leaguers in out-of-the-way places, eager to earn a commission for any prospects they found. Branch Rickey worked as a bird-dog scout from 1910 to 1913 when he coached baseball at the University of Michigan. John McGraw built the New York Giants into a powerhouse with his vast network of scouts trolling different geographic regions. Over the years, as baseball grew into an ever-larger business and fewer surprise talents lurked out in the sticks to be discovered, the real action in scouting turned to what might be called tactical scouting: studying opponents to gain an edge. Teams came to rely more often on the evaluations of special-assignment scouts, as they were sometimes called, or simply pro scouts, who would study upcoming opponents with the cold, appraising eye of a butcher looking for a good place to start slicing. In one famous story, the Dodgers sent three scouts to analyze the A's before the 1988 World Series, Steve Boros, Jerry Stephenson, and Mel Didier, and in a scouting report now on display at the Baseball Hall of Fame in Cooperstown, New York, the trio sized up closer Dennis Eckersley this way: "Likes to 'backdoor' slider to LH hitters with 3-2 count." Kirk Gibson found that information very interesting.

Schueler told Beane he would write up reports on teams the A's were about to play: how to position the infield and outfield against particular hitters, how to pitch which batters, what to expect against which pitchers, and so on. A pro scouting job would be a good way to start working toward a GM job down the line, but the work was demanding. He would be on the road for weeks at a time.

"At some point that's something I'd be interested in," Beane said.

"Well, I think you'd be good at it," Schueler told him. "So when you're ready to stop playing, let me know."

Beane went home that night and talked about the idea with his wife at the time, Cathy, a former all-American tennis player at UC San Diego, where Beane had also taken some courses. The more he turned it over in his mind, the more he thought: "Why wait?" He knew he could eke out a couple hundred more big-league at bats over the next season or two, run up some more big-league service time, but Beane didn't care about any of that. He cared about doing what felt right for his future—and for his family, which was about to grow. Cathy was due to give birth that May to their first child, a daughter they would name Casey. The next day at Phoenix Muni, Beane found Schueler and told him he'd love to try advance scouting. "I'm ready now," he said.

"You're kind of young," Schueler said. "You've probably got some time."

"No, this is what I want to do," Beane said.

"Well, let me talk to Tony and Sandy."

Alderson presided over a meeting of all the coaches and front-office people to go over which players they wanted to keep on the twenty-five-man roster and which had to go. They went through every player in camp one by one and anyone in the room was free to speak up. "The conversation turned to Billy Beane," Schueler told me, "and out of twelve guys in the room, I think there was only one who wanted to keep him."

"Ron, you've been around every day watching him, what's your opinion?" Alderson asked.

"He has not performed well, he has not earned a spot on the team," Schueler said. "But I think he has a great baseball mind and with some training he could work in the front office or possibly even in scouting."

"OK, are you the one who is going to teach him how to scout?" Alderson cracked.

The general manager wasn't sold just yet, but he did know Beane had a knack for evaluating talent. The previous season, La Russa had often asked Beane about different young players on other teams. Having spent so much time at Triple-A, he'd played against many of them and had lucid enough insights to keep La Russa and his pitching coach, Dave Duncan, coming back with more questions. La Russa and Duncan favored Beane getting a shot as a scout. That left the general manager.

"He came in and in one breath said, 'I want to retire and I want to be the advance scout,'" Alderson recalls. "I knew Tony was pretty excited about the possibility. If I had any skepticism, it was that as a player who had not hit for power or taken walks, Billy would not embrace this approach we were trying to inculcate in the organization."

"Sandy had his shorts on and everything," Beane remembers. "He looked at me and goes, 'No promises from here on out, but we'll give it a try.'"

Alderson's skepticism fired Beane up.

"I was bound and determined to make myself valuable enough to where they'd want to keep me on," Beane says now. "I literally went from stretching with the players and having the conversation to the next day walking in to the staff meeting in my uniform. I have not swung at a pitch since that day. And I have never looked back."

A lot of baseball men had the eight-months-pregnant bellies to prove they were never going to break a sweat if they could help it, but even the rare few who did try to get in a little exercise would never dream of venturing outside the hotel. Then there was the Alderson approach. "He'd go running and I'd go running with him, because I ran, too, or we'd sort of bump into each other running," Beane says. "That was part of the adventure of Sandy. One of my favorite ones was when we were in the Dominican Republic and we were driving by the old Olympic Stadium and we stopped and went for a run. We didn't have a route, but we were running the streets of Santo Domingo for forty or forty-five minutes."

They ran together at different spots around the country in Beane's years as an advance scout, and as the two got to know each other, Beane impressed Alderson with his energy and curiosity. "Billy was a sponge," says Jay Alves. "Billy was sharp enough to understand: I can learn from that man. Any of us who were around Sandy, it changed us. It helped us be better. You'd be crazy not to follow Sandy."

Walt Jocketty, hired by Charlie Finley, moved on in June 1993 after thirteen years with the A's, taking a job as assistant general manager of the Colorado Rockies. Jocketty agonized over the decision. "I felt it was a good time to try something different," Jocketty told me. "When I talked to Sandy about it, after they had offered me the job, he told me he didn't know how much longer the Haas family was going to own the ball club. He said I should go for it."

Beane started as assistant general manager that July, and his timing couldn't have been much worse. "We were soon to be sold," Beane told me. "We were going from a high payroll team to a low. I was thinking, 'Great timing, Billy, right? My front-office career will be a year.'"

Beane's education in statistical analysis under Alderson's direction started with sitting him down to talk to Eric Walker. "He will walk you through it and you'll understand everything we're doing," Alderson told Beane.

Walker wrote up a sixty-six-page report specifically for Beane on "Winning Baseball," described on its cover as "An objective, numerical, analytic analysis of the principles and practices involved in the design of a winning baseball team." Walker then added, right there on the cover, a quote from James Boswell's *The Life of Samuel Johnson*: "A thousand stories which the ignorant tell, and believe, die away at once when the computist takes them in his grip." Walker might as well have included the rest of the quote on "computation": "Cultivate in yourself a disposition to numerical inquiries: they will give you entertainment in solitude by the practice, and reputation in public by the effect."

Beane, handed the report just before he and Alderson flew to Toronto for Game 1 of the 1993 World Series, devoured it all. If he'd always felt a battle between his restless mind and the don't-think-just-hit athlete's mentality, now under Alderson's tutelage he'd found a system of thought in which he could truly come into his own. At one point in our interview, Beane joked that his whole career had been almost like plagiarism, so much did he glean from Eric Walker and Bill James and Alderson, before putting his own stamp on it. And not just the statistics. "Working out, the shorts, those are all Sandy's things," Beane told me. "To this day I still work out every game during the game. This all started when Sandy did it—and even not watching the games."

Alderson and Beane also bonded while driving from Oakland to go see prospects in action. Often when the A's were on the road the two would drive eighty miles east together to Modesto in the great, sprawling valley of California, Alderson behind the wheel, Beane riding shotgun. They'd have the radio tuned to the A's game— sometimes. Beane wanted to listen to the games. Alderson didn't and kept changing the station.

"What are you doing?" Beane would ask him.

"Nothing good can happen when we're pitching," Alderson would say.

The compromise was to listen only when the A's were at bat. "That was sort of our détente, driving out there to Modesto," Beane says. "So whenever our team was pitching, Sandy would turn it off. Inevitably, I'd try to work on him."

"We've got to have three outs by now," Beane would say.

"We've got to give it a little more time," Alderson would say.

Beane, looking back more than twenty years later, laughs at his young self. "So that inevitably morphed to where as a GM I couldn't watch anything. Watch it? Forget it. I realized when you are the GM, it was sort of protection from yourself, from the intensity and the idea you can't control anything."

I started covering the A's as a full-time beat writer for the *San Francisco Chronicle* ten games before a strike ended the 1994 season. I was at spring training in '95 when Alderson's young protégé, Beane, would follow him around in the stands at Papago Park, the Arizona buttes in the background, wearing the exact same straw hat, khaki shorts, madras cotton shirt, and sandals. "It's like watching a baby duck following the big duck around!" my friend Pedro Gomez of the *Sacramento Bee* would say to me, laughing as we watched them go by. We weren't making fun of Beane. Others, notably the great big-game pitcher Dave Stewart, had wished they could find themselves in the role of apprentice to the master, following him around (literally) and watching everything he did and emulating it. Beane's boyish good looks and charming openness were pronounced back then, and he was eager to learn, devotedly working his way through the fat Victor Hugo novel *Les Misérables* on team charters and more than a little proud of that fact.

I mixed it up that spring in a memorable pickup basketball game with Alderson and Beane. Alderson was forty-seven, five years removed from having been named American League Executive of the Year a third time in a row after the 1990 season. He was a fit and fierce competitor, and he grinned at the prospect of teaming up with Beane to take on some sportswriters. Opposing them was a group that included three of us born in August 1962, Mike DiGiovanna of the *Los Angeles Times*, Gomez, and me.

"Check out the Marine!" Gomez and I said to each other a couple of times running up and down the court, staring in wonder at the meticulous defense Alderson was playing on DiGi. Finally at one point, a stunned DiGi turned to run up the court and muttered over his shoulder: "At ease, soldier!"

Gomez and I stared: Did you hear *that*? Oh my god! He just said *that* to the Marine?

Alderson was not even sure if DiGi said what he thought he did. But just in case, he dialed it up a notch. It was a small gym, the walls barely a foot beyond the out-of-bounds line, and one time down the court Alderson flexed his knees and squared his shoulders and set a pick that sent DiGi flying into the concrete wall. "From that point on he was guarding me like it was Game 7," DiGiovanna says now. "I was beaten up."

I went over to DiGi afterward to ask him: "Don't you know Alderson's a Vietnam vet?"

He turned pale. He'd had no idea. Gomez and I, buddies on the beat in those years, had already taken to calling Alderson "the Marine" between us now and then, but after the DiGi game it was "the Marine" every single time: That's who he was. That was the key to understanding him.

"Playing basketball with Sandy was part of his leadership," Billy Beane told me. "He wants passing, he wants movement, he wants setting picks, and he's very intense. Taking a thirty-footer on a break-away, you don't want to be on Sandy's team, because he's going to let you know about it. He wants to win, but he wants to do it the right way. If you were on the other team or even if you played for him the first time, you'd go, 'He's kind of kidding, right? He's really not *that* into this, is he?' And if you knew him, you'd go: 'No, no, he's *into* it. He is into it.'"

Gomez and I used to joke about "Señor Sandy!" moments, because we always pictured Alderson waking up to coffee and the morning paper at his home in Tiburon, pounding his fist on the kitchen table as the maid, Esmerelda or Lupita, tried to calm his nerves.

"Señor Sandy!" Pedro would cry out with Latin drama, laying on a thick Spanish accent to mimic the maid's voice. "Your blood pressure!"

The joke was that we all knew Alderson could shift from calm and collected to enraged in a heartbeat, and we all marveled at how he did that and retained both an alert intelligence and wicked sense of humor. We'd all been on the wrong end of an angry Alderson outburst. But no matter how pissed off he got, he could usually laugh at himself and avoid taking himself too seriously. He had seen the world and seen combat, we all knew, and it earned him an eye that saw through the superficial or fleeting in a way we envied. When problem child slugger Ruben Sierra, frustrated at Alderson for push-ing him to take more walks, made the grievous mistake of taking a verbal shot at Alderson in 1995, telling my *San Francisco Chronicle* colleague Joan Ryan that he'd like to pitch to Alderson to throw one "over his head," Tony La Russa called Sierra "a village idiot" and let loose with a diatribe.

"Every time he opens his mouth he makes a fool of himself," La Russa said. "In this one case I'm going to say how full of shit he really is. He gets on Sandy because he never played. Here's a guy who went to Vietnam. If Ruben ever went to Vietnam, he'd alternate between vomiting and shitting his pants."

Alderson ran marathons and kept fit. His Vietnam record and his status as literally a former poster boy for the Marine Corps set him apart and ruled out a certain kind of flak. The Sierra outburst was the exception that proved the rule. No one wanted to mess with Alderson, and the name the Spanish-speaking players had for him—"Sandy Anderson"—was often half whispered in a cadence of singsong reverence, as if they needed to have respect even in speaking about the man behind his back.

Probably the topic that best brought out Alderson's angry sense of humor in his years with the A's was their cross-bay rivals, the media darling San Francisco Giants. "They haven't even negotiated his salary yet," Alderson cracked in February 1997 when the Giants announced they were paying Barry Bonds upwards of $11 million a year. "That was just a bribe to keep his mouth shut."

Late every off-season there was a media luncheon with team officials from both the Giants and the A's, and it was the rare year that passed by without Alderson getting in his licks against his rivals. One February the luncheon was hosted by comedian Rob Schneider, who missed with just about every joke. Bob Quinn, the Giants' general manager at the time, used the occasion to talk up a recent Giant acquisition, left-handed hitter Mel Hall.

"He could fall out of bed and get a hit," Quinn said.

Alderson, flashing a little smirk, was up next.

"I'd like to thank Rob Schneider for his jokes about the Giants and Bob Quinn for his joke about Mel Hall," he said.

By 1995 Walter Haas was almost out of time. He had more than lived up to the family tradition with his successful tenure as the leader of Levi Strauss & Co., with his public works, including building the A's franchise into the pride of Oakland, and, above all, with his modest, gentlemanly style. Jay Alves remembers the owner spotting a stash of baseballs on a visit to the A's clubhouse.

"You think I could have a couple baseballs?" the owner asked.

"Mr. Haas, you can have the whole bag," Alves told him.

Haas, seventy-nine, was fighting prostate cancer and in sharp physical decline by 1995. The Haas family sale of the A's verged on the surreal. The buyers who emerged—tract-housing developers Steve Schott and Ken Hofmann—had, like Walter Haas, been approached about buying the team in the hope they would keep the A's in Oakland. The team had been valued at $115 million and higher, but the Haas family consented to sell for a discounted price of $85 million—on the condition that the new owners agree to keep the team in Oakland for at least ten years. In January 1995 came the announcement that Schott and Hofmann had agreed to buy the A's from the Haas family for the agreed-upon price. Then, as Walter Haas grew sicker, negotiations dragged out. Wally did his best to reach a settlement, but Schott and Hofmann had shifted their terms so often, it was getting to be a joke. At one point, Schott said to Wally. "You must think I'm a real prick." Wally did not contest the point.

"At that point I said to my dad, 'We shouldn't sell to these guys. They are so not cut from the same cloth as you.'"

Walter Haas was so ill by that point he could not speak. He gave his son a hand gesture, a kind of hand chop, to indicate: They had to sell the team.

Finally, an announcement came on July 22 that a "final agreement" had been reached on the sale, and Wally Haas explained to a *Chronicle* reporter: "We made concessions from the original terms that are several million dollars less."

The Schott-Hofmann program was to gut as much of the A's organization as they could, including baseball operations. Here they ran into an obstacle: Alderson would stay only if they left the front office alone. If they wanted to slash personnel in baseball operations, the way they wanted to elsewhere, then they'd have to do that without Sandy Alderson in the organization.

Billy Beane's tradition of working out during every game dates back to that period. For years Alderson had made a habit of watching games in the owner's box with Wally Haas. They were friends, comfortable with each other, and it all worked somehow. Moving forward, Alderson needed to watch games elsewhere. "So I started working out in the clubhouse," he says.

It was clear Alderson could not work long for Schott and Hofmann, but he also did not want to duck out without a thought for where the franchise would go next. "It was just a very different environment," he says.

Alderson did his best to soldier on. For years he'd given Beane more and more of a voice in decisions. They worked together the way that Alderson had worked with John Grinalds as an intelligence officer in Vietnam, each an extension of the other, but no one in doubt of who was in charge. Beane passed up potential GM jobs in Montreal and San Diego to keep learning. "A lot of guys move on from assistant GM not so much just because they want to be a GM, but because they're so frustrated," Beane says. "It's just like a teenager: At some point you feel like you need to get out and break out on your own. One thing about Sandy was there was never any frustration internally. I knew I was never going to be as smart as Sandy."

For those covering the team during Beane's years making the transition from assistant GM to GM in his own right, it all seemed the most natural thing in the world, the two of them fitting together so well, Beane's ascension so inevitable. "Billy had been tremendously loyal through those years and had opportunities to leave and be a general manager elsewhere," Alderson told me. "I did feel a responsibility to make a transition."

Mark McGwire had led baseball with fifty-two homers in 1996. His contract ran through the end of '97 and then he would be a free agent. The general consensus was that the A's would never keep him because tightfisted owners Schott and Hofmann would never shell out enough money to land him. That was not quite accurate. The truth was, as I knew from multiple conversations with him that year, McGwire had loved playing for the Haas family and felt a deep loyalty to the organization. He would have loved to play his whole career in Oakland, if only the owners would pay up to field a decent team. What he needed was a break from the stench of mediocrity. The A's were on their way to a ninety-seven-loss season in 1997. McGwire wanted to know the team would spend enough to make a real effort to improve. Alderson had no cards to play: He could give McGwire no such assurance.

The Angels should have made a major play for McGwire. He was a Southern California boy all the way and would have loved to be back in Southern California—and was not the kind of player who was obsessed with money. But the Angels briefly got hot without his bat and figured: Why bother? I'd tracked down McGwire in the tunnel leading to the clubhouse in mid-July and asked if he was disappointed the Angels were pulling out of trade talks. He was feeling good after hitting two homers to give him a league-leading thirty-four.

"Would it be disappointing to me?" McGwire told me, smiling. "No. I haven't ruled out the other teams that are interested."

Who but the Marlins and the Cardinals were interested?

"There are a couple of others you'll hear about," he told me. "We've got two weeks left."

It didn't work out that way. "To their credit, the Cardinals started figuring out: Listen, we might be the only guys in this game," Beane recalls. "That's the art of the deal. If you're in and you know there's no one else, you sort of hold firm on what you're gonna give up."

Beane couldn't stand it. A few days before the deadline, it was looking bleak, the Cardinals offering a package of three undistinguished pitchers.

"We can't do this deal," he told Alderson. "This is not a good deal!"

"Listen, we need to make this trade," Alderson said.

Three hours before the trade deadline on July 31, the A's made the deal. They had a home game at the Coliseum that evening and lost 4–0 to run their losing streak to six straight. "For me it was probably the lowest point in the organization I remember being a part of," Beane says. "We weren't a good team, and here we're trading one of the best players in the game. Sandy was doing all these media interviews, and I felt bad. It was a good time to be an assistant GM and not the GM, but it wasn't any fun being the assistant GM either."

After the game, Alderson and Beane walked together to the parking lot for team officials.

"You won't have to deal with that now," Alderson told Beane. It was the passing of the torch.

"At no point had Sandy said, 'You're going to be the GM,'" Beane told me. "He never said anything. He just said, 'You won't have to deal with that now.'"

Jocketty, who had moved on from the Rockies to become the Cardinals' general manager, still thinks it could have worked out much better for the A's. "I firmly believed the players I gave Oakland for McGwire would have been better," he told me. "That worked out good for me. To get McGwire and then being able to sign him turned that franchise around."

A few months later Alderson gave his job to Beane. Alderson was still president of the A's, the man in charge, but he relinquished the title—and duties—of general manager. For a man as competitive as Alderson, the move was not without its painful aspects; a Marine never retreats. But it was the only way to complete Beane's education and development, to give him some time as general manager in his own right, but with Alderson still there. Only then did Beane fully grasp what Alderson had meant the night of the McGwire trade. Only then did he comprehend just how ugly it could have got for him as a general manager just starting out to be the one who couldn't re-sign McGwire and had to let him walk.

Commissioner Bud Selig offered Alderson a job late in the 1998 season working at Major League Baseball as executive vice president for baseball operations. "I admired his work," Selig told me. "I had a lot of respect for him, which is one of the reasons I hired him."

Alderson's farewell press conference was surprisingly emotional.

"It's going to be a little hard," Beane told me that day, his voice catching. "We're talking about losing a mentor, a friend, and possibly the brightest mind in baseball today. This isn't easy for me."

It wasn't always easy for Alderson, either. Working at Major League Baseball headquarters on Park Avenue in New York, even with an impressive title like "Executive Vice President for Baseball Operations," in some ways represented a comedown from the buzz of running a team. Alderson's physician had warned him about grave consequences to his health if he continued to live and die with every pitch, and he had tried to back off some, but the truth was he loved caring that much. He reveled in the intensity of competition. MLB was a great, new challenge, intriguing in many ways, but an office job in New York, especially with Commissioner Bud Selig 850 miles away in Wisconsin, had an almost hollow feeling.

"That office was somewhat leaderless," said John Ricco, who worked twelve years in the commissioner's office. "Sandy had a presence. If it was someone's birthday, as the ranking guy, he would make a speech. He really, you could tell, embraced that role of being a leader. We had a blackout, the whole city went black, and I remember him kind of taking the lead there. We went through that together."

Ricco considered Alderson a potential successor to Selig as commissioner of baseball. This was an idea that had been kicking around for years. Back in September 1989 when Commissioner A. Bartlett Giamatti died suddenly at age fifty-one, Ross Newhan wrote in the *Los Angeles Times* that among the likely replacements were only a few names: league presidents Bill White and Bobby Brown, Brewers owner Bud Selig, and three general managers: Harry Dalton, Frank Cashen, and Sandy Alderson. Dennis Eckersley, inducted into the Hall of Fame in 2004, was one of many who favored Alderson in the job. "He's tough, he's just so sharp, and he has that poker face," Eckersley told me in 1999. "I think he would be great as commissioner. He has the passion for the game."

One of Alderson's areas of responsibility at MLB was working to internationalize the game, an effort he promoted by organizing a game in Cuba between the Baltimore Orioles and the Cuban National Team. I was among the contingent of baseball writers on hand March 28, 1999, in Havana's Estadio Latinoamerica to witness the odd spectacle of Cuban leader Fidel Castro and Orioles owner Peter Angelos standing side by side during the playing of the U.S. national anthem as both the U.S. and Cuban flags were raised. It had been more than four decades since a big-league team had played in Cuba. The U.S. economic embargo, imposed in October 1960, was still very much in effect. Alderson sat a few rows away from Castro at the game, but had time to talk to him at a reception the night before.

"I was impressed by his command of detail," Alderson told me in Havana. "He seemed to know a lot about the development of baseball in the United States and other countries. My whole point of view is that this is recognition of a cultural bond that exists between the two countries. It doesn't speak to our economic systems. It doesn't speak to our political systems. It speaks to what we have in common."

Alderson also squarely put to rest the myth that Castro was an outstanding pitcher. "He said he was perhaps a better basketball player than a baseball player," Alderson said. "That was illuminating."

It was easy at the time to dismiss the game as a mere stunt, a chance for ESPN to set up its cameras in an exotic locale like Old Havana, largely unchanged in the forty years since Castro led a revolution to topple the Batista government. But the game represented an important step forward in bringing more Cuban players into major-league baseball. At the time, Cuban-born players in the big leagues were still rare, despite the success of Luis Tiant, Tony Pérez, and Jose Canseco. (A record nineteen Cuban-born players would be in the big leagues in 2014, up from a record fifteen the year before, and whereas in the '90s Cuban-born players sometimes showed up in the U.S. past their prime, Yoenis Céspedes, Yasel Puig, José Abreu, Alexei Ramírez, and Aroldis Chapman were all All-Stars.)

Alderson covered a wide variety of issues in his six and a half years working on Park Avenue, but it was his handling of the umpires union for which he was most remembered. The headline over a January 1999 Murray Chass article in the *Times* read COMMISSIONER'S OFFICE WON'T TAKE ON UMPIRES. Maybe the office itself wasn't going to do that, but MLB's point person on the issue was. By July 14, 1999, tensions had escalated to the point where more than fifty of sixty-six big-league umpires, goaded by umpires union chief Richie Phillips, voted to resign en masse from their jobs, effective September 2. It was a classic case of overplaying a weak hand. Alderson, delighted, responded: "This is either a threat to be ignored, or an offer to be accepted." MLB accepted the resignations of twenty-two umpires and hired replacement umps from the minor leagues. The mass-resignation gambit had backfired, leading to the demise of the Major League Umpires Association, which was replaced by a new union, the World Umpires Association.

Alderson had started mulling the problem of how fans and media would react when technological progress imposed more accountability on umpires, showing the progress of pitches over home plate and highlighting the accuracy—or inaccuracy—of an umpire's call. As every fan knew, different home-plate umpires had different strike zones. A knee-high fastball an inch off the plate might consistently be called a strike by one ump and a ball by another, or an umpire might shift the zone he called from game to game; pitchers and catchers paid close attention in the early innings to see which pitches were being called strikes, and adjusted accordingly. Alderson wanted more consistency. He felt it was important for the credibility of both the umpires and baseball itself.

"My goal with the umpires, which I stated periodically, was to have them perceived to be the best officials of any sport, amateur and professional, anywhere in the world," Alderson says. "That was our aspiration. We emphasized four things."

One, the strike zone. "The most important factor in an umpire's credibility is calling balls and strikes," Alderson told me. "If they're not consistent with balls and strikes, there are 130 chances for a fan or viewer to agree or disagree."

Starting in 2001, under Alderson's supervision, Major League Baseball began to implement an Umpire Information System developed by QuesTec, a company in Deer Park, New York, that used data culled from four video cameras installed at ballparks to track the flight of each pitch. The data could then be compared to the actual "ball" and "strike" calls made by each umpire working games at ballparks equipped with the QuesTec system and they could be given a score.

"At the time we had the ability to grade them on the strike zone but it wasn't available to the public," Alderson says. "I told them, 'Look, eventually the technology is going to catch up with us, the technology will be available to the networks, and you will be judged on that basis, in the same way instant replay came along and subjected you to second-guessing.'"

Two was what Alderson called nonconfrontation. "We had to tone down the confrontations between umpires and managers, umpires and coaches, umpires and players," he said. "They had to manage themselves and have a higher standard of conduct than we would normally expect from players and managers."

Three was hustle. "Just hustling creates the impression that they're motivated to do the job and to get the call right," he said. "It's like the perception when an umpire runs out to the outfield on a trap play to get in the right position. They needed to hustle. Part of that was physical fitness. To hustle, you have to be physically fit."

Four was getting the call right. "When there was a play, get them together to talk about it," he said. "That sort of flies in the face of the old umpire ethos, which was that you stand and fall on your own call and you never make a mistake, which flew in the face of technology. To get them together was not easy. But when you get together, it looks like you're trying to get the play right, and people identify with that. The fact you tried earns you a lot of points."

Taken together, the four added up to a major shift in how umpires did what they did. Of the four, the single most telling aspect was the Alderson edict that umpires confer far more often to discuss close plays. That one stuck. "That was an important part of the program and something that has continued, which is nice," he told me. "Sometimes you have these jobs for three or four years and leave and the whole thing goes to hell in a handbasket."

Alderson's time in baseball's New York office wrapped up in early 2005 when John Moores, a Texas-born businessman who owned the Padres, asked Bud Selig for permission to talk to Alderson about coming to work in San Diego. The Padres at that point had been in the playoffs only three times in their thirty-seven years in existence and Moores wanted Alderson to do for San Diego what he had earlier done for Oakland, and hired him as CEO starting in April 2005. "I was intrigued by the opportunity," Alderson says. "And in retrospect I'm very happy I took it."

As CEO Alderson had broad responsibility for the organization, but it was understood he would take a close look at baseball operations and revamp where he thought it was needed. "I made very few changes, actually," he says. He left in place the longtime tandem of general manager Kevin Towers, a former minor-league pitcher the Padres promoted from scouting director in 1995, and field manager Bruce Bochy, a former catcher for the Astros, Mets, and Padres, who was by then in his twelfth season leading the Padres. Bochy, NL Manager of the Year in 1996, had established a reputation as an easygoing leader good at connecting with players, a manager who believed in trusting his gut to make key choices. He had skippered the Padres to the 1998 World Series against the New York Yankees, only to be swept in four games. Each of Alderson's first two seasons in San Diego, 2005 and 2006, the Padres reached the playoffs, and both years lost the National League Division Series to the Cardinals, 3-0 and 3-1.

Soon after the Padres were eliminated in 2006, Giants general manager Brian Sabean, looking for a replacement for manager Felipe Alou, set his sights on Bochy, who had one year left on his contract with San Diego. Alderson gave Bochy permission to talk to the Giants, since at that point he was not prepared to extend his contract. Before October was even out, the Giants were announcing Bochy as their new manager. Alderson's reservations about Bochy as manager had in part to do with a sense that Bochy and Towers, who had known each other since they were teammates on the 1988 Las Vegas Stars, were such good friends, an almost incestuous atmosphere had developed that was not always ideal for team dynamics.

But when I caught up with Bochy in the summer of 2014 and asked him if there had been any issues between him and Alderson, he grinned at the question. "I've heard more than once that Sandy and I didn't quite see eye to eye," Bochy told me, almost laughing. "I really felt like we had a pretty good relationship. He would come down to the clubhouse, we would talk. I never felt that we didn't get along or that we weren't on the same page. Sandy, he's a smart man, and he would talk about baseball, about hitting, and he's got his philosophy and his thinking. But Sandy really loves the game. That showed. He was always a guy waiting for the players when they come off the bus right after a road trip. He felt like these were his guys, his troops, and he was always behind anything we did."

The playoff appearances in Alderson's first two years in San Diego turned out to be a high-water mark. The Padres were third in 2007, despite finishing 89-74, and then in 2008 plunged to 63-99 and last place in the NL West. Alderson had an inkling that Moores might be selling the team, and by spring training 2009 the deal had gone down. Jeff Moorad, the former agent, put together a group to buy the team and took over as the Padres' new CEO, and Alderson moved on. San Diego had been a good fit for him in many ways, a beachside California city much to his liking, one with a strong military presence, but he'd also been jarred at times with the differences between San Diego, down near the Mexican border, and his Northern California stomping grounds in the Bay Area.

In San Francisco, Alderson was known for his dry wit. As Edvins Beitiks, a columnist and former A's beat writer at the old *San Francisco Examiner*, once put it to me: "It's one of those senses of humor that's so sharp, you're laughing even as your head is tottering because he's cut it right off of you. To think that there are people who believe they are sharper than he is just makes me want to fall over and grab my sides."

Tom Krasovic, a beat writer who covered Alderson in San Diego, found him to be "fair, wry, sometimes contentious" with print media, but compared his radio presence to Spock, the half-Vulcan, half-human character on *Star Trek* devoted to logic. "I used to make light of those interviews," Krasovic says. "They could be torturous for the listener but also fascinating. . . . On the radio, he could come off as stilted, overly mental, almost robotic. He has a great dry sense of humor—but it translates better in person."

Alderson finally had time in 2009 to do something he'd always wanted to do: teach. He was asked to teach a sports marketing course at the University of California at Berkeley's Haas School of Business, and found he loved engaging with the students. "The undergraduates were tremendously enthusiastic and the MBA students were very accomplished and creative," he says. "I really enjoyed it. It was stimulating, it was challenging, and I learned a great deal myself." Alderson continued teaching at the Haas School even after Bud Selig asked him in March 2010 to oversee an effort to reform baseball in the Dominican Republic, and he would commute back to Berkeley to honor his commitment.

Alderson was deep into his work in the D.R. when word reached him that Baseball Commissioner Bud Selig was pushing his name as the ideal candidate to take over as general manager of the Mets. The friendship between Selig and Mets owner Fred Wilpon went all the way back to 1980, the year Wilpon first became an owner of the Mets. "We got along beautifully right from the start," Selig told me. "It transcended baseball and went to the rest of our lives. Our families get along, and they're very close." Over the years Selig and Wilpon remained close, though they did sometimes disagree on baseball matters. Selig was angry, for example, when the Mets ignored an MLB edict and announced the hiring of Art Howe as their new manager during the 2002 World Series.

The Mets payroll had gone up to $149 million in 2009, second in baseball, but came down to $134 million in 2010, fifth in baseball, and the team finished that season in fourth place for the second straight year. Wilpon dismissed general manager Omar Minaya in early October 2010 and named assistant general manager John Ricco acting GM, then asked Ricco to help search for his own successor. Thanks to Selig's nudge to his old friend Wilpon, the job looked to be Alderson's if he wanted it.

"Fred Wilpon is an extremely close friend, and I told him, 'You'll never do better than Sandy Alderson,'" Selig told me. "My view was it was important for the National League club in New York to be good, and you can't put a club in better hands than Sandy Alderson. It was as simple as that. Fred thanked me for it and, I'm happy to say, hired him."

Selig's tenure as commissioner was marked by an often deceptively iron fist. It was true he worked hard to generate consensus among owners on issues. It was also true that he built up a power base that meant that when he acted, his will was rarely defied; votes of the owners always went Selig's way. Wilpon was in no position to spurn Selig's directive.

I asked Selig if, at the time he gave Wilpon his advice, he knew if Alderson would be interested.

"I didn't know," Selig said at first, then elaborated. "You know, once you're a general manager, you always want to be a general manager. I knew that he'd be interested."

Alderson at first did not know what to make of media reports that Selig was pushing him for the job of Mets general manager. He put in a call from the Dominican Republic to Major League Baseball and wound up on the phone with Rob Manfred, then a top Selig lieutenant, now the commissioner of baseball.

"He was the one who told me, 'Don't worry about your commitment in the D.R. Go ahead and pursue it,'" Alderson recalled.

At his farewell press conference in a Santo Domingo hotel conference room in early November 2010, Alderson told reporters: "Well I was only here for about eight or nine months but I think we made great progress during that time. We came here to restore the integrity of the baseball system here as well as the rest of Latin America. I think it's important to keep in mind how important the Dominican Republic is to baseball and how many prospects come from the Dominican Republic, so it was logical for us to start here because there are so many players here."

From talking to Dominican reporters before and after the press conference, it was clear Alderson had made headway in his mission of demanding a higher level of accountability. Reporters I talked to said they hadn't been sure what to think of Alderson when he was brought in as a Baseball Czar for Latin America, but he'd won their respect with his focus and his genuine interest in engaging a variety of parties in dialogue. On his watch, they told me, progress had been made in pursuing identity fraud, cracking down on the the use of performance-enhancing drugs, and bringing the scouting bureau to the D.R.

"My job is to ensure that if a player says he's sixteen years old, he's sixteen and that if the player has a certain level of talent, that it's a level of talent that is not enhanced by drugs, so as far as the market is concerned, it is what it is," Alderson said. "The baseball community here knows more about me and feels less threatened than it did eight months ago and I certainly know more about the Dominican Republic and all of Latin America than I did eight months ago and I'm much better for it."

Juan DeJesus, manager of Latin American operations for Major League Baseball, worked closely with Alderson in the D.R. and received a crash course in taking unpopular stands but still being effective. "To go in and implement policies that are disruptive and put a process around what's going on, you're going to ruffle some feathers," he told me. "But overall I think people appreciate that the game has been preserved, the integrity of the game, and that it's in a better place and it will continue to grow and do well."

As Pedro Gomez of ESPN, who often reported from the D.R. for the network, put it: "It was widely considered the Wild West down there when it came to players using PEDs and falsifying their records. Who knew how old anyone was? Order was needed—and Alderson took some big steps in cleaning that up and bringing credibility."

There is no way of knowing for sure how much the Madoff situation was on Selig's mind in pushing the Mets to hire Alderson, whom he had long regarded as an upright figure. "He's very honest, very blunt, very direct," Selig says of Alderson. "There is never a scintilla of doubt about his integrity. Never. I really mean this, I have a very, very high regard for him as a person and I like him a great deal."

Asked directly if he favored Alderson for the Mets because he was worried about the damage the Madoff fallout could do, Selig told me: "I've said this over and over and I am particularly close to the Wilpons, particularly Fred. I never had any genuine concerns about the Mets' financial situation. Knowing what I know, and I know every club's financial position, I wasn't worried. And I say that to this day."

PART II

"COME ON, BLUE!"

When the New York Mets announced Sandy Alderson as their new general manager in October 2010, it was assumed his emphasis would be "Moneyball with money"—then came an era of dramatic belt-tightening.

9

ALDERSON'S BRAIN TRUST

For New York fans, Sandy Alderson was far from a well-known figure. He had a can-do reputation, but with the low profile of a behind-the-scenes operator, despite his stint from 2005 to 2009 as CEO of the Padres. Alderson was known to well-informed fans for his work in putting together the powerhouse Oakland teams of the late '80s, but a lot of seasons had come and gone since then. For most fans, the work of general managers was like the work of architects: easy to ignore, unless a structure suddenly collapsed and it was time to look for accountability or scapegoats. Alderson had earned headlines with his work at Major League Baseball—in particular his firm-handed showdown with the umpires, leading to a number of reforms that together added up to a major shift, all part of his high reputation among baseball insiders—but few fans gave this much thought. For them the only relevant questions are: When is my team going to start winning again? And if it doesn't, who can I blame?

For Mets fans there was a certain amount of relief in seeing an end brought to Omar Minaya's tenure. Minaya was probably underrated overall as a Mets GM. No question he was a skilled evaluator of talent. Did he make some mistakes? He did. Above all, signing Jason Bay to a four-year, $66 million deal in December 2009, based mostly on one good season with the Red Sox. Before long he would be weighing down the Mets like a cement overshoe. Rewarding Oliver Pérez for unspectacular work for the Mets with a new three-year, $36 million contract in early 2009 was another unwarranted move that turned into a full-scale headache. Then again, also in December 2009, Minaya made a move that might have seemed like a footnote at the time, signing a thirty-five-year-old pitcher who had been with three different teams the three previous years, an enigma named R. A. Dickey. "He knew Dickey from way back and he made the judgment that he was better than his record and possibly on the verge of something, from a friendship, from knowing the guy as an athlete, but also as a human being, knowing what was in his heart," *New York Times* columnist George Vecsey told me.

Still, at the time the move was greeted with the media equivalent of a Bronx cheer.

"On a day when the Yankees acquired the Atlanta Braves' ace, Javier Vazquez, to be their No. 4 starter, the Mets neared a deal with a converted knuckleballer who is missing a ligament in his right elbow," Ben Shpigel reported in the *Times*.

Minaya was hindered by his shortcomings as an administrator, which led to constant backbiting; his penchant for getting too chummy with too many of his players; and his lack of an early-warning system: Time and time again, he let issues play out in the press instead of keeping them out of the headlines in the first place. This was not all his fault; the hunger of the New York media is justly celebrated. But once the pattern was established, there was not much Minaya could do to avoid the death-by-a-thousand-paper-cuts torture of tabloid treatment, nothing short of winning the World Series.

One thing the Mets had never quite mastered in the Wilpon years was branding. That is, if they'd had a deeper, underlying vision of who they were and what they represented, they never let on. The Mets forever fell into a cycle of reaction, sending mixed messages, or trying too hard, as many felt they were when they tried to evoke Ebbets Field in their designs for Citi Field, which was fine enough, but then also added a Jackie Robinson Rotunda, although of course number 42 never played in Queens.

The buzz in baseball when Alderson's name started kicking around as a possible new Mets front-office figure focused less on Alderson's attributes and more on his availability. Would he really take the job? "When Sandy's name came up, I think from my perspective, it was just a matter of if he wanted the job," John Ricco says.

"There wasn't anybody more suited to come in and handle what he needed to handle." Alderson was not without mixed emotions about tackling so major a challenge, that much was obvious. Part of the job was going to entail waiting out some big, ugly contracts that were best forgotten sooner rather than later. It all shaped up as an exciting creative and intellectual challenge, not just trying to piece together enough good moves to rebuild a farm system and create a future winner, but far more fundamental, to reshape an entire culture and rebrand the Mets, creating a new identity as a team that was calm and determined and patient, focused on having a plan and sticking with the plan, not jumping to react every time sports talk radio or the tabloids hit the alarm button and hiring whichever aging, over-rated free agent was being talked up that year.

To the satisfaction of Mets ownership, the news of Alderson's hiring was greeted with general acclaim in the press and among fans. The players reacted well, too. "It was exciting, because he came in and said that he was going to turn the team around and we were going to start winning," recalled Ike Davis, a rookie that year. David Wright, the Mets' leader in the clubhouse, applauded the hiring. David's father, Rhon, was intrigued as well. "For Christmas that year my dad got me *Moneyball*," Wright told me. "I figured I'd better start walking more and getting on base a little better."

It was a little like Danny Ocean was back on the move—and all the best guys wanted to be involved. Alderson had established Oakland as a rich breeding ground for front-office talent, opening the doors to Ivy League graduates who had earlier been shut out of baseball. Now that he was back in the saddle as Mets general manager, looking to assemble a team around him, he had his pick of bright executives. The ground was shifting so quickly, statistical analysis and data-driven decision-making evolving so rapidly, it was essential to be always looking for the next big thing, and Alderson set about putting together a formidable brain trust of Paul DePodesta, the former Dodgers general manager; J. P. Ricciardi, the former Blue Jays GM who had worked with Alderson years earlier in Oakland; and Ricco, who had been the Mets' acting GM when Alderson was hired.

Ricciardi almost said no.

"Sandy, I have to be honest, I'm not the guy you knew sixteen years ago," Ricciardi told him. "I don't need the job. My family is more important to me. Baseball's not going to take precedence over that. If you want that, I'd rather not come over."

Ricciardi was chosen by the Mets in the same draft as Billy Beane, 1980, and the two were teammates that year playing A ball in Little Falls, New York. Ricciardi, two years older than Beane, was through playing by the following year, but he caught on in the Yankees organization, coaching in 1982 for the Fort Lauderdale affiliate and then a year later for the New York–Penn League team. In 1986 Ricciardi contacted Dick Bogard, the A's director of scouting, and started as an East Coast scout and roving instructor and worked his way up from there. He was, everyone agreed, a great natural evaluator of talent. He had the eye.

"It was an opportunity," Ricciardi told me. "Oakland had no scouts on the East Coast, and they were trying to build their scouting back up and get in the real world."

He did not hit it off with his new boss right away. "It was different," he says of their first encounter. "It was the first time I ever met somebody who was not a traditional baseball guy, so to speak. This guy was running the A's and he wasn't a guy who had played, he wasn't a guy who had been in the game from a scouting or player development background. He was a lawyer. I didn't know what to think."

Ricciardi had flown to Arizona that October for organizational meetings, and somebody had handed out flimsy hats as gifts for everyone in the scouting department.

"That's a pretty cool hat," Alderson said.

"It's a piece of crap," Ricciardi replied.

Alderson, Ricciardi, and Beane became a three-man unit in Oakland. That was when the analytical framework Alderson had been developing for years truly came into its own. "We first began to implement this extensively when Billy became the assistant GM and we got much more active in the six-year free-agent market,"

Alderson says. "We signed Billy Taylor and Geronimo Berroa this way. Basically the way we allocated responsibility was we would do these statistical analyses, J.P. would go in the field, cross-check from a traditional scouting point of view, and then Billy had the assignment of signing the players. So he wasn't really evaluating, but one of Billy's qualities was he could talk anybody into anything. He had been a car salesman in the off-season."

The Blue Jays signed Berroa out of the Dominican Republic at age eighteen, and the Braves, Mariners, Indians, Reds, and Marlins all acquired him and let him go. He was on the proverbial scrap heap, with only 189 big-league at bats spread out over five years when the A's signed him as a six-year free agent in January 1994. He had great wrists, and his power potential was never in question, but he lacked plate discipline. What the A's noticed, though, was that over nine seasons in the minor leagues he'd only once notched a walks total that was more than 10 percent of his at bats—but that was his most recent season, 1993. He came to spring training, won a spot on the team, and by 1996 was a leader of the offense with thirty-six home runs, 106 RBIs, and an on-base percentage of .344. He had twelve big-league walks before he joined the A's, but sixty-three in '95 alone.

The A's did it time after time, finding value where others had missed it. Once Berroa was due for a bigger paycheck, the A's unloaded him, trading him to Baltimore for right-handed pitcher Jimmy Haynes in 1997. It was a pattern they repeated again and again, a major part of how they reloaded in the mid-1990s. By the time Alderson handed the team over to Beane, the farm system had been restocked. The key to that rejuvenation was a combination of an analytic-driven approach, good scouting, and intense focus.

"Back then it was always *Full Metal Jacket*, let's win, let's do this, let's do that," Ricciardi says.

Pondering his future in 2010, Ricciardi felt no temptation to return to that kind of existence. He told Alderson: "I want the job for the right reasons, because I have a chance to work with you and learn."

They had a series of conversations and Alderson persuaded Ricciardi that he, too, was a little less single-minded about baseball.

"I've known Sandy since 1985," Ricciardi says. "It hasn't been until the last four years that I've really gotten him to open up. I've asked him a ton of questions about Vietnam. Going to work in New York. I wanted to be around good people again."

Ricciardi liked the idea of taking the relationship forward and also of being there for Alderson to talk through ideas, almost the way a bench coach does with a field manager.

"My role is more to be a right-hand man to Sandy," he says, "maybe be the guy who can see the big-league club and not only assess the big league, but be able to talk to the coaches, talk to the managers, be able to give him some insights into where we are."

Paul DePodesta's epiphany came one day in the offices of the Baltimore Stallions of the Canadian Football League, where he worked as an unpaid intern. The year was 1995 and DePodesta had just graduated from Harvard. "I really went there to play baseball," he says. He played some shortstop, some outfield, but hurt his shoulder during his freshman year and was never really the same, though he stuck it out through his sophomore year. He also found he missed football, so started playing for the Crimson team as a sophomore, gradually earned the respect of the coaches, earned regular playing time his junior year, and was a starting wide receiver as a senior until he got hurt.

DePodesta got along well with his coach, Mac Singleton, and by the end of his time at Harvard the econ major had decided to rule out a boring desk job in favor of following his love of sports. "What I really wanted to be at the time was a football coach," DePodesta says. "I spent a lot of time watching film. I loved the strategy of it and I loved the physical competition that went along with it. I was trying to get that experience in the CFL. My hope was to get a graduate assistant coach job somewhere in football, get a graduate degree, and start coaching somewhere."

Aric Holsinger, the Stallions CFO and a former Baltimore Orioles CFO, happened to have a collection of Major League Baseball media guides. "I was thumbing through some of the media guides, and I came across a bio for Sandy Alderson," DePodesta told me.

"He was a Dartmouth grad, a Harvard grad, a Marine. I remember being so struck by that and thinking, 'This is my kind of guy!' It was much more my profile than anything I was used to seeing in professional sports. At the time it definitely served as inspiration to me that a career path like that would actually be possible. I don't think it's something I'd ever contemplated previously."

DePodesta's thoughts turned more toward baseball, even as he continued to work for the Stallions during the day, doing a little of everything. At night he was also interning for the Baltimore Bandits of the American Hockey League, a role that entailed throwing T-shirts into the stands and propping up fans as they walked out onto the ice between periods to participate in contests or whatever else came up.

He had an in with the Indians, who had just gone to the 1995 World Series, and was hoping to land an internship. "I was ridiculously lucky," DePodesta says. "I sent my stuff in, went in and interviewed, and while I was there I found out it was for the whole year, not just spring training." It had all seemed like a lark, but suddenly it looked much more serious when Mark Shapiro, who had interviewed him, offered him a job in the Indians' front office.

"I thought, 'This isn't something I can turn down,'" DePodesta says. "I'm in the Canadian Football League. These guys were just in the World Series."

DePodesta took the job, which involved working closely with Josh Byrnes, the assistant in baseball operations. "It was a great, great learning experience, my equivalent of graduate school in baseball," he says. "In spring training, I was the minor-league van driver! Once the season began, I charted all of the major-league games and helped assist in various areas of player development. As the year continued, I started working on projects for the major-league coaching staff, John Hart and Dan O'Dowd. At the conclusion of the season, I became the major-league advance scout."

He was, without a doubt, a new breed, a thinker but not a geek; he'd played college football and could take a hit. He may not have been as gregarious and socially at ease as Billy Beane always had been, but he did just fine taking to his new environment. The Indians sent

him out late in the 1996 season to do a little pro scouting and at first
he felt some culture shock. He was watching the Yankees and the
Sox at Fenway the last week of the season, and no one was talking to
him in the scout section until a smiling, intense, hawk-nosed Mas-
sachusetts local approached him. It was J. P. Ricciardi, at the time
special assistant to Oakland A's general manager Sandy Alderson.

"I was a twenty-three-year-old who was clearly out of place,"
DePodesta told me. "J.P. was the one guy who actually introduced
himself to me and said hello. We struck up a friendship."

Billy Beane was hiring an assistant in 1999, Ricciardi recommended DePodesta, and soon Beane and DePodesta were running
the show in Oakland. "Paul and I kind of had that *Risky Business*
moment, you know, Tom Cruise in his underwear, where we realized, 'You mean we've got the house to ourselves?'" Beane told me.

"There's no doubt that Sandy, going back probably fifteen years
previous, had been the one to introduce a systematic approach to
decision-making," DePodesta says. "There had to be information
out there that would facilitate better decision-making. All that was in
place by the time I got there. It's almost like he went through everything he had to do to build the first personal computer. And then
when Billy and I were there we said, 'We could also write software
for this thing. Who knows what we could do with this thing?' The
perseverance, the smarts, everything it took to create that framework,
Sandy had done, and then we kind of ran with it."

Alderson later recommended DePodesta for the job of Dodgers GM, though they'd never actually worked together, and hired
him in San Diego, where he was working when Alderson took over
the Mets.

"When Sandy called and asked if I would go to New York, to
be honest it wasn't that difficult a decision," DePodesta says. "First,
the opportunity to work with him again was a real lure. He was
also bringing J.P., which was a real attraction. It was a chance to do
something with those people and to do it in New York. I've had my
share of both big market and small market, so I don't necessarily
believe that the grass is always greener, but I was excited about the
opportunity to do something special in a place like New York."

DePodesta was running player development and scouting and was doing a lot of scouting himself; Ricciardi oversaw pro scouting, handled special assignments, and also did pro scouting himself; Ricco, assistant general manager, handled many of the adminis- trative aspects of the big-league operation and was also involved with salary arbitration. Ricco had worked at Major League Baseball headquarters in New York at the same time as Alderson had and knew him from there, but it was still an odd transition, going from interviewing him for the Mets job, as acting general manager, to working with him. "In the early months we'd go out to dinner and I'd pick up the check, because I had the credit card," Ricco says. "I was doing all the budgets. I was signing his expense reports."

As with every other aspect of the team, Alderson's experiment in stockpiling so much brainpower in the front office hinged on what the players did on the field. If the team failed in Alderson's bid to return it to championship form, then Alderson and his brain trust would clearly take the heat. Having three general managers in their own right, all working together, helped guard against arrogance.

"One of the very first steps is acknowledging how little we know and how limited our ability is to predict the future," DePodesta told me. "We're talking about human beings playing baseball and we're talking about situations that those human beings may never have encountered before. A big part of our jobs is getting our arms around that uncertainty so we can make calculated decisions even in that atmosphere. It's not unlike playing blackjack: You never have all the information, but to the extent we can take a framework to have an idea that one decision would be better than the other, that's what we strive for. But we still know that the future is fundamentally unknowable—and the use of metrics needs to have that in mind."

10

THE MADOFF MESS

The 2011 Mets season, Alderson's first with the team, played out against the depressing backdrop of the Bernie Madoff scandal. When the whole thing blew up in December 2008, with Madoff being arrested, the Wilpon family investments with Madoff reportedly totaled half a billion dollars. That money was gone. The Wilpon family had been averaging a return of around 10 percent, some of which they could invest in the Mets. Suddenly that cash flow was gone as well. Early coverage of the scandal focused on how the Wilpons, along with other wealthy clients of Madoff's, had been duped by the scheme, and how losses incurred through Madoff's malfeasance could make it difficult for Fred Wilpon to handle the debt he incurred when he bought out Nelson Doubleday Jr. in 2002 to become the club's principal owner. The scandal percolated in the press for the next two years and, from a Mets standpoint, began to look more ominous soon after Sandy Alderson was hired as GM in late October 2010. Alderson had known about the Mets ownership's involvement with Madoff when he took the job, but he had not grasped the scale of the impact it would have on the club's finances, leading to one of the largest one-year drops in payroll in baseball history. I've known Alderson since I covered him in the '90s in my years as an A's beat writer for the *San Francisco Chronicle*, and I knew just how frustrating he had to find this shift in fortunes. But I also knew he was stubborn. Discussing it later during one of our more than one hundred interviews for this book, Alderson told me he would have taken the job even if he'd understood what was coming on the financial front, just out of love for a good challenge.

If Alderson had been president of the Mets, his former role in Oakland, he would have been neck-deep in dealing with the fallout and its financial repercussions for the Wilpons and the Mets. As it was, he was only the general manager. His job was heading up the baseball operations staff. "The nice thing about being involved in just the baseball end is that I can separate myself from the Madoff situation by just being direct and honest with people and saying, 'OK, I knew about Madoff, I knew the Mets owners had lost money with Madoff,'" Alderson told me in 2011. "I can't have any credibility with the public if they think I'm a shill for Fred, Saul, and Jeff. I think that's why they brought me in here in the first place, because I had some independent credibility. I wasn't going to come here as a 'Yes man.' On the other hand, they own the team, and I respect that."

By February 2011 the heat had turned up considerably, with a billion-dollar lawsuit by the trustee of Madoff's victims accusing the Wilpons and partner Saul Katz of looking the other way when they should have known better. As the owners went from sharply ruling out a sale of the team to announcing they were seeking additional minority investors, it became clear that the Mets would have significantly less money to spend on payroll. The prospect of an extended—and expensive—court fight that could push the Mets' financial outlook deeper into trouble had many around the team queasy. Team finances were so shaky, Bud Selig had to bail out his old friend, and it became public in February 2011 that in November 2010 Major League Baseball had extended the Mets' ownership a $25 million short-term loan.

"It was definitely something that hung over the franchise," Alderson says. "The uncertainty of active litigation, stories being written frequently about the merits of the case, where it was procedurally—all of it was a big distraction. The team on the field, the team that was being put together in the off-season, was secondary to the conversation about Madoff."

As *New York Times* columnist George Vecsey put it to me during this period, "The franchise now has its own curse of Babe Ruth, the curse of Bernie Madoff. The fun hasn't survived for the Mets. The fun is long gone. Alderson is coming in after the party is over and he's had to kind of open the windows and hose it down. In a way I feel sorry for him."

The financial repercussions of the Madoff scandal were enough of a blow to the franchise's fortunes, but this being the Mets, a team that had all too often in its brief history been the target of derisive humor, the ridicule factor was also devastating. In fact, this was one area in which the team was probably without peer. In the fifty-three years since the Mets were born, even in the periods when they've fielded a strong team, they had been the butt of more jokes, gibes, and sarcastic laments than any team in baseball, more so even than the "lovable loser" Chicago Cubs. Being a Mets fan meant caring so much, you shrugged off the jokes and the losing seasons; the very words "Mets fan" at times sounded like a punch line.

What was it about the Mets that inspired such an unrelenting supply of gallows humor? The Mets, after all, twice won the World Series—the Miracle Mets of '69 and the thank-you-Bill-Buckner Mets of '86—not a great record, but nowhere near the worst in baseball. The Pirates, Marlins, Tigers, Twins, Blue Jays, and Phillies have all won two, same as the Mets, during the lifetime of the Metropolitans. Five teams have won fewer. If only the Mets could see themselves as just another team, free to rise or fall like any other club, their record of accomplishment would balance between infamy and glory, fan heartbreak and fan rapture, as in so many other marketplaces, but that of course has never been the case.

"We're the punch line in a lot of jokes because we're viewed, and rightfully so, as kind of the little brother in the city with the Yankees," David Wright told me. "There's not too many teams that could compete both on the field and with the aura of the Yankees. You could put any team you wanted in New York and they wouldn't be able to live up to the history or the accomplishments that the Yankees have. But deep down I think that this is a National League city. There's just a different feel and a different kind of blue-collar enthusiasm that this city has for the underdogs, and in many ways we're viewed as that. I think deep down inside this city yearns for a

National League team, the New York Mets, to do well for a number of reasons, and one is probably for all the Mets fans out there to finally be able to stick their finger in the Yankees fans' faces and give them the bragging rights for that period of time."

The Mets' very colors are emblematic of pain: orange for the heartbreak of losing the New York Giants to the heathens out on the coast, blue for the heartbreak of losing the Brooklyn Dodgers to the heathens out in La-La Land. From day one the Mets were a weirdly conceived exercise in franchise as citywide therapy, except shattered innocence can't be glued back together again. "Once we had Ebbets Field and a way of life," Pulitzer Prize–winning columnist Jimmy Breslin wrote in his 1963 book *Can't Anybody Here Play This Game?* He later added, "This is why the New York Mets come out as something more than a baseball team as far as an awful lot of people are concerned. The Mets are a part of life. You can start keeping track of time with them. They are not going to move for money."

There was something oddly thrilling about the Mets' complete break with mediocrity in 1962, their inaugural year. It takes real distinction to finish a season 40-120. Only the nineteenth-century Cleveland Spiders lost more games in a season (20-134 in 1899) and no team since the Boston Braves in 1935 finished a year with fewer victories. With manager Casey Stengel and players like Choo Choo Coleman, Richie Ashburn, and Marv Throneberry, these Mets were never dull. "Nobody wants to be a laughingstock, but the fact is the Mets were fun and it was a New York thing and they were a product of people they hired, Casey and Marvelous Marv and Ashburn," remembers Vecsey, then a young reporter covering the team for *Newsday*. "It was so much freaking fun in '62. The Yankees were still hard-ass and stuffy."

More than anything, it was the crosstown presence of the imperial Yankees that tended to unnerve the Mets and their fans, though in good times it was fun having the Yankees as a foil. When the Mets picked Tom Seaver's name out of a hat, winning a three-way lottery to see which team could claim the young Californian, and Seaver went from 1967 Rookie of the Year to the foundation of the '69 team, it was easy to tune out the mediocrity in the Bronx. Those Mets also featured another exciting young pitcher, drafted in the twelfth round of the 1965 draft out of Refugio, Texas, a hard-throwing right-hander by the name of Nolan Ryan.

For all the Mets' futility in their early years of existence— and they lost a hundred games or more in five of their first seven seasons—their first big break came during secret meetings of National League owners, when a separate National League East division was established, starting in 1969, making a spot in the playoffs more attainable. Through ten games, the '69 Mets were mucking along at 3-7, following 11–3 and 4–0 drubbings by the Pirates. Late May saw the Mets run their losing streak to five with a 3–2 loss to the expansion San Diego Padres before a desultory crowd of 11,772 at Shea Stadium, dropping their record to 18-23. It looked like yet another season was leaking oil fast. Then the next night they caught a break in the eleventh inning: Bud Harrelson's ball down the third-base line was called fair, Cleon Jones came in to score, and the Mets had a 1–0 win.

The extra-inning win was a turning point. The Mets then swept both the Giants and Dodgers in three-game series at Shea to run their winning streak to seven games, capping a 7-1 homestand that was the best in the Mets' short history. Out on the coast, the Mets took three more from the Padres in San Diego with their ace, Tom Seaver, pushing his record to 9-3. "The New York Invincibles, once known as mere Mets, made it ten straight victories today in their newly accustomed fashion, as they defeated the San Diego Padres, 3–2, with a two-run burst in the eighth inning," Leonard Koppett wrote in the *Times* after the final game in San Diego.

The win streak reached eleven before the Mets faltered against Gaylord Perry and the Giants at Candlestick Park, but by then the team was on a roll that would not be stopped all season. Seaver, just twenty-four that year, would pile up twenty-five victories on the way to his first Cy Young Award. Left fielder Cleon Jones batted .340 with sixty-four walks for a .422 on-base percentage, and center fielder Tommie Agee had a team-high twenty-six homers, but no Met had as many as eighty RBIs. Even as they piled up victories over the course of the summer, no one could figure out how they had ground out so many wins. How unbelievable a season was it for the Mets? The Chicago Cubs were in first place in the newly formed National League East Division on September 2 with an 84-52 record and were still five games ahead of the second-place Mets. But the Mets finished the season on a 23-7 roll, compared to a wretched 8-17 close for the Cubs, to finish the regular season in first place by eight games.

The giddy sense of disbelief only escalated when the Mets stunned the Braves in the first National League Championship Series, sweeping them in three games with an average of nine runs scored per game. The winning pitcher in Game 3 was twenty-two-year-old Nolan Ryan, who came on in relief in the third inning. Henry Aaron already had a homer and double in the game at that point, but Ryan held him to two pop-ups. In the World Series the Mets had to face a Baltimore Orioles team full of established stars like Boog Powell, Frank Robinson, and Brooks Robinson that came into the Series 8-to-5 favorites after having won 109 games in the regular season. Manager Earl Weaver said, "Bring on the Mets!" and indeed in Game 1, with Tom Seaver matched up against Baltimore's Mike Cuellar, the Mets lost—but then they came back to win the next four in a row.

The Payson family, original owners of the Mets, sold the team in January 1980 for $21.1 million, a record at the time, to a group headed up by majority investor Nelson Doubleday Jr., the book publisher. Fred Wilpon, a real-estate developer and boyhood friend of Sandy Koufax's, came in as a minority investor and CEO and president of the club. The new owners hired Frank Cashen as general manager and he scored some immediate coups, drafting Darryl Strawberry in the first round in 1980 and Dwight Gooden in the first round in 1982, along with supporting players like center fielder Lenny Dykstra in 1981. Cashen also pulled off some big trades, sending Neil Allen and Rick Ownbey to the Cardinals in June 1983 for first baseman Keith Hernandez, who had won both the NL batting title and MVP award in 1979, and on December 10, 1984, trading Hubie Brooks, Mike Fitzgerald, Herm Winningham, and Floyd Youmans to Montreal for catcher Gary Carter, already a seven-time All-Star at that point. The Mets were twelve games over .500 in '84, their first winning season since 1976, and improved to 98-64 in '85, but still finished second in the NL East.

If the '69 Mets were an amazement, the '86 team was simply a powerhouse. They rattled off an eleven-game winning streak in April with an 8–1 win over the Braves in Atlanta that featured a 5-for-5 day from Strawberry and Gooden's fourth win of the season against no losses, and after that 13-3 start they just kept piling on the wins. Their 108-win regular season put them in rare company. In big-league history, only six times to that point, and twice since, has a team amassed more regular-season wins.

What tends to get lost about the 1986 World Series is that Bill Buckner's famous through-the-wickets error took place in Game 6. The Mets, having lost the first two games of the Series at home, had come back with two wins at Fenway to even the Series, then lost Game 5 in Boston and were two runs down and one out away from elimination in the bottom of the tenth inning with the bases empty. Gary Carter, Kevin Mitchell, and Ray Knight strung together three singles against Calvin Schiraldi to make it a one-run game and send Mitchell to third. Bob Stanley came in to pitch and promptly uncorked a wild pitch to score Mitchell and send Knight to second base. Only then did Mookie Wilson hit a spinning grounder to the right side of the infield that Buckner, almost visibly wincing as he crouched after the ball, was unable to field.

For all the lamenting in New England, all the talk of the Curse of the Bambino, there was one game left to be played. The Red Sox had already taken two from the Mets at home, and all they had to do was win Game 7 at Shea to win the Series—and in fact, Ron Darling gave up back-to-back solo shots in the top of the second inning and Boston added a run on Wade Boggs' RBI single to take a 3–0 lead that held up through five innings. Finally in the bottom of the sixth, the Mets tied it up on Keith Hernandez's bases-loaded single and Gary Carter's RBI groundout, and in the seventh the Red Sox had no choice but to go again with Schiraldi, the previous night's loser, who gave up a solo shot to Ray Knight that gave the Mets their first lead of the night. The sight of Jesse Orosco out on the mound, throwing his glove in the air after the last out of the 8–5 victory, will always stay with Mets fans.

In the all-important area of New York bragging rights, the Mets had nine years to enjoy the sweet taste of '86. The Yankees finished fourth in the AL East in '87 and fifth in '88 and '89, all the while Steinbrenner going through managers like Liz Taylor through husbands. By 1990 the Yankees were a truly bad team, finishing 67-95 under managers Bucky Dent and Stump Merrill, and did not have a winning season until 1993, under Buck Showalter. They won their division in the strike-shortened '94 season and then in 1996 won the World Series again, starting an incredible run under manager Joe Torre.

Given all the great Yankees teams of the past, the Torre-era run of dominance vaulted the Yankees to an entirely different realm, one that left the Mets all the more in their shadow, especially after the 2000 Subway Series. The Mets had won ninety-four games that season under manager Bobby Valentine, compared with eighty-seven for the Yankees, but went down meekly in the World Series, winning only one game. Up at Yankee Stadium for Game 1, the Mets took a 3–2 lead in the seventh, but the Yankees tied it in the bottom of the ninth and won in the twelfth. The next night came the bizarre spectacle of Yankees starter Roger Clemens, amped up on some combination of adrenaline, amphetamines, and steroids, moving in after he broke Mike Piazza's bat and throwing a fragment of the splintered bat at Piazza as he ran down the line toward first. Piazza's bewilderment was understandable. Clemens never has given a decent explanation for what happened. The Mets were down 6–0 going into the ninth inning of that game and mounted a five-run rally in the ninth, but fell one run short and found themselves down 0-2 in the Series. The near-miss theme continued when, in Game 5, Piazza came up in the ninth against closer Mariano Rivera and belted a drive to deep center field that looked like it was going to be a game-tying homer, but the ball didn't carry, and the Yankees had their fourth World Series title in five years.

The Mets did not have a lot of highlights in the coming years and lacked a clear sense of direction. There's an old rule in politics that says the voters, in choosing a president, often tend to overcompensate, like women seeking men as different as possible from their ex-husbands. The Mets did this with managers, deciding after six years with Bobby Valentine as skipper that they wanted someone as unlike him as possible. Whereas Bobby V loved to cultivate friends and contacts in the media and could be impulsive, the Mets figured that Art Howe, having won more than a hundred games each of his last two seasons managing the A's, would be the anti-Valentine in just the ways they wanted and would bring a winning tradition. Howe was startled to find when he joined the Mets for the 2003 season how much sourness surrounded the team.

The Mets' big off-season acquisition was left-hander Tom Glavine, who pitched Opening Day at Shea Stadium. Unfortunately, it was a few degrees above freezing that day. "They booed Armando Benitez and Roger Cedeño that day when they lined up along the base lines before the game had even started," Howe told me. "The fans weren't real happy with the team. Tom was one of the best pitchers in baseball, but he was a finesse guy who needed to feel the ball. It was so cold, it was like a cue ball. He got knocked around. I know it was probably the first time Tom was ever booed on a baseball field when he walked off the field that day." Glavine was pummeled for four runs in the first inning, the Mets lost 15–2, and the punishing headlines the next day in effect declared the season over.

Steve Phillips, the GM who hired Howe, was fired that June 12 when the Mets got off to a 29-35 start. Jim Duquette handled the job for a while, and then starting in late 2004 it was time for Omar Minaya, their former assistant GM, to get a shot. Minaya came in on a mission to mix it up with plenty of high-profile deals and also to work in more Latin players if he thought it would help the Mets win. His philosophy of trying to acquire as many gifted athletes as he could was essentially the opposite of the *Moneyball* approach. There was no question that he knew talent—he even said Ozzie Guillén could be a successful major-league manager when Guillén was still playing—and he built the Mets into a contender, starting with some splashy moves. He signed three-time Cy Young Award–winner Pedro Martinez to a four-year, $53 million deal in late 2004, just months after he took over, a move that was like a lightning bolt, making the Mets look formidable again, and hired Willie Randolph to take over when Howe was let go after two disappointing seasons.

Shortstop Jose Reyes made his big-league debut in 2003, the day before his twentieth birthday, and by 2005 he was a full-fledged phenomenon. Reyes was the rare player in the Rickey Henderson mold who could lead off, hit for power, and make things happen on the base paths, doing it all with a grin that made everyone feel good. He had a league-leading seventeen triples in 2005 and every single one felt like an event. His running was so explosive, so beautiful to see, as he'd fly around second on his way to a stand-up three-bagger. Never had such speed looked so easy. Reyes also led the league in stolen bases in 2005 with sixty and ranked fourth in singles with 142.

Reyes again led the league in triples in 2006 with seventeen, but he also boosted his batting average from .273 to .300 and his on-base percentage from .300 to .354. David Wright, just six months older than Reyes, was putting together his second straight impressive season, finishing with an OPS of .912 for the second year in a row. He had twenty-six homers, 116 RBIs, and a .311 average. Carlos Delgado, acquired from the Florida Marlins in a November 2005 trade, added thirty-eight homers and 114 RBIs, and Carlos Beltrán, signed by the Mets as a free agent before the 2005 season, had forty-one homers, 116 RBIs, and ninety-five walks. This was a team with plenty of power and just enough starting pitching, led by forty-year-old Tom Glavine and thirty-five-year-old Steve Trachsel (both fifteen-game winners that season), to finish 97-65 and face the St. Louis Cardinals in the NLCS, which went to seven games. Wright singled home Beltrán to give the Mets an early 1–0 lead against the Cardinals in Game 7, but St. Louis tied it up in the second. Finally in the ninth, Yadier Molina skied a two-run homer to give the Cards the lead. The Mets loaded the bases in the bottom of the inning and had Beltrán coming up. He worked the count full and then promptly struck out looking, frozen by a wicked Adam Wainwright curveball, and the season ended with him standing there with his bat on his shoulder.

In 2007 Beltrán, Wright, and Reyes all had strong years, with Carlos Delgado and forty-year-old Moises Alou adding power; left-hander Oliver Pérez, acquired by Minaya in a July 2006 trade, joined John Maine and Glavine to anchor the rotation. The Mets won their first four games, thirty-three of their first fifty, and were 57-43 after 100 games, heading into the last weeks of the season in a commanding position. Their lead over the second-place Phillies stood at seven games on September 12 with only seventeen left to play. They went into a tailspin, but still had a 2½-game lead going into the last week of the season, and had a seven-game homestand against teams with losing records. They lost six of seven to cap off a season-ending collapse that ranked among the worst in baseball history. They won only five of their last seventeen games, and the jeers at Shea when they were eliminated from playoff contention were unrelenting.

"It hurts," David Wright told the press afterward. "But at the same time, we did it to ourselves. It's not like it blindsides us. We gradually let this thing slip away. In all honesty, we didn't deserve to make the playoffs." Later he went on *The Daily Show with Jon Stewart* and said he had "nightmares every night" about the collapse, and that probably was not much of an exaggeration.

Alderson took the job of Mets GM in no small part because he knew how much his father, retired military pilot John Alderson, was going to enjoy hanging out at Mets spring-training games. Baseball was a lifelong passion of both men, and it had brought them closer together after Sandy's mother, Gwenny, died in April 1997. John was a star of his senior softball team in Florida. "Somebody might have said, 'Taking the Mets job is not a good idea,'" Alderson told me. "I took it in part because I thought my dad would enjoy it. Of all the intangible factors, that was probably the major one."

But Sandy's father never had that chance. In fact, Sandy had only one opportunity to talk with his father about his excitement about the team following the October 29, 2010, press conference in New York announcing him as Mets general manager.

Sandy had been invited to be the guest of honor in Santo Domingo for the annual celebration of the founding of the Marine Corps on November 10, 1775. The next morning was Veterans

Day—and Sandy got a call from his father. "We didn't talk long. He was excited about the Mets. He was in good spirits," he says. "He always called me to wish me a happy Veterans Day. If he didn't call me, I called him."

From Santo Domingo Sandy and Linda flew to Puerto Rico to take part in a fund-raiser for Carlos Beltrán's baseball academy in Florida, Puerto Rico, an hour's drive from San Juan. Back at the hotel that night, it was long past midnight when the phone in the Aldersons' hotel room rang. It was Sandy's sister Kristy calling from Florida with horrible news.

"That was the night my dad was killed," Alderson told me. "Emotionally it was a huge blow, as you can imagine."

John Alderson had been crossing Fourth Street, a six-lane thoroughfare a few miles from his home in St. Petersburg, Florida, when he was struck by a car and killed. John was eighty-seven, but he was still playing softball three times a week in a senior league. Jim Brice, general manager at Harvey's 4th Street Grill, said he and John got to be good friends and would often head to a hamburger joint called El Cap, a little redbrick corner place with a white-on-red neon sign out front. That's where John Alderson went on the night of November 12 to watch sports with friends.

"Somebody else had driven from home," Sandy says. "He got in an argument with somebody and just kind of left in a huff and decided to walk home. It's quite a walk, actually, but it was something he could do. He was in great shape. And he got hit crossing the street."

11

ANATOMY OF A TRADE

Sandy Alderson and the Mets were sliding toward the abyss in the summer of 2011, and the former Marine combat officer in Vietnam was far too open-eyed a leader to soft-pedal that grim reality to himself or anyone else. He'd watched teams spiral downward into hopelessness. He understood that, as surely as running a team in California had meant bracing for earthquakes, taking over the Mets meant living with a weird combination of perpetually high expectations and searing negativity.

Alderson had not expected a honeymoon period, which was a good thing. So much had gone so wrong so quickly by July 2011, it was enough to cause whiplash. Alderson's hiring as Mets general manager the previous November had inspired much talk of "*Moneyball* with money," a reference to the statistics-oriented, do-more-with-less approach that his protégé in Oakland, Billy Beane, had made famous. Soon it became clear that the "with money" part of this formulation could be deleted.

No real progress could be made, Alderson knew, until the team started winning. Everything that happened before then was mere prologue. Until the club took the field with respect and confidence, playing each game with the talent and attitude of a team capable of going to the World Series, all efforts to redefine the culture of the Mets would be Sisyphean. Alderson was, famously, a realist. He dealt in that which was, not that which might be. He knew he needed to make the team better fast, to communicate his message, but suddenly he was in cost-cutting mode. This was going to take time.

Who *were* the Mets in the summer of 2011? Casting a neutral eye on the team on the field was like gazing out on a nondescript stretch of landscape along an interstate highway with few landmarks. Third baseman David Wright, going on twenty-nine that year, was a former Gold Glove winner and a beautiful hitter. Wright was part of the future. Shortstop Jose Reyes, still boyish at twenty-seven, was one of the more captivating players ever to put on a Mets uniform. The fans loved him, and for good reason. He could turn even an ordinary late August game between two noncontending teams into something exciting. Reyes, too, was a player the Mets would love to have in their future, if they could afford him. The rest of the infield was a work in progress—two twenty-six-year-old contact hitters, Daniel Murphy and Justin Turner, could plug in at multiple infield positions, and Ike Davis, son of former big-leaguer Ron Davis, was a young prospect with power the Mets hoped to develop into their first baseman of the future. As their regular catcher they'd given the nod to twenty-four-year-old Josh Thole, trusting he'd work well with the pitchers and hoping he'd show enough offense not to be a liability.

The outfield looked more promising. Switch-hitting power hitter Carlos Beltrán, now thirty-four, had missed much of the last two seasons with injuries, and knee issues limited him to three games in 2011 spring training, but the hope was he'd rebound to the form he'd shown with the Mets from 2006 to 2008, finishing each of those years with more than 110 RBIs. Angel Pagan, the Mets' fourth-round pick in the 1999 draft, hit .290 for the Mets in 2010, though with only forty-four walks, and was a dynamic presence in center field. Left fielder Jason Bay had run into fresh trouble after being limited to six homers in ninety-five games for the Mets the year before in his first season after signing a four-year, $66 million deal with Alderson's predecessor, Omar Minaya, following Bay's thirty-six-homer, 119-RBI season for the Red Sox in 2009. Bay opened 2011 on the disabled list with a strain of his oblique muscle and never found himself at the plate; he was batting .223 on June 3 and .232 on July 18. His bat speed and entire approach were off.

The expectation for 2011 had been that staff ace Johan Santana, out of action with a shoulder injury, would be pitching for the Mets by midseason. The Mets had packaged Carlos Gómez with three other players in a February 2008 trade with Minnesota to land Santana, and he was 16-7 that first season with a league-leading 2.53 ERA. He was effective each of the next two seasons, but as of July 2011 the Mets were still waiting for him, hoping that a short outing in Port St. Lucie late that month meant he would soon be back in the big leagues. Six-foot-seven right-hander Mike Pelfrey, their first-round pick in 2005, was coming off a breakthrough 15-9 season in 2010, but he struggled in 2011 and fell to 5-9 by July 17. Left-hander Jon Niese, a seventh-round pick in 2005, recorded his tenth win by July 26, but the surprise of the 2011 rotation was little-noticed Dillon Gee, a control pitcher with no overpowering pitches the Mets had picked up almost as an afterthought in the twenty-first round of the 2007 draft. Gee was off to a 9-3 start in 2011, his ERA at 3.67 through July 19. As for the bullpen, the intriguing names were Bobby Parnell, a reliever with a 2.83 ERA in 2010 and clear late-inning ability, and Jason Isringhausen, originally drafted in 1991 by the Mets and part of the highly touted "Generation K," who was re-signed by the Mets in early 2011 to a minor-league deal after he'd been out of baseball the previous year rehabbing following Tommy John surgery. Over the course of the season, the thirty-eight-year-old Isringhausen mentored Parnell in the art of closing games, reminding Alderson of the value of veteran leadership in the bullpen.

At the other extreme was closer Francisco Rodríguez, whose presence had developed into a full-blown distraction. Signed under the Minaya regime in December 2008 to a three-year, $37 million deal following his sixty-two-save season for the Angels, Rodríguez was an All-Star for the Mets in 2009, but by August 2010 he had become an out-and-out liability. K-Rod, who had also mixed it up in the bullpen with easygoing coach Randy Niemann that season, was arrested at Citi Field on August 11 after punching Carlos Peña, the grandfather of his children—a ruckus that confirmed the Mets' worst fears about his judgment and commitment to the team, and led to season-ending surgery. Rodríguez had to go, but the Mets' options looked bleak. The way his contract was written, he had to finish only fifty-five games for the Mets in 2011 to trigger an option for 2012 that would pay him $17.5 million. One possibility would have been to keep him out of action, but that risked a beef with the players' union. "Everybody said we're never going to be able to get rid of him," Alderson told me.

Rodríguez switched agents, opting to go with Scott Boras, who told baseball writer Ken Davidoff, "Francisco Rodríguez is a historic closer. He's not going anywhere to be a setup man."

Oh yes he was. Rodríguez's prior agent had failed to clarify which teams Rodríguez was ruling out for trades, and that left the way clear for Alderson to act. On July 12, 2011, the Mets traded Rodríguez to the Brewers along with cash for two players to be named later, who turned out to be pitcher Danny Herrera, a five-foot-six screwballer, and minor-leaguer Adrian Rosario. "We moved him and saved the money," Alderson explained. "It wasn't clear what Boras knew or didn't know about the no-trade list, but I wasn't prepared to wait to find out."

That was deft work, but only a small start in making progress on the formidable challenge of pivoting the Mets toward a brighter future. *Baseball America* had ranked the Mets twenty-fifth out of thirty teams in its 2010 Organization Talent Rankings, with the explanation, "Most of the Mets' top prospects are products of the international market—RHP Jenrry Mejia, SS Wilmer Flores, OF Fernando Martinez—where the club has spent more of its resources." A year later the Mets were up to twentieth out of thirty, but still had a lot of work to do in developing their farm system. One highlight was the team's first-round pick in 2010, Matt Harvey, a hard-throwing right-hander out of the University of North Carolina who in 2011 was 8-2 with a 2.37 ERA in A ball. Minaya had landed a good one there.

Alderson's biggest quandary in 2011 was what to do about Reyes, so electric a presence in the lineup. The truth was, even in the face of bad financial news for the team, Alderson hoped to keep Reyes. So when in mid-June he put in a call to Reyes' agent, Peter Greenberg, to see if they could make progress toward a new contract, it was not PR and it was not going through the motions. But Reyes was having a career year, batting .345 to lead the National League as of June 15, and decided to wait for the end of the season to test the free-agent market. Reyes and his agent said that they wouldn't talk contract until after the season. Reyes thought he could snag a long-term deal for more than $20 million per year.

That was probably more than the team could afford. Then again, in that period of sudden contraction in payroll, Alderson really did not know what was possible and what was not. He knew he needed to try to unload either Reyes or Beltrán, also a free agent at year's end, before the July 31 trade deadline, but there, too, lay great uncertainty; the market was often volatile when it came to what in baseball were called rentals, big-ticket free agents a team would be acquiring only for the remainder of that season. Back in his days as general manager of the Oakland A's, Alderson had wound up in that worst of all positions, needing to unload a star no matter what, and ended up trading Mark McGwire to the St. Louis Cardinals for three obscure pitchers in 1997, the year before he set a single-season home-run record and revived that franchise. Alderson knew he needed to play his hand strong on Beltrán. That meant he could not dangle both Reyes and Beltrán going into the trade deadline, not if the Mets wanted to get as much as they could for Beltrán. Getting real value in return for Beltrán was going to be challenging enough. As columnist Joel Sherman put it in the *New York Post*: "Alderson will have to be a magician in the next few days to pull a no-doubt, high-end prospect out of a hat."

There were a lot of reasons to be skeptical about the Mets getting much value for Beltrán, starting with lurid memories of his postseason failure five years earlier. It's one thing for a role player to strike out with the bases loaded to end a season, but when a star does it—when he goes down *looking*, the way Beltrán did to close out Game 7 of the 2006 National League Championship Series—that puts a DEFECTIVE GOODS stamp on a player. Beltrán's talent was never questioned and it seemed understandable for the Mets to award him a $119 million contract in 2005, the largest in franchise history at the time. But for all the talk in certain quarters about how postseason success is a question of luck, the fact is there are players who bring an added competitive fire to the big moments, and Beltrán had branded himself as the guy who hadn't even taken the bat off his shoulder with the season on the line. It wasn't fair, since he'd proven himself before, batting a torrid .435 for the Houston Astros in the 2004 postseason with eight home runs, but life for sports stars in New York was often not fair.

Weeks before the trade deadline, the picture remained uncertain. Many teams were interested in adding Beltrán to the mix for the stretch drive, but how interested? So much was based on rumor, on teams working reporters to create the perceptions they wanted, and many reporters played along, happy to throw speculation out there on the off chance they might end up being right. Teams by this point all had pro scouting departments that studied the assets of each big-league team. It wasn't enough to know which club might be looking to get Beltrán, either to fix a glaring hole in its lineup or simply to make an incremental upgrade out of sheer habit; the key was identifying teams that wanted Beltrán enough *and* had valuable trade fodder. That analysis led Alderson and his staff to focus their attention on five teams: the Milwaukee Brewers, Philadelphia Phillies, Boston Red Sox, Texas Rangers, and San Francisco Giants. These were teams with prospects to offer and they were teams that might meet Beltrán's criterion of only wanting to waive his no-trade clause if he was being dealt to a team headed for postseason action. Early on Beltrán had indicated he would waive the no-trade only for Milwaukee or Philadelphia, which gave those teams bargaining leverage, but there were growing indications of greater flexibility from Beltrán.

One of the keys to deal-making is not to come across as too eager. "These baseball deals travel at their own pace and I always try to be careful about how I try to market the players," Alderson says. "One of my beliefs is that if I do all of the calling, eventually the value of the player gets discounted. One of the ways you really learn about people's motivation is when they call you. But there has to be a balance."

The Mets had a road trip to California that July just before the All-Star break and took three of four from the Dodgers at Chavez Ravine before closing out the first half of the season with three games against the Giants at their ballpark by the Bay. Beltrán went 3-for-5 in the series opener to help the Mets win, and the Giants made the unusual move of offering Beltrán a ride to the All-Star Game after the series. As John Shea reported after the game in the *San Francisco Chronicle*, "Carlos Beltrán will be taking Air Bochy to Phoenix for the All-Star Game, and along the way he'll mingle with the Giants' All-Star contingent, which includes four pitchers, an entire coaching staff and manager Bruce Bochy." Shea, a veteran writer, came close to openly campaigning for the Giants to deal with the Mets: "Beltrán is among the marquee names in the rumor mill and exactly what the Giants would love—a middle-of-the-order switch-hitter with pop and a willingness to waive his no-trade clause to join a contender."

Alderson laughs looking back on the charter-plane episode. A furious round of speculation erupted in the press that the Mets were foolish to accept the offer and have Beltrán take that flight down to Phoenix with the Giants. Insinuations were made that the Giants were pulling a fast one on the Mets and that Alderson was letting himself "be had."

"I said, 'These guys think that this is really going to help *them*?'" Alderson recalls. "It's really helping *us*."

Both the media and the Giants would warm to the idea of a trade, the more they got to see of Beltrán. "The Giants are going to get infatuated with the idea that they can get Carlos Beltrán, who is going to the All-Star Game. It was almost like a baited hook. From my standpoint, let him get on the plane, let him get cozy with the Giants."

The pas de deux between Alderson and his Giants counterpart, Brian Sabean, had been traipsing along through its choreographed steps for weeks. Sabean did not call Alderson and Alderson did not call Sabean. The flickers of mutual interest found other expression. The Giants' longtime vice president of player personnel, Dick Tidrow, a former relief pitcher for the Yankees and Mets, called up J. P. Ricciardi, the former Blue Jays general manager, now working as a special assistant to Alderson with the Mets, and let it be known there was interest in getting Beltrán. Obviously, Ricciardi would pass that on to Alderson.

But eventually Sabean did call and leave a message on Alderson's cell phone saying the Giants were sincerely interested in Beltrán.

Soon after the All-Star Game, Alderson called Sabean directly to talk about a deal.

The Giants' three top prospects were outfielder Gary Brown, first baseman Brandon Belt, and pitcher Zack Wheeler. Alderson made clear the Mets would need one of those three prospects at the very least to move Beltrán. Alderson was just sure that, loaded with talented young pitching as they were, the Giants were more likely to agree to deal their blue-chip pitching prospect, Wheeler, who was only at Single-A that year, than either Brown or Belt. Still, the Mets were intrigued by Belt, a Giants fifth-round pick in 2009, who batted an impressive .383 for the San Jose Giants in 2010 with an on-base percentage of .492 and a slugging percentage of .628. His 2011 numbers in San Jose were even better. "Belt had such a terrific record and he was so close to the big leagues, you had to think about asking for him," Alderson remembers. "But when I called Brian, he said, 'Yeah, we're very interested and we'd consider Wheeler.'"

"Well," Alderson told him. "We've got to get something else, too."

"It would be tough for us to do anything else," Sabean replied. "But I've got ownership here, I've got everybody together, so I'll be able to give you an answer pretty quickly."

"Would you consider Belt?" Alderson asked.

"No," he was told.

The call took all of five minutes, because both Alderson and Sabean like to get straight to the point. "Brian's a man of few words," Alderson says. Asking for Belt was, Alderson explains, "partly tactical," though if he'd been surprised and the Giants had been willing to part with him, the Mets would have been happy.

In the Bay Area, many were high on Beltrán but leery of paying too high a price. Wrote Tim Kawakami in the *San Jose Mercury News*, "There's no way they should give up Brandon Belt or Zack Wheeler in such a deal." This was more than a week before the trade deadline and these things tended to have a momentum of their own, but Alderson was thinking: "Why not do the deal a week early?" Even in five minutes, Sabean and Alderson had time to go over some details of compensation; Alderson said that even if they pulled the trigger on a deal right away, the Mets would pick up all of Beltrán's salary—about $100,000 per game—for the days up until the trade deadline and the two teams would share Beltrán's compensation for the rest of the season. As much as the Mets were having to look for ways to save money, they were ready to make a sizable outlay to move Beltrán for the right prospect.

The Mets continued to size up trade possibilities with other teams, but Alderson had heard real purpose in Sabean's voice and had been assured the Giants general manager would call him right back.

"I didn't hear from him," Alderson says. "That's never a good sign."

There weren't many other players out there the Giants could pursue to add offense down the stretch run, which was why they were so interested in Beltrán. Alderson knew another possibility was Astros outfielder Hunter Pence, an All-Star in 2009 and 2011 who was hitting better than .300.

Alderson finally called Sabean to ask what was up.

"We just can't do that deal," the Giants GM said. "We're not prepared to part with Wheeler."

Alderson thought the Giants' hesitation had to do with Pence, so he called the Houston Astros directly to get a bead on the situation.

"Hey, we may trade Beltrán," Alderson told his counterpart with the Astros, Ed Wade. "But if we do, we might have an interest in Pence as a guy we could hold on to for more than one year."

Sounds logical enough, doesn't it?

"We had absolutely no interest in Pence, but we were trying to engage in a dialogue so we at least had some intelligence," Alderson recalls. "So we told Houston, 'OK, we'll keep you in mind, we'll talk tomorrow.' The upshot was that the Astros went back and forth. I finally got a call from Ed saying they were not going to trade Pence, which they knew was good for us because it made Beltrán the only guy on the market. Later they reconsidered and decided that if they got a good deal, they were going to trade Pence. I had the information I was looking for, which was that Pence was on the market."

Zack Wheeler loved being part of the San Francisco Giants organization. To be a highly touted Giants pitching prospect in those years was to have the feeling of standing on a conveyor belt pulling you inexorably toward stardom and, who knew, maybe a Cy Young Award or two. The Giants tabbed Tim Lincecum with their 2006 first-round pick; he hopscotched through the system and by 2008 was winning the first of back-to-back Cy Youngs. In 2009 the Giants used their first-round pick on Wheeler, taking him sixth overall a week and a half after his nineteenth birthday.

Wheeler and Lincecum could not have been more different in personal style; Wheeler is as likely to grow his hair out to ponytail length or visit the Spirit Rock Meditation Center in Marin County, California, as he is to ride a magic carpet over the Manhattan skyline. Yet out on the mound, talent feeds talent, and the example of little Tim Lincecum pitching his ass off start after start in the black and orange, snapping off pitches that earned blank, bewildered stares from hitters, inspired a young pitcher like Wheeler. Hard-throwing Matt Cain, the Giants' first-round pick in 2002, made his major-league debut by late 2005 and was selected to the All-Star team by 2009. The Giants nabbed Madison Bumgarner, a big lefty with a distinctive slinging pitching motion, tenth overall in the 2007 draft and in 2010 he became the fourth-youngest starter in baseball history to win a World Series game, leading the Giants to a Game 4 victory by pitching eight shutout innings against an explosive Texas Rangers lineup. Later on, he would pitch his way into the record books with his jaw-dropping performance leading the Giants to victory in the 2014 World Series.

Wheeler's first A-ball assignment was to the Augusta GreenJackets of the South Atlantic League, three hours from Dallas, Georgia, where he'd grown up and most of his close-knit family still lived, including his parents and his older brother Jacob, who often got to see Zack pitch that year for Augusta. "The initial excitement for the family was, 'Hey, he got drafted in the first round,'" Jacob says. "A couple days go by and you start to hear about the organization and who they drafted the last few years. You realize it means a *lot* that the Giants drafted you."

Zack's two older brothers were seven and nine years older than him. Zack didn't have a real growth spurt until he was thirteen years old, so for many years he was always the little pipsqueak trying to keep up with the gifted athletes who towered over him. "We played some video games, but we were always out in the street playing basketball or baseball until dark and then we'd turn the lights on," Adam Wheeler says. "At that age, before he was ten, Zack was out there, trying to be as good as we were."

Adam, also a hard-throwing right-hander, was drafted by the Yankees in the thirteenth round of the 2001 draft and spent four years working his way through the system, including a promising season with the Staten Island Yankees in 2003, appearing in fourteen games and finishing with a 1.80 ERA. But the next season he pitched in only five games, his career cut short by a torn labrum in his shoulder.

Being the youngest in the family helped Zack get over himself. Former teammates describe him as down-to-earth and modest. Catcher Alex Burg, drafted by the Giants the same year as Wheeler, met him in Scottsdale soon after Zack flew out for his physical. "Usually the first-rounders are a little arrogant, a little full of themselves," Burg told me. "He just wasn't that kid at all. He wants to just be Zack. He's the same guy as the day he signed, regardless of how much money he might be making."

The year pitching for the Augusta GreenJackets was not altogether smooth for Wheeler. His first professional start was the kind you try hard to forget: six batters, four walks, three earned runs, and that was that. His second and third starts were rocky as well, then Wheeler bounced back and threw shutout ball in three of his four next starts before landing on the disabled list. He developed an ugly blister underneath the nail on one of the fingers of his pitching hand and was out of action from May 18 to July 9. He finished that first season with thirty-eight walks and seventy strikeouts in 58$\frac{2}{3}$ innings with a 3.99 ERA.

It's one of the great puzzles in sports: Which qualities push a future star along the path toward fulfillment of his or her talent while other prospects, also talented, also promising, get off track? Young Zack Wheeler offered a fascinating case study. He had the lanky build of a future big-league pitcher, the explosive fastball and easy athleticism, but at every level on his way up the baseball hierarchy he battled wildness, often throwing pitch after pitch up and out of the strike zone. Something enabled him to look within and continue to find new ways to make himself better. He had none of the ready-made swagger of other young phenoms. He liked to fly under people's radar. But Wheeler had that quality of many who succeed, a kind of foreknowledge of his own eventual success, a certainty that if he kept working hard, kept learning, kept gaining more of a mental edge, he would get the chance to let his pitches speak for themselves.

By the time Wheeler arrived in San Jose in 2011 to play for the Giants' Class A affiliate in the California League, he could feel how close he was. On his first flight into San Jose, he could see the expanse of San Francisco Bay stretching out, framed by green hills that would soon turn a deep shade of hazelnut in the summer heat, and sense how close he was to the Giants' spectacular ballpark, with its exuberant sellout crowds every night, only forty-five miles away from where Wheeler's plane touched down. He was not one to boast. That wasn't his style. For him it was more like being alone with a secret, a secret he shared with his brothers and parents, and the secret was: He knew he was going to be starting and winning games up at that beautiful ballpark on the Bay with its new World Series banner flying.

Wheeler's time in San Jose got off to an awkward start. When he showed up at the house of the host family he'd been assigned, the place gave him the creeps. Early on in his stay there Wheeler opened a door and bats came flying out. The shower was just big enough for someone six-foot—Wheeler, at six-foot-four, had to contort himself just to get in there. One time he stepped into the shower and saw a massive spider. "He hates spiders," Alex Burg says. "He freaked out."

"No matter what age they are, they really are kids when you get them," says Joyce Morgan, who regularly hosts San Jose Giants players along with her husband, Doug. "Zack and Tommy [Joseph] were in a home that had spiders. They were deathly allergic and scared of spiders, so they wanted out of where they were. One of my other players asked if they could come, and I said yes, I'll open up the house to any of them."

The house was on a quiet street with shopping malls nearby and easy access to the 280 and 880 freeways for a quick seven-mile drive over to the stadium where they played their games. "Instead of going to the bars with the players, he'd do other stuff with Tommy Joseph," Doug Morgan says. "They'd go to the movies instead of going out partying."

A generation earlier, the whole valley was given over to orchards, prunes and apricots and cherries. The same gentle baking sun-splashed heat that made the climate perfect for fruit trees also made San Jose Municipal Stadium a picturesque setting for the summer game. The dugouts may be tiny, the place decades past its prime, but the little stadium has been updated with slides and other amusements for the kids and perky signs like this, quoting Tallulah Bankhead: THERE HAVE BEEN ONLY TWO GENIUSES IN THE WORLD, WILLIE MAYS AND WILLIE SHAKESPEARE. The thin air gives passing planes the look of being suspended midair on their approaches to nearby San Jose International Airport and, in the background high in the Santa Cruz Mountains, the shuttered radar atop Mount Umunhum looks so close a hitter really connecting with a high fastball could almost hope to reach it.

Wheeler started 2011 on fire, pitching five no-hit innings to pick up a win in his first game. He went to 2-0 and then started to run into control issues. He wasn't bumped to the bullpen as he had been the year before, nothing as extreme as that, but he did walk way too many hitters. Sometimes it was as if he needed to be reminded of how high the stakes were, and just such a reminder came early in the year. The San Jose Giants were in Bakersfield, a city forever plagued by a pall of acrid, fresh-from-the-smokestacks smog, a city often referred to as the armpit of California. Shortstop Brandon Crawford, an amiable, upbeat sort, was there with his San Jose teammates and then he heard from Giants assistant general manager Bobby Evans.

"We were down in Bakersfield, and he called me late, close to midnight, and was like, 'Hey, how quick can you get to Fresno?'" Crawford recalled for me. "I'm like, 'I don't know, I'm in Bakersfield.

We took the team bus down, it's not like I have a car.' He was like, 'All right, we'll figure it out. We're going to call you up to San Francisco tomorrow.' I was like, 'All right, wow, cool.'"

Crawford showed up in San Francisco just before game time and watched from the dugout. The next day in Milwaukee, he started at shortstop for the Giants and remembers he was so nervous, it felt like an out-of-body experience until Rickie Weeks, the Brewers' leadoff hitter that day, hit a ground ball and Crawford threw him out at first and snapped out of his reverie. "I was like, 'All right, all right, it's just baseball again. We're in Milwaukee now, not Bakersfield, but it's still baseball.'" He won that game for the Giants with a grand slam, the kind of debut kids dream about.

For Wheeler and his teammates, it was a shot of adrenaline to see Crawford hop straight to the big leagues and make so huge a splash. Soon Wheeler was mowing them down again, and the team was hot. "Zack Wheeler struck out twelve in seven innings on Sunday, and the Giants won their tenth straight, one shy of the San Jose franchise record," the *San Jose Mercury News* reported on May 30, 2011, which was Wheeler's twenty-first birthday. To celebrate, Wheeler went out with a group including Alex Burg to the Yard House, a popular spot at Santana Row, a nearby upscale mall. "We had a rule: If our manager showed up, we had to leave," Burg says. "The night of Zack's twenty-first birthday, we were already at the Yard House and our manager comes in. He looked at us, winked, and then he finished his beer and left."

On July 18, thirty-seven-year-old Giants shortstop Miguel Tejada strained an abdominal muscle and landed on the disabled list. That prompted Brian Sabean to send minor-league pitchers Jason Stoffel and Henry Sosa to the Astros for middle infielder Jeff Keppinger, batting .307 that year in Houston in limited duty. Sabean explained to reporters in the Bay Area that he'd first talked with Houston about Keppinger a week earlier, but then had been sidetracked by talks with another club on "something we thought was much bigger." Hmm, what could that have been?

"I think the Giants wanted to see if Keppinger would be the tonic their offense needed and they could say: 'OK, we don't *need* to go after Beltrán and really give up our top guys because this guy is going to be a catalyst,'" Alderson says. But Keppinger went 1-for-4 in each of his first four games as a Giants starter—not the lift they needed.

Throughout these weeks Alderson had regular talks with Philadelphia about a Beltrán trade, but as much as they thought they might be helped by adding the switch-hitting outfielder, the Phillies were not willing to part with the kind of top-level prospects the Mets hoped they could get. This was the stage at which Boston and Texas, both powerhouse teams with stacked lineups, became more interested in Beltrán. The Red Sox were loaded offensively, but when right fielder J. D. Drew hurt his shoulder in mid-July, Boston developed more interest in talking to the Mets. "They didn't really have a right fielder," Alderson says.

"But Texas was just looking. You know, it was almost overindulgent. They had this incredible offense. They would get him and move some guys around, because they had decided they couldn't get a starting pitcher that they really liked. They were also intent on improving their bullpen. So we're talking now about five or six days before the deadline. Philadelphia eventually went quiet."

At that point the Giants had not gotten back to the Mets except to let them know they were mulling other options. That left the Mets two alternatives, Texas and Boston, who were looking at Beltrán to pad their lineup, not fill a glaring need. And in both cases, it was questionable Beltrán would accept a trade, since both teams were in the American League and he didn't want to DH.

Alderson broke this down later that season. His Citi Field office, beyond the outfield, still showed boards with detailed information on available players from Boston, Texas, and San Francisco, illustrating that all three were very much in the hunt for Beltrán down to the wire. Boston general manager Theo Epstein was offering infielder Chih-Hsien Chiang and pitcher Alex Wilson, along with one more player from a list of seven; plus, the Mets were going to throw in more than $1 million in cash considerations. The Mets continued to negotiate with Texas, focusing on starting pitchers Joe Wieland and

Robbie Ross. The teams agreed on those two names, but the Mets wanted a third player, and asked for third baseman Mike Olt or a very young Venezuelan, Rougned Odor. "If we had gotten Olt or Odor, we would have made the trade with Texas. But they wouldn't give us the third guy," Alderson says.

Boston by this point was out of the running, with less appealing options than what Texas was presenting, and the Giants seemed out of the picture, too. Rangers general manager Jon Daniels, widely respected as one of the best young GMs in the game, was pretty sure the Mets' other options had dwindled and thought the Rangers were in the driver's seat. Alderson called again to make one more stab at getting a third player in the deal and Daniels did add another name, but it was neither Olt nor Odor. Alderson mulled the offer and called Daniels back with news that came as a surprise.

"We're just not prepared to make the deal at this point," Alderson told Daniels. "I'm going to have to call you back and let you know."

This looked like the best the Mets were going to do, but there was no harm in making some more calls. John Ricco, the assistant general manager, suggested trying the Giants again. In the every-hour-things-can-change pace of the week before trade deadline, the Giants and Mets had not talked in ages. So Alderson called Sabean. He needed a pretext and decided he'd say he was calling to ask if the Giants would trade outfielder Gary Brown, the third of the top prospects identified by the Mets. They'd already been offered Wheeler and asked for Belt, but had not made a pitch for Brown.

"Well, would you consider Brown?" Alderson asked Sabean.

"No," came the reply. "But we'll do Wheeler."

In a sense they were back to square one. They'd been in this spot more than a week earlier—but with a difference. Sabean had made clear he needed to discuss the move with Giants ownership, and when no call came back, Alderson assumed Sabean had been shot down by the higher-ups. Now the trade was back in play. Alderson pulled the trigger and made the trade. Bottom line, the Mets would have been happy with Belt, Brown, or Wheeler—Belt was their first pick, given how close he was to big-league-ready, but the Mets saw all three as among the top prospects in baseball.

Alderson called Jon Daniels to let him know he'd made a deal with San Francisco.

"They were shocked," Alderson says. "They thought they had it."

The Beltrán trade was finalized on July 28. The Giants, so intent on landing Pence, did just that the following summer, and he ended up playing a key role in the team's World Series championships in 2012 and 2014. Beltrán, after his short stint with the Giants, became a free agent and signed with the Cardinals in December 2011 and led them to the World Series in 2013.

Wheeler had a feeling something was up. One constant of his life during the weeks he stayed with Joyce and Doug Morgan in San Jose was that he got his sleep. The house was big and comfortable, and Wheeler had his own room and he loved to take full advantage. "Zack doesn't wake up before noon unless it's absolutely necessary," Alex Burg says. But on the morning of Wednesday, July 27, something nudged him awake early.

"I woke up at like nine A.M., which I never do, and looked at Twitter," Wheeler told me. "They said I was about to get traded, so I went downstairs."

Burg was already down there.

"I think I just got traded," Wheeler said.

"Shut up," Burg told him. "You didn't get traded."

They turned on the TV and saw the scroll: Beltrán traded for prospect Zack Wheeler.

"Holy crap, I got traded," Wheeler said.

They sat there stunned. Wheeler called his agent and waited to hear back. It was strange: He was scheduled to start that day and went to the ballpark, suited up, and just sat in the dugout waiting to get a call making the trade official. He was there and not there, gone and not gone. "My head was up," Wheeler says. "I wasn't down about it."

"Our family and Zack, everybody loved the Giants," Adam Wheeler says. "It's saddening at first, and then you move on."

Brandon Crawford understood the move, which may look one-sided in retrospect, but at the time was just the kind of trade you wanted your general manager to make, going for it in the here and now at a time when the team was loaded and wanted to repeat as World Series champions. Still, Crawford hated to see Wheeler go. "He was probably one of our biggest pieces in the minor leagues," he said. "He had a great fastball. He was kind of working on his off-speed stuff still, and really locating his pitches, but you could definitely see his potential."

Joyce and her husband were in the Sierra Nevada foothills town of Sonora, having breakfast at Jeb's Hill Country Cooking, famous for its waffles, when the news hit. "They had TVs in the restaurant and across the bottom it said the Giants had traded Zack Wheeler," Doug Morgan told me. "We called home and they said, 'Yeah, we packed him up and he's gone.'"

"It was hard not to be able to say good-bye," Joyce says. "He was a very happy individual." It went with the territory. One week you have one group of players and then the team makes some moves and you have new kids. For Joyce and Doug, part of the enjoyment of hosting young ballplayers came in keeping up with their former charges and watching them climb the ladder—or not. They'd known them when they were unformed in many ways and would always have unique insights into their personalities and character. About Wheeler, Joyce told me: "He was just really focused and you knew he was going to go places."

How much anyone knew or didn't know then about Wheeler's future was a riddle, but it was the riddle of baseball, the mystery that made the games worth watching. The Mets could not know for sure if Wheeler would grow into a quality big-league starter, but at least with the trade they'd turned some heads; for seasons to come, GMs mulling their options going into the trade deadline would resolve not to give up as much as the Giants had in the Beltrán-Wheeler deal. The Wheeler trade offered hope for the future. It offered excitement. But for it to count as a great trade, Wheeler would have to make huge leaps forward. Alderson would have to build a championship-caliber team around him with a new attitude and a new approach, a team that could give Wheeler the chance to dominate in postseason games. Only then could a verdict on the trade be offered.

In August a federal appeals court decision opened the door to the possibility that Wilpon and Katz would have to pay back as much as $300 million. "Immediately after the Madoff litigation was made public, I realized that was going to have some impact on what we were going to be able to do," Alderson says now.

This complicated the Reyes picture but so did the injury issue. Balky legs were always a concern with Reyes, a particularly glaring concern for a player whose game relied so heavily on speed and whose mobility was likely to decline with age anyway. He was limited to just thirty-six games in 2009, and injuries took him out of action regularly in 2010 and 2011 as well. That was bad for the Mets—and might give other teams pause before throwing a lot of money at him.

"It should have, but you never know," Alderson told me in September 2011. "It only takes one team. But you have to recognize that signing Jose is not an end in itself. Maybe we play well with Jose. Maybe not. We have a payroll this year when everything is said and done that is roughly $140 million. Our bullpen is seven players, which is more than 25 percent of the team, but we're only paying them about $5 million total. Our bullpen is terrible. It's killed us. It's the reason why we're not going to finish over .500. But if we were to sign Jose, David Wright, and some others, we'd be back in the same boat, spending too little on our bullpen and scraping by with two secondhand catchers. The sad thing is if we sign Jose, we're just maintaining the status quo. We're not improving the team."

Soon after the season, Alderson would note that the team had lost $70 million that year, a sobering fact. Even for Alderson himself, who came to the Mets expecting to have substantial financial resources, it was not easy to come to terms with the post-Madoff era. Looking back, he said that contrary to Reyes' comments after the Miami Marlins signed him to a six-year, $106 million contract, the Mets did make a concerted effort to sign him. True, the Mets did not make an official offer, but talking to Reyes' agent after the season, Alderson made clear that a contract right around $100 million was a possibility.

"We actually went pretty far to try to sign Jose, further than most people realized," Alderson says. "We telegraphed our position pretty clearly, but I think what I told them was shopped. The Marlins were opening a new ballpark and were looking to make a splash."

The consensus around baseball was that the Marlins had probably overspent. As Tyler Kepner wrote in the *Times*, "Cutting loose Reyes, at a time when the Mets are hemorrhaging money and unlikely to contend, is probably the right move." Still, it was jarring, especially when Reyes talked about not feeling wanted by the Mets.

That Madoff-rocked year for the Mets, there was the whiff in the air of a team that knew it was bleeding and knew for the time being it could not stanch the wound. How much blood would be lost? Would the scandal forever distract from building a winner? The answers finally came the next spring when Wilpon and Katz reached a settlement with Irving Picard, the trustee who had sued them for $300 million. "The Mets owners, in a deal announced Monday, agreed to settle the lawsuit for $162 million and a pledge that Mr. Picard would drop his claims that they were 'willfully blind' to signs that Mr. Madoff was carrying out a fraud," the *Wall Street Journal* reported on March 20, 2012.

For Alderson and the Mets' baseball operations department, it was finally time for a sigh of relief. They did not know how long it would take to overcome the damage to the franchise represented by the Madoff morass, but at least they knew it would get no worse. They also knew that without clear signs of progress, the fans and the media would not tolerate many more losing seasons, Madoff or no Madoff.

12

WINTER MEETINGS 2012

If a hotel called the "Gaylord Opryland" sounds like a punch line, it's that and much, much more. For all that has changed in baseball since Sandy Alderson started attending baseball's annual winter meetings more than thirty years ago, the Opryland remains, timeless in its callow bad taste. Where to begin? Just inside the reception area, the almost understated elegance of a wedding-cake-white low ceiling and balustraded square columns opens up onto a gorgeous tableau of tacky excess. What is that sustained dull roar? Not a man-made waterfall, surely? Indeed not: It's *two* fifty-foot-high man-made waterfalls, side by side, bookending an odd slope of shrubby greenery, topped off with a cluster of palm trees looking as fake and out of place as if they'd been pulled from the set of *Gilligan's Island*. The waterfall runoff feeds a network of shallow streams patrolled by pellucid carp, with footbridges and faux-gas-lamp-lined pathways in abundance, looking down at giddy agglomerations of fountains, here a starburst-patterned geyser lighted red from below, there an intermittently squirting column filling a gurgling indigo cauldron. The unending inanity of it all springs from some garish amalgam of miniature-golf-course aesthetic and family-fun-era Vegas, the whole spectacle topped off with a glass ceiling (anyone seen *Willy Wonka*?). The ambience conveyed by such a place runs to the forced and pinched even on good days, but on the regular occasions over the years when the hotel complex hosts baseball's annual meetings, the mood swings sharply toward the farcical.

For days on end the raised walkway sloping up from the lobby is clotted with the twitchy, furrowed brows of sportswriters. They stand around hour after hour with nothing to do but worry and wait and swap rumors, an assemblage of humanity resembling nothing so much as the passengers of an airplane suddenly evacuated from a flight because of equipment failure, standing around with the directionless mien of those who would rather be anywhere else but can do nothing about their plight. The good sportswriters find a way to ferret out the occasional scrap of actual information or insight from scouts or midlevel executives they know, but such infusions into this closed ecosystem are passed on dozens of times and soon feel stale. Unlike during Alderson's first winter meetings in the 1980s, when reporters waited for the adrenaline-rush inevitability of deadlines so they could get bombed in one of the many bars on the premises, nowadays the need to tweet turns many or most into prim teetotalers, thumbs kept ever at the ready, primed to unleash such vital communiqués as "Four-team trade brewing." It used to be that the posturing of the sportswriting fraternity hinged on such clichés of road life as capacity for prodigious late-night drunkenness, ballplayer-like devotion to tales of fictional or actual hookups, and now and then an old-fashioned scoop, but these days it's all about numbers: How many thousands of Twitter followers do *you* have? Whose gnomic news flashes get retweeted the most? Who has statistically proven influence and the plump salaries it brings? Danny Knobler, a former Tigers beat writer for Booth Newspapers who had moved on to CBSSports.com, told me on my first night in the echo of the waterfalls ("*What?*") that he'd heard of a paper that actually tried to determine sportswriter salary based on the number of hits an article received.

Ever hungry for scraps to feed the Twitter beast, these media professionals who grew up idolizing people like Roger Kahn and Tom Boswell now put in hours of patient vigil to tweet the occasional one-liner about someone from the A-list eating potato chips or wearing a loud shirt. Along the way there is time for swapping jokes with ex-ballplayers now plying a trade for regional baseball networks, catching up with a scout one genuinely enjoys, or just following the prime directive of the media pack to intermingle and share, to swap, like members of the Borg Collective ("Resistance is futile!"). "What do you hear?" comes the half-whispered aside, and notes are compared on this pitcher's perceived value-of-the-moment, or the current odds on this or that past-his-prime slugger's chances of landing a four-year deal. These micro-adjustments cancel themselves out over a day or two, which is just the point. It would be as pointless to criticize practitioners of the new media arts for shallowness as it would be to object to a ballplayer ducking out of the way of a 90-mile-an-hour fastball thrown at his head.

We can lament, however, the absence of an element that not so long ago was seen as part of a sportswriter's job: thinking. Often during my three-plus days at the 2012 winter meetings, I mentioned this sad shift to sportswriter friends, expecting them to be offended, and was bowled over by their reactions. "Who has time to think?" one told me, only half ironically, and then looked down at his smartphone. Who indeed? If by thinking we mean reflection, time for creative perspective and original point of view, then we've crossed the Rubicon. The conversation and camaraderie of the swarm staking out the walkway were not without enjoyment and fun, but it was trumped by a palpable feel of agitation and uneasiness, and what I got talking to veterans of the scene was an almost desperate hatred of the idiocy of the ritual.

Several hundred yards above the conga-line klatch of sportswriters huddled along the railing of the walkway leading away from the Opryland lobby, Sandy Alderson spent his days sequestered in a sixth-floor suite, spacious and neat but nondescript. The drapes were as likely to be pulled shut as not, since the interesting action took place inside. The week before, Alderson told me he would probably have some extra hours to meet and talk about the goings-on. He was kidding himself. He ended up hunkered down in a suite upstairs for far longer than he expected, mulling the possibilities and running the numbers on various permutations with his team of smart young guys. Such moments are the times he enjoys the job of Mets general manager the most.

"It is like a puzzle or a chess match, I guess, but it's not like you're trying to outdo the other side, you're trying to find a deal that appears mutually beneficial," he told me one night during the meetings, his brain trust behind a door in the next suite, their voices rising and falling as they got more or less excited about different trade possibilities. "But it's also the camaraderie. At my age, it's fun to be with twenty other guys who are all involved and have a common purpose. It can be a great morale builder. But you have to be prepared not to make a trade. You have to be prepared to do less than hoped. Sometimes it happens that you do more than hoped, but doing more isn't always better."

Alderson's first winter meetings were held in Hawaii at the Sheraton Waikiki in 1982, but back then he was finding his way. Alderson was secure enough, during those years in baseball, not to pretend he was anything he wasn't; he listened and learned. "When you're a first-timer or a second-timer, everybody else seems to be an iconic baseball figure," he says. "I imagine it's like coming into the big leagues and pitching or hitting for the first time against people you've grown up hearing about. Al Campanis was the general manager of the Dodgers at the time. Guys like Phil Seghi of the Cleveland Indians, Buzzie Bavasi—he'd have been with the California Angels at the time—Trader Jack McKeon of the Padres. Just a lot of old-school personalities. I basically kept my mouth shut and listened."

Alderson's second season leading the Mets, 2012, in some ways represented a step backward. The team finished fourteen games under .500 and was clearly a long ways from contention, but there were glimmers of excitement, starting with the unlikely late-career ascension of knuckleballer R. A. Dickey, who finished the year 20-6 with a 2.73 ERA to win the Cy Young Award, all at age thirty-seven. It was a feel-good story that made Dickey a sentimental favorite of fans and writers. Dickey even published a book in early 2012—with Wayne Coffey—that was honest and funny, featuring a winning self-mocking sense of humor ("I spend seven years—seven!—as a member of the Triple-A Oklahoma City RedHawks, and some people in town are seriously suggesting I run for mayor") as well as jarring revelations of Dickey's abuse by a babysitter.

The single most exciting highlight of the season was something no one could have seen coming. The Mets' ailing ace, Johan Santana, took the mound at Citi Field against the St. Louis Cardinals and was unhittable. Given the green light from manager Terry Collins to pitch a complete game, even though it meant throwing 134 pitches, Santana tossed the first no-hitter in Mets history. He was aided by a great catch from left fielder Mike Baxter, who darted back to snare a hard-hit ball from Yadier Molina and then slammed into the wall at full speed and slumped to the ground. When Santana struck out David Freese on a 3-2 changeup for the final out of the game, and the no-no went in the books, the ovation from the crowd of 27,069 was among the giddier moments in Citi Field history. Santana was swarmed on the mound by his teammates, and the thrill he felt was contagious. "I don't think I've ever even thrown a no-hitter in video games," he said afterward.

Another jolt of energy came from the debut of Matt Harvey, their first-round pick in 2010, whose raging self-confidence fell somewhere between joke and wonder. During spring training in 2012, Alderson told the *Daily News*, "Aside from Matt himself—and I love that he thinks this way—there is no one in the organization who feels he is ready to be in the major leagues." Harvey's confidence was an asset but also presented a risk: Take a player like that and put him in a position to fail, and the confidence can crumble in a hurry. That was why the Mets had been leery of having Harvey make his major-league debut in New York.

"We put it off, we put it off, we put it off," Alderson told me. "We waited and finally pitched him in Arizona because we didn't want him making his debut at home with a big crowd and big expectations. Then of course he came out and was just dynamite that first game and went from there."

Harvey made his debut on July 26, 2012, and blew past Tom Seaver (nine) and Bill Denehy (nine) to finish with eleven strikeouts against the Diamondbacks, giving him the record for most Ks by a Mets pitcher in his first game. He hit 98 on the gun with his fastball and recorded his first victory, but lasted only 5⅓ innings. He finished the season 3-5, but with a 2.73 ERA and seventy strikeouts in 59⅓ innings, against twenty-six walks. Harvey was in some ways a work in progress, but in the critical area of electrifying the fans and getting them excited for the future, he'd already made huge strides.

"I remember at the All-Star break we were sitting around discussing when would be the right time to bring him up," Paul DePodesta recalls. "I remember saying to the room, 'If we bring him up now, there are going to be some clunkers. There will be gems, but there will also be clunkers and he'll learn more at the major-league level.' As it happened, I was totally wrong. There were no clunkers."

Among the dizzying array of challenges looming for Alderson that off-season after 2012, two of the top priorities were signing the face of the franchise, David Wright, to a long-term deal and finding a way to keep Dickey, if at all possible. Dickey had one year left on his contract, and the Mets hoped to sign him to a new deal without having to overpay. Nevertheless, the first order of business was getting Wright signed to a long-term contract that would keep him happy and establish him as the cornerstone of the team's rebuilding plans. Wright was not only a gifted all-around ballplayer, a two-time Gold Glove–winning third baseman and a hitter who anchored the Mets lineup, but he was also a capable team leader.

"He leads by example," Alderson says. "He's not somebody that talks a good game. He backs up his leadership with action. If somebody is going to get hit in the back for retaliation, he wants it to be him. He's respectful of people across the board, he doesn't go out of his way to be critical or intimidate people. And he's got a personality that most are naturally drawn to."

Wright, the oldest of four boys and the son of a police captain, was impressed with the details he'd heard about Alderson as a Marine officer in Vietnam and found out for himself via Google. "I come from a military town in northern Virginia, so that was big for me," Wright told me. "The structure, the organization, the leadership ability of the military is something I know firsthand being from that town. So I was excited. Then obviously I read *Moneyball*. I saw the movie."

Alderson needed time to get to know his franchise player, so he packed up his golf clubs in October 2012 and hopped a flight from

Newark down to Norfolk International Airport, where Wright met him. They piled the clubs into the back of Wright's big pickup for the quick nine-mile drive over Lake Smith Reservoir to Bayville, a private course in Virginia Beach where Wright belonged and played occasionally. "He wanted to come down and talk to me one-on-one, no agents, no ownership, no nothing, just me and him playing golf," Wright told me.

"It wasn't that intensely competitive, it was quietly competitive," Alderson says.

"He plays ultracompetitive," Wright told me.

The course starts with a challenge right off the first tee: a water hazard. They both got off good drives and Wright was able to par the 429-yard par 4. "I was obviously very pumped about that," he told me. "I'm not a very good golfer. I would say Sandy is a better golfer than me, but I probably played the best nine or ten holes I've played in a long time. You get two competitive guys out there. I could tell he wanted to win. I wanted to win. And I think it just brought the best out of me."

An empty golf course is a great place for wide-ranging conversation and they touched on many topics. Wright mentioned the big amphibious base only five miles to the south of where they were playing their round, and Alderson discussed his years in the military. Afterward they went for a bite to eat at a nearby fish place, Chick's Oyster Bar. "Sandy, I have a love for this organization that runs deep," Wright told Alderson inside. "I want to be here, but if I'm going to go all in and put my chips in, I want the same in return from you, I want you to go all in and give it to me straight. If you say that this is how it's going to be and this rebuilding process is going to take longer than expected, then you know what? Maybe this plan is better without me."

That was exactly what Alderson wanted to hear. Yes, he believed deeply in the plan they had in place to build toward a team in 2014 that would have deadwood millions in salary off the books at long last. The Mets in 2013 would still be paying Johan Santana $31.5 million in salary and buyout, even though he wouldn't pitch at all; $16 million to Jason Bay for having released him; and another

$6.5 million to reliever Frank Francisco, who would be limited by injury to less than seven innings of work. Once they cleared that salary, they would have more options.

Alderson was not going to tell Wright he thought the Mets had a realistic shot at going to the World Series in 2013, but he did believe they would be a playoff-caliber team by 2014. "We had Matt Harvey coming, Zack Wheeler was well known at the time," Alderson says. "David knew what else we had on the team currently and some of what was coming in the system, so he had a pretty good handle on things. I think he just wanted to hear from me that I thought this could be done."

The plan to build for 2014 had a number of steps, starting with growing the roster of minor-league talent and developing those players to where they could either join the Mets and contribute or be packaged as attractive trade bait. This approach would take time and it would not allow for missteps or backsliding. "Whether or not you want to hear it, he's not going to give you the BS version of what he thinks, he's going to give it to you straight," Wright told me. "That brutal honesty meant a lot to me. I'm in this thing for the long run. I'm all in. And when we do get to the point where we're competing for the National League East and going to the playoffs, I want that to be a yearly occurrence, not just in my case a 2006, kind of done and then you take a step backward from there."

Ownership was fully behind signing Wright, but it took many calls back and forth between the Mets and Wright's agents before details were worked out on an eight-year, $138 million contract extension, the largest contract in team history, which would make Wright a lifetime Met. It was a so-called team-friendly contract in many ways, with deferred salary and a middle-loaded structure. "Spending that kind of money almost never proves to be worthwhile in a pure performance sense, but if you factor in the brand value, particularly in light of what's happened with the Mets over the last three of four years, it's definitely the right move with the right player," Alderson told me.

He was not trying to make friends with Wright, or with any other players. He'd learned from experience that could be a bad idea.

But they could still get along. "It's the relationship I try to have with everybody, and this is true of players and staff as well, which I call friendly but professional," Alderson told me. "I'm sure I got that from the Marine Corps.

"The service is similar to baseball. There are so many different types of people you meet. I've met the president of the United States through baseball, but guys on the grounds crew can be just as interesting. If you're not a player, you're not really central to the story. I do believe, though, that the people around the players have value and I sort of identify with, you know, Steve Vucinich and Mickey Morabito."

For the hordes hanging out at the Gaylord Opryland, clotting up the walkways in search of rumor, the Wright signing was nothing like a blockbuster trade, but still a story worth running down: The press conference announcing Wright's new contract was packed. Wright was asked if he could ever picture himself playing with a team other than the Mets. "No, no," he said. "I made it very clear after Sandy visited me in Norfolk after a round of golf and sitting having a late lunch, that was the first step. After I heard the conviction, the plan moving forward, I was all in. . . . So to me there was no thought of ever putting another uniform on."

One characteristic of the Wright contract was that his salary for 2013 actually dropped, giving the team more payroll flexibility. The larger strategy was to aim toward 2014, but Alderson was also focused on the hard reality that the team was only going to improve long term by steadily showing tangible gains in competitiveness on the field. If they could be a winning team in 2013, it would accelerate their overall organizational progress. Wright's deferment increased the chances that the Mets could also sign R. A. Dickey to a long-term deal.

It was a challenging situation for the Mets. Dickey had just won the Cy Young, winning twenty games for a sub-.500 team, and better yet, he had one year left on his contract, at $5 million, which made him a relative bargain. "We have a very valuable one year left on his contract compared to what teams are paying for pitchers of his caliber, but having him for a year doesn't really fit our timetable for strong competition," Alderson told me in Nashville.

"Sandy is paid to make the Mets better," Dickey said that week on *The Daily Show with Jon Stewart*. "If I can help him do that by being traded, then that's what's going to be done."

The Mets were not going to trade Dickey just to look like they were being active. Some teams distrusted knuckleballers and were leery of them. Plus, Dickey's age had to make teams wonder about his continuing durability. If no team impressed them with an offer, they were ready to make a serious run at landing Dickey for at least two more years. The trick was to test the market without doing it in a way that shaped the market. Dickey could boost attendance, but only when he pitched—at best every fifth day. The Mets knew he was unlikely to repeat his 20-6 breakout season in 2013, but what loomed larger in their calculations were 2014 and 2015. How would he fare in 2014 at age thirty-nine? Would he hold up at age forty in 2015? Dickey represented a tremendous amount of value for 2013, but that value would decline after that—and if the Mets were going to stick with their program, they needed to look for ways to add talent to the system.

The winter meetings broke up with no resolution on the Dickey question, which meant the negative press could not be long in coming. Deadspin checked in on December 11 with an article THE METS ARE LOWBALLING R.A. DICKEY WHILE HE WORKS THEIR CHRISTMAS PARTY. The article cited as an affront the idea that the Mets had offered Dickey a two-year contract extension worth $20 million, compared with the $26 million he was requesting, though it was not clear how many fans at home would consider it an outrageous insult to offer a man $10 million a year to throw a ball.

"We have beaten the Mets up for so many years over bad business practices—I'll see your Oliver Pérez and raise you a Luis Castillo—that we should acknowledge how well they are playing the R.A. Dickey negotiations," Joel Sherman wrote in the *New York Post*. "Are the Mets low-balling their best and most popular pitcher? Yep. And that's clearly making Dickey edgy and miserable. But this is a rare moment when the Mets have all the leverage, so why shouldn't they use it, like the majority of players do when the power swings in the other direction?"

Among the possible trade partners were the Orioles, who had a top prospect the Mets coveted in right-handed pitcher Dylan Bundy, chosen fourth overall in the 2011 draft. "They toyed with the idea," Alderson says, "even though he was one of the top five prospects in baseball."

Texas was also interested, but not offering enough. The Mets were intrigued by right-handed pitcher Cody Buckel, a second-round pick out of Simi Valley, California, rated the Rangers' eighth-best prospect. "Had we gotten the players we'd asked for from Texas and made a deal, we would have regretted it," Alderson told me. Later that season Buckel developed epic control problems, walking twenty-eight batters in just $9\frac{1}{3}$ innings at Double-A in one stretch.

Trade talks with the Blue Jays flopped around, pivoting on the Mets' insistence that they land Toronto's top prospect, catcher Travis d'Arnaud. But the Blue Jays wanted the Mets to take another catcher as well: They had just landed veteran John Buck one month earlier in an eleven-player deal with Miami that sent Jose Reyes to the Blue Jays, and Toronto insisted on unloading Buck and his $6 million salary. He could provide veteran leadership, and his years of experience could be helpful when it came to keeping young pitchers calm and confident. On the other hand, he was a free swinger whose approach was generally at odds with the approach Alderson and the Mets favored. To take on such a player at such a salary, the Mets would need to be compensated.

"Once we accepted that Buck had to be in the deal, we tried to extract another player from them," Alderson explains. "That's how we ended up with the Venezuelan kid."

The heart of the deal was d'Arnaud, but the Mets wanted another blue-chip prospect and got one in pitcher Noah Syndergaard, a 2010 first-round pick out of Legacy High in Texas. The "Venezuelan kid" Toronto agreed to throw into the deal was Wuilmer Becerra, eighteen, a shortstop turned outfielder Toronto thought highly enough to pay a $1.3 million signing bonus. The Mets for their part added catchers Josh Thole and Mike Nickeas to the trade, which finally went down December 16. "Like it or not, the Alderson regime has been looking to 2014 and beyond since it took over after the 2010 season, determined to build a contender that will last," John Harper wrote in the *New York Daily News*. "And acquiring d'Arnaud should go a long way toward accomplishing that goal."

13

SPRING TRAINING 2013

More than sixty years after New York writers started celebrating spring training in Florida or Arizona, the quiet rhythms of another season of baseball rejuvenation remain unchanged. Pale-faced fans fresh off planes from the north still mill about the complex with grins plastered on their faces, overjoyed that baseball, at least on this day, at least for them, still provides a mysterious bridge to the raw emotion of youth, the anticipation and hope and freedom from regret. The Mets' spring-training complex lies near Florida's Atlantic coast about midway between Orlando and Miami along the edge of a fast-growing suburban sprawl called Port St. Lucie, rather rudely dubbed "Port St. Lousy" or (by a *New York Post* columnist) "a pathetic waste of map space." There is no port; in fact Port St. Lucie isn't even on the coast and has no downtown, but Fort Pierce and its picturesque waterfront fish restaurants are a ten-minute drive away. Sandy Alderson showed up at Tradition Field on the morning of February 23, 2013, nursing an ages-old mixture of anticipation and apprehension. This was the day when Zack Wheeler was going to make his spring debut and, as it happened, the Mets regional network had announced that this would be its first game broadcast from spring training.

"A lot of people will watch because Wheeler's pitching," Alderson tells me in his Port St. Lucie office. "Fortunately he's the kind of guy who I don't think is going to be fazed too much by it. But command will be an issue."

Alderson then had one of those jolts of unfortunate association that are unavoidable for a man with decades in the game. He flashed back on the excitement in A's camp when another hard-throwing right-hander, Todd Van Poppel, was being touted as the next big thing. Alderson drafted Van Poppel out of Martin High School in Texas in the first round of the 1990 draft and signed him to a $1.2 million deal. Van Poppel made his major-league debut in 1991 at age nineteen and was shelled for five runs in 4²/₃ innings, which proved to be an accurate indication of what was to come. By 1996 the A's gave up on him and placed him on waivers.

"I remember this with Todd Van Poppel way back when: *OK, here comes the savior*," Alderson said. "It didn't work out all that well in his case."

Managing expectations is an art form, as far as it goes. The risk is to taste a little success with spin and think it says more about you than it does. Alderson has a precision with language befitting a man who had three years of Harvard Law, but he's allergic to out-and-out bullshitting; it bores him silly, and one thing Alderson has never, ever been able to abide is being bored. This is probably a weakness of Alderson's. Slogging through boredom is often an important skill. But Alderson also turns his aversion to boredom into a strength: He finds ways to keep himself interested with his knack for the biting one-liner, even if in New York so far he'd mostly kept this side of his personality hidden.

When he moved in 1998 from Northern California to a job working at baseball headquarters in New York City, handed the title of executive vice president of baseball operations, he toned down the wit. He had a little more of the lawyer in him in those years, a little less of the guy in shorts who was always going to play by his own rules. Then he moved to San Diego to take over as CEO of the Padres and, through some quirk of the media market down there, gained a reputation for being disagreeable and remote. That may in part have had to do with the role of CEO, more like being a general, far from the front lines, removed from the daily give-and-take that field managers and even sometimes general managers have with players and media types. His mixed reception in San Diego also had to do with his own missteps, he's quick to point out.

"When I was in Oakland I developed a reputation for some humor," Alderson says. "Then I went to the commissioner's office and my reputation was more for being direct and unfiltered. Then I went to San Diego and I became a hard-ass." His appearances on a weekly Padres radio show were often contentious. "I'd basically end up saying, 'You guys don't know what you're talking about.' I would get into it with callers. I don't know why. It was stupid."

It made sense for Alderson, now in his sixties, to tone it down stepping into the pressure cooker of the New York media market, but at times it seemed as if he was too successful in avoiding his mistakes in San Diego. When Alderson in his Oakland days would go off on someone, it usually made great copy. He was letting off steam, but there was a message in it, too.

In November 2012 Alderson showed up in Palm Springs, California, for baseball's annual GM meetings and let it fly. It did not take remarkable skill at filling in the dots to hear anger in jokes like this one about Lucas Duda, a Mets prospect who was said to have broken a bone that off-season moving furniture around his apartment: "We like Duda, although he does come with a lot of furniture."

This was a period of time when, improbably enough, the Mets were talking about going into the season with an outfield of whomever they could scrounge up off the baseball scrap heap in right field, unproven Kirk Nieuwenhuis in center, and Duda, whose competence was limited to handling first-base duties, in left field.

"Outfield? What outfield?" Alderson retorted in Palm Springs.

The comment was funny because it sounded like something Alderson would say behind the scenes to Ricciardi or DePodesta, even as they scoured the options to improve the situation. That November there had been much speculation about the Mets signing Michael Bourn, a center fielder who had posted a .348 on-base percentage with some power the year before for the Braves. The trouble was, depending on how the rules were interpreted, the Mets would have had to give up a draft pick as compensation for signing Bourn; they mulled challenging the rules, and probably would have if Bourn had not insisted on a four-year deal, but in the end the Mets passed. Instead, they kept looking—and took a chance on outfielder Marlon Byrd, a former All-Star for the Cubs in 2010 whose 2012 season was disastrous, featuring both career-low numbers (a .210 average with just a .245 slugging percentage) and a fifty-game suspension for testing positive for a banned substance. The February 1 announcement that the Mets had signed Byrd to a minor-league deal did not exactly set off fireworks among the press or fans.

As with all reclamation projects, Byrd was iffy, but no one questioned he had the tools to be a productive hitter if he could get his career back on track, and there were inklings of character, the kind of toughness needed to put a miserable year behind him and rebuild his approach. Tattoos were everywhere in baseball clubhouses by this time, but Byrd had gone out and added a most unusual tattoo to his right arm: Featured there was an excerpt from former president Teddy Roosevelt's "Man in the Arena" speech.

On February 1, the same day they signed Byrd, the Mets also took a chance on forty-year-old reliever LaTroy Hawkins, another move mostly met by yawns. The *New York Post* sniffed, "Add LaTroy Hawkins to the Mets' rag-tag bullpen mix. . . ." The article went on to explore the question of who might close games for the Mets, without hinting that Hawkins had any hope of landing that role, and also not talking about Bobby Parnell, a ninth-round draft pick of the Mets in 2005 who had come into his own in 2012, finishing with an ERA of 2.49 and seven saves, second on the team behind closer Frank Francisco. A major factor in Parnell's development was the steady advice of veteran closer Jason Isringhausen, who took an active interest. Parnell had hit 103 on the radar gun, but it takes far more than velocity to handle the pressures of late-inning work. Hawkins, if he could make the team, was the kind of solid citizen who had impressed teammates at every stop along the way as level-headed and professional. Then again, there was no telling what he had left at age forty.

Mets chief operating officer Jeff Wilpon, looking to find new ways to connect with fans, started encouraging top-level figures in the Mets organization to take to Twitter and mix it up, including Mets PR man Jay Horwitz, who joined the team in 1980. Horwitz was the subject of a hilarious *Wall Street Journal* article in the spring of 2013 making fun of his prodigious habit of butt-dialing.

"Several times per week, and sometimes several times per day, Horwitz accidentally calls a current or former member of the organization," Brian Costa wrote in the *Journal*. "He has mistakenly awakened team executives at 4 a.m., roused coaches late at night and left former Mets around the league puzzled by missed calls from him. Horwitz may be the Cal Ripken Jr. of public-relations men, hardly ever taking a day off. But he is the Barry Bonds of butt dialers, putting up staggering numbers and shattering all records. By now, his career butt dials number in the thousands. 'I swear to God, I don't know how I do it,' Horwitz said. 'I'm not real mechanical.'"

The article attracted such attention, the *Today* show on NBC did a segment on Horwitz, sending a reporter and crew down to Port St. Lucie to interview Mets players about the team PR man's ways with the phone. "I've been butt-dialed probably close to around 150 times," explained a smiling Ike Davis.

Later Horwitz switched to an iPhone, which did put an end to the butt-dialing, but created new issues. "I don't hang up, but think I have," he told me. "Sometimes people hear me talking about them and sometimes I'm saying not nice things about them."

Horwitz checked in with his first tweet in January 2012: "Joined the twitter world. My dog Tiki and cats Leo, Stan and Lilly can't wait 34 years from Doug Flynn to David Wright. I am old." The new medium brought out a puckish side to Horwitz's sense of humor. Soon he was tweeting "I once went through 79 cans of whiteout in one year. Still a pr record" and "My cat Leo is speechless."

By February, Horwitz was mixing in more pictures with his tweets. On February 6 he posted a shot of the palm trees outside Legends Field and wrote, "In St. Lucie. Going to beach. Please don't tell Sandy."

Alderson joined Twitter that same month and sent his first tweet on February 9: "Getting ready for Spring Training—Driving to FL but haven't left yet. Big fundraiser tonight for gas money. Also exploring PAC contribution."

Three days later, he followed up with: "Will have to drive carefully on trip; Mets only reimburse for gas at a downhill rate. Will try to coast all the way to FL."

The tweets, coming as they did at a time when Mets finances were a grim subject, might have been too much for some. A *New Yorker* blog post that spring by Seth Berkman mentioned the tweets and asserted, "But no one expected the opening salvo to come from Mets general manager Sandy Alderson, a man usually characterized as a no-nonsense numbers cruncher."

"People don't understand: He's funny," David Wright told me. "He got a lot of backlash on Twitter for some of the things he said. Like I said, I love this organization. I bleed blue and orange. But I was cracking up."

Like the tweet about gas money?

"Uh-huh. I think he's hilarious in a dry sense. You can tell when he's ready to crack one because he kind of gets this little smirk on his face before he says it. He's got a good sense of humor. I wish more people could see that side of him, but I guess you can't really, because he's got to come off as this kind of stoic leader, general manager."

It all circled back to developments on the field: If the Mets continued to struggle on Alderson's watch, not too many Mets fans or reporters were going to want to laugh at his jokes.

One afternoon early in spring training 2013, prospect Travis d'Arnaud was catching at Tradition Field. Everyone was eager to get a look at him in action so soon after the trade that brought him to the Mets the previous December. He had a puppy-doggish look as he hopped up to confer with the pitcher. A fly ball to left sent the outfielder back toward the fence and d'Arnaud shouted out, "You got room!"

"To me he just looks like he's not having fun right now," Alderson told me. "He's feeling the pressure. He's swinging at bad balls. The first pitch went off his shin guard. Right now he knows he's this top prospect and either he's overcompensating, trying not to be Johnny College, or something else. We've got plenty of time to figure that out."

It was another perfect 86-degree Florida spring afternoon and Alderson was incognito in his white cotton golf shirt and shades, sitting with his posse of smart young men. Behind him was Adam

Fisher, the director of baseball operations; Jon Miller, the director of minor-league operations; and DePodesta.

"Adam's from Harvard, Paul's from Harvard, Jon Miller is from Princeton," Alderson told me later. "They replicate themselves."

The key to the Mets' future was development of talent, starting with Zack Wheeler. "He hasn't done anything to disappoint us," Alderson said on the morning of Wheeler's spring debut. "Prospect status is a function of past evaluations and past performance. It's a dynamic label. Once you get it, you're not entitled to it forever. You've got to keep performing. Zack has kept performing and he's moved up the list of top prospects across baseball.

"He's kind of laid-back. He tries to maintain his sort of low-key, low-anxiety approach to things. The contrast is with a guy like Matt Harvey. He's very outgoing, he's always asking questions, he wants to be part of the group, he's a joiner. I think Zack is a little more of a loner. Harvey is a very mature twenty-three years old, very self-confident. Wheeler I don't think thinks about what he projects, whereas with Harvey there's a little more posturing that goes on. They're both good guys."

Alderson took a break from talking about the future to take his dog, Buddy, outside. As soon as we got out into the parking lot, Buddy took advantage of the opportunity. Alderson pulled a little plastic bag out of his pocket and went over to clean up. As Alderson squatted down with his baggie, a friendly voice called out in the near distance.

"Hey, that'll be a good tweet for Jay!"

It was David Wright. Alderson, uncharacteristically, had no comeback and just shook his head and laughed.

"The nice thing about the Wheeler trade was that the press kept saying, 'They'll never get a top-line prospect for Beltrán because it's a two-month rental,'" Alderson says. "We kept saying we're shooting for the best prospect we can get, but media commentary lowered expectations. So when we got Zack nobody could believe it. The same thing happened with the R. A. Dickey trade."

Alderson's point was not to take any of it too seriously. In the same way media expectations can help you by being overly low, they can hurt you by being too high. Either way, you'd be wise never to congratulate yourself and instead keep focusing on the next step.

"Making a deal is different than putting a good team together," Alderson said. "You can be good at making deals and lousy at other things, but making good deals does give you credibility and credibility is an organizational requirement. The defining criteria are winning and losing and I understand that, but at the same time you have to have the discipline to see where you are and where you have to go. . . . Who knows what's going to happen this year. We were talking the other day and said, 'OK, if we have a winning season, will that be a good season?' Well, yes, unless the prospects, on whom all the future is predicated, go in the tank. If we have a winning season and the d'Arnauds of the world, the Wheelers of the world, all tank, we're back to ground zero. So a good year for us would be a winning record, yes, successful at the major-league level, but just as important would be the continued development of our farm system, and not just the top three or four guys, but other prospects that we have below them who have to develop into better players."

Alderson gave me a tour of the Mets' complex in Port St. Lucie. Across from Tradition Field we walked past several different diamonds, and maybe it was the perfect weather, or the steady stream of cheerful fans poking around the palm-lined paths in search of a star of tomorrow, or the bright orange foul poles and Mets-blue batting cages, but there was a jaunty, upbeat feel to the place. Along the way we passed a big sign, flanked by a full-sized cutout of a grinning Mr. Met, with such helpful tips as STAY ALERT AT ALL TIMES FOR THROWN OR BATTED BALLS. Then as we completed the circuit to head back into Alderson's office, he was set upon by a knot of fans. Despite the cheery mood, I was expecting some pointed questions. But these were not that type of fan.

"I like what you're doing," said one fan in a Mets cap, squinting in the Florida sun as he held out a pen for an autograph.

"Building up the farm team," another chimed in.

"Fifty million coming off at the end of the year," said another.

Boom, boom, boom, as if on cue. I had the momentary sense it had to be a setup, paid actors hired for my benefit, but if so Alderson would surely have looked like he was enjoying himself, instead of vaguely at ease, like it was a little more belief and excitement than he quite bargained for.

Later he talked about not wanting to bring young players along too quickly in part because fans love to believe in the future. "I'm not ready to wholly convert the myth into the reality at this point, because these guys of mythical status are what's carrying our plan in the minds of all of these fans out there," he said that week in Florida. "It's not just, 'Are they going to be good enough?' It's, 'OK, they're good, they're here, what's next?' So stretching it out has as much to do with maintaining that belief on the part of the fan base, but you can't stretch it out unreasonably. People see right through that."

I caught up again with Alderson the next day down the third-base line. I'd been watching from the front row as Wheeler warmed up in the bullpen before he entered the game in the third inning. I'm no scout, not by a long shot, but there are certain things you notice when you've spent many years watching baseball players for a living. One is balance. Wheeler had command issues at every step on his way up, befitting a thin six-foot-four power pitcher, but his motion itself had a tightly coiled ease to it and it was easy to see that his fastballs had that most valuable quality: late, explosive movement. Todd Van Poppel had a straight fastball. Wheeler's ball had life.

Out on the mound, Wheeler looked just fine getting ready to face his first Nationals hitter, Steve Lombardozzi, but for all the appreciative murmuring in the stands about the way his fastball made catcher John Buck's glove snap back with a pop, Wheeler was showing signs of wildness. Behind in the count, he threw a breaking ball that looked like a strike.

"Squeezing him a little?" Alderson asked conversationally.

Wheeler walked Lombardozzi and then, with Bryce Harper up, threw a fastball Buck couldn't handle. Lombardozzi moved to second when the ball glanced off Buck's glove for a wild pitch. David Wright and the rest of the infield converged on the mound for a meeting to calm the young pitcher down.

"You a little amped up?" Buck asked him. "Your heart beating?"

"Yeah, just a little," Wheeler said.

"Good, you should be," Buck told him, getting a smile.

"You're good enough to beat these guys," Wright told him. "Just relax and go."

Harper grounded out, moving the runner to third, but it didn't matter. By then Wheeler had started to look comfortable and hit 96 on the gun with his fastball.

"He's not a finesse pitcher," Alderson told me. "He's got enough movement on his fastball. He's looking for a strikeout here with a man on third and one out."

He got it, too, striking out Tyler Moore. Then he struck out Chad Tracy to end the inning.

"Well, what looked like an inauspicious beginning turned out well," Alderson said, leaning back in his chair. "Will he settle down and start throwing strikes?"

David Wright, due to hit in the bottom of the inning, was taking his warm-up swings with a winning combination of grinning nonchalance and quiet fury. "We talk about friendly but professional," Alderson said. "He's got a casual but professional demeanor, exactly what you're looking for. He's got a lot of self-confidence, but it doesn't consume him. He's a pretty humble guy, so he carries himself like he's done it before. It impacts the other players."

This was shortly before Wright was named team captain, becoming only the fourth in team history, after Gary Carter, Keith Hernandez, and John Franco.

Justin Turner, the grinning redhead utility player out of Lakewood, California, was playing second that day, taking grounders with his usual bouncy good cheer, as if it was all great fun. Turner threw to first base and we both paused to consider the case of Ike Davis, one of those players who comes along now and then and everyone seems to hope he'll make it. Ike played college ball at Arizona State, where he was batting .394 with sixteen homers when the Mets drafted him in the first round of the 2008 draft. Rated the third-best collegiate power hitter in the draft by *Baseball America*, he hit nineteen homers in 2010 as a rookie, a promising enough start, but saw limited action in 2011 because of an ankle injury, though even then he showed more than glimpses. Davis was healthy in 2012, but he muddled through a horrible start to the season. By June 10 he was batting just .162 with five home runs and calls were multiplying for the Mets to send him down to the minor leagues. He bounced back.

"He's got a lot of upside," Alderson told me. "He's still young. I think he has a chance to be a leader on the team as well, a leader among the younger group of players, sort of a lieutenant to Wright's captaincy, but he's got to perform. He doesn't hit left-handed pitching very well. He's got to improve that substantially. He has a pretty good eye at the plate. He's not a free swinger. Last year he missed a lot of pitches, got out of sync, jumping out in front of the ball, but he wound up with thirty-two home runs. If you can hit thirty-two home runs by mistake, we'll take it."

We talked about the plan of everything pointing toward the 2014 season, with Wheeler and Syndergaard another year along, d'Arnaud showing what he can do, and the deadweight of failed contracts coming off the books. Everything pointed toward a patient and disciplined approach, as Alderson and I had discussed, but I wondered, sitting there with Alderson at this spring-training game, if sometimes he tired of the discipline and patience.

"Is there part of you that wishes you could just get to that now?" I asked him.

"Oh sure," he said quickly. "That's the temptation. That's where the discipline comes in or, alternatively, the question of whether the discipline has been taken too far and it's time to do something different, still within the framework of what you're trying to do long term."

Wheeler came back out to start his second inning to a big hand from the crowd and then got things going with two straight groundouts. Then he gave up a single.

"So the leadoff walk, five outs, and then a single," Alderson said. "He's keeping the ball down. If he keeps it down there at 95, he won't have to worry about the next hitter."

Wheeler got a groundout to put his second scoreless inning in the books, clearly an impressive debut for the first televised spring-training game of the year.

"He handled himself very well, especially after digging a hole for himself with the first five pitches," Alderson said.

"What is fun for you here in spring training in general?" I followed up.

"Almost everything. I like to walk around and communicate and engage with people, and spring training is the perfect place to do that."

Building a team amounts to a series of freeze-frame shots you hope to put together to form the right movie. Wheeler's solid first outing in the spring of 2013 was a small step forward for the organization and helped build the narrative power of the young-pitching-can-build-the-future story line. Then again, Wheeler did not pitch again for the Mets that spring. A minor strain of the oblique muscle in his abdomen shut him down.

The problem with the rotation was at the top. Santana, the staff ace and intended Opening Day starter, due $25.5 million in salary for the year, came into spring training talking about wanting to pitch for his home country of Venezuela in the World Baseball Classic in March. On February 22 the team announced that Santana's first appearance would be pushed back. It was a tune Mets fans knew all too well.

Wheeler found his name on the list of ten young players demoted on March 9 from the Mets' big-league camp to minor-league camp, a world away. Among the others sent down were some names that might never be known to anyone but Paul DePodesta and a few other insiders, and some who had a shot at getting a call-up that year or the next, like the Dominican right-handed pitcher Gonzalez Germen, a fastball guy, mostly, known for his changeup ("very good," Alderson dubbed it) and for his inconsistency. At the time Alderson saw him as "an up-and-down guy who might develop into a seventh-inning option." Another name on that list of players was the intriguing twenty-four-year-old Juan Lagares, also Dominican, who was signed by the Mets when he was seventeen years old. Lagares was a shortstop then, and he wasn't converted to the outfield until three years later.

Lagares did not impress at first. He hit .210 for Single-A Savannah over eighty-three games in 2007 and, dealing with some pain in his arm, was sent down from Savannah to low-A Brooklyn, where he was still a shortstop but did play five games at third base. His progress was slow, mostly because he kept getting hurt. He had some ankle trouble and recurring elbow issues. The organization loved his athleticism, but injuries were getting in the way of his play, making him more inconsistent. He had issues throwing the ball to first.

"When I first met him he was an infielder," said Josh Satin, Lagares' teammate on the 2008 Brooklyn Cyclones and 2009 Savannah Sand Gnats. "Obviously he had all the talent in the world, but he had so much athleticism, he didn't know how to harness it. He had a really good arm at short, but he would throw the ball away a lot."

That was when the Mets decided that the large volume of throws a shortstop makes might be part of the problem. Why not try him in the outfield? At Savannah in 2009, Lagares was all over the place—twenty-three games in left field, seventeen in right, two in center, two at shortstop, and one at third base. But suddenly he looked like a player with a future. "I was a little surprised to be moved and at the beginning it was a little hard, but you never know what is going to happen in this game," Lagares told me.

"When they moved him to the outfield, you could see right away he was more comfortable," Satin said.

Playing for AA Binghamton in 2011 after a call-up from St. Lucie, he had only one game in center field, the rest in right or left, and batted .370 over thirty-eight games. Only in 2012 did he finally play more in center field than elsewhere, getting seventy games there and hitting .283 in 130 games with four homers and forty-eight RBIs. He learned center field in a hurry because of his focus and intensity. "He works hard," Satin said. "Everything he did was hard. He played hard, he ran hard, and he was hard on himself."

It was enough to get noticed in the system, but not enough to establish Lagares as the Mets' top prospect at center field, a distinction held at the time by Matt den Dekker. "Lagares was still behind den Dekker in the minds of most of us," Alderson said.

14

SWEEP

It did not take long for the Mets' 2013 season to turn into the Matt Harvey show. There were countless other questions the team needed to resolve before it could take a step forward, but Harvey's drop-what-you're-doing-to-check-this-out starts had a way of canceling all that out. In his first start of the year, the second game of the season for the Mets, he struck out ten Padres batters and gave up just one hit and no runs over seven innings for the victory. Up against Roy Halladay in Philadelphia his next time out, he limited the Phillies to three hits and one run in seven innings, striking out nine and getting the win. By his third start, in which he carried a no-hit bid into the seventh inning against the Twins in Minneapolis, he had everyone's attention.

Harvey was 3-0 for the year with twenty-five strikeouts and just two earned runs allowed in twenty-two innings, and as impressive as his numbers were, they did not begin to do justice to the Harvey phenomenon. Like Dwight Gooden in the 1980s, Harvey could blow hitters away with a dazzling fastball, and like Gooden he was so dominant, so transcendent, every start of his became an event. He might have no-hit stuff, or he might be merely devastating, but one thing he was always going to be was deeply entertaining. He was a showman and he was a winner. He won each of his first five starts in 2013, pitching at least six innings per game, never giving up more than four hits or three runs.

Matt Harvey had a hard-luck loss in Miami in his sixth start of the year, giving up just one run in 5⅓ innings, then bounced back in style his next time out. It was a warm, cloudy day, 70 degrees at Citi

Field when Harvey took the mound on May 7 against the White Sox, and the crowd of 23,394 buzzed with expectation from the first inning, when Harvey picked up a bloody nose but seemed as locked in as ever. Each of the first two Chicago batters made contact, sending balls to the outfield, but both were caught, and Harvey struck out Álex Ríos to end the inning. Harvey worked a 1-2-3 second and a 1-2-3 third, adding three more strikeouts. It was the same in the fourth and fifth—Harvey was still perfect. All over New York, Mets fans were receiving texts and phone messages saying "Turn on your TV!" Sports bars filled up with the curious and the avid.

Even more pumped up now, Harvey struck out two of three White Sox hitters he faced in the top of the sixth and opened the seventh with another strikeout and a groundout. Ríos then reached for an outside slider and grounded the ball into the hole, where Mets shortstop Rubén Tejada backhanded it and leaped and twisted to throw to first. Ríos just beat the throw. Harvey's no-hit bid had expired, but he struck out the next batter, Adam Dunn, and worked a total of nine innings of one-hit, shutout ball with twelve strikeouts. But the Mets had not been able to score either, so it went into extra innings. Bobby Parnell pitched a scoreless tenth and Mike Baxter singled home Ike Davis in the bottom of the inning for a walk-off win.

Harvey took a no-decision for his work in that game, dropping his ERA to 1.28, but he did earn a *Sports Illustrated* cover. The following week, there he was, "The Dark Knight of Gotham," captured on the mound mid-delivery in his Mets uniform, along with the subhead: "In an era dominated by the power pitcher, the Mets' Matt Harvey has the ferocity of stuff and will to rise above them all."

Another Mets player getting off to a torrid start was veteran catcher John Buck, the throw-in on the trade that sent R. A. Dickey to the Blue Jays. A month into the season, Buck was leading the National League with twenty-three RBIs and had eight home runs. It was clear he would come back to earth at some point, but watching a player get that hot was fun for everyone—and only served as a reminder of how little struggling first baseman Ike Davis was contributing. Speculation was kicking around in the media by mid-May that Davis, known for his slow starts, was about to be sent down to Triple-A Las Vegas, and Alderson used the occasion of that road trip to Chicago to have a talk with him.

"Look, it's not imminent," Alderson told him. "Don't worry about it. Go play."

Next up were three games back in New York against the Reds and, unfortunately, Davis' epic struggles and their lead-weight impact on the team were by this time becoming the dominant story line. The Reds jumped out to a three-run lead against journeyman starter Shaun Marcum in the first inning of the series opener, a rally that would have been limited if Davis had not been called for obstructing runner Joey Votto. Davis came up in the bottom of the inning with the bases loaded, a prime chance to atone. He was at that point tunneling deep into the agony of a 1-for-30 streak, but all it would have taken was one good swing. Instead, Davis grounded out weakly to end the inning. He struck out his next two at bats and was pulled from the game by the sixth.

One day later, his frustration continued. The game got away from the Mets early when David Wright of all people let a ball squirt between his legs in the top of the first for an error that scored two runs, putting the Mets down 3–0. The best chance to rally came when John Buck doubled with Lucas Duda on first, giving Davis runners at second and third. Davis then hit yet another weak grounder to first to snuff out the would-be rally, earning a hearty round of boos on his way back to the dugout. The Latin players have an expression, "*un out vestido de pelotero*," and Davis that game, and in so many others that month, was an out dressed up as a ballplayer.

The Mets were 7-1 in games started by Harvey or left-hander Jon Niese, their Opening Day starter, and 1-7 in their other games. Niese was in his fourth full season, coming off solid but unspectacular showings of 9-10 in 2010 and 11-11 in 2011, then a major step forward in 2012 with a 13-9 record and an ERA of 3.40, compared with 4.40 the year before, a development made possible by his refinement of a cut-fastball that he threw more often and with far more effectiveness. Harvey and Niese were shaping up as bona fide front-of-the-rotation guys, but after that, there was no there there.

Dillon Gee was coming off a strange injury. A twenty-first-round pick of the Mets in 2007, he'd had a sudden opportunity to make an impression after Mets starter Chris Young required shoulder surgery early in the 2011 season. Up to that season, Gee had appeared in only five big-league games, but after Young's injury he stepped in beautifully, going on an 8-1 run with a 3.32 ERA through the end of June and finishing that year 13-6. But in July 2012, tests revealed that Gee had a blood clot in his right shoulder. It was a scary time for him. He had surgery to remove the clot and finished the year on the disabled list.

Alderson was CEO of the Padres when they selected Jeremy Hefner in the fifth round of the 2007 draft out of Seminole State College in Oklahoma, but he didn't stick in San Diego. By late 2011 he was available for the Mets to claim off the waiver wire, and as a rookie in 2012 he finished 4-7 with a 5.09 ERA. Hefner had neither an overpowering fastball nor an obvious out pitch, and gave up 110 hits in $93^2/3$ innings his first year.

In late January 2013 the Mets had become the last team in baseball to sign a free agent that off-season, buying a little insurance for their starting rotation by agreeing to pay veteran Shaun Marcum $4 million for one year. Marcum, with the Blue Jays for five years and then the Brewers, had won twelve or more games three times in his eight seasons and had a career ERA of 3.76 with 746 strikeouts. He was coming off a year marked by elbow issues, and in 2009 he'd had Tommy John reconstructive elbow surgery. In spring training with the Mets, he developed a pinched nerve in his neck and missed thirty-six days, including some of the regular season, before finally joining the rotation and losing game after game.

Alderson would have liked to stay in New York after the three straight losses to the Reds and manage the situation the best he could; in fact, he'd have loved to do that, but he'd given his word that he would attend a ceremony honoring Walter Haas, the former owner of the A's, so he and Linda went straight from the ballpark that Wednesday to JFK for a flight to California. He wasn't sure how much he'd actually enjoy this Bay Area Sports Hall of Fame Enshrinement Banquet, but it would be good to see Wally Haas and his wife, Julie, as well as Roy and Betsy Eisenhardt and some other old friends.

"I didn't want to miss it," he says. "First of all I wanted to honor Walter Haas, but also I wanted to be there for Wally and Julie. They had come to my dad's funeral. It was important to be there."

Alderson flew back to New York the next day in time for a long night at Citi Field. Hefner gave up a two-run homer in the first, and the Mets looked doomed to roll to their fourth loss in a row, but to their credit they hung in there. Under a pelting rain that made playing conditions a step beyond ludicrous, they strung together an eighth-inning rally to tie the game. Second baseman Daniel Murphy, the team's hottest hitter to that point of the season, singled home John Buck and moved shortstop Rubén Tejada to third, where he scored on a wild pitch to even it up.

The heavy rain finally forced a delay. Alderson hoped the game would resume, of course, given the way his team had come back, but instead, following a seventy-six-minute delay, it was suspended—to be completed the following day. Davis struck out four times in the incomplete game, and if ever there was a day when a player came to the plate looking like an automatic out, this was it. After the game Davis went straight to the batting cage and swung the bat for close to two hours. Whether those swings were more about getting himself back on track or merely demonstrating that he knew something had to change was not clear. To Alderson, the time to send him down to Triple-A Las Vegas was getting very close.

"Ike had looked awful," Alderson says. "He came into the club-house afterward and walked into the indoor batting cage. There were like five players giving him suggestions what to do, which was part of the problem. Hitting coach Dave Hudgens was in there to protect him from this onslaught of advice. One of the reasons to send him to Vegas was to get him away from all that. Ike just looked completely lost."

The Braves resumed the suspended game the following afternoon—but not the Mets, not really. They came out looking like sleepwalkers. The ninth inning passed without signs of a pulse, and then in the Atlanta half of the tenth, Freddie Freeman worked a walk to lead off. Ike Davis, visibly removed from the action, was near the line to hold him on when Brian McCann lifted a line drive his direction. An alert player would have timed his leap and snagged the liner—or, if he was a poor jumper, at least made an effort at it, maybe knocking the ball down. Davis, sluggish and absent, reacted too late. Alderson's frustration mounted.

"He was now taking his offense out on the field and it was affecting his defense," he told me the following week. "In fact, that had been the case for some time."

The Mets lost and it was a galling outcome: not so much the fourth straight L as the giving-it-away flat performance.

"I told Terry I didn't think we were ready to play," Alderson said at the time.

The Mets still had to play that day's regularly scheduled contest against the Braves. Dillon Gee matched zeroes with Braves starter Mike Minor for four innings and then grooved a fastball down the middle that Minor himself stroked for a two-run homer to carry the Braves to a five-run fifth and an easy 6–0 win, all shown to a wide TV audience via Fox Sports. The Mets had now lost five in a row. Then a strange thing happened in the series finale: With the Mets trailing 2–1 in the bottom of the eighth, five outs away from making it six straight losses, they loaded the bases and sent up Davis, hitting all of .148 as of the start of the game. Davis did not rip the ball. The grounder he hit to the right side of the infield could safely be characterized as weak. But it found its way to the outfield grass, two runs scored, and—for the moment—Davis was a hero. It was like a mountain had been lifted from his shoulders.

"You say to yourself, 'OK, he's going to build on this,'" Alderson said.

Davis was not the only Mets player who was making a case to be sent down to Las Vegas. If a team is staking its future on young players, few developments are more alarming than the kind of overt regression that shortstop Rubén Tejada was demonstrating. Tejada, a Panamanian signed by the Mets in 2006, made his big-league debut at age twenty in 2010, and in 2012 he hit a respectable .289 in 464 at bats, though with only twenty-seven walks, fielding his position solidly enough. Tejada had another 0-fer in the win against the

Braves, dropping his average to .218, and his play in the field was becoming a glaring issue. Like Davis, he was letting his funk at the plate carry over to distracted, muddled play in the field.

"We were suffering from the same problem at shortstop," Alderson told me that month. "We'd talked about sending Tejada out, but we were sort of hostage to Ike. If we weren't going to send Ike out, we couldn't send Tejada. They were both going to have to go. To me that would be a stronger statement about the team and what level of performance was acceptable and what was not. In Ike's case, we thought it would be short term and in his interest."

The 2013 Yankees, ravaged by injuries to key veterans, were an odd hodgepodge coming into their June series against the Mets, with Jayson Nix at shortstop, David Adams at third, and Lyle Overbay at first base, but still they were ten games over .500. At Citi Field on May 27 for the first of the games, David Wright helped everyone tune out the gloom hanging over the Mets with a solo shot in the seventh inning to tie the game 1–1. Daniel Murphy knocked in the go-ahead run in the eighth, and the Mets pulled off a 2–1 win against their crosstown rival. Davis, far from building on his game-winning hit the previous night, struck out in all three at bats to drop his batting average to .155. Tejada went 0-for-4.

Alderson, one of the more competitive men on the planet, has always been especially competitive when it comes to rivalries. Any game with the Yankees was a teeth-gritting marathon for the nerves. The Monday night win over the Yankees at Citi Field was sweet, but Alderson was not about to be satisfied by a split in the two-game series in Queens before the teams moved to the Bronx for two more games. From the first pitch the Tuesday night game against the Yankees at Citi Field had the sort of crisp, attentive intensity so rare for the Mets in recent years. A good number of the 31,877 in attendance were no doubt pulling for the Yankees, but so what? It was a packed house and with Matt Harvey on the mound the Mets were a team transformed, more purposeful and more confident, less likely to half-ass their way to poor play. Harvey, amped up by his first start against the team he grew up cheering on, started Yankees leadoff batter Brett Gardner with a 96-mile-an-hour fastball that missed, then came back with another fastball that Gardner smoked to center field, but recent acquisition Rick Ankiel, always a good glove man, made the play. It was a 1-2-3 first for Harvey and a 1-2-3 second, punctuated by strikeouts of Lyle Overbay and David Adams, both looking, at high-octane fastballs (97, 98) that had the place buzzing. The Yankees broke through for two singles in the third, but Harvey struck out the side to keep his shutout going, all three strikeouts coming on hard-biting sliders.

Harvey's command of the game was so intense, so startling, it was almost tempting to forget about the festering problem of what to do about Davis and Tejada—almost. Both kept making the case they needed to be sent down, Davis with strikeouts his first two times up, Tejada with more shoddy play. Alderson, watching the game in his box with assistant general manager John Ricco, was ready to credit Davis or Tejada with anything to weigh in the plus category, but nothing came. If Davis' big hit the night before was going to open the floodgates, now was the time—but nothing.

"It was like *Groundhog Day* for Ike and Tejada," Alderson said. "It was sort of business as usual for Ike, strikeouts and looking terrible at the plate, and Tejada looked particularly bad in the field and did nothing at the plate."

Yankees right fielder Ichiro Suzuki jumped on the first pitch he saw in the top of the seventh, a 93-mile-per-hour fastball, and hit a line shot right back up the middle. Harvey twisted so the ball hit him in the back, a smart play. He collected the ball, threw to first for the out, and then glared at the Mets dugout and waved off any visit from the team trainer, but Ray Ramirez trotted out dutifully anyway just to be sure Harvey was fine. Safe to say, no way was he coming out of the game.

It's a firm general rule that a shortstop takes any ball he can; if there's any doubt about whether it's his play or another infielder's, it's the shortstop's play. This is the kind of thing burned into any player when he's young, along with knowing that three strikes means you're out. Yet with Robinson Cano at first after a sharp single in the top of the eighth, Vernon Wells hit a grounder up the middle, and Tejada suddenly gave up on the ball. It was a startling lapse, especially when you noticed: The grounder was clearly on Tejada's side of the bag! That's *his* territory! Yet he glanced up at Daniel Murphy and let the ball scoot up the middle for what was scored a hit. It was a mental error, the worst sort.

By the eighth inning Alderson was through trying to be patient. This was the key frame, one inning before the Yankees could bring in the best closer in the history of the game. The Mets badly needed to get something going, but both Davis and Tejada grounded out.

"It's time to get this done," Alderson told Ricco. "We've got to send these guys out. We have to change the dynamic."

The kicker was: The Mets didn't even know which players they planned to call up. No automatic options presented themselves. Las Vegas had its own game in progress at the time, so they couldn't even check in with Wally Backman to see what he recommended until later, but Alderson felt so strongly about the need to make the move, he was ready to go.

Alderson walked down to the clubhouse to talk to Terry Collins, who was watching the game there, having been thrown out.

"Let's do this," Alderson said to Collins of the move. "Let's get this over with."

Collins adamantly agreed.

Alderson took his dog, Buddy, down to the parking lot to have him wait in the car until the game was over, so Alderson could be on his way. With Mariano Rivera about to take the mound, statistically speaking, the outcome was as close to a foregone conclusion as it could be. Baseball's all-time saves leader was 18-for-18 in save situations that year, and forty-three years old or not, Rivera's looked as unhittable as ever. Alderson went back into the clubhouse so he and Collins could talk with Davis and Tejada after the game. He had even spoken to vice president for communications Jay Horwitz and arranged to have the usual postgame interview procedure changed up so that instead of Collins speaking first to reporters in the press room, Yankees manager Joe Girardi would, giving Alderson and Collins time to give their two troubled players the news that they were Vegas bound.

Rather than watch in the plush expanse of the main clubhouse, which looked like an airport VIP lounge with its leather sofas and recessed lockers, Alderson ducked into the adjoining coaches' office to watch as Daniel Murphy poked a 1-1 pitch from Rivera down the left-field line. The ball looked ready to go foul, but it landed a yard inside the chalk line and the Mets had a leadoff double. The crowd seemed as stunned as it did excited, but got louder as David Wright worked the count to 2-0 against Rivera, both balls missing inside. Rivera tried coming in on Wright again and he ripped the ball up the middle for a single that scored Murphy to tie the game. Rivera, so used to being automatic, didn't even back up on the throw home, which squirted away from the catcher, enabling Wright to scamper down to second. That brought up Lucas Duda, a natural first baseman asked to play left field early in the season, who fisted a single into shallow right to win the game. Wright came around to score on a hands-out slide like a kid coming down a waterslide, and the Mets had done the unthinkable: They came back to beat Mariano Rivera, knocking three straight hits without him getting a single out against them!

"It all happened within two or three minutes," Alderson said. "Murphy got the double down the line, David Wright singled him in and went to second on the throw, and then Duda on the second pitch hit that dunker behind second base and it was over. Boom!"

Alderson was elated. He watched for Collins walking in from behind the dugout and flashed him the safe sign, meaning: *Not tonight.*

"He totally agreed," Alderson said. "We didn't even have to discuss it. We didn't want to screw with what was going on in the clubhouse. The Yankees had not lost a game they'd led after six innings until that night. It was the first time in Rivera's career that he had not got a single out in a save situation. That is incredible. It was a big win, historic in a way, given Rivera's history."

Davis and Tejada gained a reprieve at the eleventh hour. That didn't mean they avoided a talking-to, just that it had no plane ticket attached to it—this time. Both players were informed that if not for the amazing comeback against Rivera, they'd have been sent out. Given Alderson's assurances to Davis just over a week earlier that no move was imminent, he now felt that the only honorable thing to do was to let Davis know the situation had changed and he was on thin ice.

"I needed to put him on notice," he said. "Adding a little pressure might make a difference. It couldn't make him worse."

The talk went well.

"Look, I don't know about hitting mechanics," the general manager told his first baseman. "I won't tell you anything, but you've got to get your act together."

"Yeah, I do," Davis agreed.

The message with Tejada was parallel, but Alderson had less sense of the young player's reaction. He seemed in a fog.

"It's time to get it going," Collins told him. "We're fifty games into it. All of the kinks should be out by now."

The Mets headed up to the Bronx for game three of the four-game home-and-home series, and the Yankees were eager for revenge. It was galling to lose to the Mets, especially two in a row. Instead, they were the ones who were spanked. The Mets erupted for an improbable five-run outburst in the first inning, made all the more improbable by the fact that two of the Mets' four hits came from Tejada (leadoff single) and Davis (single to drive in two runs). If nothing else, the team clearly had Tejada's and Davis' attention—but maybe too much so. (Tejada had been upbraided for his passive play on that ground ball up the middle. "You've got to make that dive," he was told.)

The Mets were up 9–3 in the bottom of the ninth inning when Reid Brignac lifted a high pop-up down the left-field line. Journeyman Mike Baxter, getting the start in left field, had plenty of time to run in and camp underneath the ball, ready to make the grab, and then right at the last second Tejada—intent on showing he could be eager—came flying into the picture. He had to throw on the brakes with a sudden slide to avoid a collision. Baxter made the catch, then deftly hopped sideways to avoid the onrushing Tejada, who winced and clutched at his leg as he labored to pull himself upright again: He'd hurt himself on the play.

"Clearly he was mindful of what had happened the night before," Alderson said.

The timing was convenient: By landing on the disabled list, Tejada staved off the indignity of being sent down to Triple-A. Some of his teammates might have questioned how genuine his injury actually was, but not Alderson.

"Based on his immediate reaction, I don't think he's jaking it," he said that week. "The way he grimaced when he slid into foul territory, that's something that's tough to contrive."

For Alderson and team officials, it was a week that confirmed their worst hunches about Tejada. "It's the second year in a row he's had a quad pull, and if you hurt it like that, it can leave residual scarring, which leads to problems later," Alderson said. "There's been criticism of him that he's not in good shape, he comes to camp late, he's not working out diligently in the off-season. Does his weight contribute to the injury? Does the lack of conditioning? Does it contribute to a lack of range at short? . . . Gradually you come to the conclusion that Tejada is just a placeholder. He's not a long-term guy for us."

A four-game sweep of the Yankees in the only games the teams would play during the 2013 regular season had seemed impossible going in, but after the 9–4 drubbing the Mets had handed their rivals, pushing their winning streak to four games, they went into the series finale with hop in their step and a gleam in their eye. They could feel that they had the Yankees reeling. If they could complete the sweep, it would be almost as sweet for the agony it inflicted on the Yankees as it would be for the wins themselves.

Dillon Gee, the control pitcher easy to overlook, was masterful against the Bronx Bombers. He gave up a third-inning solo shot to their best hitter, Cano, and then set down fifteen Yankees in a row, finishing with a career-high twelve strikeouts. The Mets cruised to what felt like an easy 3–1 win, buoyed by Marlon Byrd's two-run homer in the second. The Yankees were now officially in trouble, having lost five in a row for their worst skid of the season.

"It's hard when you lose to your crosstown rivals," a glum Girardi told reporters afterward, adding, "It's going to happen, but you don't want to be the team that it happens to."

For many of the Mets, it might not have been clear until the media reaction kicked in just what they'd achieved with the four wins.

WHERE NO METS HAVE GONE BEFORE ran the *Star Trek*–evoking headline in the *New York Times*.

Added *Newsday*: "The Mets' season, an afterthought only last weekend, suddenly has gained some relevance thanks to a most improbable sweep of the Subway Series."

Alderson likes to talk about how over the course of a season, certain key games stand out, in either a negative way or a positive way. They punctuate a season and give it color and texture and meaning, whether they end up defining that season or not. In four games against the Yankees the 2013 Mets had found something in themselves they didn't know was there, and the discovery made a lot of things easier. They were a team with too many holes not to be up and down and all over the place. The whole season would not feel this sweet. But even a little dose of this kind of giddy exuberance had a way of making the longer-term waiting easier to endure. The fantasy of a dominant rotation fronted by Matt Harvey and Zack Wheeler, one that might power the Mets on a years-long run of success, might still just be a fantasy, but it was one that somehow felt a step closer, a step less mad, after those final two victories in the Bronx.

15

PATIENCE

Like Matt Harvey in 2012, Zack Wheeler found himself sent down to minor-league camp in March 2013, following his single spring appearance for the Mets and a mild issue with his oblique muscle. Getting sent down was not a surprise, but it was still a jarring turn of events for the former first-round pick. A week later he was seeing game action again, throwing three innings of one-hit ball in a minor-league game and announcing via Twitter that he "felt great."

Wheeler ran into more difficulties once he was assigned to the Triple-A Las Vegas 51s, as in Area 51, surely one of the cooler sports team names ever. Vegas is notoriously hard on pitchers, and a painful blister developed underneath the fingernail of Wheeler's middle finger on his pitching hand, making it hard for him to throw his slider and disrupting his rhythm during his first two starts with Vegas. He did better his third time out, giving up three runs over 5⅓ innings and not walking a single batter. Dillon Gee and Jeremy Hefner were both struggling for the Mets, so by mid-April 2013 the pressure was mounting on Alderson and the organization to bring Wheeler up right away.

TERRY PUSHES FOR ZACK, ran a *New York Daily News* headline on April 18 with a subhead: "Collins wants Wheeler, but Alderson may balk." Reporting from Denver, where Alderson had chipped in to shovel snow so the Rockies and Mets could avoid a rare snow cancellation, Kristie Ackert wrote: "With the back end of the Mets rotation struggling through the first two weeks of the season, calls for top pitching prospect Zack Wheeler are getting louder. Even Terry Collins said he might have to think about asking for some of the young, quality reinforcements the franchise has stockpiled in the minors if the struggles continue."

The following day, I set out early from where I live near Santa Cruz, California, to make the 530-mile drive down to Las Vegas to see Wheeler pitch against the Sacramento River Cats, Oakland's Triple-A affiliate. Before I left, I called Alderson to get his up-to-the-minute take on where Wheeler was, given the blister under his fingernail that had caused him trouble early in the Las Vegas season. "We're concerned that it's recurring and we can't seem to be able to resolve it," Alderson told me that morning. "If it continues to happen from time to time, it will have an impact, but at this point it doesn't seem to be anything serious. We'll see how he pitches the next two, three outings, and if he pitches well in those outings then we might take a look at him."

What did he need to work on?

"I think it's more about command than anything else, command of all of his pitches," he said. "He needs fastball command. Everybody needs to have fastball command on both sides of the plate."

Matt Harvey had just been named National League Player of the Week after going 2-0 with a 1.20 ERA over fifteen innings, striking out fifteen and giving up just four walks. In one of those perversely detailed stats it so often comes up with, the Elias Sports Bureau let it be known that Harvey was the first pitcher since 1900 to win his first three starts in a season allowing six hits or less over those three games and striking out at least twenty-five. Matt mania was beginning to brew. I asked Alderson if Harvey's success made it easier for Wheeler to advance.

"Yes and no," he said. "In one sense the fact we didn't bring Harvey up until July is a precedent for Wheeler. The one perception we don't want to create is that we rushed Wheeler. To me, if he pitches well three or four times in a row, there is no reason to keep him down. I actually think that having both of them together in the big leagues would be a big positive for Wheeler. He could become almost a protégé."

Vegas is a strange place to play baseball and an even stranger place to watch it. The thin desert air lifts everything, like helium, so that the time-honored balance between hitter and pitcher goes out the window. A nasty breaking ball anywhere else becomes a hittable pitch here, and a safety-hack poke at an outside pitch can easily yield a down-the-line opposite-field flare home run. It was 74 degrees at game time the night I watched Wheeler pitch, with almost no breeze, and felt warmer. In the distance the horizon glowed with a fringe of desert sunset the color of melted cheese. Just a few hours earlier that day, a suspect in the Boston Marathon bombing had been apprehended, and the announced crowd of 4,979 had a confused, edgy mood to it. As Wheeler peered in for the sign before throwing his first pitch, President Obama was addressing the nation about the Boston tragedy.

Wheeler, always relaxed-looking on the mound, coiled and unleashed his first pitch of the night: a high fastball, so high in fact that it glanced off catcher Landon Powell's mitt and rolled away. Unfortunately, I wouldn't get to see d'Arnaud play. He'd broken his big toe the night before and was due to be out four to six weeks, meaning that as far as his chances of joining the Mets any time soon, "d'Arnaud has become a moot point," Alderson told me that morning.

Again Wheeler peered in, saw the sign for fastball, and again let a fastball fly that was up and away. He talked to himself on the mound a little, tried to shake it off, and then for the third time came in up and away with his fastball. A 3-0 count on the first batter, a .194 hitter named Conner Crumbliss, was no way to send the message to the Mets' front office that he was ready for a promotion. Wheeler came back with two good fastballs, low and on the corner, to run the count full and then got Crumbliss on a flyout that right fielder Jamie Hoffmann nearly misplayed into a hit. From there Wheeler started to settle in, jumping ahead 1-2 against second baseman Grant Green, then getting him to fly out to center, though Juan Lagares, in a rare lapse, misjudged the ball badly before recovering to make the out. Then it was straight cheese to strike out .372-hitting Shane Peterson, a 97-mile-per-hour fastball.

Back out for the second, Wheeler looked calm and collected except for his occasional habit of hitching up his belt buckle distractedly, a move that made him look boyish. Again he started the inning off with a fastball missing up and away. The problem with showing that much wildness, especially with fastballs hitting 97 on the gun, is that you're not going to catch a break from the umps on close pitches. Sure enough, two more fastballs that could have been called strikes were not, making it 3-0, and Wheeler came back with the same pitch, again called a ball, to put Michael Choice on first. That brought up catcher Stephen Vogt and Wheeler walked him, too, then gave up a flare single to right to load the bases. Daric Barton got a hittable breaking ball and scorched it to right-center, but Lagares, showing the moves that would make an impression on the Mets later in the season, ran it down to limit the damage to one run on a sac fly. Wheeler walked two more in the third and another in the fourth, again missing by a lot, to bring his total for the game to five. Then in the top of the fifth he walked one more and was pulled with one out, having thrown 108 pitches. If the Mets were watching to see if he could string three good starts together, this was clearly not going to count as one of the three: four earned runs in 4⅓ innings with six walks to go with four strikeouts. He was 0-1 with a 4.91 ERA after four starts.

Alderson had cautioned me not to think of Triple-A players as a bunch of kids, and looking around the no-frills dressing room at Cashman Field, there were players at all stages in their career. Infielder Omar Quintanilla, for example, Oakland's first-round pick in 2003, was thirty-one. The Mets signed him as a free agent in January 2012, traded him to the Orioles that July, then signed him as a free agent again in January 2013. He was hitting .250, but hoping still to get a shot with the Mets. Over near Wheeler's locker stood Josh Satin, who had grown up in L.A. and played at Cal. He was hitting .350 for Vegas, but at twenty-eight, with only a handful of big-league games under his belt to that point, he could hear the clock ticking. Satin had been around and he knew enough to assume the visiting reporter was there to talk to Wheeler, not him.

"Last year I lived with Matt Harvey and he didn't do very well in the beginning," Satin told me. "He couldn't throw strikes. He was throwing 95. Zack's throwing 97. But it took Matt some time to really figure out how to pitch and I think that's benefited him. Yeah, Matt could have gone there last year at the beginning of the year and thrown his 95-mile-per-hour fastball and probably done pretty well. But there's no way that he could have done what he's doing right now without his time here in Triple-A.

"I was telling Zack today during the game: 'It's not that easy, no matter what. So learn what you've got to do and keep working. I think the biggest thing is the precise control with all your pitches.' He can throw a fastball at 97 by anybody, but when you get there and, I don't know, Chase Utley is up, you have to do a little something when you get to a 2-1 count. You need to be able to throw a breaking ball for a strike to keep him off guard or he's just going to cheat. So I think the more Zack figures out what he needs to do and really harnesses what he has, the sky is the limit. I think the world of Matt and I think Zack has equal or better stuff than him. Once he gets that down, those two in the future is an incredible deal."

Satin, a former political science major, tries to dial down his articulateness at times. He doesn't want to stand out as a Cal guy. But he'd spent years taking the long view and he'd had a front-row seat the last two years watching the growing pains of both Harvey and Wheeler.

"It's hard for a guy sometimes," Satin said, shouting over the music. "I don't want to say the franchise's future is in his hands, but that's what they make it seem like. They're banking the whole future on these guys."

Wheeler came out once he was finished with his shower, and after he'd put some clothes on I asked him to show me his fingernail. He smiled and held it up for me right away, and I was startled to see how black and blue—how ugly—it looked.

"You can see underneath it," he told me. "The blister gets underneath the nail and it pops. When it first happens, that's when it's really sore because the nail is actually detaching from the skin underneath. So that's not very fun. But that's already passed. I think it's still in the back of my head a little bit if I'm finishing pitches. So I'm still not getting around on my slider. It's a pain right now."

I didn't expect Wheeler to offer much in the way of self-revelation, but I was wrong. He has a quiet to him, not so much shy as self-contained, and it's easy to fall into that sportswriter habit of overvaluing lively quotes. More important than a gift for aphorism is the relaxed self-awareness to really show something.

Wheeler and I started talking about how he compared himself— and didn't compare himself—with Harvey. The two were going to throw together in Atlanta the previous off-season, since both had been living there, but Harvey decided to work out in New York for the off-season, so that didn't work out.

"He loves what he does," Wheeler said. "He gets up there and just pitches well every time. He's a competitor and he thinks he's the best. I think that's the mind-set you've got to have. That's what I've always had. I think like that. It's just I came off it a little bit, because coming in to pro ball that's what I had."

Too often ballplayers dealing with reporters—or authors—give quote, rather than actually speaking, like squeezing something out of a tube. Wheeler was speaking, directly and honestly, the telltale proof coming in how he paid attention to his own words. His eyes took on a different look, pointing toward some murky far-off corner of the locker room, and he almost flinched, so visibly did his demeanor suddenly change.

"Now that I've said it, it clicked in my head just now," he told me. "You've got to go out there and think that nobody can hit you. It got away from me the past year. You've got to just go out there and say: 'Hit it if you want. I'm me for a reason. I've worked my way to get to where I am. Try to hit me.'"

A week did not go by in May 2013 without a fresh call in the New York media for the Mets to get Wheeler up to the big team. The blister issues made it hard for Wheeler, who tended to start slow every season, to get in a groove. If he put together three straight commanding starts, that would be enough to signal to the Mets he was ready, and he finally did that over three starts leading up to May 11. Then he complained of discomfort in his right shoulder and was flown to New York for an MRI, just to be on the safe side, and scratched from his scheduled start on May 17. He was given a cortisone shot, but made two more appearances for Las Vegas by the end of the month, struggling again.

Wheeler's twenty-third birthday came on May 30, but the 51s were busy grinding out fifteen hits in an 11–1 win over Reno, so by the time the game was over, Wheeler didn't feel like doing much to celebrate. "I didn't do anything," he told me. "We played the game, and I went back to my apartment and packed for the road trip."

After the next night's game it was time for an all-night bus trip four hundred miles west to Fresno, through places like Barstow and Bakersfield.

"Do you ever sit on the bus thinking, 'Man, when I'm in the big leagues, it's going to be a little different'?" I asked Wheeler around then.

"Nah, not really," he said. "I just pass out."

By the night of that bus ride, the need for Wheeler in Queens—even a rough, unpolished version of Wheeler—was acute. The brief dopamine surge of the Mets' four-game sweep of the Yankees, an authentic achievement no matter how you looked at it, won them exactly nothing in the way of new momentum, confidence, or sense of purpose. They flew down from New York for a three-game set with the Marlins, the worst team in the league and losers of nine in a row at that point, and handed away the first game in the series, 5–1. Worse yet, reliable left-hander Jon Niese, the Mets' Opening Day starter, was scratched from his start with shoulder trouble. Wheeler's time was coming soon, and everyone felt it.

"We could bring him up for one day, but his last outing wasn't very good," Alderson told me on May 31. "Is this the best time to bring him up for a spot-start?"

Wally Backman, manager of the Triple-A Las Vegas 51s and a man who at times left the impression that he was campaigning in the press for a promotion, chose this juncture to proclaim that it was time to promote Wheeler. WALLY BACKMAN: ZACK WHEELER READY FOR THE BIG LEAGUES, ran the headline in *Newsday* on May 30, with the article declaring, "Zack Wheeler has nothing left to do at Triple-A Las Vegas. That's the take from his manager, Wally Backman. 'This kid's ready,' Backman said. 'He's ready to pitch in the big leagues.'"

If there was doubt about how ready Wheeler was, it made sense for the Mets to delay bringing him up. The so-called Super Two cutoff would occur shortly before June 15. Simply put, players who make their big-league debut early in a season become eligible for arbitration a year sooner than those who are brought up midway through the season, past the cutoff. As ESPN New York's Adam Rubin summed it up that May 12: "Ike Davis, as a frame of reference, did qualify for the extra year of arbitration and is earning $3.125 million this year because he debuted April 19, 2010. Teammate Dillon Gee—who missed the 'Super Two' cutoff because he debuted that September—is at a team-imposed $527,325."

If Wheeler had taken a major leap forward down at Las Vegas and gotten past his minor injuries and shown consistent command, the Mets would have been happy to call him up before the Super Two cutoff and put him to work helping them win games—and helping get the fans excited about the future. Wheeler was coming along, but not enough to force a decision on Alderson just yet. The Mets wanted to win as many games in 2013 as they could, since that was essential to moving forward, but the focus continued to be on building up talent to be ready in 2014.

"We're going to be judged on how we handle Wheeler and his success over time," Alderson said. "It's exactly what happened with Harvey. Let's bring him up at the right time. The worst thing we could do is rush him and take all the expectations people have about a pitcher like Wheeler and throw them in the trash. If we bring him up and he doesn't perform, those expectations are not just diminished, they are dashed. I'd like to do something impactful. In a way I'd love to bring up Wheeler and d'Arnaud at the same time, so the focus is: Let's look to the future! But if they're not ready, then you're simply digging a deeper hole."

The next evening, June 1, Wheeler took the mound in Fresno against the San Francisco Giants' Triple-A affiliate, the Grizzlies. At first pitch it was still 99 degrees at Chukchansi Park, a little gem of a ballpark built in 2002 in the post–Camden Yards wave of intimate venues with great sight lines. Just beyond the 324-foot left-field home-run pole, a view opened up of the handful of high-rises making up Fresno's downtown, with a lineup of old shops in the foreground, including such picturesque local institutions as Luftenburg's Bridal, open since 1941.

Wheeler figured at the center of the story the Mets wanted to promote about a bright immediate future, starring Harvey and Wheeler, two young guns who could hit 98, but that evening in Fresno Wheeler was surrounded by players likely to join him with the Mets before the year was out. Everyone knew Kirk Nieuwenhuis could play the outfield, but what about hitting big-league pitching consistently? He was batting only .233 for the 51s at that point. Pitchers David Aardsma, Gonzalez Germen, and Josh Edgin would all get a shot in the Mets bullpen before long. Maybe the hardest player to figure out was Josh Satin, who had struck me the first time I saw him as a lock to become a Mets fan favorite before long.

Satin could hit, hence his .312 average in Triple-A as of June 1, but his swing was not a thing of elegance—a scout would talk about extra motion; anyone else would say he reminded them of a beer-league slugger. Back at Cal, Satin had sat out a year because of injury, which put him a little behind schedule. He expected a major-league team to draft him after his redshirt junior year with the Golden Bears. "To be quite honest, he said his goodbyes," Cal coach David Esquer told the *San Francisco Chronicle*'s Steve Kroner. Satin admitted to being "really, really angry" when he was not drafted that year, but he told Kroner, "My work ethic turned up, like, twenty times." His last year at Cal, at age twenty-three, he hit .388 with 18 homers, and the Mets took him in the sixth round of the 2008 draft. Then at every step along the way, he'd hit well, but scouts would downgrade him because he was a little older. Satin was also hobbled by a lack of grace or easy athleticism and a lack of home-run power, though he was always good at knowing the strike zone and working a count. As a twenty-five-year-old, he hit .316 for Port St. Lucie in high-A with a .406 on-base percentage and .459 slugging percentage. At Double-A Binghamton the next year he batted .325 with a .423 on-base percentage and .538 slugging percentage. He'd had twenty-six at bats with the Mets by then, in 2011 and 2012, eking out just five hits, and all his efforts were focused on getting another shot.

"I think sometimes people overblow the fact that I'm an over-achiever," Satin told me. "Why am I an overachiever? I killed in high school, killed in college, killed in the minor leagues. I don't run well. I don't throw that well. Maybe that's what they're talking about. But I think that sometimes people see athletic ability and ability to move out there, and if you don't have it, then you're a huge overachiever. But for me, I think I definitely over time have figured out the best way for me to succeed offensively. I'm not saying by any means that I've mastered hitting or I'm like this hitting whiz, but just the way I take at bats I think in the long run is effective."

We talked a little about the Alderson philosophy of plate discipline, yes, but above all of looking for a pitch to drive. Call it controlled aggression.

"I know he teaches that philosophy and I don't do it because our *general manager* wants me to hit that way," he said. "It's just something that I've created for myself over the years. I was always very patient. I've really tried to hone in on how to manage patience with aggressiveness, because you can't just be patient all the time. I think sometimes people get a bad view of what Sandy wants. He doesn't want you to take pitches just to take pitches. He wants you to swing at your pitch. That's the whole key. I think in our minor-league system that gets lost in the shuffle. It gets misinterpreted a lot."

Satin, when he's done playing, might make a good coach or front-office executive.

"The whole key is early in the count, get something you can drive," he said. "That's what I live by: I'm not going to swing early unless it's something that I can really drive. Obviously, sometimes I get fooled, but that's the key to my philosophy of hitting."

It was *Star Wars* night at Fresno's Chukchansi Park, and as Wheeler warmed up down the line, the field swarmed with Imperial Stormtroopers. Obi-Wan and Darth Vader exchanged small talk. Something had clicked for Wheeler, whether it was that night in Vegas when he thought it had or at some other point in that stretch of the season. More and more Wheeler displayed the attitude he told me he had to have, an attitude of going with his best and letting that be enough, never in the flamboyant manner of Harvey, but in his own way. He came out in the first inning in Fresno with his fastball hitting 98 and recorded three straight infield groundouts, two of them on off-speed pitches, a sure sign of a pitcher trusting his stuff.

Fresno took a 1–0 lead in the bottom of the second when Wheeler couldn't get cleanup hitter Roger Kieschnick out on a full-count fastball, which he fouled off. Kieschnick singled, moved over on a ground ball, and then scored on a single, but Wheeler got out of the inning without further harm and was able to atone in the top of the third. I looked down at the stat sheet and noted Wheeler was hitting .222 with a .364 on-base percentage, not bad for a pitcher, and then looked up to watch Wheeler's big left-handed swing connect. He stroked a ball over his former teammate Gary Brown's head in center field and busted his butt running, wanting to stretch it to a double. He legged his way to second at full speed and then—unbelievably!—went up in the air and into a hard slide into second: safe. Somewhere, Alderson's heart stopped.

"That was probably the first time I slid since Little League, honestly," Wheeler told me. "After I slid I stood up and I looked back, and my slide mark went back a long way. I would have kept on going if the bag wasn't there. I got a little strawberry on my knee, so I felt like a real ballplayer."

Kirk Nieuwenhuis, up next, ripped a no-doubt-about-it home run to right and it was a good thing, too, because there were still no outs, and once Wheeler came around to score, he had a chance to hunch over in the dugout, drink some water in the 99-degree heat, and take a breather. Back on the mound for the bottom of the third, he had a languid, relaxed look throwing his warm-up tosses, even as he wiped his face on his uniform sleeve every so often. He turned to look toward center field for a minute, staring out at the Fresno skyline in a bid to calm himself even more. He had the confident, purposeful look of a pitcher who knew he had a lead and knew he wasn't going to give it up. He backed up that look, too. A 1-2-3 third, followed by a 1-2-3 fourth. In the fifth Fresno shortstop Carter Jurica came up with two outs and poked one through the left side of the infield for a single, but Wheeler struck out catcher Jackson Williams on an outside breaking ball to end the inning, leaving the crowd of 11,174 with nothing to cheer except Luke and Darth Vader having it out with lightsabers up on the roof.

Wheeler has an unusual mound presence for a tall power pitcher, low-key almost to the point of invisibility, but he also made it clear that he felt as comfortable out there as he would on his living-room sofa watching *Baseball Tonight*. That night in Fresno, he went through a routine before each inning, hunching his shoulders, throwing his last warm-up tosses, and then taking a few paces toward second base, having a small séance with himself, wiping his face, then kicking at the dirt just in front of the rubber, first with his right foot then his left, smoothing, smoothing, smoothing, and whether he was smoothing the dirt more or his nerves and focus more didn't really matter. This was not the same pitcher I saw in Vegas six weeks earlier. Back then Wheeler was searching for himself. In Fresno his focus was absolute.

"So you know what your batting average is right now?" I asked Wheeler after the game, which wound up a 2–1 victory for the 51s.

"No," he said with a smile.

".300—it says right here," I said, flapping the postgame box.

"After tonight?" he asked, grinning.

Wheeler knew how major a hurdle he had just cleared. He gave up only one walk in his six innings of three-hit ball to go with six strikeouts. He ran his record to 4-1 with a 3.86 ERA; he'd shown he was healthy and he knew the drill: He was almost spitting distance from his big-league debut. I asked him if he could almost taste it. "It's surreal that right now I'm only two good starts away," he told me. "You know what I mean? It's something I've looked forward to my whole life."

The major-league draft, often a splashy occasion, once again had a muted, underwhelming aspect for the Mets in 2013. Selecting eleventh overall, the Mets chose first baseman Dominic Smith, and once again they chose someone unlikely to show up in a Mets uniform any time soon. Smith was seventeen years old and had advanced as far as playing for Serra High School in Southern California. He was obviously talented, with scouts raving about his smooth swing, and had tremendous upside. But it was the third year in a row the Mets had used their first-round pick to select a high school student, following their choice of six-foot-three outfielder Brandon Nimmo out of Cheyenne, Wyoming, in 2011 and shortstop Gavin Cecchini from Lake Charles, Louisiana, in 2012, and that was a potentially frustrating development for fans seeing other teams use their picks to get players who could contribute within a year or two. High school picks were riskier, in general, besides taking longer to develop. The Mets said they were not drafting high school athletes as part of a larger plan, just taking the most talented player available when their turn came up. That was true as far as it went, especially with an organization pointing toward 2014 and then 2015, but it also fit with a deeper truth about the Mets under Alderson. They had Paul DePodesta overseeing a tightly run, analytically efficient, organized system for developing minor-league talent, based on the organizational goal of using every tool at their disposal to improve that talent by 30 percent. In stocking their farm system with risky but high-end young talent, they were showing how much they believed in that systematic approach and the value it could produce over time.

16

THE BEST DAY OF THE YEAR

In 2012, Alderson had opted not to have Matt Harvey make his big-league debut at home in New York, since as exciting as that might have been for the fans, far better to be on the road with less media attention and less pressure. In 2013, he would follow the same thinking on Zack Wheeler. For weeks Alderson had been talking about a doubleheader June 18 in Atlanta, when the Mets would need an extra starter, as a prime spot for Wheeler to make his debut, just sixteen miles from his boyhood home in Smyrna, Georgia. As it turned out, Matt Harvey would be starting the first game of the doubleheader, so calling Wheeler up to pitch the second game meant the day could turn into a showcase of young pitching talent.

Harvey, coming in with a 5-1 record and 2.04 ERA, started off Braves leadoff hitter Jordan Schafer with three straight fastballs to strike him out in nothing flat and looked so impressive that one out into the game, broadcaster Ron Darling was already thinking about seeing a special pitching performance that day.

"It's interesting," Darling observed, "the home plate umpire, Eric Cooper—an outstanding pitcher's umpire—he has been behind the plate for Hideo Nomo's no-hitter, both [Mark] Buehrle's no-hitter and perfect game, so I'm just saying."

"You're just saying," Gary Cohen replied.

It took Harvey all of ten pitches to work a 1-2-3 first with two strikeouts. He took care of the Braves in order in the second as well, then ran into a little difficulty in the third, walking two, but struck out Reed Johnson to end the threat. The Mets had picked up one run in the third on a Marlon Byrd RBI single and added another in the fourth on John Buck's leadoff homer, then Harvey really started to impress. Facing the heart of the Atlanta lineup, their 3-4-5 hitters in Jason Heyward, Freddie Freeman, and Chris Johnson, Harvey struck out all three, all three of them swinging, and did it in style. He got Heyward on three pitches—a 100-mile-an-hour fastball, a curve, and a changeup—then took care of Freeman on three pitches as well, striking him out on a high fastball that hit 98, and then needed six pitches, including two fastballs that hit 99, before he struck Johnson out on a breaking ball.

"He had no-hit stuff," Alderson said the next day. "This wasn't the first time he went deep into a game with no hits. Every time he goes out there and gets into the middle of the game without giving up a hit, it's a plausible result."

Gerald Laird put up a nine-pitch struggle before going down swinging in the bottom of the fifth, with Harvey mixing in a good slider and an excellent sharp-breaking curve, all enough to make Darling exclaim, "That's like a not fair kind of pitch there." Harvey struck out Dan Uggla, too, to run his streak to six straight strikeouts, all swinging, ten total.

By the sixth, it was getting interesting. David Wright made a nice play at third, roaming to his left to throw out pinch-hitter Tyler Pastornicky on just the kind of little infield chopper that so often seems to break up a no-hit bid, then Harvey struck out Scha-fer again. By this time, Gary Cohen was pointing out that Harvey was on the verge of having an ERA of less than 2.30 after the first twenty-five starts of his career, becoming the only Mets pitcher other than Dwight Gooden ever to do that. The game broadcast cut to a close-up of the Turner Field scoreboard showing a big "0" for hits for the Braves. Reed Johnson struck out with a wild swing on an outside breaking ball, and Harvey walked off the mound having tied his career high of twelve strikeouts.

For Zack Wheeler, watching all of this on the day he was about to make his big-league debut was both exciting and nerve-wracking. A tough act to follow! But Wheeler was never that kind of worrier. The night before, out for dinner with team captain David Wright, he'd told him he didn't even feel nervous. It all felt right, the way

he saw it, getting to pitch in the big leagues for the first time just
down the road from his hometown, the place loaded with relatives
and friends. Harvey's masterful performance through six just added
to the buzz in the air.

Heyward came out to lead off the bottom of the seventh for
the Braves and Harvey started him out with a breaking ball that
missed, but soon had him 1-2. This was a game of great sounds;
any time the Braves were up to bat, Harvey's fastball was popping
Buck's catcher's mitt with such force, it made almost a ringing
sound, like the sound of marimba music. The SNY team, to their
credit, picked up on it and put together sequences of the music of
Harvey's best fastballs. Then suddenly Harvey's 1-2 pitch struck a
discordant note. Heyward reached for an outside pitch and stroked
a ground ball that thudded off home plate awkwardly, making an
awful sound, and skittered up the first-base line. Harvey was off
the mound quickly, hurrying over to barehand it cleanly and toss
it to first—only no one was there to catch the ball. Lucas Duda,
despite seeing Harvey come off the mound to field the ball, had
just stood there, rather than going over to cover. It was an "error"
on his part as clear as day, but a mental error, so this one went in
the books as a hit.

The magic mood of the day evaporated, but Harvey got a
strike-'em-out, throw-'em-out double play and ended the inning
with a groundout. The Mets scored two runs in the top of the eighth
to make it 4–0, and in the bottom of the inning Harvey came out
after loading the bases on a walk and back-to-back singles. "He
ran out of gas," Alderson said at the time. "It's tough to strike out
thirteen in seven innings and pitch a complete game." All three
of those runners came around to score against LaTroy Hawkins,
working in relief, but the Mets held on to win the game 4–3. Harvey had now brought a no-hit bid into the seventh inning for the
third time in the season, having earlier done it against the Twins
and the White Sox.

The evening end of the doubleheader was a Wheeler fest. He'd
lived in Smyrna through junior high, then gone to East Paulding
High in Dallas, Georgia, only thirty miles away, and he'd played a

season of A ball for the GreenJackets in Augusta, 150 miles away, so people he knew from different places all converged on the Braves' home field for the game. "I probably knew a thousand people there at the game," Wheeler told me.

"There were family there we only see every few years at a family reunion," Zack's oldest brother, Jacob, told me. "Everybody was there. If anybody was going to be there, they were there."

Finally all the buildup was over and it was just Braves leadoff hitter Andrelton Simmons in the box and Wheeler out there on the mound, peering in for the sign from backup catcher Anthony Recker. "During the game, it was just me and the batter," Wheeler told me. "I didn't hear anybody. It's all the same noise when you're out there."

There wasn't too much suspense about which pitch he was going to throw for his first big-league toss. Wheeler bounced sideways a little, keeping loose, and then went into his motion and let fly with a low fastball that came in knee-high but missed outside by a couple of inches. His second pitch, also a fastball, was low and away. He took his time, trying to look cool, whatever the truth of the matter was, and came back with another fastball to the same spot, but this one caught the corner and home-plate umpire Paul Schrieber did not hesitate in raising his right hand and making an emphatic strike call. For the fourth pitch, Wheeler nodded quickly, as if he and his catcher were on the same page, but Recker set up inside again and this time Wheeler missed way outside. Simmons watched a low fastball go by for ball four and trotted down to first base.

Wheeler, clearly struggling, fell behind Heyward 2-0, but came back to strike him out on a 97-mile-per-hour fastball. He fell behind Justin Upton 2-0 as well, but got him to swing at an inside fastball for a groundout to Wright at third. Wheeler walked Freddie Freeman on four pitches, none close, and then stood on the mound using the back of his arm to wipe away some sweat from his face to try to collect himself in the warm, humid Georgia evening.

Wright came trotting over from third for a little mound conference to calm down the rookie starter, who had told him the night before he wasn't nervous.

"You're a liar," Wright told him, flashing his amiable grin. "You *do* look nervous."

Wheeler had to laugh at that.

"It calmed me down a little bit," he later told *Newsday*.

Facing B. J. Upton, Wheeler missed high again, as I'd seen him do back in Triple-A when he was struggling, flying open as the baseball people like to say, and again he fell behind 2-0. But he came back to get Upton on a groundout to third to end the inning. The two walks may have been the last thing he wanted for his debut inning, but the "0" worked out just fine.

"I've always had a problem walking people," Wheeler told me. "When you do that, people are going to score a lot of times. So I have this mentality: *If someone gets on base, whether by a hit or a walk, they might get to second base, but they're not going to get any farther than that.* You have to pull back and get in that little area in your mind where you know you have to concentrate a little more and just go after that guy."

Out for the second inning, Wheeler still had the blank look of someone fighting back a certain amount of raw terror, but everything else about him had changed. His first pitch was a good, crisp breaking ball that snapped in place for a called strike against Brian McCann. He followed that up with a well-placed fastball, in on the hands, and McCann could do nothing but foul it off harmlessly. It was Wheeler's first 0-2 count and he made the most of it, not messing around with a setup pitch, but coming right back with a 96-mile-per-hour fastball up above the belt to strike out McCann.

"He knows Heyward and McCann, he's been around hanging out with them at different events or whatever," Adam Wheeler told me. "It might have made him feel a little more comfortable facing people he actually knows."

Dan Uggla went up looking for a fastball, got one, and drilled it to the wall in left-center for a double, but then Wheeler struck out third baseman Chris Johnson on three pitches. That left only the pitcher, Paul Maholm, and Wheeler struck him out.

"Watching him shut down the team he grew up watching, you couldn't have written a better script," Jacob Wheeler told me.

Wheeler did not have a single 1-2-3 inning. But every time he had to have an out, he got it. In the fourth McCann and Uggla both flied out, then Johnson reached on a flare single—and Wheeler struck out the pitcher Maholm again. An inning later, Simmons led off with a single, but Wheeler got Heyward to hit into a double play and Justin Upton grounded out. Finally, in the sixth B. J. Upton singled with one out and stole second, and Wheeler walked McCann—but he ended the threat with a strikeout and a pop-up.

It was easily the best day of the year for the Mets: Harvey at his most dominating and Wheeler showing his talent, yes, but more important, his poise under pressure in pitching six shutout innings to pick up a victory in his major-league debut. "What was impressive was the way he got himself out of trouble," Alderson told me. "Unfortunately, his mechanics were not as tight as he would have liked, but that's a function of his youth and the circumstances. Given the number of base runners he had, his ability to focus and get out of trouble was terrific. It had the potential to be either a very good day or a very bad day for us, with all the pomp and circumstance surrounding Wheeler. It turned out to be very good."

Over his next two starts, Wheeler served to demonstrate why the Mets had left him in Triple-A as long as they had. He took a no-decision in Chicago with a rough outing against the White Sox and then pitched for the first time before the Citi Field fans on June 30 against the Nationals. Other than Josh Satin, who went 2-for-4 to lift his average with the Mets to .375 in the three weeks since his June 11 call-up, the rest of the lineup eked out only three hits against Gio González, and the divisional rival Nationals coasted to an easy win after putting up four runs against Wheeler in the second. He'd looked in control in the first inning, then Adam LaRoche swung at the first pitch he saw to open the second, a belt-high fastball on the inner half of the plate, and lofted it to right field for a home run. Wheeler looked rattled after that and the Mets were never in the game, which ended up a 13–2 Nationals rout.

Among the fans at Citi Field for Zack Wheeler's first home start with the Mets was his brother Adam, a former pitcher in the Yankees organization. As far as Adam was concerned—and he'd had his look at plenty of players working their way up to the big leagues—the Mets had waited just long enough to bring Zack up, giving him enough starts for him to get over struggling with his command. "The timing was perfect," he told me.

Everyone loves a great story line, and as compelling as it would have been if Wheeler simply dominated in his first weeks with the Mets, there was something raw and unpredictable—and very human—about watching him feel his way. A lot of the best information that can be gleaned during a baseball game comes from indirect observation: You listen to the sound of bat on ball and watch the outfielder tracking a deep fly to get a sense of whether you're looking at a home run or a long out, or you watch how hitters react to a fastball to get a sense of how good a pitch it was. Technology has gotten us to the point where cameras can track not only the exact path of a thrown ball and the exact speed, but also the exact spin, to plot total kinetic energy, and for all that mind-boggling analytical capability, still the best single test is to watch how hitters react. Wheeler's fastball has that late action that makes it hard to hit, and time and again, hitters were surprised to see that action up close for the first time.

Wheeler himself kept offering glimpses of being more of a potential star pitcher than first met the eye. For example, one of the traditions of baseball is that accomplished veteran pitchers routinely get calls that rookies do not. In a sense it sounds crazy: A ball either catches the corner or it doesn't. But the way it works is often rookies get hazed, in effect, by having to deal with unfair calls. In his time overseeing the umpires as Major League Baseball's executive vice president for baseball operations, Alderson tried to curtail this practice, but it was too deeply embedded in the culture of baseball.

Wheeler, in his first starts in the big leagues, faced a large number of such calls, especially in his first game in Atlanta. He was, as the saying goes, getting squeezed. The interesting part was how he reacted. Often young pitchers who don't get a call they think they deserve come unglued. They let it get to them. Wheeler was just the opposite. Again and again he shook off any agitation and put it behind him.

"I had a kind of routine before every start where I'd walk out to stretch before I went to the bullpen before the game," Wheeler told me. "John Buck and the pitching coach, Dan Warthen, would be there and every time I'd say, 'Who is behind home plate?' Buck and Warthen would tell me who the home-plate umpire was and how to act. Sometimes you could throw it down the middle and he's going to call it a ball, just to see how you'll react. So just get the ball back and go about your business and throw another pitch. And that's exactly what I did. Just get the ball back and pitch again, and pretty soon they're going to call it. They're great umpires and you have to respect them. They've put their time in."

Alderson noticed how Wheeler reacted—and was pleased. We talked about how during that first outing in Atlanta Wheeler was clearly getting squeezed and not getting some calls, and Alderson replied: "We commented on that as well. There was a check swing. There was a play at second where we didn't get the call. He also didn't get the call on some pitches just off the plate."

Facing the Brewers in Milwaukee on July 5, the Mets having lost back-to-back games to fall to 35-47, Wheeler had to fight through more adversity. He ran into trouble early, giving up two runs in the bottom of the first after a Daniel Murphy error made a bad situation worse, and had some control issues, finishing with three walks to go with only three strikeouts, but he held Milwaukee to three runs (one earned) over five innings to put the Mets back in the win column and earn the victory. Wheeler was not wowing anyone with his pitching lines at that point, and he was not going to wow anyone with his postgame quotes. That was never the point.

"He's doing OK," Alderson said that week. "He does not have the same savoir faire as Harvey. Zack is a country boy. That's how he sounds and that's how he portrays himself."

But Wheeler may have understood his role better than people thought. Alderson himself talked often about the delicate balancing act to keep expectations hearty, but not let them get out of hand. Harvey fired himself up by letting everyone know he wanted to be the best; he raised expectations and then set about living up to them. Wheeler's style was in a way more human: He never cared much about expectations; he cared about going out there and pitching well. He accepted both ends of the spectrum, the days when all his pitches felt like yo-yos on a string, he had so much control over them, and the days when he kept blankly staring at another fastball tailing way out of the zone. "Sometimes when you have better control that day, you can overthrow, because it's more than likely to be a strike," he told me. "There are certain days you can do that and days you can't do that. You just have to know how you're doing that day."

If it was simply a matter of will, he'd have eliminated the wild days long ago. But a pitcher's development is more complex and inscrutable than that. Wheeler had to live through days of wildness to get to the next step, and he understood that necessity. There was no cutting in this line: He had to put in the time to know himself and the intricacies of pitching at the big-league level. His first Mets season was only a first step. "I should have done better, but I'm happy with it," he told me. "There's always something you can get better in."

17

"COME ON, BLUE!"

August 13, 2013, was a date to circle on the calendar: Matt Harvey, the talk of baseball, was pitching at Dodger Stadium against Hyun-Jin Ryu and Alderson would be there in the stands to watch. From a few weeks out it looked likely to be exciting, but by the week beforehand the buzz was almost overwhelming: The Dodgers, a team listless and lost through some stretches of the season, twelve games under .500 on June 21 despite a payroll well over $200 million, were now playing with a giddy, reckless energy most attributed to the arrival of young Cuban force of nature Yasiel Puig. The Dodgers had won six straight and were hoping to push it to their first seven-game winning streak in three years.

Harvey stood in the way. Based on everything they'd seen from him so far that season, the Dodgers might as well have been going up against Jason Bourne in a fistfight. Fans have been heading down to spring training for generations in search of the thrill of watching young talent unfold before their eyes, but it was rare to see a player come into his own so convincingly over the course of a big-league season. As recently as the year before, many scouts had projected Harvey as a number two or three starter. Now he was looking not only like a true ace, but the kind of ace who can single-handedly take you deep into the postseason. Whatever new thinking had come along to transform baseball, some ages-old baseball truisms remained on the money: Big-game pitchers win big games. An outsized sense of confidence and mission on the mound really can pay off in key moments when a player has all the physical tools to back up the strut.

Harvey's performance in the 2013 All-Star Game four weeks earlier on July 16 was one that sent a message to every hitter in the game. It all sounded so perfect: the first All-Star Game held at Citi Field, David Wright starting at third, and the young gun Harvey on the hill for the National League. It was audacious of Harvey to have his eyes set on the prestige start his first full year in the big leagues, but Harvey's audacity was as much a part of his persona as Woody Allen's glasses were of his.

Often the All-Star Game is boring, but from the first pitch this one was riveting. It was comical in a way, watching Harvey go through his warm-up tosses as American League leadoff hitter Mike Trout got ready to take his chances. Harvey loves the attention, loves being at the center of the spotlight, so much so he seems like a guy who would take up fire-eating if it was the only way to draw a crowd—and he'd be the absolute best fire-eater around, count on it. Standing on the mound at Citi Field, surrounded by a packed house, his every twitch captured on national television, he was grinning underneath the poker face. He wound up and unleashed his first pitch—a fastball, of course—and Trout hit it crisply to right for a leadoff double. That brought up Robinson Cano and Harvey promptly drilled him. His 1-0 pitch, a 96-mile-an-hour fastball, darted right for Cano's knee. There was a horrible instant where everyone, Harvey included, flashed on what it would mean if a Mets pitcher's errant toss exploded the knee of the franchise player of the Yankees. The ball just missed the more delicate structures of Cano's knee, but still left a contusion on the leg. No one thought Harvey was trying to hit Cano, but even so, as Cano trotted down to first, Harvey made a point of telling him he was sorry.

The stage was set for a fascinating range of possibilities from wizardry to epic collapse. Harvey had hungered for this chance and here he was wobbling badly. Two runners on base, no outs, and now he had to contend with the best hitter in the American League, Miguel Cabrera. He worked Cabrera to 2-2, showcasing his slider and changeup as well as his fastball, and then struck him out. Harvey had found his focus now, and he got Chris Davis to fly out to center and then struck Jose Bautista out to end the inning. David Ortiz stroked a ball to deep center to lead off the second, but Bryce Harper ran it down, then Harvey struck out Adam Jones and Joe Mauer lined out to left for a 1-2-3 inning. It was a virtuoso performance, a showcase of all his pitches and all his nerve, and it confirmed what many were saying about Harvey: This one has something special.

Five days later, back at Citi Field, Harvey worked seven shutout innings in the Mets' 5–0 win over the Phillies and the next night Dillon Gee threw six innings of no-hit ball against the Braves before the bullpen faltered late. Eight days later in Miami, it was Zack Wheeler's turn to put on a show: A 1-2-3 first, a 1-2-3 second, and a 1-2-3 third. He walked a batter in the fourth and one in the fifth, but still no hits for the Marlins. Could it be? Could Wheeler do what Harvey and Gee had threatened to do?

"He was incredible the first three innings," Alderson said later. "I think he only threw four balls. His pitch count was low throughout the entire game, just pounding the strike zone, hitting the corners. His command was phenomenal."

Wheeler went out in the sixth and again it was 1-2-3.

"He got through six with the no-hitter and was dominant," Alderson said. "Then in the seventh he got [Giancarlo] Stanton out, walked the next hitter, and gave up an off-field single to Ed Lucas, who was actually a teammate of Bryn's at Dartmouth."

Wheeler gave up two runs in the seventh and ended up with a no-decision, but the Mets came back to win. Still, it was a breakthrough game, clear proof of how Wheeler was developing—and signs of what was to come. Alderson had told me he expected Harvey and Wheeler to challenge each other and that was just what was happening.

"He's very quiet, Zack," David Wright told me. "He has an inner confidence about him, which is what you want in a pitcher. Whereas Matt is probably a little more outgoing, they have that same confidence. They feel like no matter who is in that batter's box, that they're better than them. The biggest part I think is they can feed off of each other. Zack can watch Matt and see the way he goes about his business and take something from that. And as much as Matt would probably never admit it, I think he could watch Zack and learn a little bit from that as well. A good competition to have at the top of your rotation is two hungry, young pitchers that want to outdo each other and grab those headlines."

All over baseball, hitters were sitting around in groups to discuss Harvey the way that fishing-boat captains talk about incipient gales. His performance against the Rockies on August 7 was the kind to have them shaking their heads. Harvey pitched the first complete-game shutout of his big-league career, giving up just four hits and no walks over nine innings, but the truly impressive part was how he did it: going right at hitters, getting outs on groundouts, and not trying to strike every guy out. The commanding performance lifted his record to 9-3 and dropped his ERA to 2.09, second in the league behind the Dodgers' Clayton Kershaw, setting up an interesting contest to see if Harvey might snag a Cy Young Award in his first full season. Since the All-Star Game he'd struck out thirty-one hitters in his four starts and walked only one.

That was the setup for Harvey's August 13 start at Dodger Stadium. I was expecting Alderson's intensity to be on full display beforehand, but he was relaxed and cheerful. We'd had a plan to meet in the long, sleek visiting-team dugout, which at Dodger Stadium extends down the first-base line, but when I arrived there Alderson was nowhere to be found, so I went looking for him and circled back around and spotted him on the Mets' bench, sitting alone in a tangerine button-down shirt and khaki slacks, his legs poking out in front of him in relaxed fashion. It was like J. P. Ricciardi had told me, Alderson has in some ways mellowed with time. He was intent on enjoying himself, at least for a few minutes, and it was the kind of evening hard not to enjoy, picture perfect in every way, the old ballpark—third oldest in baseball after Fenway and Wrigley— looking its age but good, like a restored '57 Chevy. It was the first time I'd been there since a $100 million renovation before the 2006 season that included replacing most of the seats and going back to the old color scheme with hues like turquoise and sky blue. Out in left field, where Alderson's gaze was directed, a huge American flag hung loosely, moving ever so slightly now and then, like a cat's tail.

We ended up meeting down near the front door to the visiting-team clubhouse, where I'd killed time looking at a lineup of the

Gold Glove Awards won by various Dodgers over the years. Dusty Baker won a Gold Glove for the Dodgers in 1981? Never knew that. Fernando Valenzuela in '86? That one I remembered. The renovation of Dodger Stadium was even more notable down here in the tunnels connecting the clubhouses with various other chambers, and the echoes of history resounded agreeably. Alderson and I looked around a little, then went to get something to eat in the bustling Dugout Club behind home plate.

Dinner with Alderson was enjoyable, but it had me thrown. Where was the man whose friend—and physician—had to lecture him years earlier that if he kept living and dying with every pitch during games, he wasn't going to last very long? Where was the man who sometimes used to get in his car and drive around rather than sit still for the end of a game? We looked for some seats well away from the Mets dugout, so as not to call attention to Alderson's presence at the game with a member of the press, but found nothing, so ended up sitting in his assigned seats, a dozen or so rows back from the dugout. We stood for the national anthem along with the 46,333 other people at the ballpark that night, and had barely sat back down when, four pitches into the game, promising young Mets center fielder Juan Lagares stunned Ryu by connecting on a 1-0 pitch that hit the top of the left-field wall and bounced over, putting the Mets ahead by a run before Harvey had even taken the mound.

As Harvey came out to take his warm-up tosses, with music ringing out in the warm evening, it dawned on me that Alderson was so relaxed and friendly at dinner in part because he was genuinely excited and upbeat about watching Harvey pitch. This was good news for the Mets, an agreeable surprise that suddenly had both fans and team officials looking ahead to many years of Harvey anchoring the Mets' rotation. He had been so impressive in his last start against the Rockies and so consistent all season, so often showcasing no-hit stuff, it was fun to wonder what he might bust out with this time.

Harvey, given a lead, took care of the Dodgers quickly in the bottom of the first, striking out Carl Crawford and Mark Ellis and getting Adrian Gonzalez to ground out. Alderson was far from at ease. When I say he was in a good mood, I don't mean he took anything for granted. Never. But Harvey had looked in command in the first, and even with the Dodgers as hot as they were, he was the kind of guy to cool them off. We started talking about his Cy Young chances.

"Even if he gets to fifteen wins, it could be hard," Alderson said. But clearly he was not counting Harvey out, any more than he'd counted out his chances of starting the All-Star Game. Josh Satin and Justin Turner both grounded out to start off the Mets' second, and then catcher John Buck worked a walk, earning sarcastic praise from Alderson, since walks weren't exactly Buck's thing.

Talking about his expectations for Travis d'Arnaud, still at that point awaiting his big-league debut, Alderson inevitably touched on what he wanted to see in his batting.

"The key is making sure like everybody else that he's disciplined, has a good approach and doesn't give away at bats," he said. "We saw that demonstrated very well in Vegas his first month there before he got hurt."

Omar Quintanilla struck out to strand Buck at first and then it was Harvey's turn to head back out. Yasiel Puig reached on an infield single, but no problem, Harvey fielded Skip Schumaker's comebacker and threw to second to start a double play. A. J. Ellis grounded out to short to end the inning, and Alderson clapped his hands together, eager to see more production at the plate. Up until this point, we'd been talking a lot, discussing his time in the Marines, the old days in Oakland, but now I felt his level of focus take an uptick or two and I wanted to let him concentrate.

Harvey struck out to start the Mets' half of the third. Eric Young Jr. worked the count full, and then ended up getting called out on a close pitch, not the first of the night home-plate umpire Jeff Kellogg had called against the Mets. I tried not to flinch when an eruption of sound next to me split the evening air.

"Come on, blue!" Alderson shouted, startling me with his intensity.

Lagares grounded out to end the inning. A one-run lead on the road never feels comfortable, especially with the way the Dodgers had been coming back in games. Again in the bottom of the inning, Harvey gave up a leadoff single, this time to Juan Uribe, and again the Mets erased him with a double play and then got out of the inning on a groundout.

Harvey got into more trouble in the bottom of the fourth inning. A walk and a single put two on, but Gonzalez flied out and Puig hit into a 4-6-3 double play. There was by then a strong sense of Harvey pushing his luck. He couldn't keep getting double plays to clean up stray runners.

"When was the last time he had a 1-2-3 inning?" Alderson asked. "Not since the first?"

Sure enough, the Dodgers put two on base in the fifth on a walk and a single, and this time, no double play. Instead, number eight hitter Nick Punto doubled to drive in both runs. Then in the sixth, two more Dodgers singled to set the table and A. J. Ellis hit a two-run single, and just like that, the Mets were down 4–1. Harvey was done after the sixth.

There was a feeling of anticlimax once he was gone. It had been like that all season, a sense of the air going out of the balloon once Harvey had departed, but this time was different. He hadn't been the life of the party this time. Something was off. He didn't seem quite like himself. He looked more like the number three starter some scouts had projected him as a year or two earlier instead of the dominating All-Star force of nature he had become.

Alderson was eager to get down to the clubhouse and find out what he could about Harvey's outing. It was a 4–2 loss, dropping Harvey to 9-4. He finished with only three strikeouts, tying the lowest for his career, and as *Newsday* reported, by way of the Elias Sports Bureau, he snapped a streak of twenty-six straight starts with at least ten swings and misses, the longest such streak in the majors. Dodgers hitters missed only five of his pitches.

Buck's wife went into labor three days later and he took paternity leave, so as planned the Mets called Travis d'Arnaud up from Vegas and he made his major-league debut on August 17, 2013, against the Padres. D'Arnaud drew a walk in his first major-league at bat, one of two in the game, but went hitless. His first big-league hit came on August 20 against the Braves.

A week later on August 27, just after the Pittsburgh Pirates dropped out of first place, came the announcement that in order to add to their offense, the Pirates were trading touted infield prospect Dilson Herrera and a player to be named later (who turned out to be hard-throwing reliever Vic Black) for Marlon Byrd. The Pirates also received catcher John Buck in the deal.

Harvey bounced back in San Diego on August 18, giving up just two runs in six innings his next start, with no walks and six strikeouts, but getting a no-decision. But on Saturday, August 24, the Tigers knocked him around for thirteen hits in 6⅔ innings. He gave up only two runs, but it was not a Matt Harvey–like performance.

Team physician David Altchek examined Harvey that Monday. At 1:23 P.M. he sent Alderson a text.

"Sandy, just saw Matt—can you call me at the office?" he wrote.

This was not the kind of text any GM ever wants to see, and Alderson, predictably, felt a sense of "foreboding" when he called and heard the bad news: Harvey had a torn ligament in his elbow and would in Altchek's opinion require surgery.

It was a huge punch in the gut for the whole organization. Harvey had electrified the season with his talent and command. He embodied the sense of hope for the future. "I was enjoying the season up to the point where Harvey got hurt," Alderson told me. "Our trajectory was upward. We'd been playing well. There was a lot of enthusiasm for our young players. They were developing. Harvey was pitching great. Wheeler was pitching better than most people expected him to pitch this early in his career. Niese was back, the whole rotation was solid, the bullpen was pitching well, and d'Arnaud had just arrived. Lagares was playing great in center. We were getting some contributions from other guys. Then Harvey got hurt and the conversation changed immediately to the doom and gloom of the Mets' history with injuries."

Harvey did not immediately agree to have Tommy John surgery, thinking he might try to rest and rehab instead, citing the example of Roy Halladay. Alderson doubted avoiding surgery was going to be an option, but it was hard to force Harvey to accept the inevitable.

He had a deer-in-the-headlights look when they met to discuss what to do, Alderson told me. One issue was that doctors did not always give players as blunt a report as they did team officials. As a result, the Mets had a communication issue on their hands—and Alderson got involved, personally writing the Mets' press release on Harvey and his choice to try rest before making the decision for surgery, then showing it to Harvey and his agent, Scott Boras.

"I drafted the release and we ran it by Matt and our lawyers and ran it by Scott," Alderson said. "Our doctor was pretty blunt with Matt: 'You've got to have the surgery.' But Matt didn't want to have the surgery."

Was it rare for him to write a press release himself?

"I don't draft every press release," he said. "In a year I'll probably do four or five, max. If I'm going to have to expand on the press release anyway, doing a draft helps me to organize my own thinking."

The news on Harvey's future was devastating and scary, but then a strange thing happened: The sky did not fall. As recently as a year or two earlier, Mets fans were so demoralized by years of losing and seeing highly paid players like Jason Bay join the Mets and contribute almost nothing, this kind of bad news would have unleashed a tornado of vitriol. Media voices used to jumping all over the Mets for another miscue or blunder would be poised to sink in their teeth and not let go. Matt Harvey, their best pitcher, was going to be out of action for all of the next season, at the very least a vicious setback, but instead of despairing, many fans instead saw it as a sign of how far they'd come. Roughly one-quarter of all big-league pitchers have had Tommy John surgery at some point, and many come back stronger than they were before. There was every reason to think Harvey—intense, young, and fit—would work hard on his rehabilitation and come back just as strong as he was.

"The injury put a dent in everything," Paul DePodesta told me in October 2013. "But there's so much more hope and optimism that surrounds the team than did twelve months ago and there are good reasons for that. That optimism is both external and internal. Hopefully for us the hardest slog is behind us, especially emotionally. Our future shouldn't hinge on one player. That one player might help, and will help, when he comes back. But we have other guys. Having Zack Wheeler step up and pitch better and better, seeing Travis d'Arnaud there at the end of the year, and knowing what Noah Syndergaard and Rafael Montero are doing in the minor leagues, the Harvey injury hurt, but it's more of a speed bump than a dead end."

Syndergaard, six-foot-six and 240, was 6-1 for Double-A Binghamton in 2013 with a 3.00 ERA, featuring an excellent fastball. *Baseball America* rated him as the Mets' top prospect, higher even than d'Arnaud, who came to the Mets in the same trade as Syndergaard. Third was Montero, more of a control pitcher, who was 5-4 with a 3.05 ERA for Las Vegas.

"The Mets believe they have as much pitching depth as anybody," *Baseball America* wrote in November 2013. "For proof, they can point to the fact that their pitchers at the full-season levels finished with a collective 2.79 K-BB ratio, better than any of the other twenty-nine organizations."

The Mets could also point to the second two-thirds of the 2013 season as offering clear signs of progress. They were 24-38 on June 14. Four days later, when Harvey and Wheeler won both games of a doubleheader in Atlanta, the season took a new direction. Juan Lagares hit better than expected and played excellent defense in center field, showing he could go back on the ball as well as anyone, sometimes spectacularly, helping jump-start the team. From June 14 onward, over the last one hundred games of the season, the Mets played .500 ball. Merely playing .500 is not enough to satisfy fans, nor is it enough to satisfy Sandy Alderson and the front office, or the owners, or anyone in the organization. But when the dust cleared, Harvey had his surgery and he was immediately proclaimed to be "ahead of schedule" on his rehab, and it started to seem like not so bad a scenario, having him back in 2015 and giving Zack Wheeler and the klatch of other talented young pitchers in the organization more time to develop.

"Matt will come back stronger, I know he will," Wheeler told me. "He's a hard worker and he's going to want to prove to people that he's strong—that's just the way he is. He's going to come back and win a Cy Young, that's for sure."

Going into the 2013 off-season, the challenges for Alderson, Ricciardi, and DePodesta were many. But at least the Harvey setback and its aftermath had given them proof of the progress they had made so far. They wouldn't get much more time to show the system-wide improvement was real, but they could look forward to spring training 2014 in a better frame of mind than any spring since Alderson took over.

Taking a smart approach to being a GM was in many ways not that different from taking smart at bats: In both cases, preparation and focus were key, and you were always going to do better if you went in looking not with one fixed idea, like crushing the first pitch you saw for a moon shot home run, but instead stayed alert and nimble. The trade that brought Wheeler to the Mets was in retrospect a home run, and so was the R. A. Dickey trade to Toronto for d'Arnaud, Syndergaard, and Wuilmer Becerra. To continue the metaphor, in both cases Alderson and his front office got pitches they could drive—and they didn't miss. It might not have worked out that way. Alderson was ready to take a less attractive package from the Texas Rangers for Beltrán, and when it came to Dickey, he was pleased that Toronto offered as much as it did. But in the work of building a team, the splashy moves were no more crucial than all the little stuff, call it situational hitting, the GM equivalent of getting a runner over or scoring a run with a sacrifice fly. This was the challenge Alderson and the Mets faced going into the 2013 off-season.

"It's very easy in New York to succumb to pressure," Wright told me. "The day Sandy got here, he said there was a plan in place. Maybe a lot of fans don't exactly agree with that plan, or like the process it's taken, the years that it's taken, but Sandy sticks to his guns. He believes in the process. I believe in the process. That, I think, is one of the greatest attributes that he's brought here. There hasn't been an impulse buy. There hasn't been an impulse trade. He hasn't succumbed to the pressure that is mounting on us to put a winner on the field now. He wants to win, but he wants the winning to be sustained. He wants to build from the bottom up and make sure that when we are able to compete that we're there for the long run."

PART III
LINE IN THE SANDY

Alderson (right) addresses a healthy throng of media before a Mets game at Citi Field during the 2014 season.

18

HANGIN' WITH JAY-Z

If Sandy Alderson was by the spring of 2014 gaining an acute sense of just how aggravating and nerve-fraying the job of being a major-league general manager had become, he was in part bearing the brunt of trends he had set in motion himself. Being smart was no longer a novelty. Thinking baseball challenges through in a systematic way, backed up by analytic tools and ever-greater stockpiles of data, did not set one apart. There were too many baseball front offices chock-full of smart young guys (and, finally, not only guys) who'd learned from the early excesses of the number crunchers and could use very sophisticated analysis in tandem with traditional baseball methods, like trusting a scout's eye, and were also well positioned to gain from the biggest revolution in the game, which was not computers but cameras: So much information was now available, player performance could be reliably evaluated as never before.

Alderson knew when he accepted the Mets job that New York was going to be a whole different world than Oakland. Alderson liked the challenge of edgy New York, compared with more laid-back California, so long as a certain built-in mawkishness to the sports media culture, forever reacting emotionally on behalf of the overly emotional fan, did not become too unwieldy. The certainty of blunt, tough criticism was not the issue. The difference had mostly to do with the toxic sludge left over from year after year after year of media negativity toward the Mets.

The wonder going into the 2014 season was that the press gave the Mets as much of a break as they did. Part of it was simple disbelief. They couldn't *really* be planning to hold their payroll down around

$85 million, could they, despite being a team in the largest market in the country with their own cable network and a shiny new ballpark? They couldn't *possibly* propose crawling into the 2014 season with a payroll among the lowest in all of baseball, could they? Maybe the excitement of one year earlier had bought a little time, Matt Harvey looking like he was ready to single-handedly deliver the franchise from the years in the desert, back to relevance and sexy good fun. The heartbreak of Harvey needing Tommy John surgery pushed everything back a year, but that didn't mean 2014 was over before it started. The fans would still be coming out and they had every right to expect a competitive, dynamic team. But caution about spending, extreme caution, would remain the rule.

Alderson found himself sustained through the winter by his sense of humor and the joy he'd always taken in the absurd. His own situation was in many ways absurd and he knew it. He took the job with the Mets with the expectation of being able to put in place a system that would twin intelligent baseball decision-making and talent-nurturing management structures, on the one hand, with a payroll robust enough to move forward in a timely way on improving the team. Instead, because of the way the Madoff scandal engulfed the Mets, Alderson was back to the baseball version of duct tape and ingenuity, trying to get by on less.

"Madoff wasn't even a topic of conversation in my interview for the Mets job," Alderson told me. "I didn't raise it. Maybe I should have. The bottom line is, I would have taken the job anyway. It just added to the challenge. At the time I took the job our payroll was about $140 million and I thought that's probably too high to sustain, based on attendance. We got down to $85 million."

To be clear, the defining characteristic of Alderson's attitude toward this shift in fortune was one of wry amusement. Maybe it was the former Marine lieutenant in him, but he took a kind of pride in shaking off even a mammoth shift in fortunes with a dry chuckle and using a fresh set of eyes to survey the landscape to take in absolutely every detail he could about the challenge now in front of him. Fresh setbacks were always a possibility.

The general manager meetings at Disney World in early November 2013 brought no breakthroughs for the Mets, who went in looking to trade one of their first basemen, Lucas Duda or Ike Davis. "The media can't understand why we would prefer Duda over Davis," Alderson told me on November 13. "The fact is the market prefers Duda over Davis. We could definitely trade Duda."

The problem was none of the half dozen potential trades being discussed was very appealing from a Mets standpoint. It was not smart to do a deal just to do a deal, especially since they were still not sure which player they preferred. Alderson leaned toward Duda, but without a lot of conviction. Still, he expected to resolve the Duda-Davis question well before spring training. On November 21, he told me the Mets were still exploring their options on a trade for either player and "that could stretch to the winter meetings" in early December.

Alderson, Ricco, Ricciardi, and DePodesta had met with shortstop Jhonny Peralta during the GM meetings in Florida. Their need to upgrade at shortstop was well known and Peralta, a veteran with some home-run pop, having hit at least twenty homers in four of his nine full seasons in the big leagues, and a consistent .260-plus batter, was in many ways a good fit. It was a perfunctory meeting and Alderson came away with the sense that whoever signed Peralta was going to overpay. Even so, Alderson openly admitted to being surprised when Peralta signed a four-year, $53 million contract with the St. Louis Cardinals that month. It was one of many signs that month that teams were willing to overpay for midlevel players. That had partly to do with an infusion of money from lucrative new local TV contracts worth from $75 million up to $200 million a year, and also to do with the influence of the so-called Boston model, the approach of buying up a lot of midlevel players and hoping some of them had breakout seasons.

Even as press speculation had the Mets emulating this model, Alderson's main focus in late 2013 was in fact Yankees second baseman Robinson Cano, one of the best hitters in baseball, who over the four previous seasons had hit better than .300 every year with more than twenty-five home runs and an average of 107 RBIs. Alderson had to play down the possibility in the press, but in fact he was deeply intrigued by the prospect of landing Cano for the Mets and saw it as a long shot, but far from out of the question. It was a little like shopping for wine: If table wine had suddenly become way overpriced, it just might be that, relatively speaking, the Vintner's Reserve Robert Parker–blessed go-for-it bottle might in fact be more cost-effective.

It would take big money to land Cano, no question, but Alderson believed that teams were being scared away by a potentially huge asking price, and the actual outlay needed to attract Cano might be far less than expected. The wild card was Cano's new agent, the music mogul Jay-Z, whose influence on Cano was hard to gauge. What seemed clear, though, was that, all things being equal, if the choice did not hinge on money, Jay-Z and Cano would be far more likely to sign a deal with the Mets than with some other clubs, so Cano could stay in New York, where he'd spent all nine seasons of his big-league career, a move that would make a huge splash in the media and swing the focus over to the Mets.

That was the backdrop for an intriguing Monday, November 20, dinner at a new restaurant in midtown Manhattan called NoMad. In attendance? Alderson, Ricco, and Jeff Wilpon on the Mets side, as well as Jay-Z and agent Brodie Van Wagenen, who worked with Jay-Z. Cano had turned down an offer from the Yankees, believed to be for seven years and $160 million, and some of the more hyperventilating media speculation had it that he'd end up signing a megadeal for more than $300 million. The dinner at least served to take this last figure out of the discussion.

"They're not looking for $300 million," Alderson told me the next day. "What a surprise."

Van Wagenen did most of the talking, making a full presentation with PowerPoint and the various other accoutrements of such sessions. Alderson, Wilpon, and Ricco played it all as a mere get-acquainted session, sizing up Jay-Z, who was new to the sports-agent business, and trying to gauge whether a deal might be possible.

"Jay-Z was pretty nice," Alderson said. "He wasn't arrogant. He came across as a regular guy. I don't even know what he sings.

I couldn't identify a Jay-Z record. It felt like just another meeting, but it's always interesting to meet a celebrity, not because I'm a big celebrity follower, but to compare the reality with the celebrity persona."

Earlier in our conversation, Alderson had made another reference to being a celebrity follower, albeit in a more aggravating context for him. I asked if there was an update on Matt Harvey. This was less than a month after the Mets star pitcher had Tommy John surgery performed by Dr. James Andrews on October 22 in Gulf Breeze, Florida, so I had in mind news on his medical recovery. "He went to Moscow with his girlfriend," Alderson said.

That would be Anne Vyalitsyna, a *Sports Illustrated* swimsuit model, who had already posted pictures of Harvey and her in Red Square with St. Basil's Cathedral in the background.

Alderson and I discussed Cano more than once in those weeks, and the idea was clearly far less of a long shot than it appeared in the press. "It would be a game changer for us," he said. "But you realize that if it ever gets down to a reasonable number, less than $200 million and more than $150, he'd probably stay with the Yankees. I do believe he would only leave the Yankees to come to the Mets."

Then again, Alderson cautioned, maybe talking to himself as much as to me, "If Jay-Z gets less than $200 million for Cano, I think he's open to criticism from another agent, who can say, 'I could have gotten more than that.'"

Alderson was serious enough about the Cano option that he told me he planned to call David Wright to discuss it, just to sound out the team captain and make sure he'd be on board with the possibility. Six days later when we talked, Alderson still hadn't called Wright—but he had called Cano's agent, this after telling me the week before they needed to "sit tight." Clearly the Cano possibility had Mets people excited. Cano's agent had put in a call to Alderson the week before and, not wanting to appear too eager, Alderson waited a few days to call back—until just before the Thanksgiving holiday.

"The conversation I had yesterday was to reiterate our interest," Alderson told me on November 27. "The agents, having seen my comments after the meeting, assumed we didn't have interest."

They ended the conversation agreeing to talk again soon, but just before that, the agents asked Alderson where they were not prepared to go.

"Anything over $200 million, we're not there," Alderson says he told the agent.

"And he didn't respond negatively," he said. "That led me to believe that something less than $200 million was feasible. There's still a pulse to this."

Cano would be an upgrade defensively at second and he would transform the Mets' offense. With at least "a pulse" still there, Alderson moved forward internally. "I explored things more with J.P. and Paul and John Ricco and talked to Jeff Wilpon about it," he told me at the time. "From a strategic standpoint, just looking at what the market is doing, the inflation in prices for midrange players . . . Cano makes some sense for us. He's the best player, the most consistent player. You're not taking on performance risk. The other players who are going to cost a lot of money—not that much, but a lot—also have injury risk, but with them there's also performance risk. It makes a lot of sense on a lot of different levels to go after Cano."

Alderson had spoken years earlier about the importance of making exciting additions to a team. Landing Cano would have been an attention-getter and a narrative changer. It did not take much reading between the lines to understand that Alderson thought that attendance at Citi Field was only going to bounce back if the team fielded a more dynamic lineup. For a clear upgrade like Cano, Alderson would have pushed hard, if he'd seen an opening. What he couldn't afford to do was let media hysteria influence events, which was why he made comments in the press saying the team was unlikely to sign any player to a contract worth more than $100 million. Sure, it was "unlikely." That hardly ruled it out, but he needed and wanted to scale down expectations to preserve room for maneuver.

Understandably, given the Mets' run of losing seasons, Alderson's "unlikely" comment led to a fresh round of negativity in the media. The Mets had a lot of work to do, if they were going to piece together free-agent signings to upgrade the team in a significant way. For their first move of the off-season, they signed outfielder Chris

Young to a one-year free-agent contract in late November worth $7.25 million. Young had batted just .200 for the A's the year before with only twelve home runs in 107 games, but the analytics suggested to Alderson that Young could be an option in center field and would be a bounce-back candidate in 2014, despite being a thirty-year-old career .235 hitter and despite his home-run totals having declined every year since he hit twenty-seven in 2010 for the Diamondbacks.

By early December the Mariners had emerged as a potential suitor for Cano, putting the Mets in a tenuous position. I asked Alderson on December 5 if the Cano option was off the table by then. "I think so, yeah," he said. "I told the agent: 'If you're still looking for 200-plus, we're out.' Seattle has been mentioned as a possibility, but I still think he'll end up with the Yankees."

Instead, the Mets turned to Curtis Granderson, who'd missed most of the previous season with two freak injuries, but had belted forty-one homers for the Yankees in 2011 and came back the next season with forty-three. He didn't hit for average but did draw a lot of walks, so if he could bounce back from his injury-marred 2013 season, he could shape up as a prototypical Alderson player. The announcement came on December 9 that the Mets had signed Granderson to a four-year deal worth $60 million. Four days later, the Mariners made the stunning announcement that they were paying Cano $240 million to come to the Pacific Northwest.

In signing Granderson, the Mets were hoping for an infusion of outfield power and clearly looking to him to provide veteran leadership and an upbeat attitude. "The game's still got to be the same way as when you played it when you were a little kid," Granderson told me the following spring, "because if it's fun, then you're going to want to work, and once you work, then you start to get the results, and once you get the results, that's more fun again, and that cycle continues all over again. I get a chance to play baseball. It's interesting when it comes like tax season time and it asks 'occupation' and I get to write down 'baseball player.' And I think the person outside is going to laugh at this, but that's my job and it's cool to say that."

A day later, the Mets announced they were signing forty-year-old Bartolo Colon, a workhorse for the A's in 2013 with 190 innings pitched and an 18-6 record, to a two-year deal worth $20 million. Colon was an oddball in many ways, starting with his rotund physique, but he'd been the ace of the Oakland staff. Colon knew how to pitch. He was described as a control pitcher, which was true to a point, but it did not explain his wizardry. He threw a higher percentage of fastballs than any pitcher in the league, but he had a full bag of tricks when it came to varying the speed, direction, and rotation of his pitches. He kept hitters off-balance. He kept his own defense on their toes because they knew the ball would be put into play.

The punch line for that off-season, good for a laugh at almost any juncture, was Stephen Drew, whose saga offered a case study in how, even in an age of alleged pinpoint accuracy in statistical analysis, a mediocre player could be talked up as a blue-chip talent by his very clever agent, Scott Boras, who actually seemed to get sportswriters to react to his repeated head fakes. Stunning! But also quite funny!

It was true the Mets would love to have upgraded at shortstop going into the 2014 season. Rubén Tejada, in showing up to 2013 spring training out of shape and overweight, in playing at times like a guy taking a phone call as he was drifting toward a pop-up, had raised questions about his basic commitment to excellence and that was a damning offense. The Mets could fill the need from their farm system with more time, but an immediate upgrade would have made a statement about the team being competitive in 2014; however, whether Drew would have actually translated into more wins for the Mets was highly debatable.

The tone was set early that off-season on Drew. Talks between Alderson and Boras had not always been civil. In fact, many years ago Alderson had once told the agent to fuck off and hung up on him. These things happen. Not a big deal. Boras preferred to go directly to owners whenever he could, it was known as his MO, and in December 2013 he had a call with Jeff Wilpon to discuss the Mets' interest in signing Drew as a free agent. This was soon after his talks on Drew with Alderson had hit an impasse.

"Stephen Drew is a long shot for us," Alderson told me that December 13, mentioning in passing that his talks with Boras had grown somewhat tedious and were yielding no progress. Alderson was aware that Boras had talked to Jeff Wilpon several times directly, trying to make a case for Drew, and was disparaging Alderson in the process. In dealing with other teams, it might work for Boras to try the whole end around, but it was not going to work in this case. So soon Alderson was back on the phone with Boras himself for excruciating conversations in which the agent attempted to make the case that a decent-fielding shortstop with a little pop but mediocre on-base percentage warranted a three-year-deal minimum worth well north of $10 million a season. They kept talking. Finally Boras budged—a little.

"The whole Stephen Drew thing keeps dragging on," Alderson told me on February 10. "Interesting, Scott has cut his years from three to two, but he's still looking for $13, $14 million a year."

This was all said just so, all the better to appreciate the absurdity of it.

"Is this guy worth $11 million more than Rubén Tejada?" he asked in a deadpan voice. "We've done the analysis. It's hard to say yes."

The Mets had their own numbers, but here were some out in the public realm: So far in their big-league careers to that point, they had about the same batting average, Drew holding a narrow edge at .264 to .259, much of the same story in on-base percentage, only six-thousandths apart at .329 to .323, both squarely in the range of "not very good." Drew showed some power, hitting ninety homers over his 936 big-league games to that point, and Tejada had only two in 345 games, but it wasn't like Drew was a big power guy, the one exception being 2008 when he hit twenty-one homers. Drew's slugging percentage and OPS were clearly better than Tejada's, but it wasn't even clear his defense would be much of an upgrade. Yet on sports talk radio and among some media personalities, the drumbeat continued: The Mets had to sign Stephen Drew to show they were serious about competing! They had to throw money away, just to get media types to back off!

19

THE NINETY-WIN
CHALLENGE

Consider the plight of the Mets by 2014: The club's payroll of right around $85 million represented not only a vertiginous dip from the $149 million payroll in 2009, the second highest in baseball behind the Yankees, two years before Alderson's first season as general manager; but it was the lowest for the team in fifteen seasons, going back to 2000 when it checked in with a payroll of about $79 million. The small-market A's checked in with a payroll of less than $32 million in 2000. Now fast-forward to 2014: The Dodgers loomed at the top of the pile with an Opening Day payroll of more than $235 million, followed by the Yankees at $203 million and the Phillies at $180 million. Sixteen of baseball's thirty franchises had payrolls over $100 million, and seven were over $150 million. The Mets started the season ranked twenty-second in baseball, with a payroll only a few million more than that of the A's (twenty-fifth).

Fan reaction had been somewhat mixed, but Alderson was pleased the Mets had signed Curtis Granderson, Bartolo Colon, and Chris Young. The moves, more off-season activity than the Mets had shown in years, were well shy of blockbuster, but were not meant to be all the team did. Adding Colon to the rotation and Granderson and Young to the lineup had the Mets closer to where they wanted to be, but still not there. The Mets went hard after former A's closer Grant Balfour, but couldn't quite get it done.

"We got the payroll up over $85 million, which everyone was waiting for us to do or not to do," Alderson told me over the phone on February 10, shortly before he left for Florida for 2014 spring training. "It sure would be nice if we could add to our bullpen. The perception of the team would be completely different. Right now people think we're incomplete, and you know, they may be right."

Fred Wilpon dropped by Alderson's office at Citi Field that week and they did a little brainstorming on how to shift the culture around the team. It was a familiar problem, often discussed, but Alderson kept turning ideas around in his head and went to Google to do a little research.

"If you Google 'winning cultures,' you come up with a bunch of New Age stuff, but you come up with things that all make a little bit of sense," Alderson told me. "If you do the research, one of the components of winning and sustaining a winning culture is by establishing very high goals, then holding yourself and other people accountable for those goals over time and measuring progress."

He flew down to Florida soon after our February 10 call and attended a meeting of the coaching staff, front office, and ownership to discuss players. This was Alderson's fourth spring training as general manager of the Mets and everyone knew the drill. Alderson and his lieutenants were all about process—crisp, clean, orderly, and reproducible process—and even when it came to meetings, that translated into a lack of variables. Meetings started on time. They were not dull—too much was at stake for that—nor were they scripted. But the participants knew what to expect. Others would speak, and then it would come down to Terry Collins and Sandy Alderson, playing off each other, mixing blunt talk about some of the organization's limitations with optimism for the season ahead. These were words as incantation, since to an overwhelming extent everyone was on the same page with a common perspective on the challenges of the season ahead. No one needed a reminder that Harvey was out of the picture until the following year. What they did need, though, was a good-natured, crank-'em-up kind of kick in the ass, and that was what the former Eighth and I Marine gave them.

"We shouldn't just try to be better," Alderson told the gathering. "Let's have the mind-set that we're going to go out and win ninety games. When we wake up and look in the mirror, let's make our goal to play like we're trying to win ninety games."

Everyone understood that Alderson was focusing not on any number, but on a mentality, one that was both basic and powerful: *Let's shift our way of thinking. Let's demand the best of ourselves. Let's make a sharp mental break with the struggles of past seasons and put everything we have into winning as many games, right now, as the team can.* As such the words were neither jarring nor surprising to anyone in the meeting, the context fully understood, but then Fred Wilpon, according to a *New York Daily News* article by John Harper, tossed out his own addendum to Alderson's message.

"We *better* win ninety games," Wilpon reportedly said.

On one level it was a mere throwaway line. Wilpon, the former competitive athlete, expected a winning team. As his longtime close friend Bud Selig told me in discussing Wilpon's intense competitiveness, "If you don't want to win, you ought not to be in this business."

Still, given the Mets' payroll, their reliance that season on young, unproven talent and a small number of free-agent additions, it seemed a stretch to demand ninety wins.

For those at the meeting, the talk of ninety wins did not leap out as an important detail. Alderson was not focused on the immediate reaction to his words; he cared that throughout the organization, from players to coaches to the higher echelons, a clock was ticking. Mediocrity, sloppiness, and underachieving would no longer be tolerated. The media lens had its way of altering that message.

"Alderson probably knows that most Mets fans are likely to scoff at the notion and dismiss it as delusional or disingenuous," Harper wrote. "Personally, I don't believe the Mets have a prayer of winning ninety games this season, but on the other hand, it's about time ownership and management raised the bar on what is and isn't acceptable after five straight losing seasons. Likewise, if this is an indication that they're going to start holding people more accountable in all areas, well, why not?"

But for its headline on the back cover of the tabloid, the *Daily News* chose LINE IN THE SANDY and the subhead "Alderson digs in, tells Mets brass team should win ninety games in 2014."

I was in Florida not long after the article appeared and asked Alderson what he thought of the headline.

"It was misleading," he told me. "The reporting is that I've 'predicted' ninety wins, I've 'guaranteed' ninety wins, we 'should' win ninety. It wasn't stated that way. It was really a challenge to change the mind-set."

We watched a Grapefruit League game together, and I tried to get Alderson to show me some excitement over Syndergaard. He wasn't biting. Again and again, he wanted to discuss a pitcher named Jacob deGrom, who sounded to me like some Flemish painter I should have heard of but hadn't. Come to think of it, the gangly young pitcher even looked like a Flemish painter, with his shock of long dark hair, the intellectual-in-a-coffeehouse facial hair (was he trying for a goatee? a Van Dyke?), and the pale, thoughtful expression. DeGrom was a converted shortstop who had started pitching only a few years earlier, so it was hard for me to take him very seriously. How many six-foot-four beanpoles remake themselves in short order to go from infielder to a big-league rotation? What were the odds? But Alderson was excited telling me about his potential.

"He's continued to make progress in the system," he said. "He was promoted to Triple-A last year for a spot-start and pitched so well he stayed in the Las Vegas rotation for the rest of the season."

As annoyed as Alderson was discussing the *Daily News* back cover that day, it was clear to me as an interested observer that he'd helped his cause with the hullabaloo. Some people were convinced Alderson had taken a hit, on the argument that his ninety-win comment came across as cynical; there were always going to be people who connected the dots however they wanted and arrived at unsupportable conclusions. To some in New York, Alderson might have come off as unserious and even flaky, given the disconnect between the team's low payroll and any perceived guarantee it would be a playoff team. But so what? If the larger message reached fans and media that Alderson was pissed off enough to draw a line in the sand and demand accountability, how bad was that? In the larger picture, Alderson's reputation was going to rise or fall on the Mets' win-loss record, not on snarky or sarcastic online commentary about a quote attributed to him after the fact. The one real risk to Alderson was that if the team bumbled through the season, he was going to be mocked far and wide for his ninety-win line in the sand. But again, so what? If they were that bad, he was going to be mocked anyway.

It's very New York to celebrate one's toughness, and then mock new ideas and turn out in the end to be a follower. This is part of the charm of New York sports fans; they grunt and scream and yell, but they also turn on a dime. Alderson did not have the luxury, given the task before him, of worrying if strangers insulted him based on caricatures of his actions or words. That went with the territory. Going back to his Oakland days, he had a track record of being more likely than most leaders to try out different ideas. Changing a culture was not easy; it required openness to an array of different approaches.

"Because I really believe in metrics, the more specific we can be about what we're going to accomplish and how we're going to do it, we're better off, so something as specific as a number has more meaning," he told me. "Would you say eighty-two? Would you say eighty-five? Those are not playoff numbers. So ninety is the default number. . . . You set a number, a high number, a reasonably high number but one that you know if you hit, you're probably in the playoffs, but the derivative of that is: 'OK, guys, here's what we have to do as a team.' You could even do it on our own Pythagorean basis, for saying, 'OK, we have to end up plus-seventy-five runs in order to get to ninety wins.' Well, that means we can only give up so many, we've got to score so many. But how do we score more runs? Or how do we give up fewer runs? Or what is the goal for Daniel Murphy? So it works its way down, but it starts with a notion that is not so abstract that it's meaningless."

20

DON'T THINK

At one level many of Alderson's choices could be understood only if one had genuine faith in numbers. A number can be a useful tool for enhancing knowledge; it is not, however, a club to bludgeon all other indicators. Alderson and his brain trust liked to look at fundamental problems the Mets faced and play around with possible solutions. Here was one set of numbers they looked at: 41-40. That was their record on the road in 2013. Here was another: 33-48. That was their record playing home games at Citi Field. The disparity was bizarre and it demanded countermeasures. Alderson was not necessarily after scientific certainty; he did not need to be able to prove that those numbers shifted through any particular step he or others with the team took. He just needed movement.

During 2014 spring training Alderson had gone to a dinner with Jeff Wilpon, Terry Collins, John Ricco, and a group of key veterans, starting with David Wright, the team captain, as well as Jon Niese, Daniel Murphy, Dillon Gee, Curtis Granderson, and Bobby Parnell. Topic A at this dinner, organized well in advance, was the riddle of why the Mets fared better on the road than they did at home. Teams are supposed to win more often at home, before their fans, but the Mets were fifteen games under .500 at Citi Field. Why was that? Why were the Mets 103-140 at home from 2011 to 2013? All participants were encouraged to brainstorm explanations and possible solutions.

"On the road by nature there are not a lot of distractions and here there's a lot of people tugging at you for different things," John Ricco pointed out.

As anyone who has followed a baseball team around from city to city can attest, the difference in locker-room dynamics between New York and places like Detroit or Kansas City was profound. The Alderson solution was to limit access to the Mets clubhouse to try to make home games more like road games. "A big part of that, coming out of that, was to try to establish a time period leading up to the game where the players have uninterrupted time amongst themselves in the clubhouse where they could each prepare collectively or individually," Ricco explained.

"There are always distractions in New York," Alderson says. "Can you say hello to this person? Can you do this? You never get to focus on the game. We're going to try to create a distraction-free environment, maybe change the pregame menu a little bit so that we don't end up giving them a six-course meal half an hour before game time. We're going to throw a bunch of stuff against the wall and see if it changes anything. Maybe something will stick and we'll win a few more games."

Fans pay to follow teams and are emotionally invested in every up and down of their team, so they have every right to make a few jokes about something new being tried. Jared Diamond wrote a *Wall Street Journal* article in early April 2014 about some of the changes and the target of faring better at home. "In the past, the team would provide a light meal and snacks when the players arrived to work, consisting of salad and sandwiches," Diamond wrote. "Then a larger meal, more akin to dinner, was served after batting practice, which ends about two hours before a 7:10 p.m. game. After consulting the team nutritionist, they reversed the menu this year, with the heavier food coming out before batting practice. Teams eat this way on the road because they hit second, leaving them with little time between batting practice and the game."

The article and its news flash about Mets players being served less food set off a hearty round of good fun.

"Memo from Jeff: How much do we save if we have the players bring bag lunches to home games?" came one quip at an online fan site.

"Bartolo Colon's trade request coming in 3 . . . 2 . . . 1."

Another area where the Mets were happy to experiment, even if it might lead to more sarcastic cracks from the peanut gallery, was in pursuing an intense off-season fitness program. Specifically, they offered to split the costs if players would fly up to Michigan in the dead of winter to engage in very intense fitness training. The Mets wanted to see what could come not just of better strength training, but just as important, better flexibility and biomechanics. This was an area where any effort to bring change faced heavy resistance. Veteran players, who had an understandably proprietary attitude toward their bodies, like violinists with their instruments, usually thought that whatever they were doing must be right. Organizations often let the whims or prejudices of their personnel dictate what programs would be employed in the off-season. The Mets were looking to put in place a framework that would, over time, translate into a systematic approach to maximize the potential not just of every big-leaguer on the roster, but every player in the system as well, through a combination of activity-specific stretching and training—year-round, highly specialized strength work; off-season work on biomechanics to improve efficiency of movement—and a far more all-encompassing approach to fitness and mental health.

The question when it came to strength training was how to find a way for players to add strength without sacrificing flexibility and suppleness, especially considering that over the course of the 162-game regular-season grind, maintenance of strength was as much as you could hope to achieve. The obvious answer was to make more use of the off-season. A generation earlier, most players took it easy from the World Series to pitchers and catchers. Some played winter ball. Those who trained usually focused on a gradual ramping up to February, doing a little running or treadmill work so their bellies didn't balloon too much.

The Mets decided to experiment with a far more vigorous kind of intervention, thanks to the efforts of Jeff Wilpon, who grew up a big fan of the University of Michigan football team. His father, Fred, was a good left-handed pitcher growing up in Bensonhurst, Brooklyn, like his friend Sandy Koufax, and earned a full-ride scholarship to pitch for Michigan. He gave up baseball after his first year there, but earned his degree and has over the years been a very active booster for Michigan sports. The Wolverines play games at the Wilpon Baseball and Softball Complex. During the 2008 Michigan football season, Jeff Wilpon approached the team's new strength and conditioning coach, Mike Barwis, and introduced himself. Barwis had an interesting background, including a purported 36-0 record in mixed martial arts competition, which definitely gave him an aura to the athletes he was coaching. As one Michigan player told the *Toledo Blade*, "He's a former MMA fighter and can kill any one of us if he wanted to with one punch."

Soon after Alderson was hired as Mets general manager, he and Jeff Wilpon visited Michigan to check out Barwis' facility and get to know the man. Barwis, originally from Philadelphia, studied at West Virginia University's School of Medicine, earning an undergraduate degree in exercise physiology, and then picked up a master's in athletic coaching before spending more than a decade as WVU's director of strength and conditioning. His program is based on his understanding of the physiology of sports, with much talk of how cells respond to different stresses, and in line with advances in technology (he tailors workouts closely based on data gleaned from fitness-tracking technology). Nutrition and diet, including supplements, are also part of his program.

"Barwis is a progressive guy," Alderson says. "He understands the science and he has a very dynamic personality."

You almost have to be a character to make a name for yourself as a trainer, but Barwis has done that and more. He's a great interview, with his growly voice and penchant for surprise, as when he told a reporter he'd bottle-fed and raised two wolf cubs. He even landed a gig starring in his own reality TV show on the Discovery Channel, *American Muscle*.

"Mike Barwis presides, and, from the look of things, if you're given a choice between doing his workout and being tortured by Jack Bauer of '24,' Jack is the less stressful option," Neil Genzlinger wrote in a July 2014 *New York Times* article.

The Mets decided to give his ideas a shot. Starting in late 2013, they would encourage some of their young players to go to Plymouth, Michigan, to work out with Barwis. Among the young Mets who agreed to leave their homes in warm places to hunker down in snowbound Michigan for Barwis' "special breed of hell" were Rubén Tejada, Lucas Duda, and Wilmer Flores, a Venezuelan the Mets had signed as an amateur free agent in 2007, mostly because they liked his bat. From the time he was playing youth baseball, Flores always stood out for his offense, not his defense. "You know those guys who, every time the ball is hit to them, they field it no problem? I was never that guy," Flores says. Even as a youth player, he'd played some shortstop, but had been sent to the outfield. The Mets thought Flores could probably hit at the major-league level, but he'd batted just .211 in 95 at bats for the Mets in 2013, with an OPS of.542.

"Typically what happens with old-school baseball is that guys change position based on their ability to play defense, as opposed to their ability to play offense," Alderson told me in 2014 spring training. "We move them to a position where they're no longer an offensive plus, so now what do you have? We keep moving Flores because he can't do this and he can't do that. Boom, he's a first baseman. Well, he doesn't hit for power, so he doesn't profile at first. The rationale behind this Michigan program was to see if we can't get players in condition to handle, in his case, a different position. Can we reverse this trend toward first base? He started at shortstop and he just didn't have the quickness and the agility."

Tejada had the most to gain in accepting the Mets' suggestion to make the trip to Michigan, having disappointed many in the organization by showing up to spring-training camp in 2013 looking sluggish and thick in the middle. Alderson ripped his work ethic on a radio show, saying it was like "pulling teeth" to get him to put in extra work, so here Tejada was, putting in extra work. Duda was smart enough to see 2014 as a potential year of transition, a time to transfer vague potential into actual accomplishment, but above all a time to turn themselves into better ballplayers. They didn't care whether the Michigan program was mocked in certain quarters as "fat camp." Try saying that to Lucas Duda's face. They wanted results and were willing to work for them.

In late January, shortly before he went down to Florida for spring training, Alderson talked about the challenges of knowing which way to lean in the Mets' ongoing first-base conundrum, ultimately boiling down to a choice between betting the future on Ike Davis, the sentimental fan favorite, or going with Lucas Duda. "Meanwhile," he said at one point, "Lucas Duda is up in Michigan working his butt off in these off-season workouts."

Alderson had hired the first mental performance coach in baseball, bringing in Harvey Dorfman to work with minor-leaguers in the A's organization in 1984, and Dorfman had worked with many Mets players before his death in 2010. Going into the 2014 season, at the behest of Fred Wilpon, Alderson sought to hire a mental skills coach for the Mets. Dr. Jeffrey Foote, whose extensive expertise included a stint as chief of the Smithers Addiction Treatment and Research Center, had put in eleven years as Mets team psychologist and did so without once having his name in the *New York Times*, but he was moving on by his own choice, so there was an opening.

Often sports franchises put psychologists to work primarily in the area of what's called EAP work, for Employee Assistance Programs. They emphasize mental health, in the sense of treating mental illness and addiction, as opposed to focusing on building up mental skills the way one can build up one's forearms or biceps. Jonathan Fader, an assistant professor of family medicine at the Albert Einstein College of Medicine in the Bronx, had been working with minor-leaguers in the Mets system since 2008 as an EAP counselor. Hired originally in part because he spoke Spanish, Fader "sort of came up in the system the same way our players do," he told me. By 2014 Alderson was ready to have him work with big-leaguers on their approach to all aspects of the game.

Fader grew up on the Upper West Side of Manhattan, rooting for both the Yankees and the Mets, but increasingly for the Mets. "My dad was always steering me in an open way toward the Mets," he says. "I have very vivid memories of watching the '86 Mets as a preteen and that being formative in terms of my childhood perceptions of what baseball was."

Fader stayed in New York for his undergraduate studies, attending NYU, but wound up on the West Coast for his graduate studies, pursuing his PhD in clinical psychology at the University of Washington in Seattle, where he studied with Ron Smith, the school's director of clinical training, who had also spent twelve years working in the Houston Astros organization developing a psychological skills training program. That was Fader's first exposure to sports psychology, and ever since he's made it a major focus.

"My interest is in helping people to find their own fire," he told me. Fader views Harvey Dorfman as the central pioneer in his field whose example he looks to uphold and build on. "For his time, he was absolutely prescient," he says. "From my perspective, he was someone who was really an emissary for what we do. Sometimes I talk about sports psychology as being like anthropology. Maybe I'm an athlete, but I'm certainly not a major-league athlete. You can't just go in there and say, 'This is how you should think about this.' You have to go in and make relationships, like anything else.

"If you're not really interested in the person first, then you're kind of missing it. People have to know you're really there to help them. That's analogous to therapy in general. There's so much research that shows that if people don't feel like you're in their corner, it doesn't matter about your worldview or what you have to sell. . . . In our field, there are a lot of questions about, is it the person or is it the technique? Harvey was both. In my mind he was just a total talent at connecting with people. It wasn't like you were talking about mental skills training; you were talking about how to be a better version of yourself."

Having come up through the minor leagues, Fader had nurtured longer-term relationships with many players and they felt they could trust him, which is essential to any meaningful conversation about the pressures that come to bear on a professional athlete, particularly the unique set of pressures that come with putting on a Mets uniform. Having the support of Fred and Jeff Wilpon was essential. "I have a good relationship with them," he says. "I'm thankful they've seen it's important and given it a good shot."

Fader's primary message for big-league athletes boiled down to: Don't think.

Or "Thinking is horrible," as a player once put it to him.

"Essentially what we're trying to do in sports psychology is helping people to not think," Fader told me. "When we're talking about hitting a baseball, whatever hitting philosophy you have, it can kind of cloud your actual adjustment when you're in the box. Whether it's selectivity, or aggression, you can have your plan, and then when you're in the box, you're trying to be nonpsychological. We focus on having people learn routines and methods, so they can get in the box and forget it all and be the talented athlete they are. It could be meditation, it could be breathing, it could be visualization, all sorts of things that help you not to think. What we work on with athletes is really having a singular focus. It can be done with anything that shuts the mind down and lets go."

The tradition of the LOL Mets was so deeply ingrained into the realities of New York that mockery and dismissive laughter were never far away. Losing Matt Harvey for a year was in this sense like losing a rudder; as valuable as he was as a stopper, the bulldog starting pitcher you could run out there to end a brief losing streak and get the club back on track, Harvey's combination of swagger and talent and charisma was also a great defense against ridicule. The man might hunger a tad too overtly for what the athletes call notoriety, but put him on the mound and conversation stopped: Everyone had to watch. That perpetual background noise around the Mets of press box–style wisecracks, and indeed actual press box wisecracks as well, had a way of vanishing when Harvey was being Harvey. Without him in uniform the Mets were far easier to mock. Alderson's "Line in the Sandy" distracted at least some potential critics from focusing on how much was already laughable about the team a few weeks into spring training.

All you had to do to make sport of the Mets was to focus on their first-base situation. A decent trade never came together for Davis or Duda, maybe not that huge a surprise given their numbers in 2013: nine homers for Davis, fifteen for Duda, and thirty-three RBIs for each, all with nearly exact at bat totals. "What I'm trying to suggest to people is if we don't get what we want, we're going to take them both to spring training," Alderson told me on January 9. "That's my story and I'm sticking with it."

All that off-season when Alderson and I talked on the phone, I'd ask about interest in Davis and the replies were invariably curt.

"There are two teams interested in Ike, Pittsburgh and Baltimore, and they're both trying to get him for nothing," he told me February 10. "If you take his numbers, and compare what other people are paying for first basemen, he's a valuable asset. There's no power in the game."

The Pirates were interested—but there were complications.

"They're still mad about what they gave up last year for Marlon Byrd," Alderson said. "They think they overpaid, but Marlon got them into the playoffs last year! He was outstanding for them. And we got a low-A second baseman and a reliever who could be good but may not be. They've gotten a little chippy! I don't think anything is going to happen with Pittsburgh."

So it was back to Alderson's plan B of going into spring training with both Davis and Duda and letting an old-fashioned spring-training competition decide the issue. For all the speculation about how it would be awkward and pathetic, none of that would matter if Duda or Davis showed up in Florida and staked a strong claim on the job. Josh Satin had also played himself into the mix in 2013, hitting .279 with enough walks to jack his on-base percentage up to .376, a right-handed bat who could platoon with one of the two lefties.

Alderson had mentioned the Davis-Duda competition could even generate a nice story line, and the prediction proved accurate— at first.

IKE DAVIS AND LUCAS DUDA SHINE AT THE PLATE IN FIRST SPRING TRAINING GAME was the *Newsday* headline from Port St. Lucie on February 28. "Davis and Duda arrived here as equals, thrust into a competition for the starting job at first base," Marc Carig reported. "And Friday, as the Mets dropped their Grapefruit League opener to the Nationals, 5–4, each proved eager to stake his claim. Duda ripped a double after being robbed of an extra-base hit, delivering the two hardest-hit balls of the afternoon—until Davis raised the stakes. When Nationals righthander Christian Garcia left a breaking ball over the plate, Davis was ready, sending a two-run homer into the rightfield berm."

It could have been a great draw for fans, watching two power hitters try to outdo each other whacking home runs in Grapefruit League games, but in that fine tradition of laughable Mets misadventures, their two candidates were in effect no-shows. Both Davis and Duda were on the shelf with injuries in no time, derailing the competition. Sometimes when it comes down to a choice between two comparable players, if detailed analysis of the numbers does not yield a clear verdict, tiebreaker considerations could come into play, like makeup and personality. As it happened, Davis and Duda were both widely liked but very different personalities.

Davis grew up around the game and was baseball smart in subtle, interesting ways; this made him confident enough not to worry about shutting up the way most young players try to do. "I might be a different player than most," Davis told me. "I'm sometimes brutally honest even to management. It's not like I'm mean. Actually I just don't lie about stuff, so I will tell them exactly what I'm feeling or what happened, where some people are more standoffish or under the radar."

Duda, in contrast, was very much an under-the-radar guy. He was fond of replying to reporters' interview requests with the heartfelt lament that he was sure, absolutely sure, that he was the least interesting person in the world. I came to understand Duda's personality a lot better when I found out he's from Riverside, California, an hour east of Los Angeles, a place where the smog pools up thick and heavy against the San Bernardino Mountains. Like my hometown of San Jose, known as the Prune Capital of the World when I was in high school, Riverside was a place where an almost Midwestern sense of modesty ran deep. As San Jose forever suffered from comparisons to fun, cosmopolitan, world-famous San Francisco, Riverside could not avoid at least some complex about being in the shadow of zany, self-confident, sprawling, exciting, everything-goes L.A. Since I'd lived in Riverside, and spent a year writing features on Riverside people for the *Press-Enterprise*, I felt Duda and I had something in common.

"There is something down-to-earth about people from Riverside," I mentioned to Duda at one point. "It's not Venice Beach, it's not Hollywood; it's a whole different world."

"Sure, I agree with that 100 percent," he said. "I think, like you said, people are kind of down-to-earth there. Being from there, being raised there and born there, I think they are. You definitely hit the nail on the head."

Duda, with his blond mop of hair, his blacksmith-who-just-wants-to-get-back-to-pounding-metal look of distracted concentration, can come across as something of a puzzle in interview situations.

The question in my mind was: Is this guy fucking with me? Plenty of guys with an easygoing exterior like Duda's were actually kind of pissed off underneath it all, and in his utterly friendly, just so "You definitely hit the nail on the head" remark, I thought I might have detected a whiff of angry sarcasm, like: *Stop asking me stupid questions and go away! Let me be!*

So I did what reporters do. I pressed on, talking about San Jose's inferiority complex where San Francisco was concerned and how if you came from the South Bay, you had to have a kind of modesty.

"I guess it's in part to do with where you live and how you were raised, but I think you are right," Duda told me in a slow, friendly tone that was anything but sarcastic, as if he were pondering my words. "Most of the people that I know from Riverside are pretty modest. I'm sure there are probably jerks everywhere you go. I think it's in part due to how you are raised and where you are from."

"Would you consider that part of your self-image, though, that you're modest, that you're not a cocky guy?"

"Yeah, baseball is such a humbling sport, and from a young age I think I always knew that. I always knew that you could get humbled daily in this game, so there's really no room for ego or that kind of thing. I just try to go out there and play hard every day and win ball games."

Here the conversation got a little surreal, which is why I'm reproducing it at length.

"Just on the attitude side, I'm older, but the word 'swag' is kind of a popular word now, and that seems very much not you," I said.

Duda laughed, a deep snort, and then he grinned, a little abashedly, as if it say: *I got me some swag!*

"First, explain the word to me," I said, regrouping.

"Swag is like style, a little bit of flair," he said.

"So you can be modest and have swag?"

"Sure, I think so."

"Do you think you have some swag?"

"I might not be too on the flairy side," Duda told me, "but I have 100 percent confidence in myself, so I guess that can be kind of a swag thing. Like I said, baseball is such a humbling sport. You can go 0-for-4, 0-for-8, 0-for-10 real quick and it's kind of a tough thing. For me, it's handling my business and going out there and playing hard."

In the end the spring competition was a dud, but the Mets made their choice between the two based in part on some interesting numbers. They looked not at some made-up statistic, rich in subjective interpretation, but one based on cold, hard fact: How hard did each player hit the ball? As part of the new era of baseball, the Mets paid close attention to the velocity of the ball just after it struck a player's bat. The resulting numbers were not always determinative, it went without saying. A guy could hit the ball hard and have it go straight into the mitt of an opposing player. That could happen again and again. But the law of averages told you that, sooner or later, if a guy ripped the ball consistently, he was going to be a formidable offensive threat.

"Both those guys were hitting around .240," Alderson told me, "but the ball comes off of Duda's bat at a much higher velocity and more consistently as well."

In the end it was, Alderson said, an easy choice—for that reason.

21

FIZZLE

Travis d'Arnaud was more than a prospect. He was a key bellwether for the 2014 Mets. Going into the season, it was already clear the team was building up to a critical mass of young pitching talent, with Harvey's projected April 2015 return looming as Zero Hour for that talent to coalesce, but pitching alone would not do it. Young Mets hitters had to develop as well. The Alderson system demanded power production and plate discipline, and for the Mets to make the leap to playoff contender, they needed to bring hitting talent along. They could go to the free-agent market to add complementary pieces, but such efforts were never going to add up to anything important unless they could build around young offensive stars. They had seen d'Arnaud as potentially just such a figure, but in 2013 he stumbled his way along to a .202 batting average, managing just one home run in his ninety-nine at bats. For a former first-rounder used to tearing up whatever league he found himself in, he had a distracted, lost air at home plate. The Mets needed his rookie campaign in 2014 to be a breakthrough. Given his added importance as the consigliere for the pitching staff, in an important sense he *was* the Mets. Manager Terry Collins penciled him in on Opening Day, batting seventh between Ike Davis and Rubén Tejada, and there was an air of anticipation to see how the catcher of the future would fare.

One of the things big-league hitters understand that few of us truly do is the relative nature of time. Yes, time is in some sense linear. It flows inexorably in one direction, despite the yellowing, dog-eared sci-fi novels some of us grew up on and their cheerful imaginings of time travel. But in fact we do have far more control over time, as we perceive it, than most of us ever come to grasp fully. Jonathan Fader, the Mets mental skills coach, emphasized to each player the importance of not thinking up at the plate. What he meant, really, was not throwing the mind into gear in that churning, clunky way of frontal-lobe A-leads-to-B-leads-to-C-and-D rational thought, but instead to focus on staying within the realm of emotional truth, of simply knowing.

"In the case of archery, the hitter and the hit are no longer two opposing objects, but one reality," D.T. Suzuki wrote in the introduction to *Zen in the Art of Archery*. "The archer ceases to be conscious of himself as the one who is engaged in hitting the bull's-eye which confronts him. This state of unconsciousness is realized only when, completely empty and rid of the self, he becomes one with the perfecting of his technical skill. . . . As soon as we reflect, deliberate, and conceptualize, the original unconsciousness is lost and a thought interferes. . . . Man is a thinking reed but his great works are done when he is not calculating and thinking. 'Childlikeness' has to be restored with long years of training in the art of self-forgetfulness. When this is attained, man thinks yet he does not think."

No one had to talk to Bartolo Colon about restoring "childlikeness." In that he was a role model to younger players. The challenge for the Mets of implementing their hitting philosophy was that, like Zen, it was a philosophy of doing, a philosophy of existence, not a philosophy of overthinking or indeed of thinking at all.

In 2014, Travis d'Arnaud offered a kind of eerie case study in the perils of letting your brain take over. He struck out twice in the Mets' 9–7 Opening Day loss to the Nationals on his way to an 0-for-3 day, though he did walk once and come around to score. By the end of that three-game series, a mini-nightmare for the Mets, with three straight losses and ragged outings from starters Dillon Gee, Bartolo Colon, and Zack Wheeler, d'Arnaud was 0-for-9 with five strikeouts. He was making contact and hitting the ball hard, but with nothing to show for it. The Mets finally broke into the win column against the Reds that Friday, with Jenrry Mejia giving up one run in six innings before handing the ball over to relievers John Lannan, Kyle Farnsworth, and Jose Valverde. For d'Arnaud it was another

0-for-3 with a strikeout. Manager Terry Collins gave d'Arnaud a day off to rest and clear his head, then he came back and checked in with another 0-for-3 that Sunday against the Reds, pushing his hitless streak to start the season to 0-for-15. That was enough for the *Post* to run a story under the headline HITLESS D'ARNAUD'S "MENTAL AP-PROACH" WORRIES COLLINS, offering the tidbit that Phil Linz started the 1968 season 0-for-26, the Mets' record for start-of-the-year futil-ity. D'Arnaud was a long way from that deep a funk, but his agony was obvious to everyone, especially his manager.

The team hit the road for a series in Atlanta and finally the cloud lifted: D'Arnaud singled to end the skid and then, in the seventh in-ning, lifted a high fly to center that looked like a sure out. Instead, the wind gave it a sudden push toward the center-field fence. The Upton brothers converged in the outfield and Justin made a diving attempt, but the ball landed cleanly for a double and the Mets were on their way to a 4–0 victory. One game later, d'Arnaud added a single and seemed to be on a little bit of a roll, but by April 18 he'd posted back-to-back hitless games and his average stood at .143.

The year before, Alderson and his brain trust had delayed as long as they could before sending Ike Davis down to Triple-A Las Vegas. This year, there would be less agonizing. D'Arnaud's struggles had the Mets considering a demotion as early as late April. The team was playing well, though, so it was not the time for a shakeup, and d'Arnaud put together two two-hit games over the next week and had one hit in the Mets' April 23 win over the Cardinals, putting their record at 11-10, not exactly red-hot, but for a rebuilding team, not bad at all. Alderson liked what he was seeing from his catcher of the future.

"He's starting to get some hits," Alderson told me on April 24. "Maybe I'm reading into it, but he looks more confident at the plate now that he's getting some hits. If he didn't come out of it, we were prepared to send him to Las Vegas to figure it out."

The Mets were happy with their other prospect at catcher, Kevin Plawecki, their second first-round pick in the 2012 draft, cho-sen as a supplemental pick in compensation for having lost shortstop Jose Reyes. Plawecki was making his way up through the system, and if d'Arnaud continued to raise red flags, with his injury history and sometimes with his approach, he just might run out of time. Josh Satin and Zack Wheeler, who had both watched him hit with confidence and power at different levels of the minor-league system, were so sure it was all going to click for d'Arnaud, it seemed unwise to doubt them, but watching the team early in 2014, and hearing Alderson's voice of caution, it was chilling to realize just how few chances the kid might get to find himself before it was suddenly too late. The previous two years, marred by injuries, had not given him enough at bats to establish any kind of continuity. In some ways he'd actually moved backward, and slipped from a *Baseball America* ranking of seventeenth among all prospects in baseball in 2012 to thirty-eighth going into the '14 season.

"In some ways it's not surprising that a guy would struggle at the outset, given that he missed almost a year and a half," Alderson told me that April. "But at some point, you've got to do it. You can't just rely on press clippings from a couple years ago."

Wheeler and d'Arnaud were roommates in New York for the 2014 season, and both were off to slow starts. Wheeler was somewhere between miffed and disappointed that he wasn't given consideration to be the Opening Day starter. In his first outing, Wheeler held the potent Nationals lineup to three runs in six innings but wound up an 8–2 loser.

Next up was a return to Turner Field, where Wheeler had made his major-league debut ten months earlier and pitched so well. That day Wheeler's adrenaline was pumping like mad and he threw six shutout innings. It was exciting, a life experience to savor, but it was at odds with his normal approach, which was to keep it free and easy. That's how Wheeler would establish himself over the long grind of a season, especially now that in his second year in the bigs, he'd earned a spot, earned freedom from wondering if, like his friend and room-mate Travis d'Arnaud, he might show up at the ballyard one day to get the news he was Las Vegas bound. Wheeler liked to be as cool, unflappable, and unconcerned about anything out there on the mound as his new teammate Bartolo Colon always looked. The two didn't talk much, since Colon's English was somewhere shy of sparse, but Wheeler watched the ageless veteran and shook his head in wonder.

"He really doesn't have a care in the world and I think that's why he's so successful," Wheeler told me that month. "He doesn't overthink stuff. He's just nice, laid-back, and relaxed. That sort of reminds me of myself, actually, just laid-back, and relaxed and whatever happens, happens, really."

For Wheeler the challenge was not to be too laid-back at times. It's a fine line. For someone with his talent, his effortless delivery and exploding fastball, the first lesson was to trust his stuff. He'd learned that one. Now he had to learn to trust his fastball and his breaking ball even on days when neither was at its sharpest. In his time with the Mets he was always good with men on base, always good at snuffing out a scoring threat, but he needed to snap back within at bats more often and cut down on his walks so he could go deeper into games.

His April 2014 start in Atlanta was nothing like his debut there the previous June. Wheeler struck out six, but gave up four runs in his five innings. He held the Braves to no walks, but they chipped away for eight hits and broke through in the fifth. It was an 0-2 start to the season, but when I caught up with Wheeler in Anaheim two days later, he seemed anything but troubled. "I'm filling up the zone, not pitching around guys," he told me. "I'm trying to get them to put the ball in play early." As we spoke in a corner of the visiting-team clubhouse, Bartolo Colon and reliever Gonzalez Germen were playing an elaborate game of hide-and-seek. Colon squeezed his porcine bulk just past me to hide in a corner locker, grinning as he pulled one door closed to hide himself within.

Even if it was clear to Alderson by the start of the season that Duda was their man at first base, by April 18 it was clear to everyone. Despite his prediction that the Pirates would not make an acceptable deal, the clubs agreed that day to a trade sending Ike Davis to Pittsburgh for pitcher Zack Thornton and a player to be named later. Thornton, a six-foot-three right-hander out of Los Angeles, pitched two years at Ventura County Community College and then moved on to the University of Oregon, finishing 9-0 his senior year with a 3.40 ERA, good enough for the A's to take him in the twenty-third round of the 2010 draft. The player named later was left-hander Blake Taylor, also from California, the Pirates' second-round pick in the 2013 draft.

It was a relief more than anything for Davis, who had grown tired of the boos at Citi Field and the protracted suspense about his future. "You're only as good as you play," he told me later that season. "It doesn't matter how good of a guy you are, if you don't play well, you're a villain. That's just the way the game is. We know that."

Davis had a good relationship with Alderson, he says, but at the same time, it had its limits. "Him compared to my first GM, Omar Minaya, definitely different personalities," Davis said. "Sandy's all business. You can tell he's got lawyer skills. He's a good guy, but he always had that line of business and friendship. Like sometimes you just weren't able to cross that with him, which is probably a good thing because I obviously watched *Moneyball* and that's actually like a point of their plan, is not to become friends with the players, because we are basically like stocks, you know what I mean? So it's tough to really become great friends with one of your players."

Alderson had been downcast going into spring training in 2014 because he understood all too well how this was going to go: Trying to field a competitive team while sorting through their promising but mixed bag of prospects, he knew that even when it went well, still there would be setbacks, disappointments, and weird frustrations. He wanted to get breaks from losing, but he also knew the larger picture was building for the following season. So as the team surged after the Davis trade, winning seven of nine to finish April with a surprising 15-11 record, he was almost waiting for the other shoe to drop.

The Mets' four-game series in Colorado to open the month of May would offer a good test. Bartolo Colon, the man with the body of a Macy's Thanksgiving Day balloon bobbing down Seventh Avenue, still doing his thing though he'd be turning forty-one that month, was a cutup in the clubhouse, a man with the demeanor of a playful seven-year-old. I'd approached Colon in the Mets' clubhouse in spring training and introduced myself in Spanish, telling him I was writing a book on the Mets. He sat there, extraordinarily immobile, and stared back at me placidly. I wasn't asking for an interview and did not have out a notepad or tape recorder. I was just talking to him, as moments earlier I'd been talking to former A's outfielder Stan Javier, now a general manager in the Dominican Republic, the two of us joking and laughing like old friends. Colon then grunted that he had to sign baseballs, as if this had anything to do with anything. I smiled at this, since we both knew how deeply redolent of bullshit it was, but moved away from him and there he sat, doing nothing, for the next half hour, not twitching a muscle. I mention the moment because at first I was annoyed, and then I just laughed: Colon, speaking in Spanish, English, or Swahili, was not about to give me a penetrating quote about anything. Nor was he going to do anything he didn't feel like doing. That was the man's genius: He didn't think too much, and he didn't care about anything except having a good time, making jokes, staying loose, and going out every five days and throwing a lot of darting fastballs. You could plug him in for twelve to fifteen wins and 180 to 200 innings, even on a sub-.500 team, but don't ever expect him to go out of his way to try harder than necessary.

The first game of that Colorado series was a rare case of Colon's attitude working against the team. His low-key ways were great going into a high-pressure game, since absolutely nothing was going to fluster him, but the simple fact is he took the mound against the Rockies like a man psyched out by the nightmarish realities of mile-high Coors Field, where a go-ahead-and-hit-it pitcher like Colon was due for a long day. It was listed as 57 degrees at first pitch, with a 17-mile-an-hour wind, and Colon was visibly off his game.

"Colon thought he was going to miss Colorado," Alderson, who was with the team in Colorado for the series, told me that week. "It didn't seem like he was ready."

The Mets threatened in the first, but David Wright's line drive led to a double play, and in the bottom half of the first Carlos González took Colon deep to make it 1–0 Rockies. The opposing pitcher, Juan Nicasio, came up in the second and singled off Colon to knock in two more runs. It was 7–0 by the fifth, all of those runs charged to Colon, and even with a late rally—including Travis d'Arnaud's second homer of the year—the Mets couldn't come back.

It was just one loss, not a big deal in a way, but the vibe around the team had suddenly shifted. Zack Wheeler, up next on the hill for the Mets, seemed to have adopted Colon's I-don't-want-to-pitch-here attitude. This was not characteristic of Wheeler, who prides himself on his preparation and his ability to maintain low-key confidence and intensity at all times. It's just how it works. Just as hot hitting can be contagious, so can sloppy pitching. Wheeler was hammered for four runs in the first and two more in the second. By the fourth it was 7–1 Rockies. The next day, the Mets jumped out to a 6–0 lead by the third with Jenrry Mejia handling the Rockies. Then in the fifth, the Curse of Colorado: an eight-run Rockies outburst, all off Mejia. The onslaught may have been enough to convince Mejia that as much as he insisted on being a starter, he might be better off taking the team's suggestion to try a late-inning bullpen role instead. The Mets came back to tie that game twice, then rallied again to go ahead—but lost in the bottom of the ninth, a punch-to-the-stomach kind of loss all the way. Behind Dillon Gee, the Mets won the final game of the series, but they were still reeling.

Alderson did not take the team flight to Florida and did not have to watch personally as the Mets lost all three of those games, their sputtering offense twice being shut out, the final game a stinging 1–0 loss that wasted five innings of shutout work from Wheeler. The team was back home at Citi Field for a weekend series with the Phillies, but Alderson was in California attending a wedding. On Friday night, the Phillies pulled out a 3–2 victory on a run-scoring double in the eleventh by former Met Marlon Byrd. For the Saturday night game, the Mets were up 4–3 through six, but again faltered late, losing another one-run decision when Ryan Howard singled in a run in the top of the ninth. The Mets had now lost five straight, falling to 16-19. It was panic time in New York—so Alderson decided to catch a red-eye back east that Saturday night.

"I thought to myself: 'This is heading in the wrong direction,'" he told me. "I felt like I'd better get back. Twitter was lighting up about Terry's job prospects and I was accused of hiding. 'Where's Sandy?'"

Telling the story on the phone, Alderson allowed himself a quick, exasperated laugh.

"I thought, 'Wait a minute, guys. I was just at a wedding.'"

The Mets had been thinking seriously about moving Mejia to the bullpen for weeks. One thing was clear: A young pitcher as emotional as Mejia, as fueled by adrenaline and enthusiasm, tended to wear down over the innings as a starting pitcher and might fare better one inning at a time. Like so many big-leaguers, he'd grown up poor in the Dominican Republic, shining shoes for a living as a teenager, and only started playing baseball when he was fifteen. The Mets spent all of $16,500 signing him as an international free agent in April 2007, and by the end of 2009 he was cracking top fifty prospect lists, and the following year, Minaya's last as Mets GM, he started the season in the Mets' bullpen. He did not stick at the time, instead getting a June demotion to Double-A to remake himself as a starter. There remained a temptation to develop him as a starter, but as Alderson had been making clear to me for three years in our talks, he was not about to tolerate mediocrity in the bullpen. By May 2014 it was past time to get results.

"There are people in the organization who think Mejia is better suited for the bullpen, and they may be right," Alderson had told me on May 6, picking up a theme he'd been touching on since spring training, the need to bolster the bullpen with young talent, not just free-agent retreads. "We've been letting him start in part because he wants to start. Part of the process is convincing him that the pen is a better idea. The sooner we get him into the pen, if we decide to do that, the sooner he's going to evolve into a late-inning option. So at that point our need may trump his desire. But it will be better if we can convince him that it's in his interests and in ours. And it wouldn't foreclose him going back to a starting role, if that's what happens."

The Mets had other intriguing options to explore in their rotation. Back in March, I'd sat with Alderson in his box at a Mets spring-training game and he kept changing the subject from Noah Syndergaard, who I wanted to discuss, to Jacob deGrom, the converted shortstop. Then I got my first look at the kid on the mound: the coltish long-limbed body, especially his legs, which had the look of stilts, lifting him up to a height of six-foot-four. How did he walk around on those skinny legs? It was hard to believe a kid with that kind of body could make it in the big leagues, given the importance of fine-tuned mechanics to a pitcher, given the necessity of repeating a pitching motion over and over with a level of easy, fluid exactitude. As great as Randy Johnson was, consistency of mechanics was not always his forte with that six-foot-ten body, and Johnson was not as scrawny as deGrom.

DeGrom had grown up on Florida's Space Coast, playing shortstop on the baseball team at Calvary Christian Academy in Ormond Beach. He kept playing shortstop at Stetson University in Central Florida through his first two seasons, making an impression mostly with his strong throwing arm. Finally in his junior year, longtime Stetson coach Pete Dunn prevailed on deGrom to pitch for him and started using him as a Friday night starter. He did well enough that the Mets drafted him in the ninth round of the 2010 draft, but after only six starts for the Rookie League Kingsport Mets it became clear he had elbow issues and was going to require Tommy John surgery. During his year off, he worked on adding a changeup, tutored by Johan Santana, and over the next two seasons turned heads with his composure, his competitiveness, and his truly formidable arsenal. Back for the 2014 season in Las Vegas, a thin-air hitter's paradise, deGrom quietly breezed to a 4-0 record and 2.58 ERA by early May.

The plan was to call deGrom up and give him a shot in the bullpen. As Alderson had explained back in spring training, the Mets were looking to use an approach employed by the Cardinals, which was to give talented young pitchers brief stints in the bullpen to give them big-league experience. The club gained from the infusion of talent and energy, and it was a great way to develop young talent. Instead, with Dillon Gee on the disabled list, deGrom found himself called on to make his major-league debut in Queens against the Yankees.

The Mets had first traveled to the Bronx and for the second straight year swept the Yankees on their home turf, winning not with pitching, but an explosion of offense. D'Arnaud, Granderson, Eric Young, and Chris Young all homered in a 9–7 victory, and the next day, it was Granderson and Daniel Murphy with home runs in a 12–7 win, giving the Mets six straight wins over their crosstown nemeses. Back in Queens to continue the home-and-home set, Rafael Montero made his first major-league start, but was no match for imported Yankees ace Masahiro Tanaka, who won 4–0. That set up the final game to close out the series, with the Mets looking to win behind deGrom in his first big-league start.

DeGrom was not even the most highly touted young Mets pitcher of the week. Montero claimed that distinction, and neither of them had anywhere near the level of buzz that followed Harvey and Wheeler in their climb from Triple-A to Queens, or even Syndergaard, who was running into some injury issues and ups and downs in Las Vegas that year. DeGrom took the mound at Citi Field and warmed up in the first looking like someone who had been out there countless times before, not a converted shortstop only a couple of years removed from Tommy John surgery. Showing a surprisingly languid motion, he took care of the first two Yankees batters in the first, including Derek Jeter, before giving up a double to Jacoby Ellsbury, then struck out Mark Teixeira to end the inning. He gave up a single in the second, then erased the runner with a double play the former shortstop started himself. Then in the third, overcoming his nervousness, he got on a roll, retiring eleven Yankees batters in a row. "He's very confident," d'Arnaud told me. "He trusts his stuff."

What happened in the seventh was inexcusable. DeGrom gave up a one-out walk to Teixeira, then got Brian McCann to hit a double-play ball that looked like it would end the inning. Murphy fielded and threw to second base, which with the shift was being covered by David Wright, their two-time Gold Glove–winning third baseman. Wright, the kind of ballplayer who goes months without making a visible miscue, gave his throw to first an awkward flick, it sailed—and the runner was safe. Alfonso Soriano then made it 1–0 with a run-scoring double, and that was the final score.

The games with the Yankees were costly in another sense for the Mets: Soriano's follow-through in the ninth inning of the Tuesday game hit Travis d'Arnaud in the head, and he ended up needing to go on the seven-day concussion disabled list. Once the initial concerns about the severity of the injury had been put to rest, there was some feeling that a break might be good for d'Arnaud, who had gone 0-for-5 in his final game to drop his average back under .200. As it turned out, d'Arnaud didn't start again for two weeks, until May 29, going 0-for-4 against the Phillies in a game his roommate Zack Wheeler won to improve to 2-5. D'Arnaud picked up a couple of hits in the Mets' fourteen-inning loss the next day to the Phillies, then mustered only one hit over his next four games, dropping his average to .184 by June 5, prompting Terry Collins to pinch-hit Bobby Abreu for him in that day's loss to the Cubs at Wrigley Field. From Chicago the Mets flew out to San Francisco, and d'Arnaud endured an 0-for-3 to drop his average to .180, which was where it would stay frozen for weeks to come. Following the second game in San Francisco, which d'Arnaud had watched from the bench, the Mets announced that d'Arnaud, their best prospect among position players, was being demoted to Triple-A Las Vegas to work on his swing.

New York Daily News Mets beat reporter Kristie Ackert, there in San Francisco with the team, summed up the reaction.

"Travis d'Arnaud was shocked," she wrote in her lead paragraph. "The Mets had been quietly mulling the idea of sending him down to Triple-A for about a week, but publicly denying it. The rookie catcher—and most of his teammates—were completely caught off guard Saturday night when he was called into the office and told to go down to Triple-A and fix his swing. . . . D'Arnaud was visibly upset after getting the news, as were some of his teammates. There was a steady stream of pitchers that made their way over to his locker to quietly talk to him, pat him on the shoulder and try to raise his spirits."

Actually, the Mets had been mulling the move far longer than a week, but it did catch many off guard. They were not going to fall into the trap of waiting too long. Instead of flying with the Mets from San Francisco back to New York, d'Arnaud spent Saturday night in San Francisco, then the next morning flew to Denver and on to Colorado Springs, where he joined the Las Vegas 51s in time for the Monday opener of their four-game series there against the Sky Sox, the start of an eight-game road trip. It was a jarring transition, which was just the point. Going into the weekend, d'Arnaud was a big-leaguer flying into San Francisco, always a favorite stop for most big-leaguers with its great restaurants and rich range of nightlife options. Now he was 6,531 feet high in the Rocky Mountains at a place called Security Service Field, which sounded like the punch line to a joke (had he wound up in Guantánamo?). His last game had been played with a view of the sleek and sexy San Francisco skyline in the background; now he was playing across the street from a Walgreens and a gas station calling itself Kum & Go.

The remote setting may have had something to do with it, but when d'Arnaud arrived and sat down for a talk with 51s manager Wally Backman, hitting coach George Greer, and pitching coach Frank Viola, he was a receptive audience.

"The first day I got there, we had like a two-hour meeting just honestly talking about the basics of baseball, where my head was at, every little thing about this game," d'Arnaud told me. "They actually got me to stop overthinking. They just said keep it simple: See the ball, hit the ball. You can only control hitting the ball. You can't control if it's hit at somebody. You can't control if it's hit in the gap. You can't control any of that stuff."

"Travis was in a situation where he was willing to listen," Backman told me. "You could get into his head a little bit. To see him struggle the way he struggled early in the year, it was a major priority for us to try to do everything we could to help him. It was just: Be himself. Be who he is and who he was when he first went to the big leagues. Just relax and be the guy I know he can be. It was really to clear his head."

They also told him to have fun. Talking about the conversation later, Backman, Greer, and Viola smiled in recollection, glad to have helped out, as if they were Androcles, the slave who famously removed a thorn from the paw of a lion and lived to tell the tale.

"He wasn't having fun, and at twenty-five, if you're not having fun playing baseball, why are you playing baseball?" Viola told me. "Travis had so much cluttered in his head. Here he is playing professional ball, he was a key component in the trade for a Cy Young Award winner. His expectations going into a big market are sky-high. It was just so much thrown at him in a short period of time."

Viola, a Cy Young Award winner himself, paused to stare off into the distance and revel for a moment in his sense of empathy for the young man.

"The thing I loved about him is he came down here ready to work," he continued. "From day one he didn't care that he was Travis d'Arnaud, that he was a superstar in the making, whatever. He came down to work like everybody else, probably harder than everybody else."

That Monday, d'Arnaud pinch-hit and—in his first at bat back in Triple-A—singled. The next day, he was 2-for-4 with a walk. On Wednesday, he was 3-for-5 with two home runs to pace the 51s to a 14–7 rout. Something had clearly changed. Through the end of that road trip to Colorado Springs and Oklahoma City, d'Arnaud remained hot, batting .394 with five homers and 10 RBIs in eight games, and headed back to Las Vegas with the 51s. He kept his new approach going and after fifteen games he had six home runs and sixteen RBIs and was batting .436. "Once the switch turned on, once he realized, 'My god, I can play when I'm relaxed,' it was a foreign experience for him," Viola told me.

"He so badly wanted to be the guy that everyone else wanted him to be, that young stud prospect who is going to come in and do something special for the team," Paul DePodesta told me. "When he got sent down, it was a chance for him to take a breath and say: *I can just be myself. I'm not here to meet anyone else's expectations.* Once he said that, ironically, he started to become that guy."

22

"THROW A GODDAMNED FASTBALL!"

A late-morning ride over the Bronx-Whitestone Bridge to Citi Field takes on an inherent sense of promise in mid-June, a week before the official arrival of summer. Soon enough the haze and lassitude of New York summer will cover everything in sight, but for the time being the sight lines are crisp, even the infamous East River looks picturesque and scenic down below, and the sight of Citi Field, glimpsed from the opposite angle of the approaching 7 train, somehow manages to kick in, from some forgotten corner of the imagination, a burst of childlike excitement in the promise of another day at the ballpark. I was attending the Mets' June 14 home game against the San Diego Padres with a friend of mine, Bronwen Hruska, a book publisher and author with close to zero interest in baseball, but up for some good New York people watching, and we were a little surprised to arrive and notice that the parking lots were very nearly empty. For a moment it felt like some damning indictment of the Mets. Less than two weeks earlier, on June 2, they'd pummeled the Phillies 11–2 to pull within one game of .500 (28-29), putting them in position to try to hit the All-Star Break with a winning record. Instead, they'd taken a sudden nosedive, losing six straight, including a 6–4 loss at AT&T Park in San Francisco that dropped Zack Wheeler to 2-6 for the year after he gave up four runs in only $3\frac{2}{3}$ innings. They limped home from that punishing road trip and won one against the Brewers, then it was two more losses in a row to send them back to eight games under .500.

Scanning the empty parking lots, I had dire scenarios on my mind. I was just sure a sudden decision had been made on behalf of all Mets fans to quit the team, to end the years of disappointment and frustration, but no, there was a simpler explanation. Game time was late that afternoon, so it was too early for spectators to arrive.

Looking to kill a couple of hours, and maybe contrite for having doubted Mets fans, when of course we know most of them hang in there year in and year out, we decided to visit a place with almost holy appeal for any Mets fan: Mama's pastry shop and deli in Corona, Queens, less than a mile away from where the Mets play and an institution for generations. Mama DeBenidettis passed away in 2009, but her three daughters have carried on in style. I first met Carmela, Irene, and Marie a couple of years ago when my friend George Vecsey, the longtime *New York Times* sports columnist and a regular there, suggested we meet in Corona so I could experience the place. They greeted me with warm hearts and warm freshly made mozzarella and I was hooked. The place offers a rich helping of what the Germans call Gemütlichkeit, as well as the kind of well-of-course-we're-passionate-about-sports vibe that comes with being a regular stopping-off point for everyone from former Mets GM Omar Minaya to any fan of the Italian national soccer team.

George had been to Mama's with Minaya many times, and in 2013, he and his wife stopped by with their friend Haruko, a "major baseball fan," as Vecsey put it, in town from Yokohama for the All-Star Game, and ran into security guards from more than one major-league team. "The other day, Joe McEwing, former Met utility man, dropped in—he's now working with the White Sox. He took a sack of pastry back to Pennsylvania with him. It's like that. I took my granddaughter Isabel there during the Open two years ago, and totally by accident ran into Omar, who was loading up to bring stuff home to New Jersey."

Irene greeted Bronwen and me like old friends, though she'd met me only once before. The sisters knew I was working on a book about Sandy Alderson. They knew it had been an especially dispiriting stretch for the Mets, so they insisted I take along a box of their lovingly prepared, authentic Italian cookies for Alderson, to buck him up, like Jewish aunties might insist I bring along a quart of chicken soup.

What to do with a large box of cookies sitting at a Mets game? During the years I'd worked on this book, I would meet Alderson from time to time at points around the country and we'd sit together to watch Mets games, but never at Citi Field. It was a kind of unwritten rule between us. He'd talk to me on the phone once a week or so through the season, we'd discuss all aspects of the team, but he needed to be left alone during home games. Often Alderson had to get up and pace, or leave the ballpark altogether and drive around; it was all too much. So I was surprised when, after I texted him about dropping off the cookies, we met a couple of innings later, and he showed Bronwen and me the way up to his private box at Citi Field, where we joined him and Linda and John Ricco to watch the game. The cookies would later be put out for the players; Alderson is not really a cookie person.

I was fascinated to be taking in a game that close to Alderson at Citi Field, but wished it had been another game, one not quite so ugly and hard to watch. Any lingering sense of promise that might have held over from the Mets' 6–2 win over the Padres the night before, behind a strong Bartolo Colon outing, vanished in the first inning. Zack Wheeler got two quick outs, then gave up a single to Seth Smith and fell behind Chase Headley 3-0, walking him to put runners at first and second. The first inning had been an issue for Wheeler throughout the season and he came into the game with a 6.23 ERA in the first. The crowd of 38,269 at Citi Field did not wait long to grow restless and edgy, bracing for the *kersplat* of another first-inning rally that put the Mets down before they'd even had a chance to swing the bat. It was bad enough when Yonder Alonso doubled on the first pitch he saw from Wheeler, a decent low fastball away, giving San Diego its first run, and putting a man on third base. But facing .184 hitter Yasmani Grandal and ahead 0-2 in the count, Wheeler threw a curveball in the dirt for a wild pitch that made it 2–0. The Mets had two on in the bottom of the inning, but Lucas Duda lined out to right to end the threat, and Wheeler continued to struggle, giving up single runs in the third and fourth.

The Mets were down 4–0 before their half of the fourth, and up in Alderson's box it was getting tense. Linda Alderson, a warm person as well as a woman with a most interesting work history, was getting on great with Bronwen, talking about Bronwen's novel *Accelerated*. I was grateful for their discussion, which relieved me of any need to make conversation with Alderson and Ricco. But by the bottom of the fourth, it got to the point where it didn't matter.

David Wright, leading off that inning, was hit by a pitch and did his familiar dance off first, clutching his batting glove in his hands, as reliable a sign of optimism as Mets fans have had in recent years. That brought up the amazing Bobby Abreu, doing a turn with the Mets at age forty. He worked a walk to put runners on first and second, and even if not too many in the stands—or in Alderson's box—really believed the Mets were about to erase the Padres' four-run lead, maybe they could at least whittle it down by a run or two. Next up was the big man, Lucas Duda, who was batting only .234 even after a 2-for-4 effort the night before. Duda struck out on a big, slow curve and I almost wanted to plug my ears rather than listen to Alderson's agonized reaction.

That brought up Chris Young, poised on the edge of the Mendoza Line with a .201 average coming into the game. Things perked up when Padres starter Jesse Hahn's wild pitch put runners on second and third with still only one out. But Young had nothing. He swung through three pitches, looking like he had no chance of foul-tipping one off, let alone getting a hit. The third strike was a breaking ball half a foot outside easy and his wild cut wasn't even close, earning him a resounding round of boos from the crowd.

"This guy has been a big disappointment!" Alderson exclaimed behind me.

A walk to backup catcher Taylor Teagarden loaded the bases, and during the Padres' mound conference the silence in the box dragged out uncomfortably. Then Matt den Dekker struck out swinging to end the inning. Alderson, like a pitcher sneaking in a changeup, let the moment speak for itself. His frustration was understandable: First of all, the Mets were playing the Padres, the franchise Alderson led as CEO from 2005 to 2009, and it was just human nature that he'd want his new team to make a strong showing against his old team. Far more important, with a concert scheduled for after the game by rapper 50 Cent, this was one of the best crowds of the year at Citi Field, an opportunity to make an impression and show off some of the young talent the organization was promoting. Instead, it was one of the Mets' worst games of the year. They had all of one hit through seven innings and looked ragged. By the top of the eighth, reliever Gonzalez Germen was in the game for the Mets and Alderson was out of patience with the horror show of a game. It tormented him just seeing Germen out on the mound.

"This guy went on the DL with an abscess!" Alderson cried out.

I'd read about Germen going on the disabled list on May 10 with an abscess. He had been more or less effective before that, posting a 3.57 ERA, a small improvement on his 3.93 mark the year before in twenty-nine games for the Mets.

"How do you go on the DL with an abscess?" Alderson threw out there, continuing his rant.

Talk was cut short when the inning began and Germen bounced a changeup in falling behind Chase Headley and then gave up a wind-blown home run to make it 5–0. With one out he walked Grandal and then started Cameron Maybin off with a changeup, which he poked to left field for a single. Alderson couldn't believe it. Dan Warthen had reviewed with Germen the need to pitch off his fastball. A changeup was named a "changeup" for a good reason. It was a change of pace, meaning its effectiveness usually hinged on first showing the speed of a fastball, getting a hitter focused on that, and then catching him off guard with a much slower pitch. A first-pitch changeup was another name for a very slow, hittable fastball. It rarely made sense.

"Why does he think it's called a *change*up?" Alderson groused, getting up to go walk around in the rear portion of the suite and watch on TV.

Warthen came out for a mound conference. Alderson was sure he was out there to remind Germen to establish a fastball. Warthen headed back to the dugout, and Germen peered in for the sign and made his first pitch to Alexi Amarista. It was a changeup.

"Throw a god*damned* fastball!" came ringing out from the deep recesses of the suite.

It hardly mattered that Amarista flied out to left or that Germen got out of the inning without further damage. Alderson steamed through the remainder of the game. It was agony, one of the worst days of the year for him. I asked him once what the hardest part of being general manager was, and he did not have to search his thoughts to offer an answer: "The hardest part is living with losses," he told me. "You live with them on a day-to-day basis during the season and you have to live with them in the off-season. Nobody in baseball goes home happy at the end of the season except if you won the World Series. I know that from personal experience."

Far from finding Alderson's outbursts in his box the day of the unsightly loss to San Diego objectionable or untoward, I thought they seemed about right. Alderson seethed with disappointment or anger when the team regressed, and that game had been a showcase of regression. Progress was harder to spot than glaring mistakes and it took longer to unfold, so it was therefore not nearly as satisfying as the bad moments were disturbing. I left Citi Field that day with two takeaways: One, I doubted that Gonzalez Germen had much of a future with the Mets, and two, I was struck by the sheer arithmetic of it all; that day's loss was the thirtieth of the year and therefore the 291st of Alderson's time as Mets general manager. He may have been at the forefront of bringing dispassionate decision-making to baseball, but he was passionate and tortured by every single one of those 291 losses. Seen from a distance, he might look lawyerly and disengaged; the truth—a little startling to witness trapped in close quarters with him—was that during games he could be Mount Vesuvius.

The next day, Curtis Granderson homered in the first inning and paced the Mets to an easy win over the Padres, giving them two of three in the series. They lost two straight in St. Louis after that, but by the time they arrived in Miami for a four-game series, they'd turned a corner from the sad, dispirited club they had been in the home loss to the Padres I watched with Alderson.

A tiny detail of that shift started that week: Granderson, the veteran, the man talked about universally as one of the most upbeat personalities in baseball, started waving a towel to encourage his teammates. It was a small thing, insignificant, it went without saying. But somehow it caught on. Somehow a team that could have moped through another series started to play like it was having fun, like it took pride in doing well, and the new attitude spread from player to player.

Zack Wheeler helped jump-start the feel-good vibe by shaking off the 2-7 start to his season and carrying the Mets to a 1–0 victory on June 19 with a complete-game shutout, his first in the big leagues. He struck out eight and walked only one, a key stat for him, but far more important, he'd clearly made a step forward. Harvey was ten months away from pitching for the Mets in a game, and the team needed Wheeler to be a formidable, reliable presence in their rotation. He'd been better than his win-loss record, but still confounding with his continuing issues; a complete-game shutout was a tangible sign of progress for him, a rallying point that he could use to build on.

The towel waving was on full display by the fourth game of that series in Miami, which saw the Mets erupt for eleven runs to steamroll the Marlins and take three of four. The white towels were waving all over the place by then, and after the game Granderson explained the whole thing this way to reporters: "It popped right from my memory of the Bulls and their three-peat championship, Cliff Levingston or Stacey King out there waving a towel all the time, it just popped in my head and we'll do that when we get a hit. . . . Now we've seen the guys in the bullpen doing it and some of the fans in the stands are doing it. Hopefully, just something to keep us going."

The difference in d'Arnaud's approach to hitting was truly amazing to behold when he was called back up from Triple-A and rejoined the Mets for their June 24 game at home against the Oakland A's. His first at bat, he struck out against left-hander Scott Kazmir—but there was no question, watching d'Arnaud swing, that he looked better in striking out than he'd looked even when he got a hit earlier in the season. Back then his swing often had a flailing quality to it, as if he were forever unsure if he really wanted to swing at a given pitch or wanted to try to poke the ball this way or that way. Now he was letting it fly. Sure enough, his next time: home run, a three-run bomb to help the Mets on their way to a 10–1 victory.

"You can see he's less under control than he was before," Alderson told me after d'Arnaud rejoined the team. "He's less tentative, basically swinging hard with his own swing. I think right now he's just trying to hit the ball hard, which is working pretty well for him."

The towel-waving thing had built by then into a full-fledged tradition, and it was funny watching the press try to respond. The *Newark Star-Ledger* wrote an article about the towel waving on June 26, explaining how it had already evolved to the point where players lined up in the dugout for a white-towel "car wash" line to welcome players back to the dugout after a big hit. The *Wall Street Journal* checked in on June 27 with an article pointing out that, traditionally, waving white was a symbol of surrender.

Above all it was a way for the players to have fun together. As Wilmer Flores pointed out when I asked about towel waving, it might feel a little silly at times, but it was a way to bring everyone together, rookie and veteran, pitcher and position player, star and bench warmer.

"It's just part of the game," he told me. "Sometimes we forget this is a game and we're supposed to have fun."

D'Arnaud echoed that point.

"When I came back up, they were doing it, so I just went along with it," he told me. "It's been fun."

Did having fun help them play better? Or were they having fun because they were starting to win? No one knew.

Alderson, taking stock in early July, saw grounds for both optimism and frustration and was having trouble sorting out the contradiction. The Mets had fallen to ten games under .500 (37-47) with a three-game losing streak when he and I talked on July 2, but to that point had scored 327 runs for the season, against 331 allowed. "If you look at our run differential, we're minus 4, and based on a minus-4 differential at this point in the season, we should be five games better than we are," he said. "I do believe we should be better in the standings. That's the frustrating part for me. It's not like, 'OK, the team stinks. We do some positive things, but we're 10-20 in one-run games.' You say, 'OK, that's going to come around.' Well when?"

In talking about run differential, Alderson was harking back to that nugget of wisdom Eric Walker had considered so important he put it on the first page of the report he'd written for the Oakland A's at Alderson's request: "It is elementary that the more runs a team scores and the fewer runs it gives up, the more games it will win." This insight was developed by Bill James into a famous formulation, as Baseball-Reference.com puts it: "The Pythagorean Theorem of Baseball is a creation of Bill James which relates the number of runs a team has scored and surrendered to its actual winning percentage, based on the idea that runs scored compared to runs allowed is a better indicator of a team's (future) performance than a team's actual winning percentage. This results in a formula which is referred to as Pythagorean Winning Percentage."

Alderson was mocked in some quarters when he told Jon Heyman of CBSSports.com that same day: "If you look at the run differential, we should be a .500 team." The word "should" was ridiculed, as if Alderson was trying to get a free pass on the team's win-loss record based on confusing statistics. I myself had mocked Pythagorean win-loss records. It's important to understand what they are and what they are not. They are a tool, nothing more; if a team's win total lags behind the number indicated by Pythagorean number crunching, it's a good time to start looking hard for reasons why. Or sometimes it might tell you that the law of averages will kick in. That was what happened with the Mets that month. They went on an 8-2 run to close out the first half, going into the All-Star break at five games under .500.

It's a given that for every step or two forward a promising young pitcher makes, he's liable to have a step back here or there. Time and again early on Jacob deGrom had been frustrated when he pitched deep into a game but lost because the team's offense was sputtering. Through it all deGrom showed an uncanny ability to let this frustration evaporate without a trace. Even behind the scenes, away from the roving eyes of reporters, there were no signs of deGrom being anything but quietly determined and intent to keep his run of strong outings going. It seemed almost to make him impervious to distraction, the trial by fire of having his early win-loss record so unjust a reflection of his performance, sagging all the way to 1-5 after a loss to the Braves on July 2 at Turner Field. But then he went on a roll, winning five straight starts, including a dazzling run of four straight starts giving up one run or less. By the end of July his ERA stood at an almost ludicrous 2.79.

That month brought another feel-good story line for the Mets: Unlike in the three previous seasons, this year the Mets had used their first-round draft pick to choose a player who had the potential to make an impact in the big leagues sooner rather than later. Michael Conforto of Oregon State, a left-handed-hitting outfielder with both power and plate discipline, was twice the Pacific-12 Player of the Year. He batted .345 with seven home runs in fifty-nine games—and set a record with fifty-five walks.

"Conforto's hitting style definitely fits us," Alderson said. "If you talk to Scott, he'll tell you that Michael picked the Mets. We didn't draft him, he picked us."

23

HANGING BY A THREAD

Terry Collins, cagey baseball lifer that he was, well understood that by mid-August his job prospects were slipping fast. Oh, in all but the most garish scenarios he was likely to limp through to the end of the season before hanging up his Mets uniform, but that would be agony. His time as Astros manager had ended badly, with the players growing tired of his overbearing style. As Joe Morgan wrote in his book *Long Balls, No Strikes*, "He was so uptight, his players thought each pitch was life-or-death." Failure, that great teacher in baseball as in life, instilled deep in Collins the importance of never losing a clubhouse, of always engaging with his top players, and he'd worked very hard to have good communication with his team and to stay positive. He wanted to be skipper of the team this group was capable of becoming. He'd kept his game face on through the long slog of rebuilding, driving a jalopy, and now he wanted a chance to go for a spin behind the wheel of the high-performance sports car the 2015 Mets looked poised to become.

First he'd have to get through August. The Mets dropped three of four at home against the Giants to open the month and then traveled to Washington for three with the Nationals. They won the series opener, riding resurgent Zack Wheeler to an easy 6–1 victory, but then were drubbed twice, the painful loss coming that Thursday when they lost 5–3 to end Jacob deGrom's run of victories in five straight starts. Ian Desmond homered off deGrom in the second, ending his streak of 67⅓ innings without giving up a home run, the longest ever by a Mets rookie. DeGrom took the loss, but far worse, after the game he told the team he had some discomfort in his pitching shoulder. He was flown back to New York for an MRI four days later.

DeGrom was sent to the Hospital for Special Surgery on East Seventieth Street in Manhattan for the MRI, walking distance from Alderson's New York apartment, so the GM headed over to pay him a visit. Alderson found deGrom and Mets pitcher Jeremy Hefner both in the hospital, two young men going through wildly different career trajectories. DeGrom's MRI results were generally positive, indicating rotator-cuff tendinitis, not a major concern, but enough of one to earn deGrom a little rest and a stint on the fifteen-day disabled list.

"Jacob should be fine," Alderson explained at the time. "It's usually from fatigue. He's a pretty slender kid. It's a function of his workload as well as his exercise program. We don't think his program was deficient, but this is the first time he's gotten to the innings level he has, so it's not unreasonable to expect that something like this would happen. It's just fortunate he was sensitive to what was going on and honest with us and we got it looked at right way."

Hefner, 4-8 for the Mets in 2013 with a 4.34 ERA, had lost a year with Tommy John ligament-replacement surgery in his pitching elbow. He'd been working his way back when he started feeling elbow pain again. "They were in adjoining rooms at the hospital, and Jeremy got the news he'd reinjured his elbow," Alderson told me. "He handled it well. It's how he handles all things, stoically."

Hefner may or may not have had much chance of cracking the Mets' rotation, given the talent the team was stockpiling there, and the immediate impact of the grim news on his elbow was to offer a loud, unmistakable cautionary note—to the Mets and to ace pitcher Matt Harvey, dealing with the frustrations of his own comeback from Tommy John surgery. Harvey missed the attention badly and seemed forever on the verge of doing something crazy to be in the spotlight; he actually got confused and did a live interview on ESPN during a Mets game, saying later he'd thought it was a day game, the kind of thing that ticks off teammates. The Hefner news was a sobering reminder to Harvey and his agent, Scott Boras, of all he had to lose by pushing the pace of his rehabbing, and for Alderson, urging more restraint was easy enough.

"I've had a couple of conversations with Matt since Hefner's injury recurrence," Alderson said then. "We're on the same page, but we've also got to tone him down a little bit to make sure he's not overdoing the rehab."

Alderson may not have been worried about deGrom's shoulder, but given the infusion of energy the young pitcher had been giving the Mets every start, losing him was no small hit. Then again, one of the weird up-is-down-and-down-is-up aspects of being in rebuilding mode is that setbacks also equal opportunity: It was because of an injury that deGrom wound up in the Mets' rotation at all, instead of getting a few innings in the pen.

With deGrom on the disabled list with that shoulder tendinitis, an opportunity was now staring the Mets in the face to make headlines and give the fans a jolt of excitement: They could bring up hard-throwing Noah Syndergaard from Vegas and give him a spot-start in place of deGrom. It wasn't just press hype. Syndergaard, one of the three players the Mets landed in the trade that sent R. A. Dickey to Toronto, was another tall, lanky right-hander with a classic power pitcher's build, and then some, at six-foot-six. He'd repeatedly hit 100 miles per hour with his fastball, a fact right there that boggled the mind. He didn't have to land at the big-league level with the kind of splash Matt Harvey did, because after all it was hard for an organization to find one player in a decade to debut the way Harvey had in 2013, but if Syndergaard could plug himself somewhere into the constellation of Wheeler, Harvey, and deGrom, all of them by this point having established themselves as big-leaguers to watch, the Mets would really have something.

"The three pitchers in this organization that you just go 'wow' are Matt, Zack, and Noah," Frank Viola told me that week, and as a former Cy Young winner his words carried added weight. "Those three you just go 'wow' because of just their pure, God-given natural stuff. Jake had to work for it a little bit. He's one of those guys you have to watch five to ten starts to realize, 'Wow, we can talk about this guy in the same breath as the other three guys.'"

As we spoke, on the outfield grass of Sacramento's Raley Field before the 51s' game with the River Cats, Viola said he thought

Syndergaard was ready, but did sound some cautionary notes. It
had been an up-and-down season for Syndergaard, nothing that led
Alderson and his brain trust to detract from their estimation of the
young pitcher's potential, but enough to give them pause about rushing him along. In his most recent start, back in Vegas, Syndergaard
had shut out visiting El Paso in six innings of work and struck out
seven. It was a step forward in a season that had included a fair share
of setbacks for the young phenom.

"This year has just been a very humbling experience for me,"
Syndergaard told me on August 5. "It's like my first time I've really
struggled in my career. I've had a few bad starts along the way, but
this was kind of an eye-opener. It's a stepping-stone. Now it's teaching me how to pitch, rather than throw."

He was 8-5 over his twenty starts at that point with a 4.85 ERA,
but over his last three starts he'd struck out twenty in 17$\frac{2}{3}$ innings
and posted a 0.52 ERA.

"Really the last couple times I've been out there and thrown,
I've had a lot more confidence and I've become a more well-rounded
pitcher," he told me. "I've been able to throw my fastball to both sides
of the plate, which I haven't been able to do consistently." He was also
learning to work in his breaking pitches even in hitter's counts, just
to mix it up. "I became too fastball happy, and it doesn't matter how
hard you're throwing if it's a fastball count and the hitter basically
knows what's coming. You're not keeping them off-balance. You're
not keeping them on their toes. When the hitter's comfortable in
the box, there's a good chance that they're going to win the battle."

It might have been the circumstances of our talk, alone in a dark
patch of parking lot just outside the visiting-team changing room
in Sacramento, but Syndergaard struck me as having an unusually
thoughtful and earnest approach. He was speaking slowly, thinking
his words through with care and then saying them with conviction.

"Do you know who Harvey Dorfman was?" he asked me at
one point.

I did a double take, half expecting to turn and see some old
sportswriter friend of mine smirking in the near distance, having put
Syndergaard up to this. But no, it was just the two of us out there.

"Sure," I said, not wanting to break the flow of conversation by noting that it was Sandy Alderson who first hired Dorfman to work in big-league baseball.

"I have *The Mental ABC's of Pitching* by him, and before every start, I just make it routine, I read a few chapters out of that book and get my head right," he told me in a quiet voice, not at all shy, but maybe not used to sharing so personal a detail with a reporter either. "I get focused. That's been a big thing for me, is being able to focus for seven, eight innings at a time. That's what helps when it comes to executing pitches, is extreme focus. That's something I think Matt Harvey exemplifies really well, his bulldog mentality out there. He just goes out there with that confidence and that focus and he gets the job done."

"The thing I love about him is he's like a magnet," Viola said about Syndergaard. "You say something to him and he takes it all in."

"Noah's a pretty thoughtful guy," Paul DePodesta told me. "Going into his senior year in high school, he was not hyped as the next best thing coming out of Texas. It wasn't until later in his senior year that his status came up. The Blue Jays surprised people with where they took him in the draft, thirty-eighth overall as a supplemental pick. I think he's more grounded than your typical top, top prospect. This is a guy who has *become* a great prospect. I don't think he's as caught up in it as some other guys."

On August 7 in his next start, Syndergaard gave up only two earned runs against visiting Albuquerque, but he picked up the loss to run his record to 8-6 and walked as many (four) as he struck out. His ERA stood at 4.79. For Alderson and the Mets, trying to decide whether to bring him up, it was actually an easy call: They had no room on the twenty-five-man roster and would have had to clear a spot for him. Plus, they didn't want to bring Syndergaard up just to get a quick look. They wanted him to come up, taste some success, build on it, and continue to develop at the big-league level.

"There's no question once he gets the call up in New York, you're not going to see him again in the minor leagues," Viola told me. "His stuff is that good. Once you start throwing different pitches in fastball counts and you become successful, it makes pitching totally a different game, and I think that's what he's close to right now. His last five starts, all those five starts, he's pitched really well. So I think he's starting to get it. We're talking about a twenty-one-year-old kid here and sometimes we're talking to him like he's a ten-year veteran. It's all a learning process and it's really fun to watch and be a part of."

Rafael Montero was called up instead to make the spot-start in deGrom's place against the Nationals on August 12, and the Mets suddenly looked like a team that was reeling. That night at Citi Field Montero coughed up a 7–1 loss marked by a five-run fifth. What the Nationals did to the Mets in that three-game series went well beyond mere embarrassment. This was more like humiliating. Bartolo Colon pitched well the next night and the Mets had chances to win—and in fact should have won, given the way the Nationals made mistakes—but fell short. The Nats had outscored the Mets 70–20 over their last ten games at Citi Field, winning all ten of those games, and the mismatch was so noticeable, it looked like the field was physically tilting toward the visitors' dugout.

Terry Collins, startled to see his players unlearning much of the progress they'd made over the season, woke up the next day to a *New York Post* headline proclaiming COLLINS EXPECTED TO RETURN TO METS BARRING COLLAPSE. The reassuring headline that Thursday morning, echoing a Jon Heyman report the day before, struck an odd note indeed since just the night before Alderson had gone off on his manager after the home loss. "I ranted a little," Alderson told me later. "It was not my best hour."

The *Post* article quoted "one official" saying, "Why wouldn't he be back?" That one official was not Alderson, who was still steaming mad the following day when he flew to Kingsport, Tennessee, to scout some of the Mets' Rookie League prospects playing there, in particular six-foot-four outfielder Wuilmer Becerra, acquired in the R. A. Dickey trade with Toronto, who at age nineteen was on his way to a fine season, batting .300 with ten doubles and seven home runs.

Soon after he landed in Tennessee, Alderson pulled his rental car over to the side of the road to vent over the phone about his frustration with where the team was going.

"Last night I told Terry that people are accountable," Alderson told me. "Something needs to change." Collins' chances of coming back for another year stood at that point at maybe 51 percent, and Alderson added, "Frankly for me, that percentage has been eroding."

Collins was far from surprised at Alderson's outburst the night before.

"We have a philosophy here," he told me later that week. "And when we get out of our offensive approach, it drives him crazy. I understand it, because we have both told our players—and we have lived it—that when they stick with it, it works."

Up until July, the Mets were among the league leaders in walks. With their meager batting average, taking bases on balls was the only way they were going to consistently generate offense. Suddenly in August even disciplined hitters like Lucas Duda were taking bad swings and bases on balls were scarce. The Mets made it through the first two games of the disastrous Nationals series without walking one time. Teams with loaded offenses can survive that kind of drought, not iffy lineups like what the Mets were putting out in 2014. A first-pitch fastball where you wanted it could be a pitch to hit. A first-pitch slider low and off the plate, which you could not possibly drive, was not. The difference between the one and the other was not subtle; it was not hard to understand and it did not shift or alter over time. Yet for some reason a collective breakdown in mental sharpness had ripped through the entire Mets lineup.

Wilmer Flores had come up in the seventh inning of the previous night's game against the Nationals with a chance to tie up the game. This was one of those weird occasions where the visiting Nats, good as they were under manager Matt Williams, seemed to go out of their way to hand the game to the hometown team. Washington first baseman Adam LaRoche misplayed a ground ball into a single, one of three errors by the Nationals, and when Juan Lagares came up next, he was hit by a pitch, loading the bases with one out, to bring up Flores. He's a bright young man who responds well to coaching, and he was fully aware that if he could hit the ball to the outfield, either on the ground or in the air, he'd bring the runner home from third and the Mets would be in business. The first pitch was down and in, not a good pitch to try to hit for a sacrifice fly, not a pitch a hitter wanted anything to do with in that situation. Still Flores swung, grounding out to third. Then Kirk Nieuwenhuis struck out and the rally fizzled.

"Flores comes up with the bases loaded, and he's up there hacking at the first pitch," Alderson told me from Tennessee. "He got jammed and hit a dribbler to first base."

That was typical of the larger pattern.

"Our whole approach to offense has deteriorated," Alderson told me. "It's just disappeared. . . . We can't just throw up our hands and say, 'We're not being selective at the plate anymore, so much for that.' I'm hoping guys like d'Arnaud and Flores and den Dekker and Lagares develop the selectivity over time. They don't have it yet."

Alderson may never have stood at home plate to face a major-league pitcher, but he'd defused North Vietnamese explosives. He'd had people shoot at him. He was no stranger to keeping his head under pressure. He understood that hitters, facing very human choices, were sometimes going to make the wrong call. Anomalies were not the issue. Repeated bad choices were the issue. Regression from disciplined hitters like Lucas Duda, whose combination of power and on-base percentage had turned him into the team MVP for the year, was the issue.

"Even Lucas Duda has become an overly aggressive hitter now," Alderson continued. "He's doing well, but in my view he's become overly aggressive. Sometimes guys get overly aggressive, sometimes they get overly passive. It's never a straight line. But at this particular moment, we've gone way off course."

I asked Alderson if he expected immediate results, meaning that night in the final game against the Nationals. He said it was hard to turn anything around in one day, but there needed to be a shift in approach soon. The Mets went out that night and again played poorly, running their home losing streak against Washington to eleven straight. Collins decided it was time to call a rare hitters' meeting. This, for professional ballplayers, was a little like being held after school for a scolding from the teacher. It's a rule of thumb that in the age of Twitter teams are hesitant to call such meetings, since embarrassing details often are leaked and the mere fact of calling a meeting can make a team look like it's panicking. But those risks were far outweighed by the need for action—and Collins felt in his gut that with a passionate, upbeat speech, he could offer a fresh reminder and help jolt the team's young players back into a better frame of mind.

"We are dealing with human beings," he told me that week. "These are not robots. So a lot of times they can go off into a different path, sometimes unintentionally."

Collins' words were not so much the point.

"Hey, look," he told his players. "We've got to stay with it. It works. You're going to get yourself behind [in the count] every once in a while, but you've got to have confidence in your ability."

The impact of Collins' words came from his conviction, his passion, and his optimistic belief that his players could and would adopt his message. That struck a chord and made it easy for the players to respond well.

"He brought us all together and kind of reminded us to wait for your pitch, not get too overly aggressive, just wait for your pitch," Travis d'Arnaud told me.

"Terry's always a positive manager," Lucas Duda said. "He's always got something positive to say. This game is built on negativity. So you kind of need that extra little push, I guess. . . . The gist of it was just be selectively aggressive."

Flores' take on the meeting was a little different, since he almost always smiles when he talks about baseball, and Duda almost never does. For Flores, Collins' message was to relax!

"I think we all have the talent and we all can hit," he told me. "We've been trying to make things happen too bad. We go out there and we have men on second and we're thinking, 'We've got to do it! We have to make this happen!' I don't think it works that way. You have to just relax and get a pitch. Sometimes we forget: It's just a game!"

The hitters' meeting was one detail of a long, grinding season. It was barely touched on in the press. But the manager's intervention with his team probably saved his job. He had demanded higher standards. In doing so, he not only ended up achieving immediate results, but he also gave the players something to think about. Over their next four games after the Collins speech, all against the Cubs, they would continue to struggle with their bats, starting a run of four straight games in which they mustered only four hits in each. But that Friday night, August 15, and then again on Saturday, they worked counts and earned bases on balls—seven on Friday, five on Saturday—and as a result piled up a total of ten runs over the two games, and two victories, despite the pathetic hit totals. In contrast, they'd cranked out nine hits each of their first two games of the Nationals series, but with zero walks, and had eked out a total of three runs over those two losses.

It's a rare case where a chart truly makes a larger point:

Aug. 12	9 hits	0 walks	Lose 7–1
Aug. 13	9 hits	0 walks	Lose 3–2
Aug. 14	3 hits	2 walks	Lose 4–1
Aug. 15	4 hits	7 walks	Win 3–2
Aug. 16	4 hits	5 walks	Win 7–3
Aug. 17	4 hits	2 walks	Lose 2–1
Aug. 18	4 hits	2 walks	Lose 4–1

"It was a great meeting," Collins told me that Wednesday in Oakland. "Our guys get it. We're not hitting the ball, but yet, one day we had four hits and had seven walks and we ended up winning the game. We scored seven runs. So it works.

"Our approach is: Hunt for a fastball, and if you get a fastball, do some damage with it. It's an aggressive patience, where you've got an attitude of 'Hey, I'm ready to hit my pitch, but if that's not my pitch, I've got to be able to say, "OK, I'm taking this."' Even if you know it's going to be a strike. If you say, 'I'm looking for a fastball away,' and here comes a fastball in, due to the time frame it takes to make the adjustment, you're not going to hit it good."

Did it bother him when Alderson turned up the heat the previous Wednesday night, saying there would be accountability?

"No, no, it's accountability," he said. "It all funnels back to the manager. I'm the guy that's got to get this point across. I make sure my hitting coaches are on board with it. OK, they are. Now they're around those guys a lot more than I am. I've got other things. But ultimately I'm the guy who has got to reinforce what they're talking about, because when it comes from me, it's got to have some pressure to it. . . . I make sure they understand: If you don't want to buy into this, I'll then go to Sandy and we will find the guys who do buy into it."

24

BACK TO WHERE
IT ALL STARTED

The 242 first-year MBA students packed into UC Berkeley's Andersen Auditorium for orientation week in late August 2014 were in for a surprise. Up onstage, Haas School of Business lecturer Gregory La Blanc was trying to build anticipation.

"Do you think that being a baseball general manager is a difficult job?" he asked the students. "Is it a job you would undertake? If you had to ask one of these general managers a question, what would it be?"

Sandy Alderson and Billy Beane, making a rare joint appearance, were announced to a jolly round of applause and walked through the auditorium to sit up onstage. Alderson, the students were told, had built the Oakland A's team that won the World Series in 1989, a fact that many of them had not known.

"He also hired Billy Beane," La Blanc added.

Introducing Beane, he noted that he's "perhaps most famous for having been played by Brad Pitt in the movie *Moneyball*," which even students born in Bangalore or Belfast knew all too well.

Alderson had not been to an A's game in Oakland for more than a decade, back in his time working for the commissioner's office as a top deputy to Bud Selig tasked with overseeing umpires. This was the day of his first return to the Coliseum as Mets general manager, a day that would churn up in him an almost feral competitiveness. For weeks leading up to this day, the A's had the best record in baseball and looked poised to make a strong run into the postseason. More than a month before the gathering in Berkeley, Beane had made a splash with a blockbuster trade with the Chicago Cubs, dealing Oakland's 2012 first-round pick, shortstop Addison Russell, widely talked about as a likely star of the future, and their 2013 first-round choice, Billy McKinney, as well as pitcher Dan Straily and a player to be named later. In return the A's landed two front-line starting pitchers, Jeff Samardzija and Jason Hammel. As if that huge deal were not enough, the A's then traded Yoenis Céspedes, their offensive leader and an electric presence in the outfield with a Roberto Clemente–like penchant for throwing out runners; in return, they landed established big-game pitcher Jon Lester from the Red Sox.

The 2014 A's, like so many other A's teams, were seen as a scrappy, plucky, fun-loving bunch of young guys, and the team was bathed in the continuing glory of being Billy Beane's team. The irony was that, by 2014, the Mets were more *Moneyball* in the truest sense of the term than the A's themselves were. As owner Lew Wolff was never uncomfortable acknowledging, the A's made money. Every year the team cleared at least a few million dollars in profit, thanks to revenue sharing,which funneled back to majority owner John Fisher and his family, to Wolff and his family, and also to Beane, who owned a small share of the team. Beane had gradually built up more and more credibility, and Wolff let Beane be Beane. By 2014 Beane could conceive of deals—and even increases in payroll—without worrying about too much nettlesome oversight from above; he and Wolff would talk things through, and sometimes the owner would talk Beane out of a rash idea, but if Beane believed strongly in a move, the move was likely to happen.

The Mets started 2014 with a payroll only a few million higher than that of the A's. Over the course of the season, as the A's made moves to improve, the teams' payrolls converged and, depending on whose math you wanted to believe, the Mets were actually being outspent by the A's, they of the dumpiest-stadium-in-baseball ignominy. These were not, however, points raised before the fresh-faced MBA students in the Berkeley auditorium that day.

"I've always thought that what you can measure, you can improve," Alderson said at one point. "The problem is the game is played by human beings. We have this approach toward hitting, which is really the *Moneyball* approach: You try to get on base, and on-base percentage is important. The last five or six games that we've played, we haven't had more than four hits, and the only two games we won, we actually had some walks in them, but we haven't been hitting. So the approach is there, the organizational concept, everybody understands what we're trying to do, and yet there are significant, hopefully episodic failures."

"You're getting madder and madder," Beane taunted good-naturedly.

They were two decades on from the years when Beane would trail Alderson at spring training, wearing a matching outfit, and yet still they looked almost as if they'd coordinated their outfits, both in loafers, button-down shirts, and khakis.

"I remember when being with Sandy, working together, some of the stuff that we used to do, it was pencil-and-paper collected," Beane said. "Nowadays it's captured with technology, so it's much more predictive and much more accurate. And really, our sort of rise was somewhat parallel with Silicon Valley and the rise of data. For us, it's not perfect, but we're trying to create an arbitrage between our decision-making, which hopefully most of the time is objective, and the subjective decision-making of our competitors. The hardest thing about using data and numbers is the first time you're wrong, everybody's like, 'Oh, that number stuff doesn't work.'"

Beane, knowing it was coming, paused for the warm wave of laughter.

"We celebrate intuition without going back and seeing how many times we're wrong," he continued. "When you have data and you have facts, you can look back, as opposed to making a decision from your gut and not really knowing why you were right or wrong at the end of the day."

A little later, Beane added in remarks that made everyone think of his recent deal-making: "Nobody cares about algorithms the next day when you trade their favorite player. So the Rubicon for sports is going over there and having quantitative evidence, and making the decision in the face of everybody. Not everybody has an opinion on the new search engines, but everybody has an opinion on sports, and it's usually very emotional."

Alderson and Beane were in a sense having two different conversations. Befitting two men who had worked so closely, one almost an extension of the other, their terms of reference and key ideas overlapped. The main difference between them was their relationship to time. Alderson had throughout his years in baseball taken an approach that sought to build over time; Beane tended to want to go for it more in the here and now.

"One of the interesting things about *Moneyball*, I felt," Alderson said, "was that, at least to the extent that it dealt with certain elements of valuation, like on-base percentage and things of that sort, the inefficiency in the market with respect to those particular elements disappeared pretty quickly. One of the reasons was the book didn't necessarily cause a revolution among baseball executives. It caused a revolution among baseball owners, owners who had thought for a long time that maybe we could bring some of the business propositions and principles that exist in my real-estate business or my financial business to baseball, but were always turned back by people like me who said, 'Hey, wait a minute, you can't really understand this game. It's unique. We have a particular set of expertise and knowledge and you just need to stay out of the room.'

"I think what *Moneyball* did was pretty quickly to confirm for owners that the business wasn't that different, and as a result it was kind of a top-down revolution in baseball. At this point everybody is trying to do it. But some are better than the others, and hopefully what is important is not just understanding the concept, but actually executing the concept. . . . How do you actually create that value, as opposed to going out and buying it?"

This was an important question. In fact, it was a moment that leaped out as being a major step forward from the familiar review of *Moneyball* concepts that had been kicking around in baseball and business. This was the very essence of the approach Alderson had been following with the Mets: creating value. It sounded homely and modest as a notion, compared to the killer-app drama of finding glaring market inefficiencies and exploiting them, which sounded almost like magic. Creating value was, in contrast, honest work: It happened only with a steady, consistent approach. The Mets under Alderson had come to understand that by investing resources into establishing a truly systematic approach to developing their minor leagues, and by taking an open-minded, try-anything-that-might-work attitude, they could remove much of the doubt of creating value in their system.

"Our goal was to take the talent and make sure it gets better by 30 percent," Alderson added. "If the talent's not any good, it's still got to get better by 30 percent."

And if the talent *is* good, the Wheelers and deGroms and Syndergaards of the world, then improving it by 30 percent counts as a potential game changer. The Mets' idea was that if you stockpiled enough talent to start, and then had a system in place to have across-the-board development, some prospects might wash out or plateau, but the net result would be acceleration toward a critical mass of talent. The organization would have top-level players to stock the big-league club and enough prospects to trade for missing pieces without leaving its minor-league system devoid of talent.

In the view of many in baseball, that was what the A's had done by going for it with the trade for Samardzija and Hammel, giving up two first-round picks. It was a calculated gamble. If it paid off with a World Series appearance, then it might well be worth it. But making changes could have unpredictable results, too. Over their first twelve games after the Céspedes deal, the second of the two trades, the A's were 7-5, but then they fell into a five-game losing streak that had people wondering if the trade had knocked the A's off their stride in some fundamental way. Now they had two games against the Mets.

"These games are big for Oakland, because they've hit a rough patch and they need to get back on track for their own peace of mind, if nothing else," Alderson told me on the short drive from Berkeley down to the Oakland Coliseum. "Whether you're in contention or not, every game matters to you. Each game has its own emotional importance to people who are on either side, if for no other reason than peace of mind and satisfaction for a few hours."

I mentioned that Billy Beane had often talked about how competitive Alderson was, and wondered if returning to Oakland for the first time since he became Mets GM kicked loose some added competitive fire in him. "Yeah, but you have to intentionally moderate that or not let on that it actually is that important," he said.

To keep the drive interesting, we talked about the kind of field manager Alderson holds in high regard. Dusty Baker, out of work that year after he parted ways with the Reds, had good plate discipline in his playing days, Alderson pointed out, but was less committed to that approach as a manager. Alderson had worked in Oakland with Billy Martin, Steve Boros, Jackie Moore, Jeff Newman, Tony La Russa, and Art Howe.

"I was more deferential to field managers earlier in my career, less so now," he said. "It's a partnership with give-and-take. I'm not really interested in micromanaging anyone, including the manager."

For me as for Alderson, it was odd taking the off-ramp toward the entrance to the Coliseum parking lot. I'd spent more than four years showing up here the way people show up to the office, my place of work, my home away from home. I'd covered a lot of dreary baseball. I'd watched the Beane-Alderson relationship develop. I'd been there in the front row of the press box after Al Davis made a deal to bring the Raiders back to Oakland and somehow got the city to pay for a huge and hideously ugly addition to the stadium, Mount Davis, as C. W. Nevius of the *Chronicle* dubbed it. The Coliseum was a concrete bowl, never in the same league as a Wrigley Field or a Camden Yards, but for years it had its charms, given the beauty of the Oakland Hills in the background. Mount Davis, which I watched being built concrete slab by concrete slab, blotted all that out.

"I imagine when you think about coming back here, when you think about the good times, you think mostly about the camaraderie and the people, like Steve Vucinich and Mickey Morabito," I asked. "Is that right?"

"Yeah," Alderson replied. "And hills that you can't see anymore."

Soon we had arrived in the office of Steve Vucinich, the team's longtime equipment manager, just as I'd expected we would. Alderson associates this spot with everything he most likes about being in baseball. It was the same as in the military: He didn't want to sit around with generals or admirals; he wanted to be out with the sergeants and lance corporals, too. "In the Marine Corps, if you were to talk to people who moved up even to become a general, they would say probably the most fun they had was at some other point in their career," he said. "It's nice to be a general, but what they really enjoyed was being a battalion commander. In the baseball world, being a GM is like being a battalion commander. Being a field manager is like being a company commander, the guy in the trenches. Being a president of a team is like being a colonel or a brigadier general. As you get further up, you're not as involved in work you find the most fulfilling or the most challenging or the most fun.

"I could have tried to be an owner. I could have tried to put a group together and buy a team, but I wasn't interested in being an owner. This is what I enjoy, being a general manager. I enjoy being on the front lines, basically being in touch with everyone from scouts to clubhouse attendants. The nice thing about baseball is you can be a colonel or general for a while and then you can go be a major again."

I used to meet Vucinich and Morabito for dinner regularly during my first spring in Arizona as the *Chronicle*'s A's beat writer in 1995. We'd head to Malee's for Thai or get Italian at La Fontanella, but mostly we had steaks at a place called the Pink Pony, which meant coming early, saying hello to Downtown Kenny Brown behind the bar (who always poured me a Johnnie Walker Black on the rocks), and pulling up a stool to talk baseball with whoever might roll in. General managers used to flock there, and more than a few big trades were inked on cocktail napkins at one of the booths in the corner long after closing time. The Pony was the first stop Morabito made when he arrived from New York, coming out to join Billy Martin.

"I remember when I first came out here from New York," Morabito told me. "I had just left the Yankees in 1980, they picked me up at the airport and didn't take me to the ballpark or the hotel, they took me to the Pony, where Billy Martin was having dinner with his coaches. Everyone in baseball you wanted to see was there that night."

On the wall behind Vuc's office at the Coliseum hung the portrait of him that for years was on the wall at the Pony, before it closed down. There was also a blown-up image of a vintage "Catfish" Hunter baseball card and a picture of Vuc with Joe DiMaggio in an Oakland A's uniform.

Alderson, Vuc, and Morabito spent some time talking about minor-league baseball cities. The Mets' choice to have their Triple-A affiliate in Las Vegas was often mocked, given the climate and distance, but there were no other attractive options. Alderson was on his way to Vegas next. "One thing about Vegas is you can get connections from there at all hours," Morabito, a logistics whiz as a veteran traveling secretary, commented.

Soon talk turned to Bud Selig, who as we spoke was upstairs having a press conference of some sort. One by one, new arrivals would pop in, and usually they'd make some sarcastic variation on the question "Did you go up to hear Bud?" which would then be met by a long stare. If you were the kind of person who hung out in Vuc's office and absorbed the vibe and the conversation, you were also the kind of person who had a pretty good idea what Bud was going to say in a press conference before he got around to saying it.

What was interesting, though, was the too-little, too-late challenges to Major League Baseball insider Rob Manfred's bid to succeed Selig as commissioner. This was kicked around, wondered about, but it was Alderson who made the decisive point: In supporting opposition candidates, some owners had served notice that they wouldn't have to find too many more votes for an ouster down the road.

"They've gotten rid of a commissioner before, remember," Alderson pointed out, referring to Fay Vincent, dumped by a faction that included Selig.

Vucinich turned to me and smiled, enjoying having his old general manager back in his office again. The two had been through a lot together.

"As I watch Sandy sitting there, and seeing all these media walk by and go, 'It's Sandy Alderson,' it makes me think of Sandy's going-away luncheon downtown somewhere," Vucinich told me. "Bill King got up there and spoke, and my name was brought up a couple of times in speeches. You talk about Steve Vucinich's office. You walk by and you never know who's going to be sitting there. It could be a Hall of Famer, it could be a politician. A prime example, Sandy sitting here and all these people walking by."

His words echoed when I found out later the occasion was being marked in a contemporary way.

"Mets GM, former #Athletics GM, Sandy Alderson is in chatting with Steve Vucinich," came the tweet from Susan Slusser, my successor as A's beat writer for the *Chronicle*, who also served as president of the Baseball Writers' Association of America.

At one point early in the game, A's owner Lew Wolff, coming out of a visit with Selig, saw us in the next box and came in to say hello. He's an amiable man and was making jokes about Selig.

"I just got back from a fraternity reunion with Bud in Wisconsin," he said. "It's been sixty years. Bud hosted some of the events at his place. They asked me if I could host, and I told them I'll host the next one."

Wolff earned a nice round of laughs. Alderson decided to do his best to set the A's owner at ease and address the elephant in the room, Oakland's two blockbuster trades and their current five-game losing streak.

"You know when I was with the A's and we traded Canseco to Texas in '92 for Ruben Sierra, we'd won three in a row before the trade and then we lost I think it was five in a row," he said. "We went into a tailspin, but then we came out of it."

Wolff, standing behind me, flashed a look that I took to mean: *Well, I hope it works out that way!* It was a look of good-natured panic.

"The purpose of the story was to uplift his spirits," Alderson told me later. "Things can go haywire, but they usually turn around."

The game was scoreless into the fourth, when Travis d'Arnaud's solo shot off left-hander Scott Kazmir gave the Mets a short-lived lead. The A's answered in the bottom of the fourth with four runs, getting one on a sacrifice fly and three on Coco Crisp's bases-clearing triple. The A's losing streak was finally over, and the Mets' own skid had quickly slid to three games.

"I don't have that much confidence in our ability to shut teams out these days," a downcast Alderson commented as we drove across the Bay Bridge back to San Francisco after the game. "Offensively, we haven't been scoring a lot of runs. Kazmir didn't look that good tonight, but we haven't been hitting anybody."

The next morning, I warmed up Terry Collins with some talk I knew we'd both feel passionately about: the unfair way our mutual friend Art Howe had been portrayed by the late actor Philip Seymour Hoffman in the movie version of *Moneyball.* "That is not him!" Collins exclaimed. "That is not him at all. He's real smart, really smart."

How is it working with young players, and developing them, knowing that by the time the team has grown into a playoff team, you might not be managing them anymore? How do you balance the need to develop talent versus the need to win right away?

"It's that fine line you walk between development and winning, getting a young player and putting him in a bad spot, to where he's going to fail, and yet, it's best for his development," he said. "That's what you face here, because people in our city don't want to talk about trying to build a team. They're about doing it right now. So it can be tough. . . .

"You've got to have some patience here. I've used that word a lot of times in New York, which they don't like to hear, but you know what? It's worked with Harvey. It's worked with Zack Wheeler. It's going to work with Syndergaard. And it's going to work with a lot of these young guys. Look, they may not be where we want them to necessarily be today, but where are they going to be in two years? I remember when I was coaching Pittsburgh. In '92 Barry Bonds was the MVP. Well, he came up in '86. So it took a little time for the best player in baseball to be the best player in baseball. You've got to have some patience. Certainly I've learned that."

25

TALENT UNFOLDS

There were times watching the 2014 Mets when it felt almost like taking a look at a time-lapse photograph sequence showing growth in progress. Wilmer Flores brought with him to the diamond a childlike quality that came across as confidence; talent had carried him along, through the way stations of baseball progress, without him ever having to stare down a sense of his own limitations, that most adult of self-awarenesses. Handed the job of regular starting shortstop for the Mets by early August, he looked like a poker-faced interloper, not jarringly out of place, but never claiming the role as his own. Then at the end of August he had a game where something clicked for him. It was his third three-hit game as a big-leaguer, but his first since that May, no small feat given its importance to a sputtering Mets offense. But Flores was always confident about hitting, so the breakout game at the plate was no real surprise. Far more surprising were the signs of defensive prowess he showed at short—once when he robbed Ben Revere of a base hit by diving up the middle to spear a hard-hit ground ball, then pulled his gangly frame up in time to heave across the diamond and nail Revere at first to end the eighth. In the ninth, with the Mets protecting a precarious lead, he turned a nifty double play, taking twenty-year-old Dilson Herrera's spot-on throw from deep in the diamond and getting it back to first with a veteran middle infielder's quickness. Who was this guy? This was not the Wilmer Flores who had so recently seemed such a quixotic choice to entrust with regular playing time at shortstop.

Such stark glimpses of progress are actually quite rare in sports. In an age of tweets and tightly edited *SportsCenter* highlight reels, few take the time to watch with close attention how much we can glean from the first awkward forward steps of young talent. In fact it's fascinating. In 2013 Josh Satin had earned playing time with the Mets by making the most of what he had, drawing more than his share of walks with plate discipline and coming through with singles and doubles; watching his progress that season, it was easy to fall into the fantasy that he could always make it look as effortless as he did that year. Satin was a likable, articulate young man, and who couldn't relate to his quandary of having a great head for sports but just not being that athletic? Satin's limitations were apparent. He had a lumbering, unsteady quality in running the bases, like a guy about to trip; his work on defense was steady but never impressive; and even at the plate, where he felt most comfortable, his swing was neither fluid nor compact, not for a moment poetic or awe-inspiring. There were no moments, watching Satin in 2013, when his forward progress had about it that time-lapse feeling of pronounced growth, of this player actually becoming something *more* before our eyes. Satin's nosedive season in 2014 came as a shock, watching him snap downward from a .279 batting average (and .781 OPS) in 190 at bats in 2013 to an .086 batting average (and .399 OPS) in just thirty-five at bats, and you had to feel bad for the guy, especially since his thirtieth birthday was coming up in December and he might not get many more chances to stick at the big-league level.

I called Satin up to discuss his disastrous year and he made no excuses. His tough year had nothing to do with opposing pitchers making adjustments. He just never found his swing. "It had nothing to do with anyone else," he said. "It had to do with me. It was just a funky year." Looking ahead, he said, "I know if I come in there ready to go, confident in my swing, and start swinging the bat like I have before, there will be plenty of opportunity."

Satin was an intriguing element in the mishmash of the 2013 season precisely because he was so much the exception. He's about as classic a *Moneyball* player as you can find, both in his deep-seated commitment to plate discipline and in his obvious limitations; the idea with that Billy Beane system, adapted from Alderson, was that talented but flawed players were undervalued, so you could win by stockpiling them. "The reason he's a Sandy Alderson–type player is because people like me are prepared to forgive the lack of athleticism and speed and versatility because of the approach," Alderson said. "That's the difference. Everybody appreciates the approach, but they don't give it a presumption that, 'OK, let's figure out how to use him because of the approach,' as opposed to, 'Well, yeah, he's got the approach, but he can't run, he can't do this, he can't do that, therefore he can't play.'"

The discussion about market inefficiencies sometimes made innovation sound more complicated than it was; it could lead you in all sorts of directions. Beane, speaking at that Berkeley business school event, talked about how in a way a focus on the present had become undervalued in the market. "We've talked about, for us, identifying shifts in the marketplace," he said. "There has been this trend to really value the future. In some cases, it may be overvalued." Alderson and the Mets do not agree: What if general managers, in thinking about their own role, placed too much emphasis on the aspects of team-building most related to their obvious handiwork, like high-profile trades or free-agent signings, and ignored the quiet, difficult work of building up the machinery of an organization that could maximize every aspect of player development? This was the Alderson project in New York.

The upward lift of young players is the only way to balance out the enevitable diappointments and setbacks, a point the Mets were riminded of repeatedly in the summer of 2014 watching thier captain, Wright, looking like a shell of himself.

"Boy oh boy have times changed for David Wright," Vin Scully said that August. "They walk the guy in front of him to get to him and then they blow him away."

It was a depressing reminder for the Mets of their unworkable financial situation. They were limited to a payroll of $85 million, a huge portion of which went to pay Wright his $20 million salary. On one level it made complete sense to pay Wright that money; fans demanded no less. But having so significant a percentage of their total salary expenditures invested in a single player did make it essential that he perform at full potential.

Wilmer Flores was a legitimate talent, it was becoming clear, a natural hitter whose coltishness and loose-limbed awkwardness afoot belied an easy athleticism that enabled him to make steady progress as a big-league shortstop. It's a subtle distinction, not one that can be converted into a logarithm, but the X factor differentiating those who improve and those who don't often hinges on the ability to accept positive surprises, to have the feeling all along that they were going to crop up sooner or later. Even in some of his more unsightly earlier games at short for the Mets in '14, Flores just about always had a sleepy-eyed, what-me-worry? expression, the look of a man used to having good things happen on the ball field, even good things as seemingly unlikely as making clear and tangible progress at handling baseball's most demanding position.

When twenty-year-old Dilson Herrera was rewarded with a surprise call-up in late August, hopping to the Mets straight from Double-A and becoming the youngest player in the big leagues, the promise in the Mets' lineup added up to a complete package: Up the middle, the key to any defense, the Mets now had rookie Travis D'Arnaud behind the plate, rookie Wilmer Flores at short, not-yet-a-rookie Herrera at second, and twenty-five-year-old second-year man Juan Lagares roaming center field with some of the flair of a young Willie Mays. "It's incredible what he's done in two or three years," his A-ball teammate Josh Satin told me.

There were no guarantees that the quartet of young players would all stick, or that they could develop into dangerous hitters. D'Arnaud finished the 2014 season with just a .242 average, but considering where he was when he got sent down to Las Vegas, he'd come a long way. Lagares, too, showed impressive steps forward at the plate, batting .281 with an OPS of .703. Flores was still a work in progress, and Herrera not even that just yet, but merely by having so many young players with obvious talent getting a chance to play in the big leagues, the Mets were developing that talent in the best possible way, toward the goal of having those players for themselves or, in some cases, putting together trades for star players.

Early September brought a jarring reminder of how precarious any progress the Mets were making might be: David Wright was finally put on the shelf, the agony of his fumbling efforts to play through a shoulder injury at last over. Wright's numbers for the year told the story: a .269 average, compared with .306 and .307 in 2012 and 2013, respectively; a career-low mark of eight home runs for the season, despite having gritted his teeth through 535 at bats; and an OPS of .698, also a career low. It was clear Wright could not simply have declined so much so suddenly; he had messed with his swing trying to play around the injury and paid the price. The question was: Was the damage permanent? By insisting on continuing to play, even though the Mets were in a rebuilding year, had he hurt the team both in the short run and in the long run?

Powerhouse teams don't generally fret about the outcomes of regular-season games. They're confident in their ability to win seventy to eighty of their games without much fuss or bother, and know there will be ample opportunity to throw in another ten to twenty wins to win a division or, worst-cast scenario, squeak into the playoffs. The Mets by late 2014 were beginning to see what it would be like to be within a few steps of championship caliber, as opposed to many years away. But caroming through the last six weeks of the season, they were painfully aware of how given to wild swings of inconsistency and backtracking they continued to be, and how vulnerable they were to one bad inning and one bad game that could send them into a funk.

The Mets had taken two of three from the Phillies to salvage a 12-17 mark for August—bad but one notch shy of disastrous, and at least they were not yet mathematically eliminated from the second National League wild-card slot. They went on the road to Miami and Cincinnati and took two of three in each series, giving them a chance to stay in the hunt with a strong showing against the Rockies at Citi Field. They swept all three games, and deGrom dominated Colorado in the middle game, pitching eight shutout innings and, incredibly enough, looking like he was actually getting stronger as the season advanced. If he'd been an intriguing Rookie of the Year candidate before that outing, he'd now vaulted past Billy Hamilton of the Reds to become the nominal front-runner.

The Nationals came to Queens on September 11 and, long as the odds might have been, fans could at least show up at the ballpark that day knowing the team still had a shot at landing a playoff berth. It was the second week of September and for a change Mets fans could still dream. Then came the cold shower, the frigid blast of another pummeling at the hands of Jayson Werth and the loaded Nats lineup, putting the tantalizingly remote fantasies to rest.

For many seasons in a row, the Mets in September had resembled an overinflated balloon suddenly subjected to a pinprick. There was every reason to think the Mets would repeat the act in late 2014, once the Nationals had placed a jackboot to their necks. There was every reason to think that the feel-good narrative of Jacob deGrom and his dazzling run of dominance could not possibly continue. The converted shortstop took the mound at Citi Field against the Marlins on September 15, and Mets fans, forever ready to believe in turns for the worse, braced themselves.

DeGrom, all gangly limbs and placid look of concentration, had the familiar puppy-doggish hop in his step as he bounced out to the mound to face the Marlins in the first and promptly set the side down in order, striking out Christian Yelich and Donovan Solano looking and then getting pesky Met-killer Casey McGehee to watch strike three, deftly framed by d'Arnaud. The Mets took the lead in the bottom of the first on a single by d'Arnaud, a walk to Duda, and a Flores two-run double, then deGrom came out for the second and dispatched Marcell Ozuna, Justin Bour, and Adeiny Hechavarria, striking out all three to run his streak to six straight Ks to open the game.

The electricity in the air at Citi Field was crackling by the time former Met Jordany Valdespin came out to lead off the third for the Marlins. This was just the kind of oddball character, talented but ungoverned, to break up a run of perfect pitching, but no, he went down looking and deGrom's streak now stood at seven. There was by now a mood of disbelief, a "Could this be real?" quality as deGrom struck out Jeff Mathis as well, which meant that all he had to do was strike out the opposing pitcher, Jarred Cosart, to set a major-league record for consecutive strikeouts to open a game. Wouldn't you know it? Line-drive single, end of streak. The Mets went on to lose, but deGrom had pulled off the unlikely feat of once again making the Mets a "Did you see that?" talking point all around baseball. He'd become the first big-league pitcher to strike out the first eight batters of a game in nearly thirty years.

"Opening the game with eight strikeouts was kind of an imprimatur, or stamp of approval, on his season," Alderson told me.

Great big-leaguers are built moment by moment. There is a chicken-or-egg aspect to becoming an established star: Yes, you have to show elite-level talent; yes, you have to come through in key games; yes, you have to turn promise into durability and a track record of consistency; but perception itself becomes part of the package. As a former voter for Rookie of the Year, I can tell you that the process is all about numbers, yes, but also about special feats that make an impression and jump out. DeGrom's eight straight strikeouts to open a game was just such a feat. It was now clear that deGrom had turned himself into a favorite for Rookie of the Year, an award that would be a wonderful attainment for deGrom himself, but even more so invaluable validation for the Mets and their grow-from-the-farm-system rebuilding effort.

"I think it would be meaningful to the organization," Alderson said in September. "It would be another indication of where we've come. I think it would be important. Back in Oakland, we got to the World Series three times, but what's always mentioned in connection to that era are the three Rookies of the Year we had in a row in Jose Canseco, Mark McGwire, and Walt Weiss."

Mets fans could be excited about having a potential Rookie of the Year, but three more games with the Nationals looked likely to bring the season limping to a close on a sour note. Sure enough, the Mets dropped two of three to Washington, and that funk carried over into the opener of their last series of the season, at home against the Astros. They lost that game 3–1, looking flat and distracted, and seemed ready to make a banana-peel slide out the last games of the season. Saturday's game brought eight more innings of Mets futility, another punchless offensive performance with no runs and few hits, and then with one out in the ninth, Eric Young Jr. tripled and stayed at third when Daniel Murphy fisted a little looper to very shallow left. Then Lucas Duda came up: *Boom!* He turned on the second pitch and sent a screaming liner down the right-field line for a walk-off home run, the first walk-off of his career, for a feel-good moment that felt like a party to anyone there or watching at home. Duda, a deeply modest man, had scarcely been seen to crack even a brief smile on the field, and now he was bounding around the base paths like a kid at recess, grinning ear to ear and looking completely relaxed at Citi Field for the first time, breaking up the huge scrum that greeted him by jumping on home plate to make it official and end the game.

"It was nice to see him enjoy himself," Alderson said that week. "Some people are guarded when they have some success. They don't want to assume it's going to happen again, or they don't want to be embarrassed when it doesn't happen again. I'm like that and Lucas is like that."

That gave Duda twenty-nine homers for the season, an amazing total for a man who went into spring training having no idea if he even would get the first-base job. He had been the salvation of the Mets' offense, its brightest light, and it was only natural to hope for a little bit of magic going into the final game of the season.

The Sunday game turned into almost a laugher. It was an entertaining game for the crowd of 34,897, the Mets twice taking one-run leads and losing them, but heading into the bottom of the eighth the Mets were up 4–3. Alderson, long since accustomed to walking around during games to help out his nerves, started pacing late in the game, impatient to have the W in the books, then took a walk in the concourse and ended up in his car in the executive parking lot.

"I turned on Sirius XM to get the game, and since it was satellite radio, there was a four-or five-second delay," Alderson told me. "I knew Duda was up, and Howie Rose and Josh Lewin were talking about how great it would be if Duda hit his thirtieth home run. They said he just missed a fastball and that the pitcher would try to get him to chase breaking balls. Because of the delay, I heard the roar of the crowd before I actually heard Howie describe the home run. I knew something good had happened, but didn't know what."

Alderson, alone in his car, could smile and take in the excitement of the moment. He could also exhale: The season was ending, and the Mets had come through with a memorable and emotional exclamation point to the end of the year.

"The last two days were great," Alderson said that week. "We didn't play all that well in Washington and were really flat Friday night against the Astros, which I think had a lot to do with the doubleheader in Washington and getting in late. We kind of slept-walked through a game on Saturday night until Duda hit that home run, which was like getting an electric shock. Then the next day, we swung the bats a little better, Bartolo Colon kept us in the game, and we broke through late. That was what made it so fun, that it all happened late. It's always nice to leave a positive last impression. We had good crowds on both Saturday and Sunday and played well, so it was great. It felt scripted in a way. Everybody's talking about the thirty home runs and boom, Duda hits it in his last at bat. We ended on a high note."

For Duda, those last two games were a chance to beam with pleasure right there in the public eye, in front of everyone. As Alderson well understood, he was a man who would rather not show anything than show too much self-confidence or too much pleasure in his own accomplishments. It was, after all, a team game, and it was a team game that would smack down anyone who thought too highly of himself. Duda, like Zack Wheeler, always had a strong sense of confidence, even of personal mission, but he kept it to himself, as he'd told me late that season.

"A little bit of confidence goes a long way," he said. "When you're helping the team out, and having a little bit of a success, I think that definitely adds to your confidence level. I think that I was kind of a little bit misunderstood when people said I didn't have confidence or I didn't show it a lot. Just because you don't show it doesn't mean you don't have it."

The end of the season brought a chance for Alderson to ask himself, like former New York mayor Ed Koch, "How'm I doin'?" It was one of the quirks of his job that, other than inarguable metrics of win-loss record and postseason success, if any, the job of baseball general manager was hard to monitor with any thoroughness, and few in the press really tried. For example, one paper hurriedly summing up Alderson's tenure mentioned his signing of Chris Young and Curtis Granderson for 2014, calling one move a bust and the other a near bust, but did not even mention signing Bartolo Colon, who ended up winning fifteen games for the Mets and giving them 200 innings, clearly a positive acquisition.

Beyond that, sometimes the most important deals were the ones you never made. There had been incessant clamoring for the Mets to sign shortstop Stephen Drew the previous off-season and it was a topic that buzzed around Alderson for months that winter like a cloud of gnats. The Mets just said no—and it was a good thing, too. Drew signed with the Red Sox during the season, later wound up with the Yankees, and posted truly dismal numbers. He batted all of .162 over 271 at bats with seven home runs and twenty-six RBIs. His OPS was a laughable .536.

If the Mets had signed him to a two-year deal at more than $11 million a season, and he'd performed like that, Alderson would have been barbecued over it all season long. But far worse, Drew would have been an anchor pulling the Mets down; it could have been Jason Bay all over again, except worse in a way because a shortstop was front and center every day—and Drew's contract would have included provisions requiring him to play a certain number of games, no matter how awful he was. Alderson and his front office dodged a bullet, but it wasn't something anyone even mentioned at the end of the year.

Probably no single development validated the Mets' commitment to their farm system as much as deGrom's remarkable Rookie of the Year season, which no one saw coming. "You become attached to him after a while," Frank Viola told me. "It's not that instantaneous 'Oh my god, oh my god, oh my god' that you have with Matt and Zack and Noah, but it does get to you after a while and you say, 'Jake's right there with them.' You can't teach keeping the ball down that consistently. He picked up the slider. He picked up the changeup.

And he's able to use them behind in the count in such a short period of time. People forget, he's only pitched for four years. He's picked things up so quick, so I think now, after what you're seeing after fifteen or eighteen starts in the big leagues, you can say yeah, he's got the stuff, maybe not the pure, natural, God-given stuff as Matt and Zack, but he can compete with them."

What was clear, assessing Alderson's years in Queens at the end of the 2014 season, was that he'd pulled enough rabbits out of the hat to put the team in position to successfully mesh its homegrown talent with well-chosen free-agent acquisitions. The Mets were now seen as a team that developed talent well. Harvey's '13 season and deGrom's Rookie of the Year award in '14 and Wheeler's progress at the big-league level all added up to an upgrade in the Mets' brand, and that meant they were now at the point where they could afford to make trades not just to plug holes but to try to upgrade in an important way.

The imprimatur of deGrom's Rookie of the Year award was like a flash of light shining the way forward to the Mets' immediate future, which even the crustiest cynic mumbling to himself on the 7 train had to admit looked as optimistic as it had in many years, but it was also a jolt to pull the Mets to the present and away from the dreariness of the recent past. The same was true of Juan Lagares and his thrilling development into one of the best young center fielders in the game. Considering he'd been converted from shortstop so recently, and therefore can be expected to continue to improve in center so long as injuries don't derail his progress, it was remarkable that he snagged the 2014 Gold Glove Award, becoming only the third Mets outfielder to be so honored. Lagares batted a respectable .281 with an on-base percentage of .321 and slugging percentage of .382; he finished with thirteen stolen bases, after a flurry of action on the base paths late in the season, and could even turn into a reliable leadoff hitter.

"I was with a friend watching ESPN when I found out I won," Lagares told me. "Within five minutes everybody in my family called me: my mom, my father, my three brothers, we are all very close." The joy he takes in playing baseball, readily apparent to anyone tuning in a Mets game, came through even in conversation. "I know I can run a little bit. I enjoy it. I like to have fun and play hard, like I always do. That's what I want to keep doing, so that I can be the best one day."

In looking to rebrand the team as fresh and exciting and likable, Lagares was a huge asset, truly a pleasure to watch at work in the outfield and also clearly a young man who was down-to-earth and likable.

Finally going into 2015 it was rational and unforced to anticipate a surge in fan enthusiasm.

PART IV

NOVEMBER BASEBALL

26

ZERO HOUR FOR THE METS

The countdown to the Mets' 2015 season in a sense began on September 11, 2014. That was the day Matt Harvey went on WFAN radio and, with a few words, cranked the temperature up to the boiling point, anticipating the team's 2015 Opening Day matchup with the Nationals in Washington. "I'm looking ahead to April 6 and counting Washington Nationals as a W," Harvey told cohosts Boomer Esiason and Craig Carton.

That, sports fans, is an out-and-out guarantee, one that was sure to get the attention of the Nationals, especially considering that on the day Harvey spoke, Washington won its twelfth straight against the Mets at Citi Field, a truly embarrassing distinction for the hometown squad. Harvey does not do embarrassment. He does not do halfway. No one dismissed the possibility that Harvey's elbow would go out on him again, but going into the year Harvey cast a shadow over everything in the Mets' world. It seemed certain that one way or another, he would play a pivotal role in the team's prospects.

If he failed to regain his 2013 form, the disappointment would reverberate loudly for the franchise and threaten to undermine any return to championship caliber, no matter how compelling a collection of other talent the team had assembled. A resurgent Harvey could not only anchor the top of the Mets' rotation, helping it achieve a critical mass of dominance, but his personality and attitude would also transform the team and its portrayal in the media. The sturdy appeal of David Wright had faded as injuries, time, and diminished production took their toll; Harvey offered up something fresh, a cocktail of youth and talent and swagger and insouciance, a little bit dumb, sure, in that way of headstrong youth, but canny and self-aware, funny and hip. If he came through in the glare of October baseball, he could have a run as one of the biggest sports stars in New York. Harvey at that point still had to decide who he wanted to be. He could be a great competitor and a great Met even if he forever divided himself between his twin loves, baseball dominance and, well, to put it bluntly, himself.

The time had come for Alderson to put himself on the line in public more often as a face of the franchise. He had no doubt been smart to come across in his first years with the Mets as half invisible. He vowed coming into New York that he was going to tone it down—and he did. That strategy had run its course, though, by the start of the 2015 season. Alderson had made his mark on the team. He had shifted the culture. He had painstakingly built up the farm system and instituted a process that brought talent along. Given the pieces he now had to put down on the board, Alderson had enough to work with—and it was all on him, ultimately. He had made some good moves as Mets GM and had also had his share of misses. He was finally seeing the fruition of what he had set in motion with two potentially decisive transactions: trading Carlos Beltrán to the Giants for Zack Wheeler, and trading R. A. Dickey, Josh Thole, and Mike Nickeas to the Blue Jays for Travis d'Arnaud, Noah Syndergaard, and Wuilmer Becerra. Those two deals tipped the balance, adding to an impressive haul of talent brought into the system on Minaya's watch.

"If you look at our rotation going into the 2015 season, we have nine guys we could legitimately use as starters," Alderson told me after the end of the 2014 season. "The five we have now, plus Harvey, Montero, Steven Matz, and probably Cory Mazzoni, another guy we like. That's nine that we have right now. We don't have to go sign the Shaun Marcums of the world. In fact, we can probably move one or maybe two of what we have. We have the quality and the depth."

In his first seasons as Mets GM, no subject tormented Alderson more than the bullpen, underfunded and undertalented, manned by a motley collection of veterans, some sublime, like the ageless LaTroy Hawkins, so good for the Mets in 2013, but far too many others forgettable. The Mets experimented in 2014 with working young talent into the pen and it turned out better than they could have imagined. Flamboyant Jenrry Mejía finally accepted that his rightful home was in late-inning relief and warmed to the closer role, taking his antic celebrations to new heights with twenty-eight saves. Jeurys Familia, imposing at six-foot-three and 240 pounds, had probably an even better year than his fellow Dominican Mejía. Familia finished with a 2.21 ERA over 77⅓ innings, and looked like he might have a better shot at being the closer of the future than Mejía. Former closer Bobby Parnell was due back from Tommy John surgery, and the Mets looked forward to having back Vic Black, the hard-throwing right-handed reliever acquired from the Pirates in 2013, who'd had a herniated disk in his neck in 2014.

The goal had been to build talent in the organization and build up a winning culture, and by at least one measure, they were doing just that: *Baseball America* pointed out in September 2014 that the Mets had recorded the highest organizational winning percentage in baseball. All seven Mets affiliates, unlike the Mets themselves, finished .500 or better. The Astros had finished first overall in this category in both 2012 and 2013.

It was all on Alderson now. He agreed with his toughest critics in New York that the time had come for the team to show something for his four years at the helm. It was time to win. Alderson needed to do a better job, moving forward, of making sure the Mets' offensive philosophy was translating down through the ranks to every coach and every player. That was hard to do during the years of weeding out, but now he could insist on going with a lineup heavy with patient hitters. Lucas Duda's thirtieth home run, a storybook end to the 2014 season, was important above all as a message: Do what Duda does: Take walks if they come, so you can get more pitches to crush into the stands. There could be no more breakdowns to the point where players get as far from basic plate discipline as they did during that telling stretch in July 2014.

A good example of the way Alderson liked things to work came in the hiring of Kevin Long as hitting coach going into 2015. Long, the former Yankees hitting coach, was an obvious strong candidate for the job, given his success and his commitment to the kind of plate discipline that was so central to the Mets' approach under Alderson, but especially because Long himself was a dynamic individual, someone who could be counted on to stay active in reminding hitters of what they needed to do. Alderson was in Hawaii on a short vacation with Linda and had a good talk with Long on the phone. He then talked to Curtis Granderson, who in his years with the Yankees loved working with Long and had often talked him up to other players. Alderson asked Granderson to call Long. Given all the other teams interested in hiring Long, the Mets knew they needed to move fast if they were going to land him—and if they had an inside track because of the closeness between Granderson and Long, so much the better.

Granderson talked to Long, all right, and they were both excited about all that Long could do with the Mets. In fact, Granderson was so energized by the talk, he then called David Wright to tell him about where it stood with Long. That led to Wright's calling Long as well. To hire Long, the Mets had to dig deeper into their budget than they'd intended, but it was worth it for several reasons: The hire showed players how serious the organization was about encouraging hitters to follow an offensive philosophy in line with that espoused by Alderson, and the Granderson-Long relationship would help Long quickly develop a rapport with Mets hitters. "Kevin has the kind of personality and experience that will allow him, within the general framework we have established in the organization, to make the hitting approach his, not mine," Alderson told me.

The Mets were long gone from the days when Alderson would joke, "What outfield?" They had a Gold Glove center fielder, a veteran right fielder who they were still hoping would bounce back to thirty-homer power, and in left field they signed veteran Michael Cuddyer, a former batting champion for the Rockies who also happened to be good friends with David Wright. The Mets knew that Cuddyer, who would turn thirty-six before the next season started, was declining with age, but with his swing and his approach they saw him as a clear upgrade. Cuddyer would also be a strong presence in the clubhouse, a veteran who had been around and a likable, articulate guy. The downside was that to get Cuddyer they had to give up a draft pick. "The ironic additional aspect to this," Alderson told me, "was the public-relations impact of actually giving up the draft pick, which in many ways was more valuable than the draft pick itself, because it was evidence to people that we're going for it. This is no longer player development. This is game time!"

Going into baseball's annual winter meetings, Mets people were upbeat about the Cuddyer signing and the sense that the hard work of developing young talent was starting to pay off. Down in the crowded lobby of the Manchester Grand Hyatt along the San Diego waterfront, which was buzzing with conversation at all hours, anyone from the Mets I happened to spot tended to have a jaunty, purposeful look that was in stark contrast to the uneasy mood for the winter meetings at the Gaylord Opryland two years earlier. Everyone in the organization was well aware that they'd accomplished nothing yet, but they had a strong collective feeling that they were close to breaking through, and it felt good.

"In past years we felt we needed to do something at the winter meetings to make a statement," Paul DePodesta said. "As we look at our club, we're certainly not a complete team yet and we're not where we want to be, but the foundation is in place and there is not the need to do something just to make news. We have almost our entire club returning and getting a year older, which in our situation means better, since most of them are young, and we have Harvey and Parnell coming back. There's certainly a lot more optimism around the organization now."

For the Mets' contingent, as for the twenty-nine other clubs in attendance, the winter meetings meant sequestering themselves in their suite around the clock to sift through fresh information coming in and to try to make creative choices about what deals or acquisitions might work. Alderson loves the camaraderie of these long sessions. Back in San Diego for the first time in years, with warm weather and breathtaking views, these winter meetings had a bouncy, lively feel. "I love walking around the lobby. The problem, now, is that when I walk around, I usually end up with two or three résumés. But I actually do like hanging around down there. It's kind of fun."

Later that off-season the Mets developed a sudden urgent need when they found out left-hander Josh Edgin would need Tommy

John surgery. So in March Alderson made two trades to help the bullpen, picking up left-handers Jerry Blevins, from the Nationals, and Alex Torres, from the Padres, whose main claim to fame at that point seemed to be that he wore protective headware on the mound, the only pitcher in Major League Baseball to do that. The trades were widely seen as a sign that the Mets planned to compete in 2015. For all the talk of the Mets going after a major shortstop, like the Rockies' Troy Tulowitzki, Alderson was content to stand pat at shortstop and see how young Wilmer Flores would develop.

Alderson's admonition in spring training for everyone around the organization to think of what it would take to turn themselves into a ninety-win club had generated controversy, but in the end it helped shift the focus to the present. The Mets had been chided in the media for cutting back on the players' pregame spread at Citi Field and limiting access to the clubhouse, all part of trying to ease distractions. Whether any of those steps worked was open to debate, but facts were facts: The Mets were 40–41 at home in 2014, compared with that infamous 33-48 mark of a year before. That was, no matter how you looked at it, progress. Alderson and those around him could focus on baseball, looking ahead to 2015, and know the team was seen in a much different light than it had been earlier in Alderson's tenure with the Mets.

"I think we've changed the mind-set," Alderson told me. "We've changed the conversation. Is it because I said something? No, I don't think really, but in a way it framed the conversation as maybe people perceived us as being a little better and we think about ourselves differently."

I'd been working on this book for nearly four years when I suddenly found myself wondering about something: Why was Alderson cooperating? Why was he talking to me? Part of the answer was simply that I'd asked him at the right time, just as he was taking over as Mets GM. Back then he was upbeat about the challenge and about working with a talented band of collaborators in Paul DePodesta, J. P. Ricciardi, and John Ricco. On a personal level, his father would be at the Mets' spring-training games, and he'd come up to New York regularly during the season to sit in Sandy's box at Citi Field with him; it would be fun. Then, when the Mets' finances went belly-up, and Sandy lost his father, the joy went out of it temporarily—but Alderson had given me his word to cooperate on a book project, and he wasn't going to back out.

`Here's the answer I've come to after thrashing this one out: I think Alderson cooperated on this book in part because he wanted to up the ante. It's not that he wanted personal glory or adulation, or that he thought he was going to get it from this book. The book traced his journey through life and the evolution of his work in baseball. Alderson got back into general manager work because he missed the adrenaline rush of a game on the line, a packed house full of fans leaning forward on the edge of their seats, hearts pumping with eagerness to have the outcome go their way. He loved the rush of knowing that it all mattered, that people cared that people were watching and paying attention. So he opened up his life to the scrutiny of this book. Having a book come out about his life in baseball represented a transition for Alderson, and there was no going back. It was time to be more present in public, and more assertive. If Alderson wanted to get back to the World Series, he was going to have to leave caution far behind—in his deal-making, in his public posture, and even in his relations with players and the coaching staff. This was not quite a Ferrari he had built for himself. Or not unless Harvey came back, deGrom picked up where he left off in 2014, Wheeler continued his progress, and Syndergaard made a splashy debut in 2015. But it was a car with some power under the hood, and it was time to do some driving.

27

A WEEK TO REMEMBER

Wilmer Flores did not think anything unusual was going to happen on July 29 at Citi Field when he stepped up to the plate for his third at bat of the game, facing Padres reliever Kevin Quackenbush. Flores had singled back in the second inning, one of the few glimmers of hope on a bad day for the Mets, with starter Bartolo Colón knocked around for six early runs. By the seventh inning the Mets were trailing by five and a crowd of 24,804 or whatever was left of it had turned restive with so little to cheer. But a curious thing happened as Flores moved toward the batter's box after Kirk Nieuwenhuis struck out looking on a slow curve. All around Citi Field, fans stood up to cheer for him, giving him a loud ovation. They were saying good-bye to him. They were calling out to him that they would miss him. To Mets announcers Gary Cohen and Keith Hernandez, working the game for SNY, it seemed clear that Flores had to know by then of a reported trade sending him and pitcher Zack Wheeler to Milwaukee for slugger Carlos Gómez, an exciting two-way talent who would be more than a rental. Flores had to know, didn't he? Everyone else seemed to know. Gómez, for his part, was on a team plane somewhere tweeting about the apparent transaction. In fact, it was during that at bat that Flores put two and two together and figured he'd been traded to Milwaukee.

"They had heard through the media that I would be traded and they thought this would be my last at bat as a Met, so they were on their feet," Flores told me. "That was when I realized that something was going to happen. Personally that day was a shock. It was a surprise."

Flores kept a blank look on his face during the at bat. He's a player who almost always looks like he's having a good time on the field. "Why not be happy?" he says. "I'm playing baseball. You can be mad sometimes and not show it out there. I don't show my emotions out there when I'm a really mad."

Whether Flores was mad, or confused, or trying to sort it out, none of it showed—not then. But after he grounded out and trotted back to the dugout, he faced the fans.

"They were saying, 'We're going to miss you!' and 'Good luck in Milwaukee!'" he said.

Cameras tracked Flores as he went into the dugout, still seeming calm, and then headed into the tunnel leading back to the Mets clubhouse. When he came back out for the top of the eighth inning to take his position at shortstop, his demeanor had undergone a dramatic change. The emotional impact had wrenched him loose from his usual carefree, happy-go-lucky demeanor, and he'd been crying, enough to leave his face red and puffy. Tears were still streaming down his face, so that he needed to wipe them away with his uniform sleeve as the TV cameras moved in close on his every move. There was something horrible about the spectacle, as if Flores were being chewed up like some reality-TV-show star, his pain the human drama of the moment, but the scene also struck many as endearing and refreshing.

Alderson's assistant, June Napoli, was listening to the game on radio, trying to figure out what was happening, when her mother called. June was in a position to know that no trade had been completed, but her mother was too upset to let June explain.

"She kept interrupting me, saying, 'What is going on? What is going on?' she was so upset," Napoli told me. "She told me, 'They say he's going to be traded. Why are they doing this to him? I feel so bad for him.'"

That was a feeling shared by just about every Mets fans watching or listening to the game, or hearing about it later.

Flores came in after the top of the eighth and Terry Collins told him he didn't know what was going on, but would pinch-hit Ruben Tejada for him so he wouldn't have to go up to bat again. The Gómez deal fell apart when the Mets' medical staff determined they did not like the look of Gómez's hip. The deal everyone was reporting was no deal at all. Flores was still a Met.

"I talked to Wilmer myself briefly after the game," Alderson told me. "I just told him, 'Look, these are the kinds of things that happen in baseball, but the good news is: There is no trade.' I apologized for putting him in a position where his emotions became so public, and I left it at that. I told him I was happy he was still with us. He didn't give me a hug or anything. Anytime a folk hero is created there's usually a wicked prince in the background somewhere, part of the narrative, and that's probably us."

"They told me there was no trade," Flores told me. "I wasn't interested in why. There was no trade, so here I am."

With the same speed that false reports of the trade as a done deal had proliferated, Flores was now widely hailed by Mets fans. He'd been relatively popular with fans, but now he was an instant favorite, widely beloved, and something more: a symbol of a young team with heart, a young team featuring players who wanted to be Mets.

"I hope I'm a Met for a long time," Flores told me later that season. "I really have to appreciate the fans. The way they found out that I wanted to stay was weird, because I was out there playing. I just didn't want to leave. It wasn't because I was going to Milwaukee. I have nothing against Milwaukee. It was just the fact that I was leaving this place. I only know the Mets. I've got love for this team. No matter how we're doing or what we're doing, I've always loved this team and loved the fans. They've seen me grow."

For Zack Wheeler, down in Florida rehabbing after Tommy John surgery earlier in the year, it was hard to know what to think. Travis d'Arnaud was also in Florida rehabbing at the time and was watching the Mets game on TV as word of the trade made the rounds. "I was able to text Zack right when I heard," d'Arnaud told me. "He couldn't believe it at first, and then once it didn't happen, he was out of it. I think he just went to bed because he didn't know what was going on."

Going into the deadline, a train-wreck vibe was starting to descend over the team. It's never good when your manager says he is "not embarrassed" by the lineup he sent out to take on Clayton Kershaw and the Dodgers at home, but that was what Collins said in defense of writing John Mayberry Jr. in batting cleanup, despite a .170 batting average (no typo), with Eric Campbell right behind him in the five hole, batting six points better at .176. For plenty of people on the Mets and around the team, "embarrassing" was just what it was, and it was hardly surprising when commentators teed off on the team.

Alderson struck a wan note on the phone when I called him that week. "It's been odd, and it's going to get odder," he told me, getting my attention. "I'm making a lot of calls, I wouldn't say I'm *getting* a lot of calls. I've been very proactive. The pricing on the market is very high, especially with regard to rental players, and as I've said publicly I'm prepared to overpay, but I'm not prepared to double-pay. There is still a whole week or so to go . . . We could still get somebody like Juan Uribe. We've had a lot of regression on the part of players this year. Lagares has regressed. Duda has regressed. Flores hasn't really improved."

I asked about Matt Harvey.

"He's having to deal with some other guys getting a lot of attention, too," he said. "I don't know what impact that has. He's one of three or four guys now; he's not the man. That could change, of course. He's pitched well. But he hasn't been the dominant force that he was."

It was interesting he added the "or four," which was an allusion to left-handed rookie Steven Matz, another hard thrower, more of a 96 guy than Syndergaard's triple-digit heat, but someone the Mets had been even more excited about than they were about Syndergaard a year earlier. Matz won his first two big-league starts, making a splash at home on June 28. He gave up two runs over $7^2/_3$ innings and also became the first big-league pitcher in a long time to have three hits and four RBIs in his debut. Matz followed that up with six innings of shutout ball against the Dodgers at Chavez Ravine on July 6. I caught up with him in San Francisco that week, and was impressed with his casual honesty when I asked him if the young Mets starters tended to feed off each other. "It's a little too early for me to tell that right now," he said. "Right now I'm just kind of sitting back and watching and seeing how they go about their business and seeing the way stuff works around here." That was refreshing. Matz clearly had poise and self-possession. He ended up having to wait for his third start, due to a strange muscle issue unrelated to his pitching motion, but having him due back late in the season was one more reason for the Mets to be optimistic about their chances in the postseason, if they could get that far.

Going into the trade deadline, Alderson was intent on making multiple deals happen to give the Mets lineup an influx of quality bats. Calling up Conforto, their first-round draft pick from the year before, was in the end not so difficult a choice, despite concerns within the organization that the Mets would be accused of rushing him because they were desperate for offensive help. Conforto had the kind of swing and maturity coming out of Oregon State that announced he'd make a beeline through the Mets' minor-league system, and he'd succeeded in trumping Alderson's concerns about the need for caution by forcing his way to the big-league club. On July 24, the Mets traded prospects for two veterans, Juan Uribe and Kelly Johnson, both role players by that point but both experienced bats, just the kind of guys you want on a team if you're playing in the postseason.

Then, on July 27, they traded a minor-league pitcher to the A's for Tyler Clippard, a closer with both the Nationals and A's who was tabbed to provide late-inning work along with Mejía. The following day came the announcement that Mejía, already busted once for juicing, had earned another suspension, this time for 162 games, for getting caught using steroids. It was a major blow, losing Mejía, though I myself, having written so much about steroids, was as surprised as I am in California when I feel an earthquake. For the Mets, it was a blow to lose an important reliever, but by then Alderson had put together a collection of players, featuring both upright veterans and youth, that handled adversity well.

Clippard, thrilled to be leaving the struggling A's to join the Mets, looked around the room when he arrived and was impressed. "It was really the perfect combination in this clubhouse, if you want to talk about what you want on a team," he told me later that season. "We have such great core veterans, we have great young guys that have all the potential in the world, just great stuff, doing good things, good teammates, but they go about it the right way, too, and they listen and they ask questions and everything in between. Guys from different backgrounds and countries—it's just a good group, a good mix, of people, and nobody feels like they're isolated on an island, everybody's got friends, everybody's talking to each other, having a good time. Obviously when you're winning it's easier, but I just really feel like it's the perfect mixture of guys."

The day after Flores endeared himself to Mets fans, Alderson was in a conference room with Jeff Wilpon and other club officials when Napoli, his assistant, saw his cell phone ringing. He'd left it with her because he was waiting for other general managers to call back to discuss trade possibilities. This was not a GM. It was Zack Wheeler. Napoli knocked on the door of the conference room and poked her head in.

"Zack Wheeler's on the phone," she told Alderson. "Do you want to talk to him?"

He stared back at her briefly before replying.

"Yeah, I'll take it," he said.

It was a brief call, three or four minutes. Wheeler wanted the general manager to know that his preference was very much to stay with the Mets. This was unusual, even unprecedented, but Wheeler was excited about the future of the team, excited enough to risk an awkward call to Alderson, worth it if it might increase his chances of staying with the Mets.

"I don't know that I had ever got a call like that before," Alderson told me a few weeks later. "It creates a difficult situation, because on the one hand you appreciate it, and the loyalty, but at the same you have to make a decision that's in the best interests of the team. The bottom line is Zack is still a Met. I think it reflects very well on the Mets when two players show very emotionally that they want to be with the club."

The Mets were in a precarious place. They needed upgrades, but they also had a lot to be excited about. Opening that three-game series with the Padres on July 28, Noah Syndergaard had pitched six innings of no-hit ball, showing just how much he'd progressed since suffering a 6-1 loss at Wrigley Field in his May 12 major-league debut. He struck out nine in his eight innings of shutout ball, earning a victory to snap his two-game losing streak and put the Mets one game behind the Nationals in the National League East. I'd caught up with Syndergaard in Sacramento the year before, back when Alderson was telling me Matz was ahead of Syndergaard, and he'd impressed me by talking about the importance of the mental side of the game and how he liked to read a chapter or two of Harvey Dorfman's *The Mental ABC's of Pitching* before every start. "I've kind of gotten away from that," he told me after freeing himself from a scrum of reporters in the Mets clubhouse at Citi Field. "I think my routine right now is pretty solid. I'm a lot more focused in my routine and my preparation for the game. I go out there and try not to do too much."

He spoke in a slow, measured tone. I'd heard other reporters talking about how Syndergaard never had much to say, but I saw in him a young guy who was smarter than people understood, with personality and a sturdy sense of self. He was progressing at an amazing rate, gaining the maturity and stability of mind to power through difficult moments on the mound. He told me that both Jonathan Fader and pitching coach Dan Warthen had helped him with this aspect of the game. "Working with both of them has been great," he said. "It's just really taught me how to remain calm and be poised on the mound, to relax and have fun with it."

On July 30, the day after the weird Wilmer-Flores-in-tears game, the Mets had to endure waterworks of a more traditional sort. The Mets had a 7-1 lead in the sixth, and were still up 7-5 against the Padres in the ninth. Their closer Familia had already recorded two outs, but nature intervened with a heavy downpour that forced a forty-four-minute delay. Following the break in the action, a Justin Upton three-run homer put San Diego up and the Mets had to sit through another rain delay, this one just under three hours, before they got a chance in the bottom of the ninth and went one-two-three. They looked punchless, badly in need of help, and the Carlos

Gómez deal that wasn't made Alderson and company look ineffectual in the eyes of many.

METS NOW FEEL HEAT AFTER DEAL FOR GÓMEZ FALLS THROUGH IN BIZARRE NIGHT ran a *Sports Illustrated* headline.

But as late as half an hour before the July 31 deadline, it was far from clear anything was going to happen. The Mets had interest in getting Jay Bruce from the Reds, or Justin Upton from the Padres, and pursued detailed discussions on both. As ever, such talks are hard to gauge. Were teams serious? Were they just looking to get lucky with a team willing to give too much? Only the ticking of the clock told the story, and in this case, the two options vanished as deadline time neared. "We were talking to teams to try maintain a set of options and they gradually disappeared on us," Alderson told me. "Cincinnati backed off on trading Bruce and San Diego decided not to trade Upton."

Two days earlier, when the Mets were on the verge of acquiring Carlos Gómez, the Tigers were still holding back on exploring trade options. Then suddenly they changed their minds. Jim Leyland, the former manager now serving with the Tigers in an advisory rule, called his longtime good friend Terry Collins to make sure the Mets were aware that Detroit was willing to trade Yoenis Céspedes, the absurdly talented Cuban whose departure from the A's the year before had led that club to collapse, a development I'd discussed many times with Alderson. Céspedes was always on the Mets' radar, now the blip was blinking.

"Detroit hadn't even decided to make their players available until the night the Gómez deal blew up," Alderson noted later.

The clubs kept going back and forth, but it was not looking promising on deadline day. The Tigers were set on forcing the Mets to unload blue-chip pitching prospect Michael Fulmer, a 6-foot-3, 200-pound right-hander who was later named pitcher of the year in the Eastern League. And that wasn't all they wanted. "We tried to get Detroit off the two players they wanted," Alderson said. "We tried all day to get them off those two names. The one kid we traded, Fulmer, is going to be really good." The other player involved in the deal ended up being right-hander Luis Cessa, a twenty-three-year-old Mexican with a 9.25 ERA for Triple-A Las Vegas.

I'd been talking with Alderson for years about just this moment: a time when there were enough top prospects in the system that the team could afford to gamble on trading one away in the hope that it would get an immediate return. Alderson went around the conference room, seeking the input of Paul DePodesta, John Ricco, J. P. Ricciardi, Jeff Wilpon, and others who popped into the meeting. "It wasn't an easy decision," DePodesta told me. "We all agreed that we needed to do something as one final move, but the options weren't to everyone's liking."

In the end it was Alderson's call—and he made it. Alderson was determined to go for it in 2015. He believed that the club's young starting pitching gave it a shot at going deep in the postseason with any kind of offensive support, and he'd been patient and deliberative enough in his Mets years. He'd earned the right to gamble—and that was what he was doing. Once he'd made clear he wanted to make the move, he asked Jeff Wilpon again, just to be 100 percent sure ownership had no objections, and he was given confirmation that he had a green light.

The announcement that the Mets had landed Céspedes sent a jolt of excitement through the fan base, and through the organization itself. He was that exciting a player. The mere fact of his joining the team seemed to take pressure off other Mets hitters. That same night, in a story line that seemed yanked from a heavy-handed Kevin Costner movie, only two days after his public show of tears on the field when he thought he'd been traded, Wilmer Flores had an unforgettable game

This was a key matchup with the rival Nationals, Matt Harvey was starting, and when Flores came up for his first at bat, the Citi Field crowd gave him a standing ovation. A new note had been struck, fan enthusiasm hitting a higher octave. "The Mets fans were definitely rallying around Wilmer and our team throughout the whole game," Harvey told reporters after the game. "I think they felt as much excitement as we definitely felt." Flores, clearly jacked up by the emotion of the day, singled in the fourth to bring in the first Mets run and also made a great diving stop on a ball hit up the middle, earning more ovations from the crowd. It was Wilmer Day at the park. Then, in the twelfth, Flores ended the game with a walk-off homer—and it was pandemonium at Citi Field, including around home plate as Mets players converged on the man of the moment.

It was the start of an amazing run. The Céspedes trade instantly exceeded Alderson's highest hopes. It helped that David Wright returned late in August and hit a home run his first time up after so many months lost dealing with spinal stenosis, but above all the Mets' magical August was a story of one hitter carrying a team. Céspedes was scorching the ball, hitting it at an average speed of 93.2 miles per hour off his bat, according to BaseballSavant.com, putting him up there with elite hitters Miguel Cabrera, Mike Trout, Paul Goldschmidt, David Ortiz, and José Bautista. He homered eight times in August, a franchise record for homers in a month. At one point the Mets scored seventy-three runs in seven games, the most they'd scored in a seven-game stretch in team history.

"This month has been quite remarkable actually," Alderson told me on the phone in late August. "I don't know if we'll realize how remarkable until we have some distance. It's remarkable to look at where we were before the deadline to where we are now."

Every single ESPN writer had picked the Nationals in 2015 to win the National League East. It was a team featuring Bryce Harper, making a case for himself as the best hitter in baseball, and formidable starters Max Scherzer and Stephen Strasburg. Yet in the end it turned out to be no contest. The Mets followed up the Flores walk-off win over the Nationals with two more wins for a series sweep that pulled them back into a tie for first place, then went on the road to sweep three from the Marlins. The Nationals just couldn't keep up. By season's end the team would be imploding, volatile closer Jonathan Papelbon choking Harper in a famous incident, with manager Matt Williams then sending Papelbon out to pitch the next inning as if nothing had happened.

The Mets were riding so high, it looked like they would reach the semi-mythical total of ninety wins well before the end of the season. In late September they traveled to Cincinnati and just pum-

meled the Reds, posting final scores in their four-game sweep of
6-4, 12-5, 10-2, and

8-1, and clinched their first National League East division title
and playoff berth since 2006.

They were at eighty-nine wins with six games left to play, going
into Philadelphia for a three-game series, but lost the first game, 4-3.
The next night, they jumped ahead in the first inning with a five-run
outburst. I was sitting with Alderson in his box watching the game
and mistakenly expected he might be relatively low-key at that point.
Not at all. "We need a shutdown inning here!" he said, showing a lot
more respect for the Phillies than I thought was warranted.

But he must have seen something coming. Sure enough, the
Phillies came back to win the game, 7-5, and that wasn't the worst
part: Céspedes, the man on whom so much depended, took a pitch off
his hand in the third inning and crumpled in obvious extreme pain.
Alderson hurried out of the box to go down to the clubhouse and
get a medical report and came back later to report that X-rays were
negative. Still, it was an ugly moment for the Mets in an ugly game
featuring seven wild pitches, four hit batters, and ten walks. Just like
that, the do-no-wrong feeling of so much that had happened with the
Mets since landing Céspedes seemed to have vanished. They looked
flat in a 3-0 loss to Philadelphia the next day, and hightailed it back to
New York, eager to ignore the indignity of being swept by the lowly
Phillies, but lost a day to a rainout, giving them more time to ponder
the sudden rut they'd fallen into. On Saturday they dropped both ends
of a makeup doubleheader to the Nationals, running their late-season
losing streak to five games. They might never win again! But in their
last chance to get something going before the postseason, a tag-team
assemblage of Mets pitcher took a combined no-hit bid into the seventh inning. DeGrom, limited to four innings by design, bounced back
with crisp command, handing it off to Colón and then Logan Verrett.
Granderson's solo shot in the eighth carried the Mets to a 1-0 win
over Washington on the last Sunday of the regular season. Alderson
had taken the Mets to ninety-win territory, just as he'd set out to do.

"If you're going to win one out of the last six, it was nice to
win the last one of the season at home," he joked to me afterward.

"You'd talked about ninety wins," I prompted him.

"Yeah, last year," he said, laughing.

But the ninety-win goal did help redirect the franchise, did it not?

"It shifted the focus last year, I believe, even though we didn't achieve it," Alderson said, "and this year I think it kept us on track, realizing what we wanted to do. Thinking about ninety, I think, helped keep us afloat during the first half of the season."

The one win was enough to break the spell. Now it was playoff time. Mets caps were sprouting up all over the city, including on musicians playing on subway platforms, as excitement mounted— until there was a no-show at the team's mandatory practice. Matt Harvey had, apparently, overslept. It was a thunderclap, a potential distraction at a time when the last thing anyone on the team wanted was distractions. Alderson took it in stride. His one priority was to make sure Harvey addressed the media immediately so that it would be a one-day story, which it mostly turned out to be, though it did put added pressure on Harvey to come through in the postseason, despite the obvious fatigue he'd been showing. David Wright and other team leaders handled the situation. It was a shocker, but it didn't have to mean anything for the team.

"I don't get surprised," Alderson told me. "It's like: Something is always coming up."

Talk radio and the press were buzzing about what Harvey would need to do on the Mets' charter flight from New York to California for Game 1 of the National League Division Series against the Dodgers. Would he have to wait on other players? Sing his contrition? Not hardly, said Alderson, who was on the flight. "I don't think there was anything demeaning that was going to take place," he said.

28

FINALLY BACK TO
THE PLAYOFFS

It was a fitting image for how everything seemed to go the Mets' way late in late 2015. Alderson was behind the wheel of his Ford rental, John Ricco had climbed into the backseat, and J. P. Ricciardi was riding shotgun. Just before they set out on October 9 from the team hotel in Pasadena for Dodger Stadium for Game 1 of the 2015 National League Division Series, Alderson was asked if he'd like to ride in the motorcade along with the Mets' team bus. Sure, why not? He pulled the car around, slid into position behind the bus, and craned his neck to see how many California Highway Patrol motorcycle cops he could spot, all decked out in obligatory shades and khaki uniforms like on the '70s TV show *CHiPs*.

"How many of them are there?" Alderson wondered.

"Six," I called from the backseat.

Then it was showtime. The six individual CHP officers darted in different directions in an elaborately choreographed display of precision. One stopped traffic at a distant intersection, one headed out in a point position, others flared out in front of the bus, now in motion, then retracted at exactly the right instant, shot forward, and resumed the tag-team work. Alderson loved it. For him this was a throwback to the tight choreography back at Eighth and I.

"These guys are good at this," he grinned at one point, happy for the distraction from thinking about the game, now three hours away.

Ricciardi, dressed casually in a white golf shirt and khaki slacks in contrast to Alderson's and Ricco's suits, grinned at the empty expanse of highway spreading out in front of their car, the L.A. Aqueduct flanking their progress on the left.

"See," Ricciardi said, deadpan. "L.A. traffic ain't that bad."

In the backseat, Ricco had his phone tuned in to the fourteenth inning of the Blue Jays–Rangers game.

"Well, the road teams have had success in all the games so far," Ricco pointed out.

The car panel showed 88 degrees back in Pasadena when Alderson pulled out of the hotel at 2:34 p.m., but soon it was up to 103. When they arrived at the ballpark, Ricco and Ricciardi hurried off. Alderson lingered, walking up to all six of the CHP officers in turn to shake hands.

"Thank you," he said to the final officer. "That was fun. You guys were great. It was like going to the ballet."

A lot of people around baseball assumed that the rollicking good fun of the Mets' late-season surge amounted to a tease of their fans. It was a nice story, the Mets sneaking into the playoffs on the heels of the Nationals' collapse, but many found it hard to believe the Mets had much chance against the Dodgers' best-in-baseball tandem of Clayton Kershaw and Zack Greinke or an offense fueled by the largest payroll in baseball. The Mets took comfort in having fared well head-to-head against the Dodgers. They'd taken two of three at Dodger Stadium in early July, one of those games the second of Steven Matz's career, and split a four-game home series later, the last game featuring seven innings of shutout ball from starter Jacob deGrom and a tenth-inning win for the Mets.

I'd caught up with Alderson in his suite at the team hotel hours before Game 1, passing Noah Syndergaard and his parents on the way to the elevator, and talked to the young pitcher long enough to get a sense that he was riding the right sort of wave—not too excited, not overtaken by the moment, ready to let it all play out.

I was a little surprised, but pleased, when Alderson made a point of talking about being glad for his manager, getting his first shot at the postseason after so many years. "Obviously I'm elated we're here and happy for the fans," he said. "I'm happy for Terry Collins, who hadn't been in this position ever before, and the coaching stuff and the players. We've got a lot of young players for whom this is a new experience. But it's going to be a tough series, facing some very good pitching, and a lot of left-handed-hitting pitching. Our young guys have actually adapted pretty well. Consider where Noah was at the beginning of the season and his role with us now. There's a lot of youth and inexperience there. But this is the crucible. We'll see how they come out at the other end."

The risk would be that, like countless teams coming into old Yankee Stadium over the years, the youthful Mets players would be intimated, but the surreal vibe of the day, with summer heat shimmering like in a Hollywood disaster movie, warded that off. It was still in the mid-90s when the Mets came off the field after batting practice. David Wright was among the last to take the steps down from field level, and as he did a Mets fan called out to him and Wright looked up and smiled, then stopped to converse. Wright was beaming. He looked totally relaxed, but there was a deep joy emanating from him, a feeling of long-deferred pleasure and satisfaction in the moment that gave him the happy glow of a bridegroom on his wedding day, intent on claiming every moment and occupying it as fully as possible. Wright disappeared into the tunnel, a noticeable hop in his step, and when Alderson appeared a few minutes later, walking into the now deserted dugout, he was all business, game-time worry now kicking in with full force.

Up in the press box, looking out over the Art Deco expanse of Dodger Stadium, even among cynical sportswriters there was a mood of palpable excitement over the matchup: Kershaw—so dominant so often, yet to date a postseason underachiever—against Jacob deGrom. I'd done an event at Litquake in San Francisco that summer along with Molly Knight, author of a bestselling book on the Dodgers, *The Best Team Money Can Buy*, and her anecdote about Kershaw sticking with his plan to have her over to his house for an interview, even though he happened to be agreeing to terms that very day on a huge contract extension, made him come across as sympathetic. Now here he is was in the 92-degree heat of an October evening, peering in for the sign against Mets leadoff hitter Curtis Granderson to open the game.

The Mets loved to work the count, putting pressure on a starter, but Granderson swung at the first pitch, a rarity for him, and smoked the ball to right fielder Andre Ethier for an out. Then David Wright, batting second, also swung at the first pitch, and fouled it back, taking a good cut. No sign of the stenosis slowing him down. Wright had a look of extreme composure up at bat, his linebacker eyes opened wide, and it was clear he was doing a good job of picking up Kershaw's pitches. He fouled off eight Kershaw deliveries and earned a twelve-pitch walk. The Mets did not score, but the game was on a trajectory where Kershaw was going to have to work.

Jacob deGrom came out in the bottom of the inning looking over-amped, missing high with early fastballs, but came back to strike out leadoff hitter Carl Crawford on a 98-mile-per-hour fastball. Second baseman Howie Kendrick poked a deGrom fastball to right for a single, and on the mound deGrom's body language was not good. He was noticeably upset, never a good place to be for any pitcher in the postseason, especially against as deep a lineup as the Dodgers'. Then deGrom went to work, disposing of shortstop Corey Seager with a high fastball and then, after a protracted battle, coming back from 3-0 to strike out Adrian Gonzalez on a 99-mile-per-hour fastball on the outside corner. Walking off the mound after striking out the side in his first inning of playoff baseball, deGrom still looked over-amped, but he also looked determined and focused.

The game's first scoring threat came in the second when ex-Met Justin Turner cracked a sharp line drive to left field and veteran Michal Cuddyer froze, then moved back awkwardly and had the ball kick off his glove for what was scored a double. This would be a test for deGrom, and he responded by striking out the side around an intentional walk to Joc Pederson. No one was happier than Cuddyer, who hurried in to congratulate deGrom. "Hey, my bad," Cuddyer told him, as he explained afterward. "The way he was dominating them, it didn't faze him one bit." Nor was deGrom nonplussed an inning later when Cuddyer misplayed a blooper by Seager, letting it fall for a two-out double, striking out Gonzalez again to end the inning.

Daniel Murphy led off the fourth for the Mets. Kershaw fell behind 2-0 and then threw a classic mistake pitch, a fastball out over the plate, about thigh-high, that Murphy belted for a no-doubt-about-it homer to right. Kershaw pulled his cap off as Murphy sprinted around the bases and used the back of his forearm to wipe sweat away from his forehead. He held the score at 1-0 through six, but he was pulled in the seventh after he gave up three straight walks to load up the bases for Wright, who lined a single off reliever Pedro Baez to score two runs and put the Mets up 3-0. As Ron Darling noted on the broadcast, it was a nice moment for Wright, who had seen his baseball life flash before his eyes and didn't know if the spinal stenosis would keep him from ever playing again, let alone stroking the game-winning hit in a playoff game. DeGrom came out of the game after seven shutout innings, having recorded an eye-popping total of thirteen strikeouts and winning the duel with Kershaw. "Ultimately Jacob outpitched him," Alderson told me afterward. "Kershaw was good, but Jacob was a little better and he had a little bit extra left in that seventh inning. That was really the difference."

It came down to a four-out save by Familia, but Alderson didn't see much of his work. He couldn't stand to watch the ninth inning, and went for a walk. As anyone who has visited Chavez Ravine knows, the parking lots go on and on, and up and up, and Alderson climbed to the far end. "I always take a walk in the ninth," he said. "I got in about eleven thousand steps at the ballpark. That's more than five miles."

"I was pretty calm, although I wouldn't let our PR guy leave the box," J. P. Ricciardi told me. "He tried to leave with two outs in the inning. I told him: You can't go anymore."

Sometimes watching the 2015 Mets on a tear over the last month of the season, it was easy to forget how new this all was to many of their players. Since coming back from an elbow injury at the end of July, catcher Travis d'Arnaud had showed he could stay healthy and contribute with his bat, and he was the linchpin that held the pitching staff together, conferring with pitchers, pitching coach Dan Warthen, and bullpen coach Ricky Bones to go over game plans and make sure he was in sync with the pitchers in his game-calling.

But d'Arnaud was so young he was still half-fan, and couldn't believe he was playing at Dodger Stadium, not far from where he'd grown up in Long Beach, just thirty-five miles away.

"I felt like I was in my backyard," he told me after Game 1. "I had my family there, all my friends there, watching me warm up. I felt like I was playing high school baseball all over again. I've been to Dodger Stadium as a fan too many times to count. Even last year when we were out of it, they were in the playoffs and I was there in the right-field pavilion crushing hot dogs."

This time Alderson knew the drill for the ride back to the hotel. He passed by the CHP motorcycle unit on his way to the car and told them, "Let's see if you can do it as well at night as you did during the day."

"Maybe better," one of them said with a good-natured smile.

It was a quiet ride. Alderson and Ricciardi were satisfied but tired. There was some grumbling over minor game details here and there, but for Alderson it was time to take at least a modicum of pleasure in the moment and once again marvel over the strange un-predictability of baseball, where his converted-shortstop, second-year starter could outpitch a three-time Cy Young winner.

Back at the hotel, having made the trip in eighteen minutes flat after leaving Dodger Stadium at 11:15, he started to walk into the lobby, then thought better of it. "I'm going to go thank the guys," he said with an almost impish grin, walking off to shake the hands of the CHP team.

Alderson had taken the Oakland A's to the World Series three straight years a quarter-century earlier, winning just once, in 1989, and he was acutely aware of the fundamental truth that in baseball, no matter how talented you might be, you never know when you'll get back to a division series or World Series. The Mets might have come into the 2015 season thinking in terms of a feel-good brief ap-pearance in the playoffs paving the way for a run at the World Series in 2016 or 2017, but with the Washington Nationals' underachieving drama leaving the National League East wide open in 2015, Alderson and his assistants planted the flag on the season.

"I give them a lot of credit: They said: 'Let's go for it now,'" manager Terry Collins told me at the bar of the Mets' team hotel that night, soon after I left Alderson.

I had informed Collins, who was ordering a celebratory round for his coaching staff as I enjoyed a quick postgame beer, that Alderson had just been telling me that morning how happy he was for Collins to be getting his first postseason managing action at age sixty-six after so many years. Collins did a quick double take, staring up into my eyes for a minute to see if I might be snowing him, saw I wasn't, and then smiled and launched into a quick, friendly paean to the front-office magic of July. He was well aware of the five years I'd spent researching this book with unprecedented access to Alderson.

"Sandy did a great job," Collins concluded, cradling his haul of drinks for his coaches and heading away with a grin and gleeful-little-boy, speeded-up shuffle.

The following night, thanks to early home runs from Céspedes and Michael Conforto off Greinke, the Mets were in the unbelievable position of carrying a 2-1 lead into the bottom of the seventh inning, nine outs away from taking two from the Dodgers in their own stadium. Syndergaard came out throwing 100 miles per hour in the first inning, but soon put on a show with more than speed, demonstrating that the giant with the flowing blond locks really was a pitcher, not just a hulk.

The seventh started quietly enough, with Syndergaard issuing a one-out walk to Enrique Hernandez and veteran Chase Utley pinch-hitting for Greinke. Utley had slowed down at age thirty-six, and was nothing like the player who helped the Phillies win a World Series, but he did his job, poking a single to right to put runners on the corners. That was all for Syndergaard, and Collins opted to go with Bartolo Colón, figuring he could get a double-play ball. As every Mets fan knows, that is exactly what he got, but Murphy's flip to Ruben Tejada was high, and the shortstop found himself with his back to first base, trying to spin around, as Utley approached. There is breaking up a double play hard but clean, and there is flying past the bag, arm outstretched with no move whatsoever to touch the base. There is sliding hard, and there is not actually sliding at all, but simply diving right at Tejada, breaking a bone in his leg.

"That's not a slide," Cuddyer said afterward. "That's a tackle."

The most bizarre part of the play was what happened next. Utley had clearly slid late, and he dutifully hopped up and trotted toward the dugout, knowing he was out. The correct call would have been to call him out and also bring the runner back from home, since he had scored on an illegal play. Instead, Utley was called out—and Dodgers manager Don Mattingly actually challenged the play.

As everyone knows, umpires give middle infielders wide latitude in turning a double play. The so-called "neighborhood" play means, roughly, that you could be in line for beer out in Section 111 and still get the call. But the umpires somehow came up with the crazy notion that the neighborhood play did not apply. Tejada, who had been assaulted mid-play, was now being punished for having his foot fall just short of the bag. It was a joke. But the appeal was successful: Utley was awarded second base! Predictably enough, the Dodgers took advantage of the gigantic gift given to them and took a two-run lead—and the game—when Adrian Gonzalez belted a Colón offering into the gap for a double that broke it open.

The Utley incident unleashed a major "Señor Sandy" moment. Alderson was fuming, waiting near the umpires' room after the game to talk with Joe Torre, Major League Baseball's chief baseball officer, and their exchange was lively. Later Torre would suspend Utley, but Utley was able to appeal and retain eligibility for the series, rendering the issue moot. There was a lot of talk, especially on the Dodger side, about how the Utley play had given L.A. "momentum." What the blown calls had done was give the Dodgers a game. They were tied at one apiece instead of down by two games heading to New York for Game 3.

Really there was not much room for ambiguity. In my days as a newspaper baseball writer I used to pass the time reading the rule book, and it amazed me how people didn't bother to study the text. It's usually quite clear, as it is in this case: "(e) If, in the judgment of the umpire, a base runner willfully and deliberately interferes with a batted ball or a fielder in the act of fielding a batted ball with the obvious intent to break up a double play, the ball is dead. The umpire shall call the runner out for interference and also call out the batter-runner because of the action of his teammate. In no event may bases be run or runs scored because of such action by a runner."

The description almost sounds like it was written with the Utley play in mind, and when Major League Baseball ruled the Utley tackle "illegal," it clearly meant the above rule should have applied and that the inning should have been over with no runs scored and the Mets' 2-1 lead intact. Noah Syndergaard should have been charged with only one run allowed, and would probably have been in line for a win in his first postseason start. The injustice of it all kept the voices loud on talk radio into the wee hours, but for Mets players there was also a deeper feeling: We're outplaying these guys.

The series moved to New York, where the mood was set by the back cover of the *New York Post*, showing Harvey and the headline DARK JUSTICE. For the Mets, the justice that mattered was winning. Harvey was not sharp early and the Dodgers took a 3-0 lead, helped by a Granderson throwing error, but half an inning later Granderson doubled with the bases loaded to put the Mets up 4-3, and from there it was a night of offensive fireworks. D'Arnaud connected on a two-run homer in the third and in the fourth Céspedes launched a three-run blast to put the Mets up 10-3 on their way to an easy 13-7 win.

The only trouble was, the next night it would be Kershaw, pitching on only three days' rest, against left-hander Steven Matz, who was dealing with not having pitched in an actual game since September 24. Matz was pretty good, holding the Dodgers to three runs in five innings, a credible performance, but Kershaw was much better, giving up a Murphy solo shot and little else on his way to seven dominant innings and a 3-1 Dodger victory.

Game 5 back in L.A. turned into the Daniel Murphy show. He doubled in the first off Greinke to give the Mets a 1-0 lead, only to see the Dodgers come back in the bottom of the inning and make it 2-1 on four straight singles off deGrom. That had Syndergaard up in the bullpen in the second, ready to come on in relief, but after the two runs in the first deGrom found a way to hold the Dodgers scoreless from then on. The biggest play of the game came when Lucas Duda drew a walk with Murphy at first base. The Dodgers had the shift on for Duda, so no one was near third base. Murphy noticed, but kept his head down as he took a slow trot to second base, almost walking, nonchalant as can be, as he neared the bag. Then—wham!—he threw it into gear and ran from second to third, stealing the base easily. It was a stunner! When d'Arnaud followed up with a sacrifice fly to right to score Murphy, tying the game, the Murphy theft loomed even larger.

His teammates were amazed, especially David Wright, who had been watching Murph play for years. "Sometimes it seems like he thinks he's invisible out there on the bases," Wright told reporters after the game. "He'll do something out there that makes you say, 'What was he thinking?'" This time he did something that made the Dodgers say: *What were we thinking?* They were reeling after that, and the Mets were energized, especially when Murphy hit yet another home run two innings later to put New York up by a run. The game was far from over—the unforgettable action included Syndergaard's turn in relief, striking out Turner on an off-speed pitch after setting him up with high-90s fastballs and working a scoreless inning, and Familia's putting the win in the books with a six-out save.

The Mets' celebration was explosive, as we would all have expected, and it was all-inclusive. Alderson made a point of rarely venturing into the clubhouse, viewing it as the players' private realm, but this was a time to head in there and soak up the moment—and he ended up soaking up a lot more than that. As soon as he entered, he was set upon by Mets players, spraying him. "I couldn't really stay out of the clubhouse," he told me. "That wouldn't have been good form. It's a small clubhouse. I sort of expected that somebody would try to get me when I went into the clubhouse. It was a combination of players and staff, but in any event I was soaked. It was champagne and beer, I think. Fortunately I was able to take a shower before our plane departed. It was a nice gesture. I felt part of a happy group of players and staff. That was really enough of a reward in and of itself."

Terry Collins had used the word "gravy" to describe the Mets making it to Game 5 against the Dodgers, and many assumed the

Mets were just happy to be there and couldn't possibly hang with the talented Chicago Cubs, led by dynamic manager Joe Maddon, in the National League Championship Series. The Cubs, like the Mets, had stockpiled young talent, but focused on power-hitting position players rather than pitchers. Many thought it would be a close series, but it wasn't. In fact, Game 1 was the closest contest, and it really wasn't that close. Daniel Murphy smoked a first-inning home run to give the Mets a 1-0 lead and Harvey worked four perfect innings before a hit batsman and a double gave the Cubs the tying run in the top of the fifth—but then they made the mistake of testing Céspedes' arm. Starlin Castro was out at home trying to score, and the Cubs were unable to take the lead; in fact, they would never have a lead in the entire series. The Mets won Game 1 4-2, and came back in Game 2 to sprint to an early lead, jumping ahead 3-0 on a Granderson single, a Wright run-scoring double and (you probably saw this coming) a Murphy home run, giving him homers in four straight games. Syndergaard was on his game, striking out nine and holding the Cubs to one run in 5⅔ innings and the Mets coasted to a 4-1 win.

Back at Wrigley Field, the Cubs' delightful century-old ballpark, fans were ready to see their Cubs pounce. After all, in winning the first two games at home, the Mets were in a sense just holding serve; now it was the Cubs' turn. Except: Not so fast. Daniel Murphy put the Mets ahead to stay in the third with a solo shot to center, deGrom held the Cubs to two runs over seven, and the Mets rolled to a 5-2 win. The shame of Game 4 was that the Mets' young left-handed starter, Matz, who gave up only one run through four innings, came out in the fifth with a 6-1 lead, three outs short of earning himself the win. This was another shellacking, with Lucas Duda launching a three-run shot in the first and d'Arnaud and Murphy both adding homers, giving Murphy home runs in six straight postseason games, a major-league record.

"It's unbelievable," Alderson said chuckling. "One or two people a decade get this hot, maybe. I do think he's been a different hitter since the middle of the season. He's looking less to punch the ball the other way and to drive the ball, whether to go the other way or to pull it. Rather than laying off pitches out of the strike zone, it's more about laying off of pitches away in the strike zone, and looking for pitches middle-in that you can drive. He's no less aggressive. He's still aggressive, but on different pitches."

"Murphy's on a different planet right now," hitting coach Kevin Long told *USA Today*. "Last at bat, he's looking for a changeup, and he hits a ninety-seven-mile-an-hour fastball out. That's where he's at right now. It's mind-boggling, it really is. He told me he was going up there looking for a changeup. I said after, 'I thought you were looking for a changeup.' He said, 'I was. I have no idea what happened.'"

The Mets, 8-3 winners in Game 4, were going to the World Series. For Alderson, the Cubs series had almost passed in fast motion, compared to the slow, agonizing grind of the Dodgers series. Against L.A. the series had been back and forth, with constant awareness that Kershaw and Greinke might both render the Mets helpless; this series with the Cubs, in contrast, zipped along as if at an accelerated pace. Whereas in L.A. when the Mets advanced Alderson had known he couldn't possibly skip out on the celebration, instead getting doused with beer and champagne, this time he felt no obligation to celebrate with the players. Jared Diamond of the *Wall Street Journal* spotted Alderson sitting quietly by himself, taking it all in, and tweeted out a picture, along with the words: "That lone man in the crowd is Sandy Alderson, the architect of this team. He's watching the party go by."

"I had no desire whatsoever to get a champagne shower again," Alderson told me two days later. "I figured once was enough. I kind of wandered around. I went to the bus to see if Linda was there. Then everyone was on the field, I kept wandering around and I thought, 'This is really nice. Why don't I find a place just to sit?' My phone had blown up and I thought I could answer some of that. I wasn't looking to have a photograph taken, but it was nice to see. The players were happy, the families were happy, the organization people were happy. That was what it was all about for me. I just sat there and enjoyed it."

29

SIXTY FEET, SIX INCHES

The prevailing opinion among baseball writers, and probably most of the country, was that the Royals were simply too good a team for the upstart Mets to challenge. Kansas City, went this line of thinking, had been there a year earlier, grappling with the Giants tooth and nail, and only falling in Game 7 because of the heroics of Madison Bumgarner. It was a compelling argument, and watching them in the first two games, it was easy to believe the Royals might run the table, snatching the Series from the Mets and never giving them a chance to snap to life.

Game 1 had started in the worst possible way for the Mets. The Royals' leadoff hitter, Alcides Escobar, loved to lunge at the first pitch, hunting fastball, and Harvey gave him one right where he wanted it, which Escobar torqued to left-center. Céspedes had volunteered to play center field when he arrived with the Mets, emphasizing he felt he could easily handle the position, and he had the physical tools. But on this ball, as on so many others in the postseason, he had a confused look and was slow to react. It was his ball as the center fielder and he should have been going for it all the way, but instead he looked over at left fielder Michael Conforto at the last minute. He never found the ball again and ended up playing what should have been a fly-out into an incredible inside-the-park home run. The Royals had already been loose and confident; now they felt like they were unwrapping birthday presents.

Harvey was not at his best, and the Mets weren't, either, but even so they took a one-run lead into the bottom of the ninth. Familia had been so good as their closer, not having blown a save since the rain-delay game on July 30. For Mets fans he seemed automatic, but the Royals apparently didn't get the memo that they should be impressed. Familia tried a quick pitch, something he had learned from ex-Met LaTroy Hawkins, only Alex Gordon didn't seem in the least surprised, and the 97-mile-per-hour sinker was up in the zone, not where Familia wanted it. Home run, Royals. Blown save. The game dragged on so long that when the Royals finally won it in the bottom of the fourteenth with a rally started by a David Wright error, the marathon loss seemed to leave the Mets depleted and wrung out. That was how they looked the next night, eking out just two hits and one run against Johnny Cueto, who worked a complete game, in a 7-1 loss, deGrom losing on a night when Royals hitters struck out only twice against him.

Back in New York, the Mets felt back at square one, in a good way. Given the depth of their starting pitching, they felt that if they could get one win under their belt, slow down the Royals' parade, they were well positioned to grind them down with their dominating young pitching. Even contact hitters can sometimes be dominated. On the off-day, Collins gave his players the day off, giving them time to regroup, so just Collins and Game 3 starter Noah Syndergaard would address the press in the interview room. Syndergaard was peppered with questions about how he would handle leadoff hitter Escobar, who made no bones about swinging at the first pitch. I'd taken an all-night flight from California to be there and was slumping in my chair, but perked up when I heard his reply.

"I've got a few things up my sleeve," he said, smiling. "Their strength is how aggressive they are. I was able to watch Matt and deGrom and see how they approached hitters ... and devise a game plan for myself. My main focus tomorrow night is to pitch to my strengths."

That was interesting. A pro forma session with the press had hit another level, and by the time the comment made the rounds via social media, the sense of expectation surrounding the first pitch of Game 1 had built to a crescendo. That was when Syndergaard unleashed the 98-mile-per-hour message pitch that sailed to the screen. He had a flair for the dramatic, a willingness to take center stage. Far more important, though, was the stubborn creativity Syndergaard showed in working past the innings in which the Royals' contact hitters ping-ping-pinged his deliveries all over the place, scoring three quick runs to take a 3-2 lead. He got himself to idle down enough to start hitting the target with his fastball and kept Royals hitters wondering which pitch was coming next, and from the third inning on Kansas City never scored again. The Mets' 9-3 win in the first World Series game ever at Citi Field, punctuated by home runs from Wright and Granderson, had the place jumping.

Back in L.A., when Chase Utley flew past the bag to take out Ruben Tejada, most saw it as a dirty play, and for good reason. Some defended it as hard-nosed old-school baseball, with a whisper that the Mets were a little soft. David Wright looks more like a choirboy than a guy who'd pull a tire iron out of his muscle car and come at you. From my vantage, it was clear that the Mets of the Alderson era possessed some of his toughness as a former marine. Alderson was gentlemanly, especially now that he was in his sixties, but he'd always had a quiet hidden toughness as well. The Utley play infuriated Alderson not just because he didn't like the impact it had on his team in that game but because it assaulted his sense of right and wrong and the rightful boundaries between being aggressive or even brutal, within the rules, and going beyond that.

The Syndergaard game generated a buzz; it demanded that you tune in to Game 4 on time and stay alert, because wild stuff might be coming. The Royals had wallowed in their sense of outrage like pigs in slop. If the Royals were so affronted, they could have come out of the dugout right then and there, instead of standing at the rail swearing a blue streak. They could have thrown high and tight when Syndergaard came to bat. Instead they pitched to him, challenged him with a fastball, and he stroked a clean single to right and came around to score. No, the cries of protest from the Royals after the game carried the whiff of all those dismal bad-acting moments we've seen in soccer, when a player writhes on the field, howling at an octave usually reserved for animals being carted away to the slaughterhouse. This was theater, but it was theater in New York City, the capital of theater, and a bunch of contact hitters from

Kansas City had an uphill struggle if they were going to out-theater the hometown New York club. They might outhit them. They might outpitch them. But they were not going to out-theater them on their home turf.

The problem was, sometimes a flair for theatricality can end up being the worst possible thing. Steven Matz pitched well in Game 4, lasting five and being charged with two runs. It was 3-2 heading into the eighth when the Mets put together all the elements for the kind of theatrical collapse that gets replayed forever. Jon Niese, Bartolo Colón, and Addison Reed had all come and gone and Collins went to Clippard, who had been struggling. He ended up issuing back-to-back walks, putting the go-ahead run on base, but when Familia came on in relief and got a ground ball to second, it looked like the Mets might be on their way to getting out of the inning after all. Murphy charged hard, avoiding the Royals base runner, and then— oh no!—the ball rolled right under his glove. One run scored to tie the game. Familia did his best to shrug off the defensive miscue, and got Mike Moustakas to hit a ground ball to the right side of the infield. A second baseman with more range—or Murphy on a better day—would have had it, but it skipped into the outfield to score the winning run.

I tried talking to some Mets in the clubhouse after Game 4, but realized it was pointless. The press contingent was thick as flies, much thicker than after the Game 3 victory, since reporters crave quotes more when a team has blown a game. I decided to make my way to the 7 train back into Manhattan, and unfortunately the record-setting crowd that night at Citi mostly had the same idea. By the time I made it into a subway car, bumped by grumpy Mets fans all along the way, I was not so much irritated as distracted.

Obviously I knew that if the Mets won the World Series, more people would read my book, which is the main thing any writer cares about, so in a sense Murphy's blunder had denied me that. But mostly, as ever when I'm around sports, I was busy trying to tune in to the narrative of it all. My first thought, hurrying away from the acrid quiet of a Mets dressing room every player badly wanted to avoid, was that no team could hand away two games in a World Series and survive to take the series deep, let alone win it. But I was starting to wonder. When I thought about Harvey and his chances in Game 5 the next night, what came to mind was a picture of him having that look again, that look of swagger and utter focus. My hunch was that Harvey was going to solve the riddle of the Royals, but would Mets batters be able to do their part?

I was mulling these thoughts as the jam-packed 7 train lurched toward Manhattan. I looked around to get a sense of the crowd. How demoralized were Mets fans? Would this epic collapse rob them of the retrospective joy of the amazing hop, skip, and jump of a march past the Nationals, Dodgers, and Cubs? As I was wondering, the guy right next to me suddenly lapsed into a theatrical voice and called out: "We've still got Harvey, deGrom, and Syndergaard!"

The hangdog looks all around the car yielded to wary smiles. Heads topped by Mets caps turned his way.

"It's not over yet!"

Then, even more improbably, he brightly declared that it was time to sing "Meet the Mets!" a song written back in 1962, and proceeded to give it all he had doing just that, straight through to the lesser-known second verse, starting with "Oh, the butcher and the baker and the people on the streets/where did they go? To MEET THE METS! . . ."

Smiles were all around now, and even, if you can believe it, clear optimism about how the rest of the Series would go. I could hear murmurs, speculation about how once Harvey won, deGrom would get another chance and look at what he'd done, and man oh man, how cool would it be to see Thor out there for Game 7 after the way he'd gotten inside the Royals' hitters?

The singer's name was Brian Manning, an editor for *Financial News* and a lifelong Mets fan, going back to 1986, which was huge for him as an eight-year-old. He was a devoted enough fan that when he had recently married, he plugged in his iPod at the reception to rock the joint with "Meet the Mets!"

"You've got to keep the hopes up when you can," he told me as the doors slid open at a stop along the way to Times Square. "Nobody in April would have said, 'Oh yeah, we'll be in the World Series.'"

Brian Manning's heartfelt optimism stayed with me, and by the time Harvey took the mound to start Game 5, who was I not to believe? Why wouldn't I start to tune in to the sweet potential of a great story line, the Series going back to Kansas City with deGrom and Syndergaard looming? Harvey's fastball had that explosive late life again. He was snapping off his breaking pitches. He could clearly throw all four of his pitches for strikes.

Granderson homered for the Mets in the bottom of the first to give them a lead and Harvey took it from there, throwing shutout inning after shutout inning. There had been an operatic quality to all the hullabaloo around Harvey. Yet here he was stepping into a rarefied realm, potentially on his way to a historic World Series performance.

It was like descending into a mine shaft, the way the pressure closed in from all around, ever greater in intensity, as Harvey worked deeper into the game. How far could he go? He recorded his ninth strikeout to open the top of the sixth, then gave up a single to Zobrist. By this point absolutely everyone was aware of the Royals' M.O., which was to start small and just keep coming, so the Zobrist single loomed large. Next up was Cain, always dangerous, and Harvey worked him to 2-2, pounding fastballs. Peering in, Harvey shook off d'Arnaud, wanting the low slider, and just as he was about to deliver the pitch, he flashed a devilish little smile, an I-got-this grin, subtle but unmistakable, that told you he was still feeling it—and he was, letting fly with a devastating low slider that bounced as Cain lunged for the strikeout. Then, facing Hosmer, Harvey got a groundout to Murphy, who was very careful in fielding and slowly throwing the ball to first to end the inning.

Harvey was doing his part, and the Mets' offense knew it had to add to the 1-0 lead—too potent was the Royals' ability to stage late-inning comebacks. Granderson led off with a walk, taking an inside pitch, and Wright singled to left to put two on with Murphy coming up with a great chance to atone for his blunder the night before. Murphy drilled one; it handcuffed Hosmer and flipped up in the air and rolled away before anyone could corral it. Céspedes had been quiet in the Series, but now he had the bases loaded with no outs, a prime chance to feast on an RBI opportunity. Céspedes, possibly out of whack with his sore left shoulder, swung and drove the ball hard into his left knee, crumpling in pain. Through the extended delay, and seeing Céspedes so obviously hobbled, it seemed odd that Collins chose not to bring in Uribe to pinch-hit, especially when Céspedes popped up and could barely limp toward first base. But Lucas Duda, next up, came through with a sacrifice fly to make it 2-0, and the Mets finally had a little more breathing room.

That was where it stood in the bottom of the eighth, at 2-0, Harvey having delivered an electrifying performance, and now the Mets were pulling him out of the game. Pitching coach Dan Warthen went over to give his starter the news—only Harvey was having none of it. He made his case to Warthen and then to Collins and carried the day: He was going back out there for the ninth. His general manager wasn't about to second-guess his manager's decision.

"My feeling is that the entire stadium was asking for Harvey in the ninth," Alderson told me that week. "You heard the chants: 'We want Harvey.' Harvey himself wanted to be out there. I can totally understand why Terry sent him out there."

Once the Mets had been retired, Harvey stepped up, pulled the towel off his shoulder, and then removed his warm-up jacket, shaking his hand out, all in slow motion, as if he were absorbing the energy of the moment, the "Harvey" chants of the crowd, trying to summon something. What was it? Will? Energy? Karma? Luck? Did he even know? He just felt something, almost like current flowing, and knew it was telling him he had to continue here and that he would be up to the challenge. As soon as he hit the top of the dugout on his way out, the Citi Field crowd reacted with a huge roar, and he sprinted out to the mound.

Facing Cain, knowing how much he needed to make each pitch count, he missed with a fastball up to make it 1-0. Soon it was 2-2, the noise level in Queens seemingly rising with every pitch, but Harvey's 2-2 pitch sailed up and away, not even close; and then with a full count he missed low. No! A leadoff walk! Surely Collins would have to go to Familia now. But he didn't. And Hosmer doubled against Harvey, scoring Cain to make it a one-run game. Murphy had swiped ninety feet unforgettably to get the Mets this far, and now they would have the favor returned. With one out and Hosmer having advanced to third, Perez grounded to the left side of the infield. Wright pounced on the ball and had plenty of time, but given his health issues, he was using a sidearm fling without much mustard on it—as Hosmer well knew. So he started cheating toward home, then broke with the throw. First baseman Lucas Duda had time to make a good throw home, which probably would have had him, but his throw sailed wide, one more costly mistake for the Mets this World Series.

The Mets came up in the bottom of the twelfth, now down by five, seeking a comeback that would be beyond amazing. The final play was all too fitting, Céspedes leaning the wrong way on a line drive off the bat of Duda and getting doubled off to end the game and the season.

I know as well as anyone how much Sandy Alderson despises losing. I called him on the Tuesday after the Series, and when I asked how he was, it was no rhetorical question.

"Not bad considering we just blew three games and blew the Series," he muttered darkly. "I know that people say they were a better team, but we had the lead in the ninth twice and blew both those games and blew a lead in the eighth. We weren't great, but we were in a position to win. You get this close, and it's even more disappointing. It's like I remembered: Nobody goes home happy except the winners."

In some ways the Mets' whirlwind ride through the 2015 World Series offered an almost clinical experiment in mapping out the subtle ways in which a team is, or is not, more than the sum of its parts. Céspedes had helped put the Mets in the playoffs with a spectacular run, and yet all through the postseason he looked like someone out on the dance floor who doesn't like the music playing: Others were dancing to the beat, but he just wasn't feeling it. Good hitters go cold in the World Series—it happens—but Céspedes had done much more than go cold at the plate. He started off the World Series by misplaying a ball Juan Lagares would surely have caught in center field into an inside-the-park home run. Then he refused to take responsibility after the game. He was a step slow reacting to any fly ball hit to him and he was a step slow in reaction to the realities of what was happening around him.

Talking one on one, Cespedes impressed me. He had big, alert eyes, he listened attentively, and he was clearly a thoughtful man. The conclusion I came to, watching his lackluster performance in the Series, was that he just did not understand what it was to be a part of a team and to experience events as a teammate. Partly, of course, that has to do with only arriving on the team in late July, but it ran much deeper than that: Juan Uribe had no such problems. Céspedes was in a sense doomed by his prodigious, nearly unprecedented talent to be in a club of one, never one of the guys; but he seemed to go out of his way to perpetuate this. No one would care if he golfed every day before games as long as he showed up ready to give his all, but kicking balls around in the outfield and striking out time after time is not giving your all. Céspedes was playing in a fog, and whether it was because of his sore shoulder, other injuries, or some other factor really didn't matter in the end.

When Steven Matz first joined the Mets, he told me that literally everyone on the team made him feel welcome, and if that seemed like exaggeration it actually kind of made sense. On a club deep into a youth movement, with so many talented prospects working their way up through the system, they all knew each other and had shared the experience of getting to the big team together. Céspedes gave the Mets one of the all-time remarkable runs in baseball history, and people I respect, like longtime *New York Times* columnist George Vecsey, felt that in so doing he'd announced himself as a player to be talked about in the same breath as Mays or Clemente. Céspedes could well have taken over the World Series as well. It didn't happen that way. He didn't even contribute in a meaningful way. But far from being disappointed, the Mets knew that the experience of playing meaningful games not into August or September, a previous goal, or into October, the classic goal, but all the way into November, had given their young players a crash course in how to carry themselves as champions. It had worked for the Royals, who fell just short in 2014 but used the experience as a fulcrum to will themselves back to the World Series a year later. There was a lot that stood in the way of the Mets pulling that off as well. But enough promise beckoned that the bitter defeat of early November shifted quickly to an awed appreciation of just what a fun year it had been.

"What a crazy year!" d'Arnaud told me a few days after the season ended. "Even from spring training, our thought process was that we wanted to get to the playoffs, and then we did so well to start the season, and then we had a losing streak, and then we came back. The last two months we were playing ridiculous baseball. I feel like with the four starters we have it's going to be like that from the get-go in 2016."

ACKNOWLEDGMENTS

I'd first like to thank Morgan Entrekin, Grove Atlantic publisher, for being the kind of reader who gets excited about writers and looks for ways to make things work. He decided he wanted to publish me based on the first chapter of *Reading in Place*, a memoir-in-books I'm writing, and suggested we meet to kick around ideas for my next sports book. As Morgan and I ate lunch, Sandy Alderson was across town in Queens interviewing for the job of Mets GM. I'd been studying Alderson since the mid-1990s and sparred regularly with him; he once tried to get me reassigned from my job covering the A's as beat writer for the *San Francisco Chronicle*. Thanks, Sandy, for agreeing to make yourself available for more than a hundred interviews for this book, for sitting with me to watch games together from Port St. Lucie and Cincinnati to L.A. and Oakland, and for doing your best to maintain wan good cheer even during some grim stretches. Thanks to June Napoli for always doing her best to connect us and for her warm heart and sense of humor, and to Jay Horwitz (keep tweeting, Jay!) and Shannon Forde.

I was lucky to be teamed up with an editor as brilliant and as committed to the long, slow build of book writing as Jamison Stoltz. He's an editor of the old school, comfortable enough to be grumpy at times, almost giddy in his enthusiasm at others, and he took on the onus of living and dying with the Mets during the four years we worked on this book. I only hope that his son Oscar, a little Mets fan, will live to see his wishes fulfilled "at the baseball stadium." So many at Grove are both talented and go the extra mile, but I'd like to thank in particular Allison Malecha, Deb Seager, John Mark Boling, Amy Vreeland, and Judy Hottensen (I look forward to more Bay Area dinners). My longtime agents Jane Gelfman and Heather Mitchell are two of my favorite people.

Billy Beane was generous with his time and insights. We've been talking about everything but baseball for twenty years now, but especially books and soccer, and it was fascinating to revisit his early days with the A's. To my best friend in baseball, Pedro Gomez, I can only flash back to 1995 when it was KGB: you, me, and the Island of Bitikos, talking ball until closing time most nights on the road ("I don't *have* a car!"). I'd have never had a clue about navigating a major-league clubhouse if not for Pedro, but above all, he passed on a passion for the game and for the quiet human drama behind the game. That's how I feel about many others from Oakland days: broadcaster Ken Korach, a future Hall of Famer, I'm just sure; Mickey Morabito, traveling secretary and best dinner companion ever; Steve Vucinich, equipment manager, team historian, and in so many ways, the soul of the A's along with Mickey. Wally Haas has so many stories, thanks for letting me share a few of them. Getting to know Roy Eisenhardt was a highlight of this project; thanks, Roy, for making me a little smarter. Thanks to Debbie Gallas and Bob Rose of the A's, and Jim Moorehead of the Giants.

My first sports editor, back at the *Daily Californian* in the 1980s, was Pete Danko, also a great sportswriter: I'll never forget a column he wrote as a student that was partly in the voice of Joan Didion. Pete, who went on to write for the *New York Times* and *Riverside Press-Enterprise*, was hugely helpful in reading versions of the manuscript, as were my other readers, Steve Vucinich, Ken Korach, Pedro Gomez, George Vecsey, Bryan Curtis, David Davis, and Danny Knobler.

Bronwen Hruska not only invited me into the sitcom of her life (and oh what a sitcom) during my many New York visits on this project, she was the ultimate sounding board for getting past the dol- drums along the way; she's never at a loss to shed light on a writerly quandary and offer possible solutions. Also, her novel *Accelerated* re- minded me of the power of imaginative, well researched storytelling. Thanks to my companions at Citi Field, the incomparable Dave Blum (*not* Darth Vader), future ace sportswriter Sam Blum, Nick Kulish, and Clay Risen for sharing insights or just humoring me. I've been a baseball fan since I was a kid growing up in San Jose, thanks to my family: my late sister, Janette Kettmann Klingner of Colorado; my parents, Gerard and Nancy Kettmann; brother Jeff, so loaded with sports insight he should have a talk radio show; and brother Dave, always my favorite choice for taking in a game at the ballpark.

It's hard to explain to a German why I think baseball matters. When Sarah Ringler and I founded the Wellstone Center in the Redwoods in Northern California in 2012, it was our hope to inspire people. It's been a challenge, but we've made some early progress. *San Francisco Magazine* named us to their "Best of the Bay" issue for my "Find Your Voice" weekend writing workshop; we've begun to host writers in residence for one month at a time; and our Wellstone Books publishing arm is off to a good start with some exciting titles on the way in 2015. We've been lucky to share our project with so many who have lent a hand and made our lives richer: Thanks to Renee Anderson, Liz Olds, Ariel Jelsma, Josh Barron, Doug Moore, Claire Sorrenson, Drew Mitchell, James Ward, Ashleigh Lowe, Drew Goldstein, Kelsey Eiland, Danielle Lerner, and so many others. We work to nurture young writers and encourage creativity in others, but so often we're the ones who gain.

Above all, thanks to you, Sarah Lisa. I can probably never persuade you to read this book, but thanks for inspiring me to put so much into trying to tell this story right. You truly do inspire me, every day, with your strength and your creativity and your beauty. We were probably crazy to move from Berlin to start a new life in California, and I hope we can always be that crazy. You and Coco make me happy like I never thought I could be. I'm already looking forward to Coco's first baseball game.